HJP
C0-AYM-610
DISCARDED
Adirondack Community College Library

AT THE DAWN OF CIVILIZATION

THE WORLD HISTORY OF THE JEWISH PEOPLE

FIRST SERIES: ANCIENT TIMES

VOLUME ONE: AT THE DAWN OF CIVILIZATION

GENERAL EDITOR (Vol. I)
B. NETANYAHU

JEWISH HISTORY PUBLICATIONS LTD.

AT THE DAWN OF CIVILIZATION

A BACKGROUND OF BIBLICAL HISTORY

EDITOR

E. A. SPEISER

RUTGERS UNIVERSITY PRESS, 1964

PUBLISHED IN ISRAEL
BY JEWISH HISTORY PUBLICATIONS (ISRAEL — 1961) LTD.

© 1963 — JEWISH HISTORY PUBLICATIONS (ISRAEL — 1961) LTD.
ALL RIGHTS RESERVED. THIS BOOK OR PARTS THEREOF, MAY NOT BE
REPRODUCED IN ANY FORM WITHOUT PERMISSION OF THE PUBLISHERS.
LIBRARY OF CONGRESS CATALOGUE CARD NUMBER 64—15907

PRINTED IN ISRAEL BY PELI–P.E.C. PRINTING WORKS LTD., RAMAT-GAN

9684

CONTENTS

CONTENTS

PART THREE: THE CULTURAL FACTOR

A. MESOPOTAMIA — EVOLUTION OF AN INTEGRATED CIVILIZATION

E. A. Speiser

B. EGYPT — THE KINGDOM OF THE "TWO LANDS"

J. A. Wilson

AUTHORS

ILLUSTRATIONS

Between pages 32 and 33

Between pages 80 and 81

Between pages 80 and 81 (continued)

Between pages 136 and 137

Between pages 224 and 225

Between pages 224 and 225 (continued)

Between pages 272 and 273

MAPS

PREFACE

The present volume, although so conceived as to form an independent unit, is also part of an integrated whole. It is the first in a series of similar volumes, each written by a different group of scholars and linked to the series by a common plan and purpose. The purpose is to present a new, authoritative history of the Jewish people from its beginning to the present time.

That a Jewish history, to be all-inclusive, must be of collective authorship, is today almost a truism. It is certainly no novelty. Since the turn of the century the creation of such a history has been repeatedly urged – and with good logic. It was suggested as an answer to our dual need for completeness and consistency, on the one hand, and for scientific reliability, on the other. In fact, the sheer magnitude of the scope of Jewish history, both in terms of time and space, precluded any other course. Yet the realization of the idea, apparently quite simple, appeared, upon analysis, to be most complex, and thus the gap between theory and practice remained unbridged for a long time. Only in 1947 were discussions begun in the United States that finally led to actual results.

Five years later, in 1952, two committees of scholars were formed to consider plans for a history of the Jewish people along the lines above indicated. One of these committees was established in Israel under the chairmanship of the late Professor Schwabe, then Rector of the Hebrew University; the other was organized in the United States under the chairmanship of Professor Abraham A. Neuman, President of the Dropsie College. The late Professors S. Asaf and J. Klausner, the late Professor Joshua Gutman and Doctor Solomon Grayzel, Professors H. M. Orlinsky and E. A. Speiser, Professor Solomon Zeitlin and the undersigned, formed the membership of these committees. Soon thereafter other scholars, although not formally associated with these bodies, were drawn into constant collaboration. They were the late Professor V. A. Tcherikover, and Professors S. W. Baron, B. Dinur, S. D. Goitein, B. Mazar, and Cecil Roth.

The fact that there were important precedents for this sort of collective writing was, of course, most helpful. Among the works considered as guiding examples mention should be made, in the first instance, of Wilhelm

Oncken's *Allgemeine Geschichte*, published 1879-93. Another model of inestimable value was the Cambridge Historical Series, planned by Lord Acton, J. B. Bury and others, and published since 1902. While these works deal with the history of mankind and not with that of a single people, a Jewish history, being global in scope, could gain, in its planning stage, by their example. But precedents were not lacking for collective authorship of histories of individual nations, too. Hanotaux's *Histoire de la Nation Française*, published in the early twenties, and Menéndez Pidal's *Historia de España*, which has been appearing since 1947, were among the works of this category consulted. Both by their clearly positive achievements as well as by some of their debatable features, these works offered the above-mentioned committees important aid in solving knotty problems inherent in the nature of such projects.

Yet the planning of the work under consideration offered difficult problems of its own. These stemmed primarily from the state of dispersion, which obtained through half the Jewish people's lifetime and resulted in a multitude of evolutionary courses, running in different or even opposite directions, here and there to be halted at different times. To present Jewish history in this period as moving along a common front is, of course, a formidable task. Surely when a history of a people is so presented, a common denominator must first be found and the major historic current identified. Could these prerequisites be noted, it was asked, in the history of the Diaspora? Portraying the life of the Jews in this period in a series of parallel communal histories, and thus dividing the material longitudinally, seemed to offer an easy way out of a difficult dilemma. Yet the consensus of the scholars consulted on the matter rejected this solution. For above and beyond the regional differences, they felt, there were unifying factors in each period that were of overriding significance; there were basic conditions that were common to vast areas; and there were influences flowing from one community to another, sweeping ultimately across the whole Jewish world, or at least across its historically most active parts. Consequently, the first principle adopted was that the major divisions of the material should be along chronological rather than territorial lines.

Another question of prime importance, and related to the one just discussed, was the measure of attention to be paid to the conditions of the world in which the Jews lived. Having never been a people that "dwelt apart," not even in pre-Diaspora times; having always been engulfed by mighty forces, whether political or cultural or both; having often struggled with these forces, primarily for the sake of retaining identity, and more often joined with them, in strife and in peace, in a mutual process of give and take — the Jews were involved in the histories of other nations perhaps more than any other people on earth. Yet this paramount and crucial fact, it seems, has never been duly reflected — either in the histories of the Jews, or in those of other peoples. To understand, therefore, more fully the inner developments that took place in Jewry itself, as well as the historic role played by the Jewish people on the international scene, much closer attention than thus far shown should be given to the general external background against which Jewish history has evolved. Also, what is called for, in accordance with the above, is a broader and fuller description of the relations between Jews and gentiles through the ages, and of the interplay of influences exerted by non-Jews upon Jews and by the latter upon the surrounding societies. Thus presented, Jewish history, it was believed, would appear more clearly as what it has truly been: not a history of an isolated people, but part and parcel of the history of the world.

With these major principles in mind, added to the fundamental understanding that the History will deal with all aspects of Jewish life — the political, social, economic, religious, and cultural alike, detailed plans were mapped out. By the time half of these plans were completed — and this was fortunate for the projection of this history — an organization was formed to finance the project — the Jewish History Publications, Inc. Largely thanks to its President, Mr. Alexander Gurvitch, who was moved by the vision of the new history, and also thanks to a few public-spirited individuals who came to his and his colleagues' aid, work could proceed uninterruptedly for several years. Then, when the History reached the stage of publication, the Massadah Publishing House of Israel shouldered most of the burden.

From the inception of the work until recently the undersigned served as general editor for the entire series. Circumstances, however, have since compelled him to limit his responsibility in that capacity to the first volume only. He is hopeful, nonetheless, that, in the course of his work, solid foundations were laid for the entire series; and perhaps, like others, he should be satisfied with the thought that *dimidium facti qui coepit habet.* It remains for him to thank all those who helped him in performing his editorial duties, and especially his assistants in recent years: Dr. E. Feldman, general secretary of the History, and Mr. J. O'Dell, secretary for Volume One. Both took care of many details, and Mr. O'Dell also checked the proofs, made a number of valuable suggestions, and prepared the volume's index.

B. NETANYAHU

Dropsie College

ABBREVIATIONS FOR BIBLICAL BOOKS

Genesis	Gen.
Exodus	Ex.
Leviticus	Lev.
Numbers	Num.
Joshua	Josh.
Judges	Jud.
I Samuel	I Sam.
II Samuel	II Sam.
Isaiah	Isa.
Jeremiah	Jer.
Ezekiel	Ezek.
Hosea	Hos.
Obadiah	Ob.
Habakkuk	Hab.
Zephaniah	Zeph.
Haggai	Hag.
Zechariah	Zech.
Malachi	Mal.
Psalms	Ps.
Canticles (Song of Songs)	Cant.
Lamentations	Lam.
Ecclesiastes	Eccl.
Daniel	Dan.
Nehemiah	Neh.
I Chronicles	I Chron.
II Chronicles	II Chron.

ABBREVIATIONS FOR JOURNALS AND SCIENTIFIC LITERATURE

AASOR — Annual of the American Schools of Oriental Research
AfO — Archiv für Orientforschung
ANEP — The Ancient Near East in Pictures, James Pritchard, Princeton, 1954
ANET — Ancient Near Eastern Texts, Ed. James Pritchard, Princeton, 1950
AnOr — Analecta Orientalia (Pontifical Biblical Institute, Rome)
AO — Der Alte Orient
AOS — American Oriental Society
ARM — Archives royales de Mari
AT — The Alalakh Tablets
BASOR — Bulletin of the American Schools of Oriental Research
BASS — Beiträge zur Assyriologie und semitischen Sprachwissenschaft
BIES — Bulletin of the Israel Exploration Society
BiOr — Bibliotheca Orientalis (Leiden)
BSL — Bulletin de la Société de Linguistique de Paris (Page numbers preceded by an asterisk refer to the reviews)
HUCA — Hebrew Union College Annual
IEJ — Israel Exploration Journal
JAOS — Journal of the American Oriental Society
JBL — Journal of Biblical Literature
JCS — Journal of Cuneiform Studies
JEA — Journal of Egyptian Archaeology
JNES — Journal of Near Eastern Studies
MSL — Materialien zum sumerischen Lexikon
MSOS — Mitteilungen des Seminars für orientalische Sprachen (Berlin)
RA — Revue d'Assyrologie et d'Archéologie Orientale
RB — Revue Biblique
RT — Recueil de traveaux relatifs à la philologie et l'archéologie égyptiennes et assyriennes
SIL — Studies in Linguistics, ed. G.L. Prager
WZKM — Wiener Zeitschrift für die Kunde des Morgenlandes
ZA 1–44 — Zeitschrift für Assyriologie und verwandte Gebiete
45 *et seq.* Zeitschrift für Assyriologie und vorderasiatische Archäologie
ZDMG — Zeitschrift der Deutschen Morgenländischen Gesellschaft

HEBREW-ENGLISH TRANSLITERATION

1. All Hebrew names found in the Bible are given as they appear in the English translation of the Holy Scriptures by the Jewish Publication Society of America, Philadelphia, 1955.

2. Those names that are familiar to the English reader are rendered in their customary, accepted spelling (e. g. Caesarea).

3. All other Hebrew names and words are transliterated as follows:

א	Not noted at beginning or end of word; otherwise by ', e. g. p^{e}'ēr or pĕ'ēr (פְּאֵר), mē'īr (מֵאִיר).
בּ	b
ב	v
גּ	g
ג	g
דּ	d
ד	d
ה	h (unless consonantal, ה at the end of the word is not transliterated)
ו	w
ז	z
ח	ḥ
ט	ṭ
י	y
כּ	k
כ	ḵ
ל	l
מ	m
נ	n
ס	s
ע	ʿ
פּ	p
פ	f
צ	ẓ
ק	q
ר	r
שׁ	sh, š
שׂ	s
תּ	t
ת	t (Except in the word בית – *beth*)

a) The *dagesh lene* is not indicated, save in the letters בּ and פּ. *Dagesh forte* is indicated by doubling the letter.

b) The Hebrew definite article is indicated by *ha* or *he* followed by a hyphen, but without the next letter doubled, e. g. *ha-shānā*, not *ha-shshānā*.

ַ	a	ֶ	e
ֲ	ă	ֱ	ĕ
ָ	ā	וּ	ū
ָ	o	ֹ	ō
ֳ	ŏ	ֻ	u
ֵ	ē	ִ	i
ֵי	ė, ēi	ִי	ī

Sheva mobile (שוא נע) is indicated thus: ^{e} or ĕ. Neither long vowels nor *sheva mobile* are indicated in proper names.

ARABIC-ENGLISH TRANSLITERATION

ء	— ' (not indicated at the beginning of a word)	ض	— ḍ
ب	— b	ط	— ṭ
ت	— t	ظ	— ẓ
ث	— th	ع	— '
ج	— j	غ	— gh
ح	— ḥ	ف	— f
خ	— kh	ق	— q
د	— d	ك	— k
ذ	— dh	ل	— l
ر	— r	م	— m
ز	— z	ن	— n
س	— s	ه	— h
ش	— sh	و	— w
ص	— ṣ	ى	— y

The Lām of the definite article ال is assimilated before a solar letter. Proper names familiar to the English reader are rendered in their customary spelling.

AT THE DAWN OF CIVILIZATION

PROLOGUE

by E. A. Speiser

RECENT YEARS have witnessed a steady growth in the knowledge and understanding of man's past. The increase in quantity is immediately apparent. By bringing to light an immeasurable wealth of monuments and inscriptions, archaeology has added enormously to the range of traceable human history. Yet the qualitative gain, while less obvious perhaps, is the more significant by far, for it has meant a radical change in perspective. History as a whole stands out today in much sharper focus than was thought possible only a few decades ago.

Man's career as a food-gatherer is judged to have begun not less than half a million years back. Some 50,000 years ago, within the last tenth of the overall span, cave deposits began to reflect a pattern of conscious social behavior. Yet history in the full sense of the term, as it can now be precisely defined, is barely 5,000 years old. It is thus the latest and uppermost of a hundred turned leaves in the ledger of mankind — the only one, moreover, of that hundred that is fully inscribed and open to decipherment.

Since history proper, as a record of established and continuous civilization, is hence but a minute fraction of man's total indicated lifetime, no part of this latest and most advanced stage is even remotely suggestive of mankind's infancy. The fumbling steps of primitive man fall within the opposite segment of the full scale. And by the same token, the events that left their reflection on our historical spectrum — within the past five thousand years — emerge as the culmination of an immemorial process of trial and error, of survival and selection, the outgrowth of a long series of social and intellectual mutations. However one may view these events subjectively, they must be regarded in an objective appraisal as the product of mankind's maturity.

It is now possible, furthermore, to single out those mutations that led up to the beginnings of recorded history. The resulting picture is by no means sharp in every detail, but it is clear on at least two basic counts. First, the changes that produced history and influenced its tempo and content were all arrived at in the same particular region of the world, the region which we know as the Near East. And second, ever since its emergence in the Near East, history has been advancing in a well defined mainstream down to our own day and age. Despite all its turns and twists, its tributaries and its backwaters, this tortuous flow remains a connected and integrated whole. As such, human history can lack neither continuity nor coherence.

It follows thus that the emergence of history in the Near East marks at the same time the beginnings of the historic age anywhere on earth. The West does not become a major factor in the process until the advent of the Hellenistic age, by which time the Near Eastern phase had all but run its course. The Hellenistic interlude marks the half-way stage in the total of recorded history. The last half, long dominated by the West, has attained global proportions. But the first, the pre-classical, half — which was in many ways a pioneering and normative experience — was centered, at first exclusively and at all times prominently, in the so-called ancient Near East.

The study of the pre-Hellenistic Near East involves in the first place the contemporaneous yet sharply contrasted civilization of Egypt and Mesopotamia. Each of these featured its own distinctive way of life which was sustained for thousands of years; each was in a sense an unpremeditated experiment on a truly heroic scale. The findings of Mesopotamia and Egypt, whether positive or negative, were not to be lost on the successor civilizations.

In the second place, such a study cannot ignore the neighboring areas which connect and complement the valleys of the Tigris-Euphrates and the Nile. Advanced civilizations cannot be shored up by means of political and geographic barriers. They interact and expand. The ultimate record is reflected as much in their external relations as in their internal achievements. It is thus that Anatolia and Syria and Palestine, among various other lands, appear first as witnesses and as pupils, and in due time also as independent actors on an expanding world stage.

The Land of Israel was to arise, above all other areas large or small, as a unique factor in world history. Its enduring impact is without parallel in the annals of mankind, and its story has therefore an importance and appeal second to none. This land was both an heir to the older cultures of the Near East and a source of new and far-reaching contributions. That country, in short, lay along the course through which the mainstream of history came to be channeled.

The world history of a people whose basic inspiration and achievement had the Land of Israel as the center must start out, accordingly, with an account of the antecedent civilizations of the Near East. These beginnings coincide, as has been indicated, with the beginnings of world history. The whole process, however, owed little to mere coincidence. Yet such are the limitations of the historian — any historian — that some of the essentials of universal history must forever remain shrouded in mystery.

PART ONE: THE ENVIRONMENTAL FACTOR

A. THE LAND OF ISRAEL — FROM "THE BROOK OF EGYPT" TO THE LITANI

1. NAME AND CONCEPT

by A. J. Brawer

THE LAND which was to become the cradle of the Jewish people and the major scene of its history for nearly two thousand years — the Land of Israel, as it came to be known by many — was considered, before as well as after that period, as a part of larger geographic units. For the Sumerians in the first half of the 3rd millennium B.C.E. it was a section of *Kur Martu-Ki*, i.e. the land of the West; for the Akkadians, their successors, the same area was regarded, from the middle of the third millennium onward, as *Mat Amuru*, the Land of the Amorites. The Egyptians of the Middle Kingdom and the beginning of the New One (i.e., until the 14th–13th centuries B.C.E.) designated this land and part of southern Syria by the name of *Retenu*, the origin of which is not quite clear, while subsequently they called the same area *Haru*, after the Hurrians who settled there in the 17th century. The name Canaan, which first appears in a 15th century cuneiform document found at Nuzi, serves in the Bible, in a narrower sense, as a designation for the area of Cis-Jordan, and, in a broader sense, also for Western Syria (Gen. 10:18). Perhaps it indicated the area of cultural, if not ethnic extent of the merchant races whose strongholds clustered along the northern shore of Palestine, just as the name Palestine (originally Philistine Syria; Συρία ἡ Παλαιστίνη) was given to the land by the ancient Greeks under the influence of their acquaintance with the maritime people who occupied the southern seaboard of the country. The latter name came into vogue especially following the loss of Israel's independence and the rise of Hellenism in the East — already centuries, curiously enough, after the Philistines had disappeared from the scene. Then again, the same territory was repeatedly broken up into various units, each of which belonged to much broader domains, extending far beyond the limits of the country. Nevertheless, the conception of Palestine as an independent entity, both geographical and historical, has never since disappeared from the consciousness of mankind. Clearly this conception owes its origin to the period when the country in its entirety was the national territory of the people of Israel. For never before or after that period was Palestine as a whole simultaneously bound up with one nation and one political power.

Although morphologically, as well as in other respects, the land of Israel, or Palestine, has a great deal in common with what is historically known as Syria, it forms an independent geographical region, with well-defined natural boundaries and characteristics and peculiarities of its own. Considering southwestern Asia and the lands around the eastern Mediterranean which formed the scene of ancient history, Palestine, one may say, was at that time at the very center of the civilized world. Because of its unique location, it experienced the impact of cultural influences that flowed through it from all the points of the circle encompassing Mesopotamia, Asia Minor and the Greek islands on the one hand, and Egypt, Cush and Arabia on the other. Yet, it was not only a center, but also a bridge linking the two great water-pathways of the ancient world — that of the Mediterranean and the Red Sea — and this partly explains the fact that the most daring navigators of the ancient world, who first reached both the Atlantic and the Indian oceans, embarked on their missions from the shores of this region. Then, again, as a mere strip of land between sea and desert, connecting Eurasia and Africa, it served as the main channel for the most important continental arteries of communication — the great routes of commerce and conquest alike. Because of this advantageous geographical position, the control of Palestine was the relentless ambition of races and rulers striving for wealth and power, and thus Palestine became the object, as well as the victim, of repeated invasions — from the North and the South, the West and the East — and a scene of battle for almost all the great conquerors of antiquity.

In this whirlpool of conflicting cultures, political interests and ethnic currents, in this relatively narrow passage where the military might of empires rumbled almost incessantly backward and forward, it was indeed a most formidable task to establish and maintain an independent nation. And yet such a nation was established, clung to this land against all odds and resisted the tremendous pressures of annihilation longer than any empire did. What is more, it was in this very country that the people of Israel developed a religious philosophy, a moral system and a way of life that was destined to influence all mankind. It was here, in the midst of a heathen world, and moreover, among a multitude of local pagan cults, conforming to the requirements of the numerous tiny kingdoms and city-states into which this country was divided, that the lofty concept of monotheism struck root and grew to maturity. It was from the central position of this land that the prophets of Israel observed, as from a mountain top, the movements of armies and the stratagems of states, saw how the mighty fall, how the great kingdoms of yesterday are crushed almost overnight, subjugated, or even completely wiped out. It was on the basis of these observations that a philosophy of history evolved which viewed power, war and expansion as ephemeral phenomena in man's life, reflecting nothing but the principle of crime and punishment demonstrated in an inevitably recurring process. Then again, it was here, under the impact of this philosophy and the bitter experience of repeated invasions, that the dream of international peace was nurtured, based as it was not on a *pax Romana*, on a regime of one empire controlling the whole world, but on the free, independent existence of all nations, settling their conflicts by fair arbitration in a supranational court of justice (Isa. 2:2–4; Micah 4:1–3). Finally, these ideas about the universality of God, the inner unity of man's history and the basic oneness of man's ideals and aspirations made this country the source of religious movements which have inspired mankind down to the present time and indeed made Palestine the *Holy Land* for many millions the world over.

Whatever influence may be generally attributed to the relationship between a country and a people in determining their historic course or cultural creativeness, it is clear that, in this instance, both land and people played a unique role in shaping the history of Israel, its moral system and the ideals it proclaimed to mankind. Perhaps nowhere else, therefore, should the geography of a country be studied so minutely to understand its history, as in the case of the Land and People of Israel.

2. MORPHOLOGY

by A. J. Brawer

A. Boundaries and Area

THE BORDERS of Palestine as drawn in the Bible,[1] i.e., the territories allotted to the twelve tribes of Israel, are in detail not altogether clear. If, however, we combine the known with the assumed, the borders of the country ran as follows: on the west — the sea, from the mouth of Naḥal Miẓraim (The Brook of Egypt; in Arabic: Wadi 'l-'Arīsh) in the south to Qāsimiyya River (the lower reaches of the Litani) in the north; on the north — from the great bend of the Qāsimiyya, along the northern edge of the Ijon Valley to the southern foothills of Mount Hermon; on the east, from the eastern edge of the Trachonitis (al-Lijja) and of Mount Hauran (Jabal Ḥawrān), circling around the southern edge of the latter mountain and proceeding along the western outskirts of the Syrian Desert as far as the Arnon River, and then along the Arnon to the Dead Sea; on the south — from the south-eastern corner of the Dead Sea, including Zoar, along the bed of Naḥal Zin (Wadi Fukra) to the Negev mountains south of the Ascent of Akrabbim (The Ascent [or Pass] of the Scorpions), thence running south of ha-Har he-Ḥalaq (the "Bare Mountain"), turning north to Kadesh-barnea and Azmon (al-Quṣayma) and then to Naḥal Miẓraim along which it continued to the sea.

The lands of Moab, Edom and the desert of Paran, up to the Gulf of Elath, were not included within these boundaries, although from a purely geographical standpoint they should be considered as part of Palestine, and historically, were repeatedly incorporated into Israel's domain. The natural borders of southern Palestine are, therefore, as follows: in the southwest — Naḥal Miẓraim and the road descending from El Arish to the Gulf of Elath; in the southeast — the road leading from Elath to Maon (Ma'an) in Edom, the railway line as far as Edrei and the south-eastern borderline of the Hauran mountains. Within these borders, the area of Palestine contains 22,800 sq. miles.

Like Syria to the north, Palestine is divided into four natural belts, stretching from north to south, almost parallel to each other. These consist of: (a) the Coastal Plains, (b) the western mountains, (c) the Jordan Valley and (d) the Transjordan plateau.

B. The Coastal Plain

Economically and strategically the Coastal Plain was undoubtedly the most important of the four longitudinal natural belts of Palestine. Unlike the fertile areas in the mountains, those of the plain are continuous and, in addition, provide outlets to the sea. The international routes running from Egypt to Syria and on to the lands of the Tigris and Euphrates also passed through these plains.

The Coastal Plain consists of undulated land transversed by numerous wadis. It is twice interrupted: once at the "Ladders of Tyre," where the mountains protrude into the sea along a seven mile stretch, and again at Haifa, by the Carmel promontory. The narrow coastal strip between the Qāsimiyya River and the "Ladders of Tyre" is known as the Coast of Tyre, while its continuation south of the "Ladders" to Acre is called the Plain of Acre. Theoretically, both these plains belong to Upper Galilee, whereas the plain between Acre and Haifa — the Plain of the Bay — belongs to Lower Galilee. Dunes along the coast obstruct the flow of the rivers in the Plain of the Bay, and, as a result, it was until recently infested with swamps. Of the two cities, Acre and Haifa, situated on either end of the bay, the former has, until the twentieth century, enjoyed the greater renown ever since it was first mentioned in the second millennium B.C.E.

From Haifa southwards to Naḥal ha-Tanninim (Crocodile Brook), a narrow strip of the Coastal Plain separates Mount Carmel from the sea. Now called the "Carmel Coast," it is historically part of the Sharon Plain. This plain extends to the watershed between the Yarqon River and Naḥal Sorek (Nahr Rūbīn), close to the Ramleh–Jaffa road. According to the fourth century B.C.E. inscription of Eshmunezer, King of Sidon, the towns of Dor (on the Carmel Coast) and Jaffa were situated in "the field of Sharon." The Sharon gradually widens southwards; by Caesarea its width is about 9 miles, while near Tel Aviv it is nearly 13 miles, its entire area being about 400 sq. miles. In ancient times the Sharon was largely covered by a forest; this is why the Septuagint translates the word Sharon as δρυμός, i.e. Oak Forest.[2] Parts of this forest existed at the time of the Crusades. Napoleon makes mention of a forest near the village of Miska and states that it is the largest in Syria; and Kitchener, in the seventies of the 19th century, could still mark on the Palestine Exploration Fund Map some remains of this forest. The Sharon also contained some good cattle grazing land.[3]

The important towns of the Sharon in the time of the First Temple were Jaffa — the port of Jerusalem — in the south, and Dor, a port and a district capital, in the north. Herod converted a small Phoenician sea-town called Migdal-Sharshon into the large city of Caesarea, which became the capital of the country after the destruction of Jerusalem by the Romans. Caesarea had no natural advantages aside from the fact that it was the terminus of the road from Transjordan to the coast, running through Shechem (Nablus). In the southern Sharon, the city of Lud became an important urban center after the destruction of the Second Temple. Its neighboring town of Ramleh, founded (ca. 700 C.E.) by the Arabs, was the capital of the country during the Islamic period up to the Crusaders' conquest. After the expulsion of the Crusaders and the destruction of the ports, the Sharon was laid waste and degenerated into sheep and camel pasture. The river outlets were blocked and as a result the swamps, whose bounds had previously been limited, spread widely and infested the district with malaria.

South of the Sharon the coastal plain of Judea, i.e. Philistia (in Hebrew "*Peleshet*"), extends along the coast to the mouth of the Besor Brook (Wadi Ghazza). The eastern border of the plain in Philistia has an average altitude of 500 ft. The length of the plain along the coast is 47 miles, the average width 13 miles, and the total area about 600 sq. m. The dunes are widest in the north (near Rishon le-Zion), and a short distance from the coast line they reach a height of over 100 feet. Resting as they do on petrified dunes, the undercutting action of the wave erosion has resulted in the formation of a precipitous coast behind a narrow beach at many points along the coastal plain of Judea and the Sharon. Beyond this chain of petrified dunes there is a gutter-like valley, about one mile wide, in which the road and, since 1918, the railway line to Egypt are located. This is "the way of the land of the Philistines" mentioned in the Bible.[4]

Unlike the Sharon, the coastal plain of Judea had only small swamps which dried up in the summer, for this part of the plain and its hinterland get less rain than does the Sharon. In both the Sharon and the Judean Coastal Plain the soil of the drained swamp-lands is black and rich with vegetal remains, while the rest of the land consists largely of red sandy soil especially suited to the growth of citrus fruits (the leading export from this region since the latter half of the 19th century). Farther south, the soil is loamy and mixed with loess which becomes more dominant as we approach the northern Negev, where it constitutes nearly all of the soil. The southern part of the plain of Judea is mainly cropland. In ancient times the cultivated fields here — mostly vineyards and olive groves — were watered only by rainfall. Until the Moslem conquest put an end to the vineyards, wine was among the leading exports of this plain; the export of olive oil, the other principal product, was abruptly terminated by the Mamelukes' destruction of the harbors in the 13th century, after the defeat of the Crusaders.

The Coastal Plain in the Negev extends eastwards approximately to the 1,000 feet altitude line; its area is ca. 1,540 sq. m., about a quarter of which is covered by marine and desert sand dunes. The most important part of this section of the Coastal Plain is the valley behind the coastal dunes and its adjoining areas. Precipitation here is greater and more stable than farther inland, and ground water is available at a comparatively small depth. Furthermore, the route to Egypt passed through this valley and the caravans provided the main source of livelihood for the people who inhabited localities along it. Farther inland in the Negev coastal plain there were, in the past, only a few small settlements. This was due to the wide expanses of sand, scanty precipitation and the absence of ground water at depths which could be reached before the advent of modern drilling rigs. Those settlements of the Negev which, in the period of the Nabateans, developed into towns serving the transit trade between the Red Sea and the Mediterranean were situated on the hills further east, and not in the Coastal Plain itself.

In the whole area comprising the coastal plains of Sharon, Judea and the Negev, along a coast line of 125 miles between Naḥal ha-Tanninim and Naḥal Miẓraim, only ten brooks reach the sea. These are the brooks of: Tanninim, Ḥadera, Alexander (Nahr Iskandarūna), Poleg (Nahr al-Fāliq), Yarqon, Sorek, Lachish (Nahr Sukrayr), Shiqma (Wadi 'l-Ḥasī), Besor and Miẓraim. The ranges of petrified sand dunes as well as the loose sand dunes along the coast force the brooks descending from the mountains to detour sideways, thus causing them to converge. The Poleg is the only one of these brooks whose catchment-basin lies completely outside the mountain area; originally it was probably merely an old canal, dug to drain a swampy area. The Besor brook has the largest catchment-basin of all the above mentioned brooks. Second to it is the Yarqon, the only river west of the Jordan with a considerable perennial flow (average annual discharge of 220 million cubic meters) over a course of nearly 20 miles.

C. The Western Mountains: Galilee

The mountain region of Western Palestine, including that part of Edom which lies west of the Jordan, is 7,350 sq. m. in area, of which 3,320 sq. m. are in the Negev, about 1,740 sq. m. in Judea, about 1,200 sq. m. in Samaria, and about 1,100 sq. m. in Galilee. The whole mountain region, from the vicinity of the Gulf of Elath in the south to the bend of the Litani in the north, is 250 miles long. Its maximum width (in the Negev) is about 50 miles, while its narrowest part (in the extreme north) is only 22 miles wide.

Galilee, the northernmost part of this belt, is divided into Upper and Lower Galilee. The dividing line, as far as Parod (Farraḍiyya), is the Beth ha-Kerem Valley, along the Acre-Safad road, and from Parod a straight line to Lake Kinnereth (Lake Tiberias, or Sea of Galilee). The land in Upper Galilee slopes northward towards the Qāsimiyya River, and the few peaks higher than 3,300 ft. — including the highest of them, Mount Meron (Jabal al-Jarmaq; 3,960 ft.)[5] — are all in the south of the area. Wadis running to the sea divide the mountains into more or less parallel ranges. The eastern slopes are steep and without counterpart in the entire country except for the even steeper shores of the Dead Sea. The area as a whole is extremely rugged, a country of ridges extending in various directions, with no wide valleys — a land ideally suited for guerrilla warfare. This partly accounts for the fact that during the Israelite monarchy remnants of various folk groups inhabited the Galilee, especially the upper part (hence the name *Gᵉlīl ha-Gōyīm* — "The district of the nations," Isa. 8:23), while after the collapse of Jewish autonomous life remnants of the Jewish rural population held out in these mountains until as late as the 14th century.

As its name indicates, Lower Galilee reaches a much lesser altitude, its highest peak, Mount Ḥazon (1,825 ft.),[6] being about half the height of Mount Meron. Three rift valleys running from east to west divide this territory into four large ridges. Of these rift valleys the largest is the fertile plain of Beth-netophah (Sahl al-Buṭūf = Plain of Asochis). In the time of the Second Temple and up to the anti-Roman rebellion of 351 C.E. which resulted in the annihilation of the Jewish population in this area, a chain of Jewish villages surrounded this valley. Among these settlements was Yodfat (Jotapata), well-known as a fortress in the anti-Roman rebellion of 66–67 C.E. Between the Beth-netophah Valley and the Plain of Jezreel to the south rises the range of the Nazareth mountains (highest peak: 1,838 ft.). The isolated mountain south-east of the Nazareth mountains, in the north-eastern corner of the Plain of Jezreel, is Mount Tabor (1,843 ft.), a limestone mass with a dome-shaped top.

So long as one journeys parallel to the ridges, i.e. in an east-westerly direction, travel in Lower Galilee is fairly easy. It is not so in a north-southerly direction. While no great city ever developed in the mountains of Upper Galilee, Lower Galilee had a number of such cities. On the slopes west of Beth-netophah Valley, there was Zippori (Sepphoris), which supported a large population up to 351 C.E. A second large city — Shefar-'am — was situated on the edge of the western foothills, and at the southern foot of the mountains of Lower Galilee was Beth-she'arim.[7]

The Plain of Jezreel (Plain of Esdraelon) is a rift valley, 155 sq. m. in area, the largest in Palestine and the only one which transects the mountains. Having outlets at both ends which unite it in the west to the Coastal Plain and the east to the Jordan Valley, it offers convenient access from the Mediterranean, to Transjordan, Syria, and the lands of the Tigris and Euphrates. For thousands of years trading and military routes have passed through this plain; it was also the scene of numerous battles from the days of Thut-mose (1479 B.C.E.) down to 1948. Resembling a triangle with its base at the foot of the Carmel and its apex at Mount Tabor, the plain is crossed from east to west by Naḥal Kishon. During the long period of desolation under Arab and Turkish rule, a considerable part of the Plain of Jezreel turned into swamps. As a result malaria infested the area, driving the peasants away. The once fertile valley (Jezreel = יזרע אל = sown by God) was thereafter used mostly as grazing land.

D. The Western Mountains: Samaria

The political border between Judea and Samaria repeatedly underwent changes in the course of time. The natural border ran from Mount Baal-hazor (Tel Asur, 3,316 ft.) through Naḥal Shiloh (Wadi Dayr Ballūṭ) to the west and through Wadi 'l-Awjā to the east. The traveller going north along the unbroken crest of the Judean mountains will notice beyond Baal-hazor that the Samarian crest is often broken by erosional or tectonic valleys, which force the road repeatedly to descend. Because of these broad valleys, the mountains of Samaria were more accessible than those of Judea to penetration from the Coastal Plain, and were less able to provide refuge for a solitary folk as did the mountains of Judea. Shechem (Nablus-Neapolis) and Samaria (Sebaste) are known to this day by their Greek names, while in Judea hardly an allusion remains to a name imposed by foreigners on one of the ancient settlements.

The mountains of Samaria are also much more alive with vegetation than those of Judea. This is due to climatic differences as well as to the fact that Samaria did not suffer as much destruction as Judea. The traveller journeying from the barren mountains of Judea to those of Samaria can see with his own eyes the "blessings" pronounced upon Joseph by Jacob and Moses: "blessings of heaven above, blessings of the deep that coucheth beneath" (Gen. 49:25); "Blessed of the Lord be his land, for the precious things of heaven, for the dew, and for the deep that coucheth beneath" (Deut. 33:13).

Two ridges branch off from the mountains of Samaria — that of the

Carmel in the northwest and of the Gilboa in the northeast. Both are triangle-shaped horsts with rounded apexes, each having on its eastern flanks much steeper slopes than on the western. The Carmel is higher than the Gilboa (1,810 ft. and 1,648 ft. respectively) and much longer. Because of its proximity to the sea, the former enjoys an abundance of rainfall and dew; hence the freshness of its vegetation which made this mountain a symbol of nature's glory. The Gilboa mountains, in contrast, are covered by poor, greyish soil and, being sheltered from the sea by the Carmel, get less rain.[8] The historic Carmel extends as far as the road between Zikron Ya'aqov and Yoqne'am (Jokneam). Geographically, the whole horst lying between the Coastal Plain and the Plain of Jezreel, as far as the Valley of Dothan and En-gannim (Jinīn), should be considered as part of the Carmel. Through the southern part of this mountain (in its larger sense) runs the Iron Valley (Wadi 'Āra), first mentioned in a document from the time of Thut-mose III, 1479 B.C.E. This valley offers the shortest route from the Sharon to the Plain of Jezreel and thence to the crossings of the Jordan. Megiddo, at the northern end of this valley, not only guarded for thousands of years the entrance to the Plain of Jezreel but also served as a post for trading caravans. This explains its past greatness and the many ruins found there in recent years.

The mountains of Samaria, south of the Carmel and the Gilboa and as far as the Plain of Shechem (Nablus), are rugged and variegated. Southeast of the Carmel is a rift valley called Dothan, connected with the Plain of Jezreel by a pass referred to in the Bible as "the ascent of Gur, which is by Ibleam,"[9] south of En-gannim. Through this valley runs the road from Shechem and Samaria to the Plain of Jezreel. The Valley (Marj) of Sanur, waterlogged during the rainy season, lies 3 miles south of the Valley of Dothan. South of the Sanur Valley and up to the Shechem Valley there is a mountainous mass about 10 miles long and 9 miles wide, making access and passage difficult, so that the routes leading northwards from Shechem circumvent this mountainous mass to the east and west. The highest peak in this sector is Mount Ebal (3,080 ft.) rising just north of Shechem.

In the eastern slopes of northern Samaria there are three ridges similar to those of Lower Galilee. At the eastern edge of the southernmost of these ridges rises the white cone of Mount Sarṭaba (1,160 ft.), the first post north of the Mount of Olives (Har ha-Mishḥa) in Jerusalem for announcing the blessing of the new month.[10] Through the Samarian mountains stretches the tectonic Valley of Shechem. From a height of 1,800 ft. it slopes gently westwards to the Sharon and eastwards towards a crossing of the Jordan, near the Biblical site of Adam,[11] now called Jisr ad-Dāmiya. South of Shechem rises Mount Gerizim (2,840 ft.), sacred to the Samaritans as the traditional Mount of Blessings (Deut. 11:29). Due to its height and location, it affords a wide view in every direction—in contrast to Mount Moriah which, lower than the surrounding mountains, has only a limited horizon.

Because of its central position in Palestine, Shechem served as a meeting place, but could not be the capital of Israel since it lacked natural protection, exposed as it was to the scrutiny of the besieging enemy from Mount Ebal and Mount Gerizim. The town of Samaria, the capital of the kingdom of Israel, was built on an isolated mountain about 6 miles northwest of Shechem, near the road leading to the north. Thanks to its naturally protected position, it was able to hold out for three years against the besieging Assyrians.[12]

E. The Western Mountains: Judea

Looking down from Baal-hazor[13] one can see the Jordan Valley to the east and the Coastal Plain on the west, and may notice the difference between the mountains of Judea with their unbroken ridge and the broken structure of Samaria. An oak grove which, due to the sanctity of its site, has survived at Baal-hazor gives some indication of the nature of the forest of Ephraim (southern Samaria) before it was destroyed. Indeed, the tribe of Joseph found wide expanses of such oak forests, but it was forced to cut them down in order to gain arable land.[14]

In Judea it is easy to distinguish between the mountain platform and the slopes, for the slopes are steep on both sides, especially on the east. Access to Judea is difficult from all sides, a fact which contributed to Judea's ability to defend itself in several periods of its history and aided in warding off foreign cultural influences. Unlike the Coastal Plain, these mountains could provide a nation with relative isolation from the rest of the world. Also, the longitudinal road in the mountains of Judea gave the kings of Judea the possibility of maintaining an effective government in this area.

The Judean mountains can be divided into three regions: Beth-el to the north, Jerusalem in the center, and Hebron to the south. The mountains of Beth-el are higher than those of Jerusalem by an average of about 330 ft. Their crest takes the form of an almost flat plateau on either side of the watershed. The village of Ramah near Geba, home of the prophet Samuel, is situated near the southern end of the mountains of Beth-el. North of it is another Ramah (the one associated with Deborah, Jud. 4:5),[15] the present Arab town of Ramallah (Rama of Allah). The area surrounding these two localities bearing the name Ramah is the Biblical Ramathaim-zophim[16] on the northern periphery of Jerusalem. Jerusalem itself is ringed by mountains reaching an altitude of 2,730 ft. and higher than the one on which it is situated.[17] The main watershed extending along the Judean mountains in a north-south direction veers around the Old City and most of the New City, forming a curve to the west. Thus most of Jerusalem is included in the Dead Sea basin. The Old City is built on a mountain surrounded and protected by valleys: in the east, the deep Valley of Kidron; in the south, the deep and steep Gai-ben-Hinnom (Valley of Hinnom), descending into the Valley of Kidron; and in the west, a smaller valley (Wadi 'r-Rabābī) which converges on the Valley of Hinnom.

The ground on which the Old City of Jerusalem stands slopes from north to south and from west to east, and is divided by the Tyropoeon Valley (whose ancient Hebrew name is unknown) which crosses it in a north-southerly direction, from the Damascus Gate to the Dung Gate. Jerusalem requires strong fortification only on the north, and it is indeed from the north that the city was stormed and taken whenever its defenders were overpowered by an enemy. On the western slope of the Valley of Kidron is a spring, 'En Gihon; from it, water was brought in an aqueduct to the southern end of the earliest walled city, where it was stored in the Pool of Shiloah. Jerusalem normally expanded to the north and west.

Besides being highly defensible, Jerusalem enjoys a certain advantage as a communications center. Here the main north-south route intersects the roads passing through the mountains of Judea on their way from the Coastal Plain to Transjordan. The most ancient historic route from the Coastal Plain to Jerusalem ran through Lower and Upper Beth-horon. It involves 2.5 miles of difficult ascent between Lower Beth-horon and Upper Beth-horon, hence the well-known battles and skirmishes at this place from the days of Joshua to those of General Allenby. A road much used during the Roman period climbs from the Aijalon Valley through the valley of a seasonal brook to Gibeon, where it joins the road from Beth-horon. This road has the advantage of a gradual slope, but is exposed along its entire length to attacks from the mountain flanks. A third road, also leading through the Aijalon Valley, goes up to Kiriath-jearim (now the Arab village Qaryat al-'Inab), and thence reaches Jerusalem after ascending and descending twice. This has been the main road since medieval times. The route in Naḥal Sorek, used at present by the railway line, is for the most part new, although Betar — which still exists today — proves that the highest part of this road was used in the days of Bar Kokhba. The road from Jerusalem to Jericho descends eastwards through the ascent of Adummim and continues to Transjordan.

South of Bethlehem there begins a gradual ascent to the Hebron mountains — the major part of the mountains of Judea. About half way between Bethlehem and Hebron is a small valley called 'Emeq Beraḵa,[18] (Valley of the Blessing), located on the mountain crest. Southeast of this valley, at 'Ayn al-'Arub, are several springs. At the end of the period of the Second Commonwealth, the water from these springs was brought down in an aqueduct, following a tortuous way along the mountain flanks, to Solomon's Pools, south of Bethlehem. From Solomon's Pools the water ran to Jerusalem. South of Mount Halhul (3,370 ft.) begins the Hebron Valley in which the city of Hebron is situated[19] and which extends southwards as far as the Plain of Beer-sheba. Toward this plain the Valley of Hebron, lying as it does between two forking ranges which form the southern part of the Hebron mountains, widens gradually and the mountains of Hebron slope gently.

The westward slope of the mountains of Jerusalem and Hebron, which leads to the Coastal Plain, is divided into two hilled terraces, one below the other. The descent from the highland plateau to the upper terrace is steep, and constitutes the main part of the descent from the mountains to the Coastal Plain. Below this terrace stretch the foothills of Judea, called in the Bible the *shefela* or the mountain lowland.[20] In the Mishnah, however, the *shefela* also includes the Coastal Plain. The roads leading up to Jerusalem are concentrated in the Valley of Aijalon, hence its distinction as an important strategic site. Emmaus, the scene of Judah Maccabee's first great victory (165 B.C.E.), is situated on the eastern slope of this valley.

The eastern slopes of the mountains of Judea are divided into a number of successive narrow terraces. These terraces are more numerous in the south than in the north. The bottom terrace is the highest and steepest, actually a precipice along the Dead Sea. The platform of the highest terrace, and nearest to the watershed, is still within the inhabited area; beyond it, to the east, stretches the Wilderness of Judea. There were only a few isolated settlements in this desert, such as En-gedi, near a rich spring close to the shores of the Dead Sea, and Masada, which subsisted on rain-water collected in cisterns. The Essenes and, several generations later, recluse Christian monks, withdrew from the tumult of life to this wilderness where the many desert caves served them as dwellings.

F. The Western Mountains: The Negev

The Plain of Beer-sheba (about 100 sq. m.) is part of the Negev highlands, and its surrounding mountains slope gently into the plain. On its western margin it is about 700 ft. above sea-level. It rises gently eastward towards the watershed between the Mediterranean and the Dead Sea, which runs near the eastern edge of the plain at an altitude of 1,800 ft. The descent towards the Dead Sea is gentle at first, but farther east the ground slopes steeply, descending 2,950 ft. within 7–8 miles. In the spring of a rainy year the Plain of Beer-sheba looks green as barley fields or pasture. Beer-sheba, situated in the heart of the plain, at the intersection of the roads leading from the plain and the Hebron mountains, was in ancient times a commercial, administrative and religious center. South of the plain the mountains stretch, in folded ranges, in a southwest-northeasterly direction. Between the ranges there are parallel strike valleys, of seasonal streams, with numerous small tributaries running down the steep slopes. Ancient routes and strings of ruined settlements run parallel to the folding; we find here almost perfect conformity of the orography to the hydrography, roads, settlements and tectonic structure.

The part of the Negev included in the territory allotted to the tribes of Israel does not rise to an altitude higher than 2,350 ft. (in the mountains of Ḥatira). South of the Naḥal Zin, where the southern border of that territory passed (Num. 34:3–4), the folded beds are much more uplifted. Here the peak of Mt. Ramon reaches an altitude of 3,390 ft. Further southward there is a large and deep syncline, into which two large seasonal brooks flow: Naḥal Paran (Wadi 'l-Jarāfī), heading east to the Arabah Valley, and the Jerāyya brook running into Naḥal Miẓraim. South of this wide syncline the mountains rise again to an altitude of over 2,300 ft. This elevation is known as the Mountains of Elath.

Among the morphological phenomena peculiar to the Negev are the erosional cirques called *mak̲teshim* (bowls), elongated closed valleys on the crests of the folds' anticlines. These valleys are surrounded by escarpments up to 1,300 ft. high. Each such cirque has on its eastern side a single gorgelike outlet with a seasonal brook running through it. The largest of the *mak̲teshim* is Ramon, formed on the crest of the highest range of the Negev mountains. It is about 12.5 miles long and up to 5 miles wide. Next to it in size is the Ḥatira cirque in the northern Negev. Third in scope is the *mak̲tesh* of Ḥaẓera, north of the Ascent of Akrabbim.

In the central and southern Negev mountains there have been no permanent settlements, only some caravan stations and military posts located near wells. In the northern Negev sedentary settlement reached the high points of its development during the second half of the third millennium B.C.E. (Gen. 14:6–7) and later, in the 700 years preceding the Arab conquest, when the *pax Romana* afforded the Nabateans the opportunity to develop not only trading and transit centers, but also agriculture. The Kingdom of Judah was unable to provide constant protection for the tribe of Simeon which inhabited this region as wandering herdsmen; therefore, all traces of this tribe vanished even before the Babylonian Exile.

Dry or partly irrigated farming was possible only in the valleys where rainwater flows from the flanking mountains, thus doubling the quantity of water per surface unit. In Nabatean times the flood water in the seasonal streams was stored in cisterns and caves at the bottom of the valleys.[21] In the last centuries before the Arab conquest towns of ten thousand inhabitants existed in the northern Negev, without the necessity of bringing water from great distances as is done nowadays. These towns lived on the transit trade between the Gulf of Elath and the Mediterranean. From the fifth century C.E. until the Moslem conquest, Christian monks from all parts of the world came and lived in the northern Negev, but their means of support were provided from the outside.

G. The Jordan Valley

The three head rivulets which make up the Jordan River, the Senir (Nahr al-Ḥaṣbānī), Dan, and Hermon (Bāniyās), emanate near the foot of Mount Hermon. These three rivulets, carrying the water of many springs in "the land of Jordan and of the Hermonites,"[22] unite near Sede Neḥemya, from which point the river bears the name Jordan. Before it was recently regulated, the river split up again, one mile below Sede Neḥemya, into a number of arms, and spread over the valley, forming the large swamps of Hula with the small shallow Hula Lake (or *Samḵo*), 225 ft. above sea-level, at their southern end. Both lake and swamps were formed as a result of a Pleistocene flow of lava that obstructed the Jordan, and to this day the river has not been able to erode down this hard basalt obstruction. As long as water was diverted for irrigation, the swamps were not as extensive as they were before their recent drainage. In ancient times there was a wide network of irrigation canals which was neglected in the days of Arab rule. The city of Paneas (later: Caesarea Philippi) drew its livelihood from this irrigated land.

South of the Hula Lake the river flows in a narrow valley. It descends here about 885 ft. over a distance of 10 miles and then runs into Lake

Kinnereth, 650 ft. below sea-level. Lake Kinnereth is about 13 miles long (north to south), with a maximum width of 7.5 miles and an area of about 66 sq. m. The maximum depth is 160 ft. The banks of the lake are steep, leaving only a narrow strip of beach between the water and the mountains to the east and west. Lake Kinnereth and the Jordan are rich in fish. In ancient times, when the shores were inhabited, fishing was highly developed there.

The distance between Lake Kinnereth and the Dead Sea is about 66 miles, but the length of the Jordan's course between these lakes is, owing to the extensive meanderings of the river, about 2 1/3 times longer. In this part of the rift valley, known as "the plain (*kikar*) of the Jordan"[23] the river flows nearer to the mountains on its western side (its right bank) than to those on the east. Five miles south of Lake Kinnereth the Yarmuḵ river flows into the Jordan. The catchment-basin of the Yarmuḵ includes practically the whole of Bashan and northern Gilead. The average annual quantity of water which flows from the Yarmuḵ into the Jordan is almost equal to that of the Jordan itself, but there are enormous fluctuations in the volume of water brought down by the Yarmuḵ. After a heavy rainfall it discharges 28,600 gallons per second, compared to 1,200 gallons per second at summer's end.

Second in size to the Yarmuḵ among the tributaries of the Jordan is the much smaller Jabbok river, whose catchment-basin is small and does not include high mountains. South of its confluence with the Yarmuḵ, the Jordan flows 50—100 ft. below the general level of the Jordan Valley. This makes it impossible to irrigate the Jordan Valley with Jordan water, except by the aid of modern techniques and at great expense. Within the flood plain of the Jordan, called *Geon ha-Yarden* — "the inundation area of the Jordan" (in Arabic: al-Zur), the river meanders, having changed its bed here — during the historic period — in many places. The banks of the river are covered with dense vegetation: trees, bushes, and tall grasses in which boars and other wild beasts are still to be found. The lions often seen here in ancient times[24] disappeared at the beginning of the modern period.

The Jordan Valley, whose average width does not exceed 6.5 miles, has a westward extension opposite the confluence of the Harod brook which comes down from the eastern part of the Plain of Jezreel. This extension of the Jordan Valley, flanked by the mountains of Galilee and Samaria, is called the Beth-shean (Beisan) Valley, after the town in its center. This valley, which is blessed with springs and perennial streams, is mostly under irrigated cultivation. It was like a bit of Egypt in the land of Canaan; hence the attraction of this spot for the Egyptians whenever they wielded power in Palestine. In the "tell" of Beth-shean more Egyptian relics from the 13th century B.C.E. were found than in any other site in Palestine. In the Ptolemaic era Beth-shean (Scythopolis) was a Hellenistic center and, even in the days of the Hasmoneans, it did not have a Jewish majority. Beth-shean served not only as the commercial center of the valley but also as a transit market to Transjordan. Opposite Jericho the valley widens on both sides. Here the area west of the river is known as the steppes of Jericho, while the area to the east is called the plains of Moab. The landscape along the borders of the Jordan's flood plain is extensively dissected, having the character of badlands on a small scale.

The Dead Sea, or the Arabah Sea, 30% of whose water consists of salts, is the evaporation basin for the waters of the Jordan, Arnon, and Zered rivers, as well as other small streams descending from the east. Its surface is today about 1,300 ft. below sea-level, its length about 50 m., its maximum width — opposite En-gedi — about 10.5 miles, its area ca. 400 sq. m., and its maximum depth 1,320 ft. South of the tongue-shaped peninsula which projects into the southeastern part of the Dead Sea, the water is shallow, its depth not exceeding 40 ft. Precipitous rock walls bound the Dead Sea along its western and eastern shores; the northern coast is slightly elevated so that only to the south does the Dead Sea have a low-lying flat coast, which is flooded in rainy years. Southeast of the Dead Sea, above the level of the occasionally flooded area, is a small plain, the soil of which is not saline, as it is constantly washed by sweet water from springs and the Zered River. This is the Valley of Zoar. The town of Zoar, which stood amid groves of palms, still existed in the time of the Crusaders. At present this plain supports only one small Arab village. The hypothesis that Sodom and its neighboring towns were submerged at the southern end of the Dead Sea has so far not been scientifically confirmed.

South of the Valley of Zoar the land rises rapidly towards the Arabah Valley, 720 ft. above sea-level. This valley, 100 miles long, extends as far as the Gulf of Elath ('Aqaba). The Arabah Valley is a desolate region. In ancient times and up to the Islamic period there were a few oases here, especially in the eastern part, where springs were more common and richer in water than in the west. The inhabitants of these oases lived by smelting copper ore brought down mostly from the eastern mountains, for the deep, soft and stoneless clay soil of the Arabah Valley lent itself to the forming of molds in which the copper vessels were cast. The laborers' vegetables and fruit were supplied by peasants who cultivated small plots of irrigated land. The oases served also as posts for caravans passing from the Red Sea and Petra. Zoar was not only an agricultural settlement but also a trading town for goods brought from the Red Sea and shipped north across the Dead Sea.[25] An important route along the Arabah Valley comes down from Beer-sheba through the Ascent of Akrabbim (Scorpion Pass).

In the past a road descended from Petra to the Arabah Valley. Between modern Elath and 'Aqaba was located the town of Ezion-Geber, a port and a leading copper smelting center at the time of the First Temple.

H. Transjordan, Moab and Edom

Transjordan, in its widest sense, includes the whole plateau stretching from the eastern border of the Jordan rift valley to the desert. It is divided into three main regions.

1. The Bashan, from the northern border to the Yarmuḵ River.
2. The Gilead and Moab from the Yarmuḵ to the Zered Brook.
3. The Seir mountains from the Zered Brook to the Gulf of Elath.

Along the whole of Transjordan there is a highland belt overlooking the Jordan Valley, dissected by short marginal streams that run down the western slopes. It is higher than the area adjoining it on the east and also than the mountains on the opposite side of the rift valley, a fact which affects the climate of Transjordan and its hydrographic pattern. Except for the mountains of Hauran in the eastern Bashan, which because of their altitude, get sufficient rain, the transition to the desert in the eastern part of the plateau is quite rapid. The higher the highlands adjoining the rift valley, and the farther south we go, the nearer the desert to the rift valley. The southern part of the Seir mountains, near the Gulf of Elath, is a barren wilderness, for it is not high enough to attract rainfall from the distant sea. Even the mountains exposed to the western winds and overlooking the rift valley are desolate here.

As a result of the proximity of the Transjordan highlands' crest to the rift valley, only a few brooks break through the highlands and flow from the inside of the plateau into the valley. These brooks which collect a large number of tributaries are: Yarmuḵ, Jabbok, Arnon, Zered and, at the extreme south of the Seir mountains, Wadi 'l-Yatīm which descends to the Gulf of Elath, near 'Aqaba. In the valley of Wadi 'l-Yatīm runs the road from Rabbah Ammon (Amman) to the Gulf of Elath. Because there are so few valleys running from the highlands of Transjordan to the rift valley, and owing to the canyon-like character of these few valleys, connections between the plateau, the Jordan Valley and Cis-Jordan are few and difficult. The Transjordan highland roads are orientated more to the north and south than to the west. Over against this background the wars of Israel with Aram can be better understood.

Transjordan, down to the Zered Brook in the south, has the character of a plateau rather than of a mountain region. The eastern flank of the rift valley appears like a mountain range to anyone looking from the west because it is highly dissected, but once having climbed this flank of the rift valley the observer finds himself on an eastward sloping plateau.

The *Bashan*, largest and most fertile section of Transjordan (area 4,380 sq. m.), is divided from west to east into three sub-regions; the Golan, the Bashan plain, and the Hauran mountains with the "Trachona." The Golan is the highland region, facing the rift valley. Its northern part, facing upper Galilee, is known as Upper Golan. In the extreme north it reaches a height of 5,260 ft., while in the south its peaks, largely extinct volcanos, reach heights of between 3,600–3,940 ft. The Lower Golan is only 1,680–2,000 ft. high.

The Bashan plain, east of the Golan, is, in its northern part, mostly a rough and rocky terrain covered by hard lava. Further south the plain is covered by rich volcanic soil, which is very fertile. East of the Bashan plain, the Hauran mountains, known since 1860 as Jabal ad-Duruz (mountain land of the Druses), represent an enormous accumulation of lava in two terraces one above the other, the southern one reaching a height of 4,900 ft., and the smaller northern one a height of 5,900 ft. Because of its altitude, this range (except for its eastern slopes) receives sufficient rainfall for agriculture. The Druses, who began to settle here in the 18th century, revived the area agriculturally; they drove away or subdued the Beduin, who had previously roamed in these mountains. To the inhabitants of Jerusalem in ancient times, the mountains of the eastern Bashan seemed a far off country, almost legendary, and its height appeared in popular imagination as the extreme opposite of the depths of the sea.[26] The Bashan mountains were included in the areas conquered by Moses. Salcah, one of these conquests,[27] is situated round an extinct volcano. The "Trachona" is a solidified laval flow over an area of about 300 sq. m., without any valleys or streams. It is a labyrinth of rocks, an ideal refuge for outlaws, as is signified by its Arabic name al-Lijja (= "refuge").

Gilead, together with Ammon to the east, extends from the Yarmuḵ almost to the northern end of the Dead Sea; its area is about 1,900 sq. m. In northern Gilead there are patches of basalt, remnants of the lava cover which formerly extended from Bashan to beyond the Yarmuḵ. The presence, in parts of Gilead, of sandstone[28] beds close to the surface keeps the soil comparatively moist. This was the main reason for Gilead's wealth of natural vegetation[29] and the existence of forest remnants to this day. Northern Gilead, sloping towards the Yarmuḵ river, rises no higher than 2,000 ft. The central part of Gilead is a large dome reaching an altitude of 4,080 ft. (at Umm ad-Daraj). Because of its great height and its proximity to the rift valley, central Gilead is more dissected by river-beds than any other part of the western highlands of Transjordan. In spite of this, the character of the landscape in the upper part is that of a plateau rather than of mountains. The Jabbok runs westward across the central part of the dome, through a fault widened by erosion, into the rift valley. Southern Gilead, facing the mountains of Jerusalem, is 300–500 ft. higher than the central region.

Moab is the country east of the Dead Sea. The region to the south of the Arnon River was outside the area allotted to the tribes of Israel. The northern part of Moab, conquered and given to the tribes of Reuben and Gad, was also called Moab later, when it reverted to Moab after the tribe of Reuben had gone into exile.[30] In Moab the plateau character is dominant. The deep valleys of brooks which, running to the Dead Sea, dissect this part of the plateau make communication here very difficult. Travellers therefore use the road east of the plateau on the border of the desert. This is the "King's Highway," along which the Children of Israel asked Sihon's permission to travel (Num. 21:22).

Moab slopes both from north and south towards the Arnon Valley. In the south, near the Zered Brook, Moab reaches an altitude of 4,160 ft. In the north, on the border of Gilead, the highest peak is 2,980 ft. Mt. Nebo is only 2,530 ft. high, but as it faces the Jordan Valley and the mountains west of the rift valley, there is a very wide view from its summit.

The *Mountains of Seir* differ in altitude, structure, and shape from the other mountains of Transjordan. They look like mountains even when viewed from the east, for on their eastern flank, too, they have strongly inclined slopes. The Seir mountains are in several places over 2,600 ft. higher than the Negev mountains opposite them. The central part of the range, called ash-Shirā' in Arabic, reaches a height of 5,690 ft.; to this day it contains relics of a large pine forest. Ancient Edom comprised the northernmost part of the Seir range, which at a later period was called Gebal.[31] This area is actually a narrow belt of arable land between deserts on the east and west. To defend himself against the Beduin, the peasant had to live in fortified settlements in "the height of the hill."[32] At times when Palestine had strong governments, it extended its rule also to this mountainous region, through which a route runs from Syria and Transjordan to the Red Sea. The golden age of the Seir mountains was during the *pax Romana* of the first centuries C.E., when the population was concentrated mainly in the heart of the region. There, in a deep and closed valley — a natural fort — near a perennial river, the Nabateans built their capital, best known by its Greek name Petra. The temples, palaces and tombs of this town, all cut in red sandstone rock, command the admiration of observers to this day. Petra served as a storehouse for merchandise brought from South Arabia, India, the Indian Ocean islands and China. From there it was sent to Palestine, Syria, and Egypt.

The southern part of the Seir mountains has always been desolate, caravan posts being confined to their foothills. However, this region, too, is served by a road which runs all along Transjordan down to 'Aqaba.

3. GEOLOGY

by M. Avnimelech

TO APPRECIATE more fully the morphological structure of Palestine, one should take into account the country's geology, since morphology is essentially the outward expression of geological changes — evolutionary or revolutionary — wrought in the course of time. This examination may have historical value too; for geological conditions not only affect the landscape, but also the quality of the soil, the water supply and the wealth of mineral resources. They largely affect a country's living conditions, and thus play an important role in determining its historic course.

A. The Geological Regions of Palestine

For environmental purposes, the area of Palestine may be divided into six physical regions:

1. The region of Igneous Rocks (granitic, metamorphic, etc.) which are present in comparatively small areas on both sides of the Arabah Valley, especially in the south.
2. The region of mountains composed mainly of limestone and dolomite.
3. The region of basalt in the north of the country — in eastern Galilee and the Golan.
4. The Coastal Plains region, composed of geologically young sand and sandstone.
5. The Inland Depressions, filled largely with sediments of ancient lakes and rivers.
6. Transjordan.

1. *The Region of Igneous Rocks.* The granitic and metamorphic rocks comprising the igneous complex represent the earliest geological formation to be found in Palestine. They date back to the Pre-Cambrian period and are estimated to be more than half a billion years old. The areas of igneous rock extending on both sides of the Arabah Valley constitute an arid desert region, barren of arable soil and useful plants. They form a wild, irregular, rocky landscape of cliffs and deep crevices — a region unsuitable for cultivation and habitation other than the occasional wanderings of nomads. Neither trading caravans nor invading armies passed through this area,

which served as a natural barrier between the regions touching on the Arabah Valley.

2. *The Mountain Region.* This name applies to the entire region of mountains running like a backbone along the length of the country. These mountain ranges are composed mostly of limestone and dolomite and, to a small extent, of sandstone. Their strata represent the older geological periods, starting with the Cambrian up to the Eocene and ending with a few remains of the Oligocene and the Miocene. A complete series of all geological periods, however, is not to be found in Palestine: some of them have not left any sediments at all, while the traces of others may have been obliterated in the course of time. On the eastern shores of the Dead Sea and northeast of the Arabah Valley, rocks of the Cambrian period occur in limited areas; they are present also on the western side of the Arabah, near Timna' (north of Elath). Some rocks, found in the same region, have been supposed to belong to Ordovician or Silurian times. Of other periods of the Paleozoic era there is no definite evidence, although Carboniferous rocks are known to be present in the Sinai peninsula and Eastern Egypt. Certain strata in the southeastern Negev may possibly belong to this period.

The Mesozoic Era is represented in all its periods, the Triassic, Jurassic, and Cretaceous. Deposits of Triassic and Jurassic rocks are present in the mountains of the eastern Negev, the northeastern part of the Dead Sea region, and the Jabbok Valley. On the other hand, layers of the Cretaceous system extend far and wide over most of the mountain areas on both sides of the Jordan. Their combined strata are more than 6,000 feet thick, and their character changes according to their position in the series. In these strata we distinguish the Lower Cretaceous, whose layers here are for the most part sandy, and the Upper Cretaceous, composed mainly of limestone and dolomite, sometimes containing quartz and flint.

In the strata of the Upper Cretaceous we distinguish a lower part of harder and darker rocks belonging to the Cenomanian and Turonian ages. Its layers are overlaid by strata of the Senonian and Maestrichtian, which are generally composed of soft, chalky limestone, conspicuous in the landscape.

The rocks of the Paleocene and Eocene are generally similar to those of the Senonian and the Maestrichtian, and they too extend over wide areas of the mountain region. Here and there they are covered with Oligocene and Miocene rocks of which only scanty remnants are still preserved on the surface.

The degree to which the various strata are exposed depends on several fundamental factors, especially on their original expansion at the time of their deposition. In Palestine, most of the rock formations are of marine origin, that is, were deposited on the bottom of the sea. There are, however, many strata which were deposited on the surface of an old continent. Most of the sandy layers of the Lower Cretaceous are continental in origin. On the other hand, the limestone and dolomite layers of the Upper Cretaceous were originally deposited on the sea-bottom. The different characters of the rock layers indicate the conditions under which they were deposited. Among other things, these layers offer evidence to the shifting borders of the sea and land during various epochs.

In some periods of geological history the originally flat layers became folded in definite directions. In the Negev these directions are usually from southwest to northeast; in the center and the north, from south-southwest to north-northeast. The basic geological structure of Palestine and the extension of the rock layers on the land surface are determined by these facts. Thus the oldest strata appear along the axis of the anticlines, i.e., the upfolded parts of the folds, while the younger strata extend along the synclines, or the downfolded parts of the folds. Accordingly, the Triassic and Jurassic strata are exposed in the erosional cirque of Ramon (Wadi Raman) — which forms a large anticline — while those of the Jurassic are laid bare in the anticlines of Ḥatira (the great *Maḵtesh*) and Ḥaẓera (the small *Maḵtesh*). The younger layers of the Senonian and the Eocene extend widely in the synclines or in the flanks of the anticlines, as, for instance, in the Judean Desert or in the regions of Ṭūlkarm and Megiddo.

The axes of the folds usually slope in a definite direction. Those of the Hebron mountains, for instance, dip to the southwest, towards the plains of Beer-sheba. The central part of the Hebron mountains is therefore composed of deep layers of Cenomanian, whereas the strata covering the plains of Beer-sheba are mainly Eocene.

The disposition of the successive layers on the surface depends not only on folding but also on faulting which is caused by the fracturing of the earthcrust along definite lines, resulting in a downwarping or upwarping of separated blocks. Different kinds of faulting play an important role in the geological structure of Palestine. The Arabah Valley, the Jordan Valley, and the Dead Sea are all part of a rift valley which has sunk along a formation of faults stretching generally from south to north. The valleys of Beth-shean, Jezreel, and Zebulun are within fault systems which intersect the area from northwest to southeast. The Beth-netophah Valley is in the main a fault system perpendicular to the former, that is, its direction is from northeast to southwest. The Coastal Plain conceals a complicated fault-system which produces a zigzag line approximately at the foot of the mountains. As a result, part of the mountainous masses sank and the rest remained elevated.

These faults, and the horizontal and vertical movements which followed them, broke the folds either crosswise or lengthwise; some of them were uplifted, some sank, and others shifted to the sides. The wildest upheaval took place in the north of the country, in Upper and Lower Galilee.

The different shapes of the folds as well as the intensity and direction of the faulting determined the morphological character of the country and its division into several major sections: the Negev in the south, the central region, comprising the mountains of Hebron, Judea and Ephraim, and the northern part, including Mount Carmel, Gilboa, and the Galilee.

The eastern and southern Negev are noted for the great intensity of their folds, which are closely packed. They run in a southwest-northeasterly direction, parallel to the igneous rocks in the areas of Elath and Sinai. In the northern Negev the direction of the folds changes; here it is from south-southwest to north-northeast, coinciding with the direction of the folds in the center of the country. The folds in the Negev are often longitudinally broken, their slopes descending steeply towards the east. They constitute one of the main reasons for the difficulty in an east-west crossing of the Negev, the routes in this direction being limited to a few passes through the mountains. The steep, longitudinally faulted anticlines were exposed in some places by erosion; in this way, the famous erosional cirques (*maḵteshim*) were formed, the largest of which — the Ramon cirque — is nearest to the region of igneous rocks.

In Ramon, as well as in the Ḥatira and the Ḥaẓera cirques, the erosion reached the heart of the anticline, exposing the strata of the Triassic and Jurassic ages in Ramon, and those of the Jurassic and Lower Cretaceous ages in the two other cirques. The multi-featured morphology of the Negev is therefore a result not only of arid climatic conditions, but also of the geological structure and the manner in which the geological formations extend.

Except for a few places, climatic and edaphic conditions in the Negev were unfavorable to the development of agriculture. Its population, therefore, was always sparse and unstable. Small and short-lived pastoral settlements sporadically sprang up in the steppes of the western Negev, where the inhabitants' main livelihood depended upon sheep-herding. Beer-sheba — in the plain, south of the Hebron mountains — was the oldest permanent settlement; it owed its uniqueness to the high ground-water, always available here because of geological conditions.

In the central part of the country, bounded on the south by the diagonal line of Ashkelon-'En Ḥaẓeva ('Ayn Ḥuṣb) and on the north by the Carmel-Gilboa line, the folds assume a different character; they become wider, and their flanks slope more gently, changing the configuration of the geological formations on the surface. In the Judean Desert, whose folds are a continuation of those in the eastern Negev, they reveal a marked complexity. The mountains in the interior of this region are mainly limestone and dolomite, and occasionally quartzitic rocks of the Cenomanian age. In both the eastern and western flanks of the anticlines, strata of the Turonian and Senonian ages protrude outwards, the latter conspicuous by their softness and whiteness. The chalky and flinty chert of the Senonian age which covers most of this region is unfavorable to the formation of fertile soils and the preservation of moisture. The Judean Desert, like the Negev, was therefore but sparsely and sporadically inhabited, and most of the inhabitants were either nomads or hermits.

Conditions are different on the western slopes where, owing to the wide expansion of the Eocene cover, the strata of the Senonian are much reduced on the surface. The hills along the Coastal Plain are made up of Paleocene and Lower Eocene strata extending into the western foothills of the Judean Mountains. Thanks to the geological structure and type of rocks, rich and fertile soils were formed and deposited on the hillsides and in the valleys. These conditions also explain the existence of many springs whose water output satisfied the modest needs of the early population. In the course of time the inhabitants learned to dig wells and build cisterns to preserve rain water. As a rule, Eocene strata do not form very contrasting landscape forms. The hills are usually well-rounded and the valleys are relatively wide, rendering the area more suitable for permanent agricultural settlement. On the other hand, such regions lack natural protection and offer easy access to invaders. In consequence, the Coastal Plain, more than any other part of the country, was a scene of battles and political upheavals.

The region of the Carmel and Gilboa presents a different picture. It is intersected by numerous faults running mainly in a northwest-southeasterly direction. Along these faults, some landstrips sank deep, while others remained in their original position or were elevated, with the result that the whole area resembles a complex of huge converging icepacks. The compression caused some land masses to be horizontally moved, making it extremely difficult to recognize the shape of the original folds of the strata.

Such faulted rift valleys produced the valley system of Zebulun, Kishon, Jezreel, Beth-shean, Beth-netophah and the depression of Lake Kinnereth, and created conditions for human existence differing from those in

Environs of Elath.
From the Archives of KKL,
Jerusalem.

A Wadi near the Dead Sea.
From the Archives of KKL,
Jerusalem.

The Negev. The Road to Timna'.
From the Archives of the Jewish Agency, Jerusalem.

The Judean Desert.
From the Archives of KKL, Jerusalem.

The Judean Desert.
From the Archives of KKL, Jerusalem.

Judean Mountains. Aerial View.
From the Archives of KKL, Jerusalem.

The Plain of Jezreel.

The Carmel (North-Western Slope).

Upper Galilee: General View at Rama.
From the Archives of KKL, Jerusalem.

The Upper Galilee. Environs of Safad.
From the Archives of KKL, Jerusalem.

Lake Kinnereth.
From the Archives of KKL, Jerusalem.

The Hula Swamps.
From the Archives of KKL, Jerusalem.

The Lake of Hula.
From the Archives of KKL,
Jerusalem.

The Hula Swamps:
Poplars (*Populus euphratica*).
From the Archives of KKL,
Jerusalem.

The Hula Swamps: Water-Lilies (*Nuphar luteum*).
From the Archives of KKL, Jerusalem.

The Ḥula Swamps: Buffaloes.
From the Archives of KKL, Jerusalem.

The Hula Swamps: Herons.
Photo Braun, Jerusalem.

The Hula Swamps: Papyrus
(*Cyperus papyrus*).
From the Archives of KKL, Jerusalem.

The Jordan leaving Lake Kinnereth (near Deganya).
From the Archives of KKL, Jerusalem.

Waterfall in the Dan River.
From the Archives of KKL, Jerusalem.

Upper Galilee: Waterfall ("The Cauldron") in the Brook of Ijon at Metula.
From the Archives of KKL, Jerusalem.

The Lower Galilee. Wadi Amud.
From the Archives of KKL, Jerusalem.

Aerial view of the lower Plain of the Jordan and the Highlands of Gilead, seen from the West. In the left bottom corner — the Oasis of Jericho. The black line in the center — the gallery-forest of the Jordan.

The Yarmuḵ.
From the Archives of KKL, Jerusalem.

the other regions. The tortuous path of the watershed in this area did not serve as a convenient line of communication, thus causing the main routes to pass through the fault-valleys leading from the passages of Yoqne‘am, Megiddo and Jezreel through the wide valleys between the Tabor and Giv‘at ha-More (Jabal Daḥī) to the Valley of Ginnosar. In contrast, diagonal transverse faulting produced convenient passages leading from the sea eastwards through the Plain of Jezreel; these routes are marked by the sites of ancient settlements and famous battles. The morphological divergence contributed also to a great variety of living conditions and limited the possibilities of attaining political and cultural unity and stability.

3. *The Basalt Region.* Considerable areas of Palestine are covered with black volcanic basalt rocks. Basalts are found in relatively small patches in the Negev, the center of the country and the Carmel. They were formed by volcanoes active at least a hundred million years ago, in the Cretaceous or even earlier period. Younger basalt rocks of the Neogene (Miocene-Pliocene) and Pleistocene ages cover large areas in eastern Galilee and the Golan. The hard, solid basalt rock produces a rough, rocky landscape which makes agricultural settlement in the area a thankless task. Also passage through this rocky country is difficult, and the springs are few and poor. The basalt region therefore has always been sparsely settled and generally avoided by caravans. The great highways of ancient times, such as the route to Damascus, ran along its borders, mainly on its southern or northern side.

4. *The Coastal Plain Region.* As already indicated, the Coastal Plain is an area in which land masses sank to various depths along zigzag faults separating plain from mountains. Deep borings and geophysical tests have made it possible to determine the position of these land masses and to ascertain that they are in fact a continuation of the folds in the mountain region. The broken mountain border was attacked by the sea, so that parts of the region were first eroded away and afterwards covered, to varying depths, by sea and land sediments. These deposits are formed mainly of sand and are therefore mostly porous and friable. The upper layer, 30 to 300 feet thick, is formed of continental sands of rather weak cementation. The landscape is subject to fairly quick changes caused by the rivers flowing down from the east, and the shifting sand dunes coming from the west, i.e., from the sea. All this has determined the topography of the Coastal Plain. In both appearance and history, this region reflects the interrelation between continental and marine geological factors. The slightest variation of the sea level, any considerable alteration in the

altitude of the inland hills, any change in the force of the river torrents, left its mark on the landscape of the Coastal Plain. Consequently, the present width of the coastal region is not what it was during the first century of the present era, for example; nor are the shape and character of the shores, rivers and swamps what they were 2,000 years ago.

Starting from the southernmost part of the Carmel, near Caesarea, the Coastal Plain constantly narrows down until it almost disappears near Haifa; then, after a slight widening, it terminates completely at Rosh ha-Niqra (Ra's an-Nāqūra).

Because of these conditions not all parts of the Coastal Plain were equally suitable for safe and convenient passage. The unstable sand dunes and the rivers which transect the region and formerly flowed into swamps have often proved an obstacle to communication. The main route, therefore, ran along the borderline between the foothills and the Coastal Plain itself. It is well marked by the ruins of famous cities, such as Gerar, Gath, Gezer, Lud (Lydda), etc. Another route, much less convenient and less frequented, passed right along the shore, circumventing areas of coastal cliffs. Both routes joined near Caesarea (a fact which may have contributed to the establishment of the town), from where the road turned to the mountain valleys of Yoqne'am or Megiddo and thence to the highways leading to Damascus. The passage along the shore of the Carmel was difficult and dangerous and, at Rosh ha-Niqra, completely blocked.

5. *Inland Depressions.* These include the Jordan Valley and other depressions in the mountain areas, which are overlaid with thick deposits of dark-brown alluvial soils. They were formed in the Miocene period or later by the fracturing and sinking of layers along faults usually running in north-south, northwest-southeast, or northeast-southwesterly directions. The most important valley system in the country is that of Zebulun—Kishon—Jezreel—Beth-shean. Also notable is that of Beth-netophah and Beth ha-Kerem in Galilee.

The natural conditions of these valleys have left their imprint on local history. On the one hand, the soil is fertile and easily cultivated; on the other hand, these valleys occasionally were turned into swamps, hindering communication and fostering pestilent disease. In addition, such areas often invited the invasion of aggressive neighbors (or even distant powers) intent on looting or transit or both. For these reasons, settlers preferred to live in the mountains surrounding the valleys, coming down only to cultivate the land and gather in the crops. Only here and there, where there was a rocky elevation in the valley, do we find a "tell" — a mound marking the site of an ancient settlement. Ancient Beth-shean, Tell 'Afula, and

[GE]OMORPHOLOGICAL REGIONS OF PALESTINE

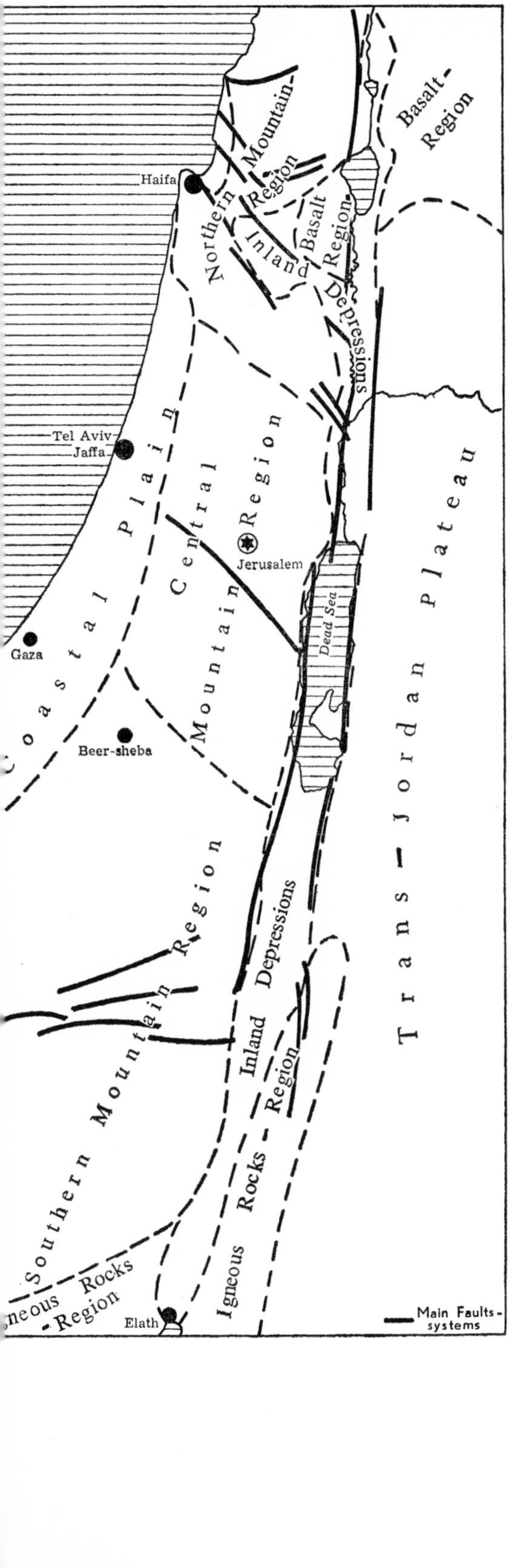

Northern Mountain Region
Inland Basalt Region
Basalt Region
Depressions
Coastal Plain
Central Mountain Region
Trans-Jordan Plateau
Dead Sea
Southern Mountain Region
Inland Depressions Region
Igneous Rocks Region
Igneous Rocks Region
Haifa
Tel Aviv-Jaffa
Jerusalem
Gaza
Beer-sheba
Elath
Main Faults-systems

GEOLOGICAL MAP OF PALESTINE

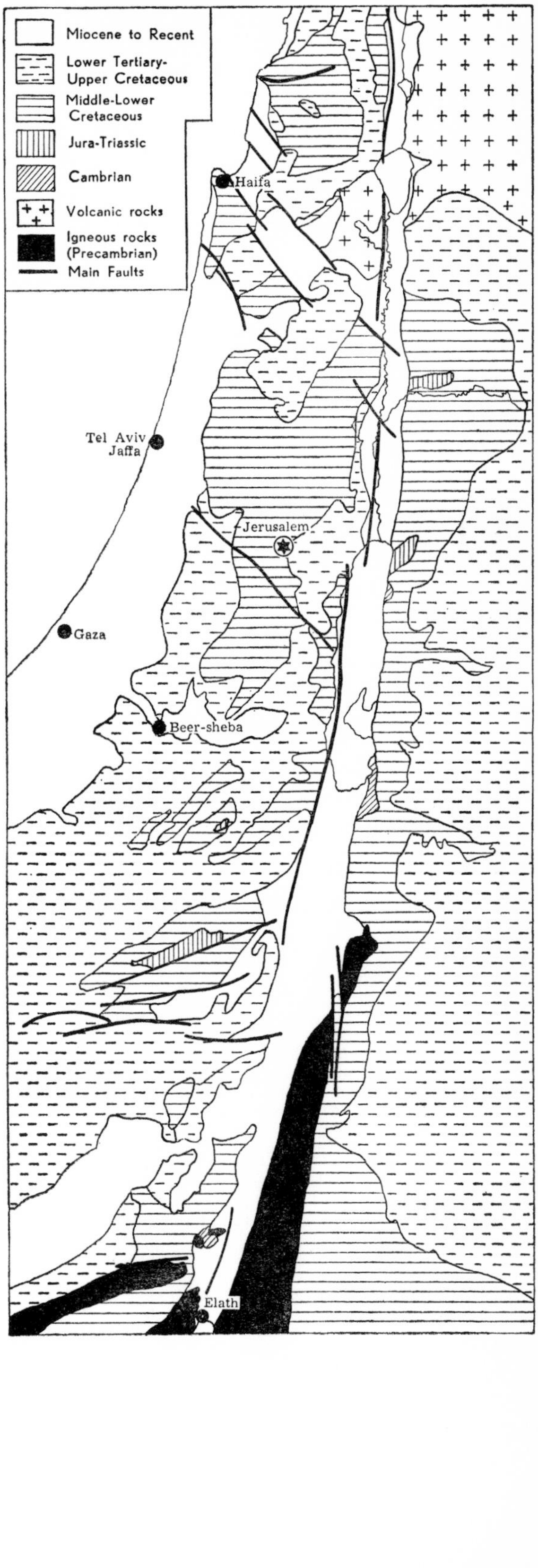

Miocene to Recent
Lower Tertiary-Upper Cretaceous
Middle-Lower Cretaceous
Jura-Triassic
Cambrian
Volcanic rocks
Igneous rocks (Precambrian)
Main Faults

Haifa
Tel Aviv Jaffa
Jerusalem
Gaza
Beer-sheba
Elath

many other mounds surrounding the valley of Zebulun are examples of such "tells."

6. *Transjordan.* The steep slopes of the Hula—Jordan—Kinnereth—Dead Sea—Arabah depression form a real barrier to east-west communications in spite of the few passages running mostly from west to east along the valleys of the main rivers or the diagonal rift valleys. Thus the route from Beth-shean leads to the Yarmuḵ Valley; the Jabbok River is opposite Wadi Far'a (Shechem-Nablus), and the Heshbon and Nimrim valleys lie opposite Wadi Kelt.

In the south of Transjordan, almost up to the Dead Sea, are long strips of archean granitic igneous rock, forming a natural fortification and interrupting the communication of Transjordan with the Red Sea ('Aqaba-Elath). This denies Transjordan the great advantages of navigation, maritime trade, and contact with overseas nations.

East of the granitic belt, in a rather narrow strip, are areas of sandstone from the Lower Cretaceous age. In this sandstone the wadis have carved high-walled canyons. One of the gorges transversing the granitic ridge leads to Petra, the famous Nabatean town.

East of the sandstone regions are wide plains formed of limestone of the Cenomanian, Turonian, Senonian, and Eocene ages. The folds of the strata, so predominant in the mountain region west of the Jordan, are here less conspicuous, although they form a continuation of the Cis-Jordan folds, gradually diminishing towards the east. The region as a whole, therefore, has a more plain-like character, its wide flat-lands being highly suitable for the grazing of cattle and sheep. North of the Yarmuḵ, as far as Damascus, the plains are thickly overlaid with basalt.

The main highways of Transjordan, as those of the central region of western Palestine, pass through the limestone plains of the Senonian strata, near the watershed. Passages through the gorges or river valleys are few.

B. Mineral Resources

Among Palestine's mineral resources of historic interest *flint* should be mentioned first. Flint was the basic raw material employed by prehistoric man for the production of tools and weapons, and it continued in general use throughout the early stages of the historic period. Flint or chert is contained especially in the strata of the Upper Cenomanian, the Senonian, and the Eocene. It is found in all the mountain regions of the country, but not in the Coastal Plain and inland valleys. No ancient flint quarries, like those of England, have been discovered in Palestine to date, probably because flint was here abundant on the surface. Primitive man no doubt distinguished varieties of flint and preferred given kinds for specific purposes.

Clay of different kinds, suitable for pottery, is found throughout the country. Various types of clay were used at various periods according to the prevailing requirements of the market. *Sand* for the production of glass is plentiful all over the Coastal Plain. *Copper* ore is found on both sides of the Arabah Valley and was used in the periods of the First and Second Temple. *Iron* ore is found in the eastern Negev, in north-eastern Galilee, and in the Jabbok Valley; which of these sources was utilized in ancient times is not quite clear. *Gold* ore in small quantities is known to exist in Midian, and certain *precious stones* (turquoise, for example) are found in the southern regions of the Negev as well as in Sinai.

Palestine is blessed with an abundance of *building stone*, noted for its variety, strength and beauty. Granite and other igneous rocks are found in the southernmost parts of the Negev. Because of the great difficulty involved in transporting such rocks through the Negev, it is doubtful whether they were ever used in the central and northern parts of the country. The granite now found in many Palestinian ruins represents mainly the remains of such rock originally brought from abroad.

Basalt was commonly employed as a building stone in the north. In spite of its hardness it was already used in neolithic times as material for domestic implements and in later periods (e.g., during the Egyptian rule) — for monuments, sculptures, etc.

The richly colored sandstone of the Lower Cretaceous, the so-called Nubian sandstone, acquired special fame as the type of rock out of which the necropolis of Petra was carved. A young sandstone, called Kurkar, was used at various times as building material in the Coastal Plain. Particularly well known is the Crusader fortress of 'Atlit, which was built of this stone.

There are also different kinds of limestone. Some are soft, white and chalky, easily cut and dressed; others are difficult to work, but strong and durable. A white marble-like limestone of the Eocene strata, not unlike the limestone of the Egyptian pyramids, was used as building material for the palaces of the kingdom of Ephraim and later for synagogues in the Galilee. It is typical of Palestinian building that flint, so frequently employed in Europe, was not used here, probably because of its unsuitability for a hot climate.

4. CLIMATE

by D. Ashbel

THE SPECIFIC climatic conditions of Palestine are determined above all by the unusual combination of its boundaries: the sea (to the west), the desert (to the east and south) and the towering, snow-capped mountains (to the north). In consequence of these heterogeneous natural boundaries, Palestine enjoys a diversity of climatic conditions, the like of which can only be found elsewhere at distances of hundreds and even thousands of miles.

Because it is situated between Egypt, which is poor in rainfall, and Lebanon, with its wealth of rain and snow, Palestine serves as a transitional land from a sub-tropical desert to a sub-tropical rainy region. Hence the great contrasts between north and south in all four orographic belts of the country, in all of which the south has a low rainfall which increases northwards.

The *rains* are caused by barometric depressions moving from the west along the longitudinal axis of the Mediterranean Sea. As they reach the eastern part of that sea, the center of these depressions is approximately over the island of Cyprus. Isobars surround such a barometric depression in a more or less concentric form, and in certain parts of the depression clouds develop, from which rain is precipitated during the cold season. The greater the distance from the vortex, the smaller the chance of precipitation. Hence the scanty rainfall in Egypt which, unlike Palestine, was exclusively dependent upon irrigation for its agriculture. The Bible was already cognizant of this distinction, and defined it as follows: "For the land, whither thou goest in to possess it, is not as the land of Egypt . . . . where thou didst sow thy seed, and didst water it with thy foot, as a garden of herbs; but the land, whither ye go over to possess it . . . . drinketh water as the rain of heaven cometh down," or "a land which the Lord thy God careth for; the eyes of the Lord thy God are always upon it, from the beginning of the year even unto the end of the year" (Deut. 11:10–12).

It may logically be assumed that already in ancient times an invisible but clearly defined boundary ran between irrigated Egypt and Palestine, watered by rains. This boundary lay then, even as it does now, in the Negev. At no stage, however, was it a border line, comparable to a political frontier, but rather a broad belt which, from year to year, moved tens and sometimes even hundreds of miles northward or southward. In 1959-1960, for example, the desert was thrust more than 60 miles northward, whilst in 1934–1935 or in 1944–45 there was also heavy rainfall in the Negev, and even further to the south, beyond the Egyptian border. In a dry year, large tracts of the agricultural region revert to complete or partial desert, whereas in years of copious rain, broad stretches of the Arabah, arid for many years, blossom into pasture land and green fields.

Had the whole of Palestine been a plain, the desert may have encroached on more extensive parts of the country than at present. The western currents of air coming from the Mediterranean are compelled, however, by the mountains to ascent and form, in winter, dense clouds which precipitate in amounts that increase from south to north. Whilst the southern Negev (Sinai) has only 2–4 inches of rain a year (during the winter months), the Beer-sheba region has 8 inches and that of Gaza 16 inches. From here to the region of Lud, the precipitation increases to 20 inches. In the northern Sharon, the figure reaches 24 inches, whilst in the Carmel range and in the mountains of Samaria and Judea, the rainfall is many inches more. Palestine's highest rainfall is in the mountains of Upper Galilee (39–42 inches). On Mt. Hermon, which feeds the sources of the Jordan and its various tributaries, there are 47–67 inches of precipitation annually; up to an altitude of 4,000 ft. the precipitation consists of rain, whereas above that height it is mainly snow which remains on the mountain throughout the winter, until the higher temperatures of spring cause the great thaw which floods the Jordan and its tributaries. From the mountains of Judea, Samaria and Galilee, the cloud-producing currents of air continue on their course eastward to the Jordan Valley, being forced more than 3,000 ft. downwards to the Jordan basin. Through descent and compression (the barometric pressure at Jerusalem is 690 mms. Hg, whilst at the Dead Sea it is 790 mms.), the air becomes hot and dry; the clouds vanish and the sky clears. In consequence, the Jordan basin has a low rainfall, although here too the amount increases from south to north. Whilst the shores of Elath and the Red Sea have only about 0.4 inches of rain a year, the annual rainfall at the Dead Sea is 1.6 inches in the south and 3.2 inches in the north, that of the Beth-shean Valley 11.2–12, of the Kinnereth Valley 16–20, and of the Hula Valley 16–28 inches.

Streaming from the west into Transjordan, which is higher than the western mountain range, the currents of air once more rise, and since the ascent here is much greater than that from the Mediterranean, heavy clouds again form, bringing abundant rain to the upper region of the mountains of Transjordan. This area is, however, surrounded by desert land on three sides. In the west, a desert dominates the entire lower portion of the slope that rises from the Jordan Valley, whilst the desert of the Arabian Peninsula encroaches on the east and south. Only the uppermost part of Transjordan's mountains has a rainfall sufficient for farming as well as for the growth of large forests in Edom and the mountains of Gilead.

Dew. There are regions of abundant dew in Palestine, such as the western Negev, the Coastal Plain, the Plain of Jezreel and the crest of the Carmel range. Other regions of copious dew are the lower Beth-shean Valley and the central Hula Valley, their fringes, however, remaining dry even when the remainder of the area is blanketed with heavy dew. The dryness of these fringes is explained by the fact that the currents of air which flow down the mountain slopes during the night are warmed up in the course of their descent, thus preventing condensation of moisture into dew. For the same reason, not only are the lower slopes of the Carmel poor in dew, but also the western feet of the entire high range of the Judean, Samarian and Galilean mountains, as well as of their steep eastern inclines. The aridity of the Judean desert during the summer months is similar to that of the deserts of Benjamin and Samaria, which likewise shelve down to the Jordan Valley. The feet of the mountains of Moab, Ammon and Gilead, the Golan and the Hauran, down to the Jordan Valley westward, remain dry.

Because cloudiness and the easterly winds are not conducive to the formation of dew, Palestine has the most dew during August and September, and the least during the *khamsin* months. In the western Negev, as well as in the Coastal Plain and in the central part of the Plain of Jezreel, the number of dew-nights per year rises to 200–250; on a dewy night, however, more dew is formed in the Negev than in the Plain of Jezreel or the Coastal Plain. In the mountain regions, there are no more than 100–150 dew-nights per year (inclusive of nights of fog). At the feet of the western mountains, the annual figure is about 100, whilst on the mountain slopes of the Judean desert, in the Jordan Valley and on the shores of the Dead Sea it does not reach even 50.

Dew has great agricultural significance. In areas where it is abundant crops may be raised in summer without the aid of irrigation (melons, durra, sorghum, sesame, and also certain kinds of vegetables); in regions devoid of dew, however, no summer crops can be produced without irrigation. The shepherd and the herdsman, too, appreciate the importance of dew for the growth of pasture for sheep and cattle.

Snow falls almost every year on mountains of 2,600–3,300 ft. in altitude, such as the mountains of Hebron or of Upper Galilee in western Palestine, or the mountains of Gilead, Moab and Edom (4,300–5,600 ft.) in Transjordan. Mt. Hermon and the mountains of Lebanon that rise to a height of close to 10,000 ft. above sea-level, receive the major part of their annual precipitation in the form of snow. Because of this, these limited areas are permanently able to feed a number of relatively large rivers during the entire year. The fall of snow on the mountains of Palestine occurs mostly during the months of January and February, although there have been years when snow has fallen in November—December and even in March—April.

Cloudiness. The frequency of barometric lows during the period of October—May and their rareness (or absence) during June—September lead to a great difference in cloud formation during these two seasons. From October to May, and sometimes even to June, high, medium and low clouds, in all their manifold forms, are to be seen; in the summer months there are only low clouds, produced by currents of oceanic air ascending to the mountains. In September, mostly at the end of the month, high ice clouds begin to make their appearance, followed first by medium clouds and then by the bulk of low, moisture-laden cumulus clouds. The summer clouds, though higher, are of the same low type — cumulus — as those seen in the winter months. In summer, too, low clouds, more laden with moisture than in winter, drift to the continent from the west, but they precipitate no rain, for during these months they lack ice-crystals and the other conditions necessary for producing rain. In the high mountain region, such as that of Hermon and the Lebanon to the north of Palestine, summer clouds reduce the force of the sun's burning rays during diurnal hours. The western slope, rising from the sea, is generally enveloped in fog at midday, and the clouds, which literally crouch on the ground, clamber and ascend from the sea along the courses of the river beds. Cloudiness in the mountains is often, especially at night, close to ground-level; during daylight hours, the clouds drift at a height of 1–2 miles. Clouds of fog which in summer mornings accumulate in the river beds of the mountain regions dissipate after sunrise. In winter cloudiness is more evident in the mountains than along the littoral, the opposite holding true in summer. Throughout the whole country, there is not a single day during the summer months which is entirely overcast.

In the coastal region there are *fogs* in winter, in the transitional months and when a *khamsin* passes over the country. In the valleys, such as the Plain of Jezreel, fogs are more frequent in summer and, in the windless mornings, occur mainly in the valleys' depressions. Like cloudiness, morning fogginess is in summer more extensive in the Upper Galilee than in the south. In winter months, fogs rise from the Dead Sea and from the Hula Valley. On cold nights, a dense fog blankets the Hula, whilst at the Dead Sea the fog forms not at night but after sunrise — in the wake of the final stage of a barometric low when a wave of cold air reaches the country, driving the local air to the slopes of the mountains on both sides, to the Jerusalem—Hebron mountains on the west and to the mountains of Moab on the east. After sunrise, the fog begins to ascend the slopes of the mountains, climbing by the river beds to the mountain summits (a difference in altitude of 3,900–5,600 ft.). The fog reaches the mountains of Jerusalem in the late morning, becomes denser at noon, and generally dissipates in the late afternoon, occasionally, however, continuing until the evening or even persisting all night. As though it were a solid object, the fog remains stationary on the mountain ridge in spite of the strong westerly wind that blows over the mountains at that time. The sharp beak of the fog faces westward (at an angle of about 60°) and its depth on the surface of the mountain at times extends many hundred of yards. In this manner the stable fog persists for hours on end until it dissipates.

Radiation. Due to its location in the northern sub-tropics, Palestine receives an enormous amount of solar radiation. The small extent of cloudiness and the length of the day (14 1/4 hours on the longest day) in summer, on the one hand, and the elevation of the sun (81.7° above the horizon on the longest day) during that period, on the other, sufficiently explain the fact that radiation in Palestine during the summer reaches the maximum values measured on the globe. In winter, too, the minimum altitude of the sun is not less than 35° above the horizon, and although the days are shorter (10 hours on the shortest day) in this period, cloudiness is not an all-winter phenomenon. On about half the winter days an easterly wind prevails, when the sky is almost totally clear of heavy clouds (there are occasionally high ice clouds on these days, but they do not greatly diminish radiation).

Palestine, therefore, may be defined as a land of abundant sunshine, and only few countries can compare with it in this regard. On a summer's day the daily mean of radiation received on a square meter of horizontal surface is about 7 1/2 million gram calories; on a bright winter's day it is about 3 million gram calories, whilst on a dull, overcast day it is no more than 0.7–1 million gram calories. Whereas this holds true for horizontal areas, the mountain slopes are subject to varying quantities of radiation, the southern slopes receiving the maximum amount in winter and the minimum in summer, as well as the largest annual total. During the period of the Second Temple, the priests at Jerusalem were already aware of these facts; hence, the Tannaitic dictum (Men. 85a): "The Omer is to be brought only from southern fields, for on them the sun shines from sunrise to sunset." The southern slopes are of especial value to agriculture in winter, for then vegetables and other growths may ripen here early and be marketed out of season.

Light. The quantities of light which Palestine receives are, as in the case of solar heat radiation, very large. In this country, as in the rest of the eastern Mediterranean, the quantity of light that reaches a horizontal surface at noontime during the summer is in excess of 100 kilo-lux-hours, while a surface vertical to the sun's rays receives more than 120 kilo-lux-hours — almost the absolute maximum light transmitted by the sun to the earth. Again as in the case of radiation, southern walls and slopes receive more light in winter than in summer, whereas those to the east, the west and the north receive more light in summer than in winter.

A comparison of light measurements taken in this region and in countries of a temperate climate shows that in winter Palestine receives three times more light than France or Germany, for instance, and in summer — although the days in the latter countries are then longer —, twice as much, this being due to the sparse cloudiness of its skies during the entire season. To avoid superfluity of light, as well as of heat, the ancients built their homes, and especially their temples, with long, narrow windows and doors, through which light and radiation could enter in sufficient but not excessive quantities, in order to achieve maximum comfort indoors during the hot season. For the same reason Solomon made for the Temple (I Kings 6:4) *hallōnēy sheqūfim 'atūmīm:* windows transparent within and opaque without.

Temperature. During the summer months the temperature of the air in Palestine may rise very high, particularly when the currents of air are forced downwards from high altitudes either in the mountains or in the free atmosphere. The descent of air from the upper levels takes place when a high barometric pressure prevails over an area, or when a wind blows from a mountain into a low-lying valley. A westerly wind blowing in May or June from the mountains of Jerusalem to the Dead Sea becomes very warm and dry, greatly increasing the temperature in the Jordan Valley. An easterly wind that blows in winter from the mountains of Hebron, for example, in the direction of the Mediterranean raises the temperature at the western feet of the Hebron mountains, thus preventing frost there even on a very cold night. The temperature in the valleys is, in consequence, generally higher than that in the mountains, and the greater the difference in altitude between them, the greater the difference in the prevailing temperatures. At Elath, for example, which has high mountains to the west and east, air masses are forced down into the bay and invariably become greatly heated in the process, so that temperatures rise to record heights, unparalleled throughout the country.

Extremes of temperature. The highest temperature measured in Palestine since 1860, i.e., since records of temperature have been kept in this country, reached (in the Beth-shean Valley, on June 22, 1942) 129.2°F. (54°C.). On that day, the temperature was 124.7°F. (51.5°C.) at the Dead Sea, 113°F. (45°C.) in the Coastal Plain, and 118.4°F. (48°C.) in the Plain of Jezreel. In the Jerusalem area, no values higher than 111.2°F. (44°C.) have been recorded during the last hundred years. In most instances of heat waves, the temperature in the Jordan Valley rises to 113°–118.4°F. (45°–48°C.) and in the Coastal Plain to 95°–100.4°F. (35°–38°C.). Values of 100.4°F. (38°C.) at the coast or in the mountains are considered very high.

The lowest temperatures recorded at Jerusalem during the last hundred years were 23° and 19.4°F. (-5° and -7°C.). In the Jordan Valley also, temperatures have many times dropped below the freezing point. On the other hand, a temperature of 32°F. (0°C.) was recorded only twice (February 1920 and February 1950) on the shore of the Mediterranean, when heavy snow blanketed the entire country up to the coast itself and even up to the shores of the Dead Sea.

Winds. The barometric pressure in Palestine during the summer is totally different from that in winter. During the hot months, no lows or highs reach the area from the sea, and in consequence of the very deep low prevailing over the whole continent of Asia, this region is then on the extreme western perimeter of the vortex. Isobars in the eastern Mediterranean show a continuous decrease from west to east, and because of this there occur (mainly over the sea and in the mountains) westerly winds that blow day and night for successive weeks and months. Due to the absence of barometric highs in the summer, the pressure remains low throughout the season, and is in fact at the same level as the pressure prevailing here on stormy and rainy winter days. The strong, steady winds that blow from the north and the northwest over the sea between Greece and Egypt were recognized already in ancient times as Etesian or "seasonal," and the part they played in the development of Phoenician and Greek oared vessels and navigation was great indeed.

Lulls in the Etesian winds in the middle of summer, as well as the occurrence of heat waves in the region, are the result of an abnormal monsoon in India and other parts of southern Asia. Local pressure cells are then formed in the area, forcing the descent of upper air masses, which consequently become heated and dry.

In winter, when a barometric depression from the Mediterranean approaches its eastern shores, a dry, and at times also cold, easterly wind springs up. However, since the currents of air in such a wind *descend* over this region, a rise in temperature invariably occurs.

When the depression is very close to the shores of the eastern Mediterranean, the wind becomes southeasterly and later southerly. As the center of the depression passes over the area, the wind changes to southwesterly and westerly, and is attended by cool, humid sea air together with a great mass of clouds. The rains that fall in this region in winter are always accompanied by a southwesterly or westerly wind. When the wind again changes its course and becomes northwesterly, the rain generally stops and the skies clear. Such is the picture in winter. A barometric depression reaches the region on an average once weekly, and it is, therefore, likely that the rain, which begins to fall on a particular day at the start of the season, will for a number of weeks come on that same day, until an interruption occurs in the system when, after a week or two of clear weather, depressions will begin to arrive in a new pattern.

It is otherwise during the summer months, when no barometric depressions reach the area and only a northwesterly to westerly wind blows continuously until the end of the season. With the disappearance of the summer pressure system over the continent of Asia, new conditions are created, permitting depressions from the Mediterranean Sea to reach the region from the west, whereupon the winter system of winds with all their variability returns: "The wind goeth toward the south, and turneth about unto the north; it turneth about continually in its circuit" (Eccl. 1:6).

5. FLORA

by M. Zohary

A. The Flora and its Environment

THE FLORA of Palestine is richly variegated. No less than 2,250 species of flowering plants grow wild in the country; some are trees and shrubs, but most are annual or perennial herbs. The specific density, i. e., the number of species per surface unit, generally decreases from north to south and from west to east, in proportion to the annual rainfall. The large number of communities in which the plants are grouped is in proportion to the numerous habitats found in the land.

The great variety of flora and the multitude of habitats are partly a result of climatic conditions which evolved and changed throughout the ages, and partly the outcome of phytogeographical, topographical and edaphic factors.

For, in the first place, it should be borne in mind that the country has undergone many climatic changes since it emerged from the sea in the Oligocene period. Every climatic period had its own flora, which later gave way to another flora when a radical change in the climate occurred. This replacement, however, was never total nor complete; certain species always survived from one period to another. This accounts for the gradual accumulation of various flora remnants down to the present time.

From the phytogeographical point of view, Palestine stands at the junction of three great floral regions, the Mediterranean, the Irano-Turanian, and the Saharo-Sindian; it can accordingly be divided into three phytogeographical territories.

The Mediterranean region, which consists of the countries around the Mediterranean basin, is represented within Palestine by the Coastal Plain, the western mountain range up to the main watershed, and the western part of the Transjordanian plateau. This territory enjoys a mild and rather temperate climate, an annual rainfall not below 14 inches and, on the whole, a fertile soil. In the past, this territory sustained not only forests and scrub forests, but also a stable agriculture, as it is capable of doing today.

The Irano-Turanian region comprises all the countries to the east of Palestine, from the Syrian desert to Central Asia and the Gobi desert in the east. In Palestine it is represented by the territory that includes the Judean Desert, the eastern slopes of Samaria, the Middle Jordan Valley, the northern Negev, and a wide strip of the Transjordanian plateau in the direction of the Syrian Desert. It has a more continental climate and the rainfall fluctuates between 8 to 14 inches. The soil is poor and arid, incapable of sustaining forests or scrub forests, and the agriculture is unstable.

The Saharo-Sindian region is one of extreme deserts. It comprises the deserts of Sahara, Libya, Egypt, Sinai and Arabia and extends as far as Sind. Corresponding to this region, there is within Palestine a territory which consists of the central and southern Negev, the Arabah Valley, the Lower Jordan Valley and the desert of Edom. Its climate is extremely hot and dry and the annual rainfall fluctuates between 1 to 8 inches. This territory has never sustained any dry farming whatever and its vegetation consists mainly of dwarf-shrubs and herbs.

The flora of Palestine has been largely determined by the wide diversity of the country's topography, as exemplified by the contrast between the Idumaean mountains, reaching an altitude of about 5,575 feet, and the area around the Dead Sea, which is 1,300 feet below sea level. Especially reflected is the ecological difference between the western mountains and the two valleys to the east and west.

Although the country as a whole is governed by a climate of the Mediterranean type, the regional climatic variations are considerable. There is a strong gradient — not only in rainfall but also in temperature, evaporation, and radiation — between north and south and between east and west. The differences are so extreme that one can, within a few hours' journey by car, pass from a subhumid region to one of extreme desert.

The varieties of soil in Palestine are no less striking. As many as 15 types of soil, differing from each other in chemical and physical properties, have been defined and described. On the one hand, there are large areas of red soils and fertile alluvial plains, and on the other, dry hammadas, sands, and sterile salines; in the one case, deep moist soil, and in the other, rocky ground with scanty soil cover.

All these factors produce a great variety of environments for the plants and contribute to the existence of floral elements belonging to different plant-regions. In addition, they encourage the formation of endemic species whose distribution is confined to the boundaries of the country. There are, indeed, as many as 150 endemic species in Palestine.

This diversity of environmental conditions has no doubt exercised a deep influence on the tribal distribution of the local population over the country, or at least helped to maintain the cultural individuality of each ethnic unit for generations. Already in ancient times the ecological differentiation of Palestine gave rise to a variegated agriculture. Situated as it is between three great centers of the origin of cultivated plants — Western Asia, Abyssinia, and the Mediterranean — Palestine has from time immemorial absorbed cultivated plants from its native flora. There are, in fact, numerous native plants in this country which are considered wild ancestors of cultivated plants.

While the vegetation did indeed have a strong bearing on the agricultural civilization of the country, it left no less deep a mark on the religion, language and literature of the people. A few examples will suffice. Forest trees serve in the Bible as symbols of worship and holiness; the oak and the terebinth, the two most common trees in the country's forests, are philologically connected with the stem *El* ("God"). Under trees incense was burned for Baal, and in their shade the dead were buried. Biblical proverbs and metaphors abound in images inspired by plant life. A great number of place names and proper names are also borrowed from the world of plants. The Halakah is full of subjects dealing with wild and cultivated plants, and many legends have grown up around trees and herbs.

B. The Main Vegetation Types of the Country

The following offers a brief account of the vegetation in Palestine's floral territories, commencing with that of the Mediterranean. This territory is characterized by forests and scrub forests which formerly constituted the main vegetal cover of the landscape. A few wooded tracts of land are now the only remnants of these forests, but with the help of vegetal relics and literary documents, it is not difficult to ascertain their former distribution and composition.

1. *The Common Oak Forest.* From the standpoint of both its distribution and composition, this is the most important type of forest. Apart from the common oak (*Quercus calliprinos*), we find here many representatives of the Mediterranean scrub forests such as the Palestinian pistacio (*Pistacia palaestina*), the common laurel (*Laurus nobilis*), the strawberry tree (*Arbutus andrachne*), the common hawthorn (*Crataegus azarolus*), the lance-leaved phillyrea (*Phillyrea media*), the Judas tree (*Cercis siliquastrum*), the carob (*Ceratonia siliqua*), and others. In this composition such a community does not appear as a tall forest but rather as a scrub forest, i.e., a formation of low trees and tall bushes which never attains the stature of trees because of constant interference on the part of man through cutting and pasturing. But as soon as man desists, the oaks grow taller and their associates disappear.

While there are many stands of oak scrub forest throughout the hill and mountain area of this territory, there are but poor remnants of the oak forests; these survived only thanks to the custom common among the Arabs of burying their distinguished dead in the shade of trees and guarding those trees from human enemies. The common oak scrub forests are the pride and glory of the country. They are not limited to the areas of red soil, characteristic of the Mediterranean territory, but are commonly found also in grey soil, though never in swampy or sandy terrain. They climb mountains to an altitude of over 3,000 feet, but never descend lower than 600 feet above sea level. According to the altitude, soil, and exposure of the mountain, one can distinguish several varieties of the common oak scrub forest differing from one another mainly by the presence or absence of certain bushes and trees.

2. *The Pine Forest.* The most important tree in this forest is the Aleppo pine — a tall evergreen whose life-span covers 120—150 years. Of especial importance in the timber industry, it has suffered more at the hands of man than did any other kind of tree. Formerly it dominated large parts of Upper Galilee, Samaria, and the mountains of Judea and Transjordan where the pine forest was connected with the greyish white calcereous soil called Rendzina. Nothing remains today of these forests except small groves in some hilly districts of the Mediterranean territory. The pine wood also harbors other Mediterranean trees such as the common oak, various species of pistacio, phillyrea, and hawthorn, as well as numerous dwarf-shrubs, herbs, bulb plants and the like.

3. *The Tabor Oak Forest* (*Quercus ithaburensis*). This is a deciduous forest whose distribution in Palestine is limited to the Sharon, Lower Galilee, the Hula Valley and the slopes of the mountains descending to it. In the Sharon Plain (between the Yarqon River and Binyamina), this forest was composed purely of oaks, unaccompanied by other trees. In Lower Galilee, some areas of woodland have survived in the region of Alonim-Shefar'am, and there we find the oak in company with the styrax, the Palestinian pistacio, the common hawthorn, the Palestinian buckthorn, and others. In the valleys of the Hula and Dan and on the slopes of Bashan and eastern Galilee the oak is accompanied by the Atlantic pistacio. This forest is found in a variety of soils, but does not climb higher than 1,500 feet. The Tabor oak is noted for its quick growth and its shallow roots. It attains a height of 60 feet and has a wide crown. There are ancient oaks in Palestine which certainly exceed 1,000 years of age.

4. *The Carob and the Mastic Pistacio Scrub Forests.* In the foothills west of the mountain range, from the Hebron mountains to the Lebanon border,

on the Kurkar hills and the consolidated sand dunes of the northern Sharon, as well as on some of the eastern slopes of the mountains of Galilee and Samaria, grows a type of evergreen scrub forest, which is composed, among others, of the carob tree (*Ceratonia siliqua*) and the Mastic pistachio bush (*Pistacia lentiscus*). In addition to these dominating species other shrubs, dwarf-shrubs and climbers, as well as a great number of annual and perennial herbs, are to be found. This scrub forest which does not generally climb to an altitude of more than 1,000 feet, has in many places been totally destroyed. In other places the carob tree alone has been spared due to its fruit, edible by man and beast.

The types of the forest and the scrub forest listed above constitute the characteristic feature of the vegetation in the Mediterranean territory. In the past, these types formed a more or less continuous cover of woods; but since this territory, by its soil and climate, has always been very suitable for permanent agriculture, man has never, since earliest times, ceased to interfere with the vegetal cover, either for farming purposes or to satisfy his need for fuel, building materials, and pasture. Some woods have nevertheless survived to this day, owing to natural conditions and the sturdiness of the trees, which regenerate after cutting and burning. Where man refrains from damaging these woods directly or indirectly, natural rehabilitation of the vegetation may take place in successive stages. Each stage produces a vegetation of higher stature and of different composition until the final stage of forest or scrub forest is reached. The most important stages leading to the reappearance of the scrub forest or the forest are the Batha (dwarf-shrub vegetation) and the Garigue (shrub-vegetation), both of which require open sunlight. These shrubs and dwarf-shrubs thus appear wherever a forest has been exterminated. They remain for many years until the soil improves and becomes capable of supporting the characteristic components of the scrub forest and the forest.

Apart from the forest and scrub forest, and those types of Batha and Garigue which are genetically connected with them, the Mediterranean territory also supports other types of vegetation, a few of which will be mentioned.

(a) *The vegetation of the sand dunes and sand fields.* All along the Coastal Plain there is a belt of light soils, so-called because they are mainly composed of sand. First of all, mention should be made of the sandy dunes comprised of quartzy sand brought from the sea. These sand dunes maintain a special vegetation dominated by shrubs and perennial herbs capable of checking the movement of the sand, such as marram grass (*Ammophila arenaria*), sand wormwood (*Artemisia monosperma*), white broom (*Retama Roetam*), horsetail knotweed (*Polygonum equisetiforme*), French tamarisk (*Tamarix gallica*), etc. These leading plants of the various communities are accompanied by many other annual and perennial plants adapted to the extreme conditions of on-shore winds and soil-movement. With the stabilization of the sand and the consolidation of the soil, different plant communities, such as those of Batha and Garigue, make their appearance and conquer the area until a special variant of the carob and Mastic pistachio scrub forest (in the north of the country) finally takes possession.

To the rear of this sand dune belt there are wide stretches of sandy clay as well as hills of calcerous sandstone called Kurkar. Here we find special plant communities composed of shrubs, dwarf-shrubs, and other sand-favoring herbs. In the Sharon the sandy clay is dominated by the community of the bipinnate spring grass (*Eragrostis bipinnata*) which comprises dozens of annual species. In the Kurkar hills there are Batha and Garigue communities of a peculiar composition.

The light soil region which, because of its barren unproductive soil, had for generations been very sparsely settled, has in the last few decades become a thriving center of irrigated agriculture, in which citrus growing is of primary importance. As a result, the natural vegetation of the region is rapidly being exterminated.

(b) *The Hydrophytic Vegetation.* Although to the south and east the country borders on extremely arid deserts and steppes, it nevertheless maintains an exceedingly rich vegetation of water-, swamp- and riverine plants. In both its hydrographic centers, the Coastal Plain and the Jordan Valley, there are several permanent rivers, as well as lakes and swamps. Among the many plant communities typical of these aquatic habitats, the following plants are the leading species: the common reed (*Phragmites communis*), the papyrus (*Cyperus papyrus*), the clammy inula (*Inula viscosa*), the prickly sea rush (*Juncus acutus*), the Palestine bramble (*Rubus sanctus*), the oleander (*Nerium oleander*), etc. On the banks of those rivers which flow the year round, a wood vegetation containing species of the willow (*salix*) and the oriental planetree (*Platanus orientalis*) is also to be found. The banks of the Jordan are noted for their thick forests of Euphrates poplar (*Populus euphratica*) and Jordan tamarisk (*Tamarix jordanis*).

(c) *The Vegetation of the Steppes and Deserts.* About half of Palestine is steppe and desert. Except under special conditions, this area has never maintained any wood vegetation. Both the Irano-Turanian and the Saharo-Sindian territories were essentially pasture land and — except in the valleys and depressions, in the vicinity of river mouths, or on artificial terraces in the ephemeral wadis — supported no agriculture. The extreme climatic conditions and the poor soil lend the vegetation, which is mainly low bushes, dwarf-shrubs, and herbs, an appearance of desolate monotony. Particularly abundant in this territory are annuals and ephemerals which complete their life-cycle within the few weeks of the rainy season, whereas the perennial plants are few in number and equipped with physiological and anatomical means of withstanding the drought and fierce heat of the long summer. The plant coverage here is poor and sparse, and yet the deserts of the country have never been totally uninhabited by man.

According to the type of their soil on which their vegetation closely depends, the steppes and deserts of the country may be classified as follows:

(i) *Grey-soil steppes*. Close to the southern and eastern borders of the Mediterranean territory there are areas of grey calcerous soil containing no injurious salts, with a vegetation composed, among others, of the herba alba wormwood community (*Artemisia herba alba*). This community contains low and mostly grey dwarf-shrubs and, in the spring, numerous annuals. This is also the case in the western part of the Judean Desert, the northern and central Negev, and in parts of the Syrian Desert.

(ii) *Loess steppes*. In the northern Negev and in the southern part of Transjordan there are wide stretches of loess-soil, especially in the valleys. Because they are relatively fertile and contain no injurious salts, man has always claimed these areas for agriculture; hence their original vegetation has been completely destroyed. With the help of analogy and some vegetal evidences, it may be concluded that, in the past, this soil also maintained a sage brush steppe. Today these areas are characterized by their special segetal vegetation (weeds accompanying field crops), namely, the community of santolina milfoil (*Achillea santolina*). Apart from the Achillea this community contains a considerable number of weeds found nowhere else in the country.

(iii) *Gravel deserts or Hammadas*. This name is applied to wide areas of the central and southern Negev having a gravelly brown or grey soil of a fine, mealy consistency, and generally containing a considerable percentage of gypsum and chlorides unfavorable to the growth of plants. The vegetation of this region is extremely poor and largely confined to rummels and wadi beds that criss-cross the plains. The plant community most typical of the plains and slopes is that of the bushy bean caper (*Zygophyllum dumosum*) accompanied by some dwarf-shrubs and herbs. The banks of the river beds and depressions are dominated by the community of the jointed anabasis (*Anabasis articulata*). In the ephemeral wadi beds there are the shaggy sparrow-wort (*Thymelaea hirsuta*), white broom (*Retama Roetam*), species of the tamarisk (*Tamarix*), and others. In the Arabah Valley, the wadi beds of the Hammada maintain among others some species of acacia accompanied by certain tropical shrubs and dwarf-shrubs.

In the Judean Desert there are slopes whose dry soil contains a high percentage of gypsum and other salts. These slopes are also characterized by a poor and sparse vegetation of succulent dwarf-shrubs dominated by the Dead Sea blite (*Suaeda asphaltica*), *Chenolea arabica*, *Reaumuria palaestina*, the Palestine orach (*Atriplex palaestina*), etc. The plants of the Hammadas and of the gypsum soils are mostly succulent and resistant to both the salinity of the soil and the extreme drought. These desert plants are most modest in their requirements and best adapted to desert conditions.

(iv) *The Sand Deserts.* The sand dune belt of the western Negev joins with that of the Mediterranean territory; in the Negev, however, the dimensions of the sand dunes are wider and, because of the low precipitation, the plant coverage is poorer. Apart from the sand wormwood and white broom bushes, certain perennial grasses also appear here in the form of large bunches, such as the triple-awned grass (*Aristida scorporia*), the millet (*Pennisetum dichotomum*), the turgid panic grass (*Panicum turgidum*), etc. In the southwestern corner of the western Negev, the loess is covered by a layer of sand which not only improves the soil but also retains a greater amount of moisture. The density of the vegetation increases correspondingly and its composition differs considerably from that of the sand dunes. In the sand dunes of the Arabah Valley (derived from the weathered igneous rock and Nubian sandstone), the vegetation is composed of bushes and small trees among which the saxaul (*Haloxylon persicum*), the bunge (*Haloxylon salicornicum*), the *Calligonum comosum* and the white broom (*Retama Roetam*) may be mentioned.

(v) *The Salines.* Although saline soils are found also in the Mediterranean territory, in the deserts they constitute a characteristic feature. Occurring mainly in the Arabah Valley and the Lower Jordan Valley, their existence is determined by drainless basins, a high ground-water level and saline springs. Except for a special vegetation (including a few trees) adapted to these edaphic conditions, the salines are unfavorable to the existence of plants. The most important plants of the Arabah Valley-salines include many species of the tamarisk (*Tamarix*), species of the sea blite (*Suaeda*), the orach (*Atriplex*), the arthrocnemum and the saltwort (*Salsola*). In the flood regions to the north and south of the Dead Sea there is a big, fairly dense tamarisk forest characteristic of the salines. There are, however, considerable areas in which the concentration of the salt (mainly sodium chloride) is so great that no plant will grow there.

(vi) *The Tropical Vegetation of the Jordan Valley.* Within the desert region of the Jordan Valley and the Arabah Valley is a string of oases containing a tropical African-Arabian vegetation. Requiring high temperature and humidity, this vegetation found these conditions in the river mouths of the above mentioned valleys. So far, about forty species of the tropical element have been listed, among them such important trees as species of acacia (*Acacia*), the moringa (*Moringa aptera*), the toothbrush tree (*Salvadora persica*), the Jericho balsam (*Balanites aegyptiaca*), etc. Comprising Jericho, Far'a, Nimrim, Zoar, En-gedi, and other spots, these oases have ever been centers of irrigated agriculture.

C. Mutual Relations between Man and Plants

The foregoing description of Palestine's natural vegetation may have enabled the reader to receive an insight into what has been man's environment in this country for millennia. Long before man became a farmer, however, his hunting, herb-collecting and shelter-building interfered with the vegetation. With the development of agriculture he was obliged to destroy natural plant communities and supplant them by field crops. There is, indeed, much evidence to the effect that in the past the forest was extensive in Palestine — evidence afforded primarily by individual remnants of forest trees spared by the woodcutter on utilitarian grounds. Such relics are abundant not only in uninhabited, but also in the midst of settled areas, and even within the larger towns (Jerusalem, Hebron, etc.). Even in the region of intensive agriculture, where the natural vegetation has been completely exterminated, one may occasionally find choice trees spared by man for the sake of their shade or fruit. Much knowledge about the past distribution and composition of the forest can be derived from the "sacred trees," that is from those groves or groups of trees held sacred by the Arabs and preserved out of reverence for the holy men buried in their shade. Further evidence for the past existence of forested areas is afforded by many literary documents (Biblical passages, travel and exploration accounts, medieval pilgrims' journals, maps, etc.).

Devastation of the forest was caused by several factors: (a) the Mediterranean forest territory bordered directly on deserts and steppes whose inhabitants, greatly in need of timber, raided the forest and damaged the trees; it should be borne in mind that timber was once exported from Palestine to Egypt; (b) several times in its history Palestine served as a battle-field and passage-area for armies of belligerent kingdoms which wrought much destruction to its forests (Turkish armies devastated large wood-lands even as late as World War I); (c) the irrational clearing of forests to gain additional farming land; (d) the charcoal and lime industries which also raised their axes against the forest trees; and (e) animal husbandry in wooded areas which seriously encroached on the forest during all the historical periods. Considering all these factors, and also the scantity of forest self-regeneration due to the deterioration of the soil, it is not surprising that the country has lost most of its woods.

On the other hand, there is evidence that devastated forests have time and again regenerated themselves when left alone by man. One finds, for instance, remains of human dwellings, wine- and olive presses, cemeteries, etc., in spots covered today by dense forest.

There are also areas of Palestine in which primary woods — never completely destroyed by man — are still extant; the trees, stronger than primitive tools, defeated man in his effort to convert woodland into fields. As a result, some of the most fertile lands from the climatical point of view, could not be conquered by man because of the difficulty in eradicating the trees with their subterranean roots and shoots, hidden in rock crevices. Such lands are, for instance, the humid mountain sides of Galilee, Samaria and Judea, which have probably never been tilled. Topography, stoniness and vegetation withstood the axe and fire of the primitive farmer, who was thus forced to look for arable land in the plains and valleys which presented no such obstacles. It thus seems highly possible that agriculture in Palestine originated not in forest areas but in grasslands or even steppes, such as the Philistine Plain and the northern edge of the Negev. This type of land gave to the semi-nomadic farmer possibilities for both pasture and tillage, which the mountainsides failed to offer.

Slighter changes were effected by man in the desert vegetation. Overgrazing and careless pasturing have caused the disappearance of good pasture plants which were replaced by unpalatable plants. This change, however, did not affect the general physiogony of the vegetation as a whole.

A feature clearly illustrating the interrelation of man and vegetation is the direct utilization of wild plants for food, industry and medicine. The history of such use begins, indeed, with man's first appearance on earth. To this very day wild plants are the mainstay of primitive tribes with no agricultural experience in the Sahara, Central Asian deserts and Australia. In Palestine, too, widespread exploitation of useful wild plants whose species number hundreds, persists to the present time not only among primitive Beduin tribes — inhabitants of the desert and the steppe — but also among villagers and city dwellers. Food plants eaten partially raw or requiring but little preparation (roasting, boiling, etc.) are particularly abundant. Of the industrial plants, some are employed in wickerwork construction and others in the production of oils, tannins, fiber, dyes, etc. Similarly, many plants are customarily used for medicines, pasture, honey-plants, etc. It may be assumed that the number of useful plants still collected from among the native flora of the country is only a fraction of the number utilized by primitive man before the introduction of agriculture. The selection of useful plants from the native flora was obviously marked by a long process of trial and error.

D. A Brief Account of Palestine's Agriculture

How the transition from this haphazard to a planned agriculture took place, we do not quite know. It is clear, however, that primitive man required no great intellect to sow, in the vicinity of his dwelling place, the seeds of plants he had collected in the field, and to realize that by so doing he simplified the problem of his subsistence. More difficult it is to trace the way in which man changed wild plants into cultivated ones — an activity which was the most crucial step in the history of agriculture — as many cultivated plants differ radically from their wild relatives, while of others no trace of the wild ancestors is to be found. No doubt Palestine's early population participated in this process of cultivating some of the local wild plants. Situated between three great floral centers which gave the world many cultivated plants — such as wheat varieties, barley, oats, beets, chickpeas, clover, lentils, beans, vetchling flax, figs, olives, carobs, almonds, and many others — Palestine was one of the spots where agricultural civilization first budded.

Although there is no vegetal evidence of primitive agricultural civilization in Palestine earlier than the Bronze Age, it may be assumed that plant cultivation already existed in the Mesolithic. This is shown by: (a) the discovery of tools such as sickle stones, weaving instruments, etc., proving, according to Miss D. Garrod, the existence of a primitive agriculture in that period; and (b) vegetal findings from the Bronze Age, which testify to a very high stage of agriculture.

Scientific opinion agrees that irrigated farming, like that of Egypt, already existed in certain parts of the country as early as the Neolithic-Chalcolithic period. It is also clear from archaeological discoveries that agriculture was fairly well developed in Palestine during the Bronze Age and included field crops and various fruit trees. No sufficient evidence is available for the Early Bronze Age. Contrarywise, the high standard of agriculture in the Biblical period, when both dry and irrigated farming were common, is well-documented. Most field plants of that period are identical with those common today; also the orchard trees and vegetable plants were to a great extent the same as ours. The number of cultivated plants has subsequently increased through introductions from Persia, India and Anatolia. It was particularly enlarged during the period of the Mishnah, though little was added during the Roman-Byzantine era. Some important plants were, indeed, introduced into the country during the Arab period, but there is authentic evidence to prove that, as a whole, Arab rule deeply harmed the country's agriculture. Dozens of agricultural settlements mentioned in Talmudic literature were destroyed by the Arab conquerors who, accustomed to their desert way of life, damaged terraces, wells and water sources, and particularly neglected the preservation of the soil.

A few words should be devoted to the large number of Palestine's floral plants (about 20% of the total inventory) which are connected with man and his culture. These are the segetal and ruderal plants — the weeds — which accompany man wherever he goes. Before man appeared on the scene only few of these plants existed here. Some were brought to this land unintentionally, together with the seeds of cultivated plants; others left their natural habitats and invaded the fields by themselves, since fields serve as large habitats free from competition with other plants. Man has consistently viewed these plants as his enemy and fought them with all the means at his disposal; he never succeeded, however, in annihilating them completely and many of them still grow in his fields.

The very existence of such a rich variety of weeds in Palestine serves to point up man's effect on the composition of the local flora. Not all of these weeds reached the country at the same time or by the same means. They arrived in waves, each plant having its own story to tell. Were it possible to trace the history of their migrations, we would gain knowledge of a most important chapter in the history of agriculture.

6. FAUNA

by F. S. Bodenheimer

THROUGHOUT the Mesozoic and early Tertiary periods Palestine was covered by the big Mesozoic Middle Sea, the Tethys. Although the earliest land-areas, which rose from the Tethys in the late Tertiary period, were still cut off from the north by the waters of the shrinking Tethys, they were solidly connected with Afro-Arabia. From this region Palestine received its first inhabitants, among them the Ethiopian cony (*Procavia*) and the Gondwana forms (e.g., the mouth-breeding fishes of the family *Cichlidae*). Toward the end of the Pliocene, a land-bridge to Syria and Anatolia was established, over which the Pikermi-fauna[1] of the vast area from Greece to North Persia migrated slowly southward to the African continent; there its offspring formed the nucleus of animal life now found in the African savanna. The bones discovered in the Mt. Carmel caves prove that in the Pleistocene period many survivors of this southward migration, such as the spotted hyena, the warthog, the Kudu antelope, the Leggada rat, and others, were still lingering on Palestinian soil; eastern elephants, wild cattle and Colchian pheasants were also extant at that time. By the Palaeolithic period, however, most of the Pikermi-fauna had already passed from Palestine to Africa, and the bulk of the present-day fauna was already established.[2] Other animals, including the lion (which became extinct in the 13th or 14th century), subsequently died out. In 1891 Conder[3] was still able to write:

> "Except for the disappearance of lion and wild bull there is no change in the fauna since Biblical times: fallow deer, roebuck, gazelle, fox, wolf, hyena, jackal, ostrich and crocodile still survive in the wilder parts of the land, with the great boars which delight in the marshes; the leopard lurks in the jungles and the cony in the rocks; the ibex leaps on the precipices, and the wild ass in the distant eastern deserts is not unknown."

Since then the wild ass, gepard, leopard, Isabelline bear, red and fallow deer, roebuck, ostrich, and crocodile have completely disappeared. The last of the larger Palestinian mammals, the gazelle (*Gazella gazella* and *Gazella dorcas*) and the ibex (*Capra nubiana*), are on the verge of extinction.

Palaeolithic man subsisted largely upon game. Glueck[4] has given a dramatic description of primitive man's elephant-hunting in the Hula marshes. The alternating predominance, in the breccias of the Mt. Carmel caves, of bones of gazelles and fallow deer — the remains of game eaten by the cave-dwellers — is often regarded as proof of climatic fluctuations which, however, were not as extensive as some are prone to maintain.

Domestication of animals had no doubt begun in Mesolithic times (8000 to 5000 B.C.E.), although no remains of human settlements or habitations have been preserved from that period. We have no idea how man lived in Palestine during the Middle Stone Age, but by the earliest Neolithic period animal husbandry (sheep, goats, cattle) was well established. Figurines of these animals were found in temples of the moon goddess at Jericho and other sites.

In Palestine, as elsewhere, the earliest companion of man was the dog. We can assume that the wild pariah dog (*Canis familiaris paria*) was domesticated by man at a very early stage. That it was used to assist in hunting is attested to by the rock-carvings of Kilwa in Transjordan (8000 to 4000 B.C.E.), but it was probably employed as a watchdog even earlier. We question the identification of Pleistocene dog bones as those of the sheep dog (*Canis familiaris matris-optimae*). In all likelihood, these bones represent a form of the wild pariah dog.

All the sheep of Palestine thus far known belong to the *Ovis vignei* of the Asiatic steppes. This includes the fat-tail, the fat-buttock and the long-tail sheep — all of which store fat in or around the tail for the lean season. It must be noted that the sheep depicted on the Roman and Byzantine mosaics are all of the long-tail variety which by now has completely disappeared to be replaced by the fat-tail species. We have no record of wild goats in Palestine. Similarly, *Capra pseudofalconeri* with upright, twisted horns, is more often represented in the ancient mosaics than the only native goat of our day, the mamber goat (*Capra aegagrus mambrica*), with its backward-curved horns and its long pendulous ears.[5]

The oldest varieties of cattle were apparently very similar to our present native Beiruti breeds. Yet in antiquity, a zeboid species with a distinct hump on its neck had already been introduced into the Near East. This zeboid cattle also predominates in the Roman and Byzantine mosaics, and the present Damascus strain of native cattle is apparently a survivor of that period; more exactly, it is a stable, though unharmonious cross of Beiruti with the zeboid species, the latter now being extinct. There is an important contradiction in historical documentation. While Macalister[6] distinguishes four strata of cultures at Gezer, each having its own characteristic breed of domestic cattle, Miss Bate [6a] could find no trace of such variety among the cattle bones of the different strata at Megiddo. The buffalo is a relatively late introduction — apparently since the Arab conquest — for St. Willibald,[7] of the 8th century, reports its presence in the Hula region.

The donkey is one of the oldest domestic animals of Palestine. It does not stem from the onagers of the Syrian and Arabian deserts, which were domesticated only temporarily by the ancient Mesopotamians, but from the wild asses of Somaliland. Essentially a desert animal by origin, the importance of the donkey as a beast of burden in the deserts of North Africa and Syria has been greatly underestimated. For millennia it crossed all the deserts of the Middle East, and Seligman[8] has collected material to prove that ass-caravans were still traversing the Sahara — from the Atlantic coast to the Red Sea — at the beginning of this century.

The appearance of the horse in Palestine and the neighboring countries was attributed, till recently, to the Hyksos who, according to the same hypothesis, brought it from Elam in the 2nd millennium B.C.E. The assumption[9] that the Hittites had independently domesticated the horse by that time is not well founded. Others again assume that the original domestication took place in the steppes of Russia. There is general agreement that the Hyksos, on their march of conquest to Egypt, introduced the horse into Palestine. Ritual graves of sacrificial horses, dating from the end of the 2nd millennium B.C.E., each containing the skeleton of one horse, with a hindleg missing, have been found at Beth Eglaim (Tell al-'Ujūl), south of Gaza. In the later history of Israel, horses were of prime importance in the employment of war chariots, their use for cavalry and ordinary riding coming much later. All these conjectures were considerably upset, however, by the discovery — in the Negev (1956) — of two molars of obviously domesticated horses, in Chalcolithic strata (prior to 3000 B.C.E.). To draw final conclusions, further evidence pertaining to bones and drawings of horses in the ancient Middle East must be obtained.

Mules were valued as mounts in Biblical times, but owing to the prohibitive laws of "diverse kinds" were not bred in Israel; they must therefore have been introduced from some neighboring area.

The history of the domestication of the camel is still obscure. The rock-carvings of Kilwa[10] include a depiction of two camels with very prominently raised humps. As the wild camel has such humps only during a very short season of the year, it stands to reason that the camels of Kilwa were already domesticated. Certain indications suggest that camels were known in Sumer and Egypt as early as the 4th millennium B.C.E.; yet from that time until the 2nd millennium B.C.E. no further traces of their existence in those areas have been brought to light. Albright[11] judges therefore that the mention of camels in the time of Abraham is an anachronism, and that the account in Judges, 6:5; 7:12, about the invasion of the Plain of Jezreel ca. 1200 B.C.E. by the Midianite camel-riding Beduins contains the first actual evidence of domesticated camels. Only about a thousand years later (in the Ptolemaic period) do camels reappear in Egypt as domestic stock. This break in the tradition can be explained by two factors. First, from the early domestication to the full symbiosis, as represented today among the Beduin of the desert, many centuries and even millennia must have elapsed. Originally camels were used for milk and wool, later as beasts of burden, as we know from the accounts about Abraham in Genesis. The last step, i.e., the utilization of the camel for ordinary riding, and then for long-distance plundering raids, was probably reached only at the end of the 2nd millennium B.C.E. Finally, due to the camel, desert travel reached its highest stage of development prior to the modern era.

A second reason for the thousand year gap in the history of the camel's utilization is to be found in the taboo placed upon the camel in ancient times. This perhaps explains the dislike shown to this day by the fellahin toward this animal. Similar taboos are mentioned in the Bible concerning the cat, the rooster, and the swine.[12] Cat-amulets were found in Egyptian temples of the Palestinian frontier fortresses from the 2nd millennium B.C.E., and there is no doubt that cats were kept in the temples of Bastis in the same areas and the same period. Its use in idolatry is the obvious reason why the cat is not mentioned prior to the apocryphal book of Baruch. The presence of the rooster in Palestine since the 9th century B.C.E. is proved by two Hebrew seals,[13] but the earliest literary reference to it is to be found in the New Testament. Here again its connection with idolatry, e.g., in the rituals of the Cuthaeans, was probably the cause of this taboo. The presence of swine in the heathen sections of Palestine is well established. For the Jews, however, it was a proscribed animal, though the origin of the strict prohibition against the eating of pork is still obscure. Certainly it was not utilitarian, i.e., the desire to prevent trichinosis, as some scholars have suggested. The Greeks suspected this taboo to have been based on a form of idolatry.

The importance of game for Palaeolithic man has already been mentioned. It was important also in later periods, especially in desert regions. The many scenes of ibex-hunts depicted at Kilwa and in later periods in the Negev support this statement. From the Bible we learn that red and fallow deer as well as gazelles were served at King Solomon's table (I Kings 5:3), while the *barbūrīm avūsīm* mentioned there were not game fowls but domestic geese.[14] King Herod is described as an excellent hunter who in one day killed forty animals: gazelles, onagers, and wild boars (*Bell. Jud.* I:21:13).

Since the disappearance in Palestine of the lion, wolf, leopard and other animals preying on herds, locusts (*Schistocerca gregaria*) and voles (*Microtus guentheri*) have been the greatest scourge to husbandry. These pests are mentioned in the Bible, and their ravages sometimes made history. A prolonged vole plague in the 12th century C.E. almost caused the collapse of the Latin kingdom in Palestine. Catastrophic locust invasions run like a continuous thread from the days of Moses through those of Joel down to the last great invasion of 1915.

Among the useful animals in Palestine's history mention must be made of the producers of Manna.[15] Certain scale-insects living upon the manna-tamarisk (*Tamarix mannifera*), excrete sweet honeydew, and the dried granules of these honeydew-excretions are almost pure sugar. In ancient times these manna grains were the only source of sugar in the desert, and sweets are the culinary dream of every desert dweller. A few hundred pounds of this manna are still collected in our times, although date-palms are now numerous and sugar can be bought cheaply by the Beduin. The Hebrew University's expedition to the Sinai in 1927 demonstrated the identity of the Biblical manna with this honeydew excreted by *Trabutina mannipara* and by *Najacoccus serpentinus*. The *selav* of Sinai, mentioned in the Bible, is of course the quail (*Coturnix coturnix*)which still arrives each spring exhausted from its flight across the Red Sea.

Another source of sugar in Palestine was honey. Yet all Biblical records refer only to honey-gathering, not to bee-keeping. Bee-keeping is mentioned several times in the Mishnah. It was never of great importance, yet we read in Mukaddasi (985 C.E.)[16] that the honey of Jerusalem was famous.

Animal dyes are mentioned in the Bible. Already in the 2nd millennium B.C.E. caravans from Tyre brought *argamannu and takiltu*[17] (in Hebrew: *argāmān* and *tᵉḵēlet*) to Assyria. The Greek name *Phoinikeos* (Φοινίκεος) is derived from the red purple, which was prepared by the Phoenicians occupying the coast between Tyre and Dor (Tantura).[18] In some ancient sites along this coast, mounds composed of broken *Murex*-shells indicate the locations of that industry which was so important in antiquity. The main purple shells of Palestine's seashores are *Murex brandaris*, *Murex trunculus* and *Purpura haemostoma*. We are still in doubt as to the actual difference between the *argāmān* and the *tᵉḵēlet*, and whether it was due to the use of different species of the purple shells, or to variations in the methods of manufacture.

Another Biblical dye was the *tola'at ha-shani* or the *karmil*, which is extracted from certain scale-insects inhabiting oaks (*Kermes biblicus*, *Kermes nahalali* and *Kermes greeni*).[19] These crimson dyes were used for coloring the priests' garments. The Fig Wax Scale (*Ceroplastes rusci*) was apparently used as a more common dye. Other dyes, namely those of the red Indian lac (*Tachardia lacca*) and of the Armenian cochineal (*Porphyrophora armeniaca*), were imported in later antiquity, while in the 18th century the Mexican cochineal (*Dactylopius coccus*) was bred around Nablus on the Nopal cactus, which was imported for this purpose.

The Chinese silkworm (*Bombyx mori*) was brought by monks in 552 C.E. to Constantinople. Justinian immediately distributed the eggs to all suitable places in the Byzantine Empire, among them Berytos (Beirut) and Tyre, where large silk weaving-mills were established. The southern coast of Palestine was among these most ancient districts of silk production and weaving. Mukaddasi mentions a flourishing silk industry at Gaza. Various travelers report silkworm breeding near Gaza in the 17th and 18th centuries. At least two independent attempts to plant mulberry trees and develop silkworm-breeding in Palestine (on the Yarqon and the Kishon rivers) were made during the 19th century, before Baron Edmond de Rothschild hit upon the same idea.[20]

Of the 25,000—35,000 species of animals that are thought to live in Palestine, slightly over 10,000 species are so far known.[21] The total number of animal species is possibly still greater. It can be roughly estimated as follows:

Group of animals	*known*	*Probable total*
Terrestric Vertebrata	660	750
Arthropoda	over 9,000	20,000—30,000
Others	about 1,000	4,000— 5,000

Not all these animals belong to one zoogeographical sphere, and not all follow the same principle of distribution. Ancient groups, such as Amphibia or Scorpions, reached the limits of their present distribution long ago, under geological and climatic conditions different from those that governed groups with recent species formation, such as mammals and birds. The latter spread out under geological and climatic conditions which much resemble those existing today. Hence our zoogeographical divisions are based on the distribution of the latter groups. Palestine is part of the Palaearctic kingdom and a number of regions, much greater than is usual in so small a country, share in the composition of its fauna. These regions are:

The Mediterranean maquis region dominates in the north and the coastal plains. It is characterized by wild rainy winters with dry summers. Mammals: the genet (*Genetta genetta terrae-sanctae*), the mole rat (*Spalax ehrenbergi*), the Syrian hare (*Lepus syriacus*). Birds: the jay (*Garrulus glandarius atricapillus*), the tit (*Parus major terrae-sanctae*), the warbler (*Locustella luscinoides luscinoides*), etc.

The Saharo-Sindian desert region occupies the south and penetrates into the lower and middle Jordan Valley. It has a short mild winter with little and very irregular rainfall, followed by a prolonged hot and dry season extending from spring to early winter. Apart from the gazelles, a number of rodents (*Gerbillus*, *Psammomys*, *Jaculus*, etc.) forms the dominant mammals; among the birds we find many desert larks (*Ammomanes*, *Alaemon alaudipes*), finches (*Carpospiza*), Tristram's grackle (*Onychognathus tristrami*), many wheatears (*Oenanthe*), etc.

The Irano-Turanian steppe region intrudes from the north-east as a narrow elongated band between the two aforementioned areas. A cold winter and a dry, hot summer interrupt the short seasons of active plant and animal life in spring and autumn, the latter being too short to be of any importance. Here belong the marbled pole-cat (*Vormela peregusna*), the Syrian pouched rat (*Spermophilus xanthoprymnus*), and among the birds — the Transcaspian sparrow (*Passer transcaspicus*), the swift (*Apus melba tuneti*), etc.

A few animals, mainly birds and insects, are Euro-Siberian intruders. More common are species of wide distribution in the Palaearctic kingdom. To these belong, among others: the badger (*Meles taxus*), the wolf (*Canis Lupus*), the otter (*Lutra lutra*), etc.; also the tawny pipit (*Anthus campestris*), the swallow (*Hirundo rustica rustica*), etc.

Tropical elements are rare. Palaeotropic is a number of big carnivores, such as the leopard and cheetah, or the ratel (*Melivora ratel*). Only a few oriental species, such as the fish owl (*Ketupa ceylonensis*), have reached Palestine. A more important element, especially among insects (of *Acacia*, *Calotropis*, etc.), is the northernmost Ethiopian, which came from the Sudan.

7. PREHISTORY

by W. F. Albright

A. Preliminary Remarks

THE RECONSTRUCTION of human prehistory has made extraordinary strides since the end of the Second World War. Among the many elements which are involved, the discovery of radiocarbon dating ranks easily first. Announced in 1948 by W. F. Libby, radiocarbon dating depends on the proportion of ordinary carbon (C^{12}) to its radioactive isotope (C^{14}). As first developed by Libby and Arnold, solid carbon was used in radiocarbon counts; this method was replaced by the acetylene process, in which the carbon material is put into gaseous form, and is now partly superseded by the use of "enriched" samples of carbon. Each improvement in technique has led to greater precision in dating and has extended the time range which can be covered. With the method of isotopic enrichment first described by H. de Vries and his colleagues in 1958, it is possible to date suitable samples of organic material as far back as 70,000 years B.P.[1] With the aid of thousands of radiocarbon counts from laboratories in many countries, it has become possible to date the end of the last glaciation of the Pleistocene (Würm in Europe, Wisconsin in North America) and the coeval end of the Last Pluvial period in Palestine about 11,000 B.P. (ca. 9000 B.C.E.). De Vries was able to show (1958) that the Würm glaciation began roughly about 60,000 B.P. and that the date 70,000 B.P. fell somewhere in the latter part of the third interglacial.

By a remarkable combination of radiocarbon counts with oceanic temperature cycles, established by Harold Urey and Cesare Emiliani on the basis of oxygen isotopes ($O^{16,17,18}$) whose ratio was measured in deep-sea cores, it has been possible (since 1957) to date glacial fluctuations through the entire Pleistocene.[2] To be sure, radiocarbon counts cover only the last quarter (or even less) of the four glaciations and three interglacial periods, but extrapolation has made it possible to work out a tentative time scale for the full length of the cores. It follows that the first ice age (the Günz glaciation) began not over 300,000 B.P. instead of over 500,000 years ago, as hitherto supposed.[3]

The antiquity of man must be correspondingly reduced. The earliest type with pronounced hominid characteristics, *Australopithecus* of South and East Africa, is now attributed to the Villafranchian.[4] With their small brains and — apparently — not quite erect posture, these creatures were not yet human, and there is no convincing evidence that they could make tools.[5] Then came — morphologically speaking — the Java Man, *Pithecanthropus erectus*, who is generally dated about the first interglacial, placed by Emiliani between ca. 250,000 and 200,000 years ago. No tools of this type of hominid are known. It is only with Pekin Man (*Sinanthropus pekinensis*), representing a somewhat more advanced hominid than *Pithecanthropus*, that there is real evidence for use of primitive stone tools. A very similar type of fossil man has been discovered in Algeria (*Atlanthropus*), where it has been dated early in the second interglacial period; it is very doubtful whether the artifacts found with it can be used for dating.[6]

The human fossil evidence from later Pleistocene times belongs to two main evolutionary lines: *Homo sapiens* and his precursors; Neanderthal Man (*Homo neanderthalensis*) and his congeners (*Homo soloensis* of Java, etc.). It is now known, thanks to the discovery of the Swanscombe and especially of the Fontéchevade skulls, that an early form of *Homo sapiens* preceded Neanderthal Man in Europe. The Steinheim skull, believed to date from the last interglacial, is intermediate between Neanderthal and modern man; it has pronounced eyebrow ridges but a quite well developed forehead.

The skulls from the first stage of the Last Pluvial Age, discovered by Dorothy Garrod and T. D. McCown south of Carmel in Palestine, are in general intermediate between Neanderthal and modern man, though at a more advanced level than Steinheim man. They are actually much more diversified in structure than the Neanderthal skulls hitherto found in Europe, though the latter are on the whole later in date. While voices are heard occasionally in support of a chronological priority for the more Neanderthal-like skulls from the Carmel area, when compared to the less Neanderthaloid examples,[7] it is very doubtful whether they are justified. Most physical anthropologists seem to prefer the view that Mount Carmel Man reflects a mixture of races between groups of the two sub-species *Homo neanderthalensis* and *sapiens*.

More and more specialists are tending to recognize only a single genetically true species of tool-making man ("*Homo faber*"), whose morphology was scarcely more varied than that of such polytypic species as *Canis domesticus* (the dog). *Homo neanderthalensis* was already upright in posture, as pointed out convincingly by W. L. Straus and A. J. E. Cave[8]; he possessed a brain that was definitely within the range of brain size found in living men. There is, accordingly, good reason to consider all tool-making men as only different races — or at most sub-species — of a single species. Geneticists have long since accustomed themselves to regard "species" among mammals as determined by sterility of interspecific hybrids: e.g., all varieties of dogs, cats, etc., interbreed to produce fertile offspring, but the horse and donkey, the lion and tiger produce only sterile hybrids (the mule, hinny, and tiglon).

Not only must we recognize the unity of man as a tool-making species as far back as 150,000–200,000 years ago — perhaps considerably more, but we must also attribute such skills as speech and such mental qualities as aesthetic appreciation to man at a very early date. The great antiquity of speech is shown by glottochronology, which pushes back the time at which such languages as Egyptian and Semitic separated to a date no later than ca. 10,000 years ago, and suggests that languages of totally different morphology must go back to a common origin many times as remote from the present. Early man's aesthetic potential is proved by the functional elegance of the best hand-axes and other flint artifacts of the Lower Palaeolithic, more than a hundred thousand years ago. It is confirmed by the wonderful cave art of the Aurignacian as well as by the remarkable baked clay statuettes of animals from Moravia, which date ca. 25,000 B.P.

B. The Lower Palaeolithic of Palestine

Very little is known about man in Palestine and Syria before the Last Interpluvial Age, about 100,000 years ago. Caves were not yet occupied, and there are no great river-valleys, like the Somme or the Nile, to provide a correlation between the Pleistocene pluvial phases and human artifacts. In spite of hopes, the Jordan Valley terraces have not provided much information.[9] It is now inferred by many that there was a close correlation between successive pluvial phases in Palestine and corresponding glacial phases in Europe, but this cannot be proved until we reach the Last Interpluvial and the succeeding Last Pluvial Age. Ancient beach lines at levels higher than the modern shore prove that Palestine and Lebanon shared the alternating rise and fall of sea-level which were characteristic of the entire Mediterranean littoral during the Pleistocene Age.

The oldest surface finds from Lower Palaeolithic come from the hill-country around Jerusalem. In the enclosed depression of the *Biq'a*, south-west of Jerusalem, R. Neuville and M. Stekelis made soundings in 1932 which established a stratigraphic sequence of "Chellean" and "Lower Acheulian" hand-axes. The nomenclature is typological, and there is no guarantee that the similarity of types reflects contemporaneity. All that can be said is that the relative antiquity and the succession of types do correspond roughly to what has been established for Western Europe.

In the lowest occupied levels of caves near Bethlehem (Umm Qaṭafa G-F) and south of Carmel (Tabun G) have been found artifacts of pre-Levalloisian (Mousterian) type, with distinctive flakes but without hand-axes, to which the French term "Tayacian" has been applied. In view of equally striking differences, the name "Tabunian" has been proposed by F. Clark Howell.[10] It can be roughly dated by the discovery of a similar assemblage of artifacts on a marine terrace of the Middle Pleistocene in Lebanon (Bahsas), which seems to belong to the early part of the third glacial period (Riss). If correct, it may be dated (according to the Emiliani correlation) over 100,000 years ago.

This cultural phase was followed in Palestine and Syria by Acheulian industries, featuring a return to the Abbevillian-Chellean tradition of hand-axes, though of more sophisticated ovate form. The earliest Acheulian remains are credited to a beach terrace at Ra's Bayrūt, gravel beds at Gesher Benot Ya'aqov in the northern Jordan Valley, and alluvial deposits near Jerusalem (see above). According to the excavator, R. Neuville, stratum E at Umm Qaṭafa is middle Acheulian, but there is some difference of opinion here. At all events, upper Acheulian is well represented at Umm Qaṭafa (D), Tabun (F-E), as well as in numerous other sites in both Syria and Palestine.[11] These remains seem to date back to the last interpluvial age, more than 60,000 B.P. On the basis of careful study of faunal remains from Tabun F-E, D.M.A. Bate has shown that they indicate a warm and damp climate, apparently tropical at the beginning but gradually becoming drier toward the end of E.

C. The Middle Palaeolithic of Palestine

With the end of the last interpluvial and the beginning of the last pluvial period, scarcely over 70,000 years ago, we find a Mousterian culture with Levalloisian traits dominant throughout Palestine and Syria. This is the culture represented in Tabun D-B, which belong to different phases of Middle Palaeolithic, all believed to date from the long first stage of the three cold stages (separated by two warmer interstadial phases) which made up the last glaciation (Würm).[12] The climate of the Carmel region was no longer warm and seems at first to have been drier, but the occurrence of fossils of *Hippopotamus amphibius*, *Bos spelaeus* and other mammals requiring plenty of water, proves that the coastal plain south of Carmel was then swampy. The evidence from Tabun is confirmed and supplemented by the results obtained in other caves south of Carmel, in the region of Bethlehem, in Galilee, and in Lebanon. Between Tabun C and Tabun B there was a sudden transformation in the fauna of the Coastal Plain, which became modern in type almost throughout. This abrupt change may be dated between ca. 35,000 and 45,000 B.P.

The most interesting finds in Mousterian levels are without doubt the fossil human remains from various caves in northern Palestine. These include some nine burials from Tabun C (besides much fragmentary material), two from Sukhul B, and a number from a cave below Jabal al-Qafza south of Nazareth. The Qafza remains closely resemble the human fossils from Sukhul B. As mentioned above, all these skeletons are intermediate between the extreme Neanderthal finds in Europe and *Homo sapiens*, but specialists are still debating the exact meaning of the facts. One thing is clear: Palestine was then just as much of an intercontinental bridge as it is today, and mixture of different races and sub-species might be expected. The date of "*Palaeanthropus palestinensis*" may be fixed roughly between 40,000 and 50,000 years ago on the basis of such datings as ca. 41,000 B.P. for Tabun C.[13] This date agrees very well with the discoveries by R. S. Solecki at Shanidar in Kurdish Iraq (1956–57), where three adult Neanderthal skeletons were found in a Mousterian stratum (Shanidar D).[14] These skeletons, dated about 46,000 B.P. by Solecki, are "classic" Neanderthal in primitiveness, and thus reflect an earlier human evolutionary phase than the Mousterians of Palestine. Apparently a more primitive type of Neanderthal survived in the Kurdish mountains, just as in Europe, whereas in Palestine mixture with *Homo sapiens* had produced more advanced types. Only future research can yield a clearer picture.

D. The Upper Palaeolithic of Palestine

Perhaps about 35,000 years ago, Middle Palaeolithic gave way to Upper Palaeolithic in Palestine. Neanthropic man then definitely superseded Neanderthaloid types, just as modern types of fauna displaced archaic types. The flint cultures of the new age in Palestine and Syria are related to the Aurignacian of Europe, though with pronounced differences, which increased with the passage of time.[15] There can no longer be any serious doubt that the break with Mousterian culture came toward the end of the first stadial of the last pluvial age (which corresponds to the end of the Würm glaciation), as held notably by Hallam Movius and F. C. Howell. The latter distinguishes seven phases of Upper Palaeolithic, which he labels as Stages 0-6, preferring to avoid the increasing confusion of terminology by using numbers rather than names.[16] Stage 0 is still obscure and has not yet been identified in Palestine; it seems to have been intrusive in Yabrūd 13 and 15, since it is intercalated in a series of Mousterian horizons. Stage 1 was first identified by Turville-Petre at Maghārat al-Amīra above Lake Kinnereth; it has been clarified by Dorothy Garrod and shown to be a natural typological advance from the earlier Levalloiso-Mousterian.

Stage 2 of Howell's series is poorly documented, but Stage 3 is very well known, both from Palestine and from Lebanon. The latter provides the best stratigraphic succession of "Aurignacian" assemblages in the rock-shelter at Qaṣr 'Aqīl, where J. F. Ewing and Hallam Movius have studied a stratified deposit over 22 metres thick, mostly Aurignacian. Three clearly demarked stratigraphic breaks occur, each composed of sterile layers of clay and stone conglomerate; they have been convincingly correlated with the three stages of the last (Würm) ice age. There is very good correlation, on the whole, between the rich series of material from Qaṣr 'Aqīl and the stratification of the Palestinian caves. Stages 2-3 correspond, in a general way, with Aurignacian finds at Shanidar in Kurdish Iraq, which have been well dated by two independent series of radiocarbon counts to the period between 35,000 and 25,000 B.P. for both the successive phases of Shanidar C.

Upper Palaeolithic 4 is considered the best documented of all "Aurignacian" cultures in Southwest Asia. Here again there is good correlation between Qaṣr 'Aqīl in Lebanon and the caves of the Carmel and Bethlehem areas. The climate was then quite dry, perhaps indicating the last interstadial of the Würm glaciation and its corresponding pluvial. Howell's Stage 5, which followed, is known chiefly from Dorothy Garrod's work near Carmel, where she isolated it in al-Wād C, calling it "Atlitian." It diverges in detail from all other known assemblages of middle and upper Aurignacian, but is definitely "Aurignacian," without a trace of the microlithic culture of the Mesolithic.

Nowhere in Palestine or Syria do we have any trace of the representational art which forms so characteristic an element in the Aurignacian of Europe after about 25,000 B.P. One cave with an alleged frieze of animals was reported from southern Palestine, but it proved to be an illusion, greatly to the relief of geologists who were troubled by the collocation of beasts from different times and climatic environments. We may perhaps consider the absence of cave art as connected with the fact that no comparable caves are known in Palestine and Syria. Yet it may some day be found, just as the Dead Sea Scrolls turned up after generations of skepticism among scholars as to the possibility of any such find.

E. Epipalaeolithic and Mesolithic Palestine

While Western Europe was probably enjoying the brilliant flowering of the Magdalenian culture, ca. 15,000-12,000 B.P., a new, microlithic culture was developing in the Mediterranean basin to the south and east. In Palestine the first phase of the Mesolithic is known as the Kebaran, from the cave south of Carmel where it was first isolated by Turville-Petre; it is characterized by long, narrow, microlithic blades with blunted backs, small end-scrapers and burins. The same culture appears in identical stratigraphic sequence at al-Khiyām near Bethlehem and at Naḥal Oren (M. Stekelis), as well as in related form near Yabrūd in eastern Syria, also below Natufian deposits. On the other hand, the Zarzian of Kurdish Iraq, which Howell associates with the Kebaran, is also related in the typology of its artifacts to Dorothy Garrod's Lower Natufian, and the radiocarbon date about 12,000 B.P. obtained for this phase of culture at the neighboring site of Shanidar, may thus apply to Lower Natufian rather than to Kebaran (Howell's Stage 6 may, accordingly, be earlier.) At Qaṣr 'Aqīl in Lebanon the same Kebaran culture appears just above the uppermost conglomerate break and it should thus be placed in the final stadial of the Würm glaciation.[17]

The Kebaran culture was in any case the last of the exclusively food-collecting economies; thenceforth men began to experiment — at least in Southwestern Asia — with food-producing, though hunting and fishing long remained the chief sources of livelihood for most regions without the right combination of soil and water. We may suppose that the beginnings of agriculture in the Levant go back even before the retreat of the glaciers from southern France some 9000 B.C.E. (ca. 11,000 B.P.). Hitherto only the Mesolithic site underlying the Pre-Pottery Neolithic of Jericho has been dated by radiocarbon; the announced dates, about 9850 ± 240 and 9800 ± 240 B.P. (i.e., between ca. 8100 and 7600 B.C.E.) for the Natufian of Jericho correspond fairly well with the date of ca. 10,000 B.C.E. (12,000 B.P.), which has been set for the Zarzian (see above), and ca. 7000 B.C.E., for the settlement of Pre-Pottery Jericho (see below). The Natufian thus seems to overlap the late Magdalenian and Azilian in Europe, which may be dated just before and just after the end of the Würm glaciation.

The Natufian culture was first discovered by Dorothy Garrod in Wadi Naṭūf (northwestern Judea) during her initial campaign of 1928. She then found rich deposits from this period in Maghārat al-Wad, south of Carmel. Her discoveries were followed with similar finds by R. Neuville in several southern caves and a rock-shelter. Most recently, the remarkable discoveries of J. Perrot at 'Enan ('Ayn al-Mellāḥā above Lake Hula) since 1956[18] have radically changed the picture in several respects, and Kathleen Kenyon's excavation of a Natufian building below the lowest Pre-Pottery Neolithic of Jericho[19] further illustrates the new picture.

Between ca. 9000 and ca. 7000 B.C.E. the climate of Palestine seems to have become increasingly like the present Mediterranean climate, in spite of minor oscillations. The fauna of the Mesolithic was substantially identical with that of today. Natufian man (of whom over 175 whole and fragmentary specimens have been found) was small and highly dolichocephalic; in general his physical characteristics were the same as those of chalcolithic man of the late fourth millennium at Byblos and Megiddo, and of somewhat earlier Badarian man in Upper Egypt. There can, therefore, be little doubt that Natufian man was a progenitor (though certainly not the only one) of the typical dolichocephalic Hamito-Semite of early historical times.

The outstanding cultural feature of Natufian life was cereal production. This is proved by the discovery of a great many flint sickle edges, as well as of the bone sickles along the inner edge of which they were set, end to end. The handle of a bone sickle was sometimes decorated with a relief carving; Maghārat al-Wad yielded a particularly beautiful representation of a fawn, hunched up in relief. "Picks" of stone were probably used as hoes lashed to the end of a short piece of wood; we may safely assume the existence of a primitive form of hoe cultivation (Hackbau). Lance-heads, harpoons, and other objects of flint or bone show that hunting and fishing remained the most important source of livelihood. The beautiful flint crescents or lunates, which form the most characteristic microlith of the entire Natufian assemblage, must have served to tip arrows used by fowlers; the relative width of the sharp edge of these tips would be much more effective against birds in motion than any other kind of missile then available.

The discovery of numerous burials with pavements and traces of wall at Maghārat al-Wad scarcely prepared us for the sensational finds of Jean Perrot and Kathleen Kenyon. At 'Enan the former has found an open-air Natufian settlement — the first of its kind in Palestine. The area of occupation appears to extend for more than a thousand square metres; in 1956–57 parts of walls, floors, and circular plastered basins were cleared. The most striking find was a well-built circular tomb with a diameter of some five metres at the top, surrounded by a plastered wall sloping inward toward the bottom, nearly a metre below. Three different strata were found at the tomb, showing constructions and pavements of stone, as well as burials from different phases of occupation.[20] At Jericho Miss Kenyon has discovered, below the lowest Pre-Pottery Neolithic, a clay platform enclosed by a substantial stone wall of apparently rectangular plan. Two solid stone sockets, consisting of stones completely bored through a thickness of some 75 cm., were set in the wall, suggesting sacred poles of some kind. The structure had used much timber, carbonized remains of which yielded a date between ca. 8100 and 7600 B.C.E. (see above). Both 'Enan and Jericho seem to exhibit only Lower Natufian, since such characteristic artifacts as the deeply notched arrow-heads of Upper Natufian near Carmel have not been found in the rich collections of material from 'Enan. Miss Kenyon considers the Jericho deposit also to be Lower Natufian.

Thanks to Jericho it is possible to establish the existence of a previously unknown flint assemblage, labeled Proto-Neolithic by Miss Kenyon, which bears a fairly clear relationship to the earlier Natufian culture but is entirely different from that of the following Tahunian. According to the excavator, this flint industry may have been in part contemporary with the Upper Natufian of the Carmel region. This scarcely seems probable, in view of the tremendous cultural superiority of the "Proto-Neolithic" as well as the difference of nearly a millennium between the Mesolithic and the Proto-Neolithic radiocarbon dates from Jericho. More likely, to judge from later analogies, would be a geographical separation between two offshoots of Lower Natufian, one of which became Upper Natufian (with analogies in southern Palestine), while the other gave rise (possibly in eastern Transjordan) to the hitherto unrecovered immediate precursor of the Proto-Neolithic of Jericho.[21]

F. The Pre-Pottery Neolithic of Palestine

Kathleen Kenyon's work at Jericho since 1952 has fully confirmed Garstang's discovery (1935) of a series of Pre-Pottery Neolithic floor levels at Jericho. She has, however, carried his stratification far down below his lowest level and has demonstrated that a fortified city larger than Bronze-Age Jericho flourished on the site (with interruptions) for over a thousand years before the invention of pottery. Today there are perhaps a dozen settlements from Pre-Pottery Neolithic known; they extend from Thessaly in Greece to southwestern Pakistan, and seem to be common along the fringes of the North-Mesopotamian alluvium. The nearest to Jericho is at Khirokitia in Cyprus, but there can be little doubt that many favorable localities in Palestine were settled during the time of Jericho A and B. Though at first opposed to the existence of such a culture at Jericho, R. J. Braidwood accepted the idea after excavating a Pre-Pottery Neolithic village dating not later than the seventh millennium B.C.E. at Qal'at Jarmo in Kurdish Iraq. Even after the announcement by Miss Kenyon of her discovery of massive fortifications, he continued to reject the use of "urban" for these early installations. (In this one may follow him, not because early Jericho was neither fortified nor a town, but because the term "urban" has been grossly misused in recent times. There is little indeed in common between any pre-Phoenician city of Syria or Palestine and such cities as Babylon, Athens, and Rome at the height of their wealth.)

Miss Kenyon's demonstration that Jericho was a strongly fortified town with well-constructed houses and a surprisingly advanced culture during the Pre-Pottery Neolithic between ca. 7000 and ca. 5500 B.C.E. has very far-reaching repercussions. Jericho is an oasis with an appallingly hot summer; it must have been isolated from similar towns, since the nearest promising rival is at Pella, south of Lake Kinnereth. Under no circumstances can Jericho be considered as uniquely qualified to be the locus of a sedentary culture which flourished on and off for two millennia.[22] It does indeed have unique qualifications for archaeological study, since it stands outside of the oasis proper, above the great fountain of 'Ayn as-Sulṭān, and the archaeologist can dig down to virgin soil without being blocked by ground water. Pella is very similarly situated, and there are probably a number of sites such as Rosh ha-'Ayin at the source of the Yarqon River, located along the eastern edge of the Coastal Plain, where we should find similar conditions. But if a little oasis like Jericho could support such a flourishing town for so long, it stands to reason that favorably located sites in the alluvial river valleys would be still better provided by nature with opportunities to expand. Of course, the alluvial deltas of Egypt and Babylonia were still marsh-land, where hunters and fishers would have a great advantage over farmers. But the upper Tigris and Euphrates, and especially the confluent streams were extremely favorable to cultures of the Pre-Pottery Jericho type. All the larger alluvial valleys of relatively recent date have risen steadily in level over the past ten thousand years, with concomitant rise in the water-table, until many of the earliest occupations are deep under ground water. This, for instance, prevented Garstang from digging down through his Pottery Neolithic at Mersin in Cilicia, where he might well have discovered Pre-Pottery Neolithic levels such as he had already found at Jericho. In general excavators have assumed in the past that pottery was the unfailing mark of settlement, so when they got below pottery-bearing levels they stopped digging. This may, for instance, be the reason why Thompson found no Pre-Pottery Neolithic at Nineveh. In other cases the excavator's money and time were exhausted before he reached the bottom even of his pottery-bearing stratification.

In the writer's view there is no basis for the opinion now being expressed by Braidwood and other scholars to the effect that there was as yet no highly developed irrigation, but only a primitive use of water coming from springs or small streams. While the people of Jericho did not need to build massive stone storage or deflector dams, much less heavy sluice-ways, they did build remarkably massive fortifications, so we may rest assured that their contemporaries in richer and more hospitable areas did build massive irrigation works of stone, sun-dried brick, and earth. It is, in fact, difficult to understand the tremendous expansion of irrigation in the Chalcolithic unless we suppose that it had a long prehistory, going far back into the sixth and seventh millennia. There is no justification for the frequently expressed view that grain-raising in the upland plains of Anatolia, Iraq and Iran played an important role at the beginning of sedentary culture in the Levant. These regions are far too arid to sustain regular crops without aid from irrigation, and there is not the slightest evidence that they were then occupied by sedentary communities. Sites such as Qal'at Jarmo and Teleilat el-Ghassul, which are now much too high above stream-beds where irrigation might be employed at certain times of the year, are the victims of intense erosion extending over many thousands of years. In Pre-Pottery Neolithic Jarmo the irrigable alluvium was much closer to the site than it is today. Even then, however, the area which could be farmed by use of simple earth dams was only large enough to support a small hamlet, not a large fortified town like Jericho. So far there is not the slightest evidence that any upland sites of Palestine were settled at such a remote period; in every town in the hill-country hitherto excavated down to bed-rock we begin with Chalcolithic or Bronze-Age remains strewn sparsely in the terra rossa between limestone outcrops.

The first Proto-Neolithic occupation at Jericho occurs in a deposit of some four meters containing a long succession of floor levels belonging to huts of clay, wood, and skins. Though only one such deposit seems as yet to have been excavated, there can be no doubt that it preceded the first buildings of Pre-Pottery Neolithic A. Houses of the latter were round or ovate, with walls slanting upward toward a lost roof of dome shape. Construction was mainly in mud brick of elongated plano-convex shape, called "hog-back" by the excavator. The flint industry was substantially the same as in the four-meter "nuclear" tell; it is named "Proto-Neolithic" by Miss Kenyon. This town was already surrounded by a wall as far back as ca. 7000 B.C.E. The wall was primitive enough in construction, but was faced with stone and surrounded with a rock-cut ditch. The most remarkable find was certainly that of a great stone tower, built in different phases. In its final form it was some nine meters in diameter, with an even more massive staircase in its centre, leading down by twenty-two steps to a horizontal passage. Each step is made from a slab over 0.75 m. across, and the roofs of the staircase and passage are made of still larger slabs, 0.95 m. across and up to a metre long. The stone masonry, though hammer-dressed, is good, and sometimes excellent.

Before the end of the seventh millennium B.C.E., the hogback-brick culture of Pre-Pottery Neolithic Jericho A had been replaced by the plaster-floor culture of Jericho B, which for the first time exhibits an industry of essentially Tahunian type, though curiously lacking the flint axe-heads with ground edges which became the hallmark of the Tahunian phase of Pottery Neolithic as well as of earlier Chalcolithic. Houses and other buildings of possible cultic function were rectangular and were paved with a highly burnished plaster. No fewer than fourteen superimposed house levels of this period were found in one area. The most remarkable find made by Garstang in the Pre-Pottery B phase[23] consisted of numerous fragments of plastic statues of human beings, apparently in groups of a man, woman, and child. The plastic statues were about two-thirds life-size *en face*, but were very thin in profile; they were made by smearing native limy marl on frameworks of reed which served as crude skeletons. Their plaster faces, with shells used as eyes, and with painted detail, resemble the slightly earlier plastered skulls found by Miss Kenyon in a family group of seven. The plastic figures probably reflect the deities of an early pantheon, whereas the plastered skulls, one of which is beautiful even by Hellenic standards, presumably reflect some form of mortuary cult. In one form or another we find this preference for skulls in Palestinian burial practice from the Mesolithic of 'Enan down to the end of the Chalcolithic.[24]

The plaster-floor period of Jericho also yielded remains of fortifications, but the town-walls of Pre-Pottery Neolithic B were much less massive than those of A. From the radiocarbon dates it would appear that the Pre-Pottery Neolithic came to an end here before the middle of the sixth millennium, and was followed by a gap of centuries. During this gap the site was apparently abandoned, and when it was finally reoccupied early in the fifth millennium, we find it occupied by makers of pottery.

G. The Pottery Neolithic of Palestine

The earliest pottery at Jericho appears in Stratum IX of Garstang's series; it is found chiefly in pits of irregular shape which had been dug by the new population in the ruins of Pre-Pottery Neolithic B. Nothing is known about these people except their pottery and flint industries. The former is very primitive in some ways; the clay was poorly cleaned and chopped straw was mixed into the paste to serve as a *dégraissant*. On the other hand, some of the better ware is decorated with geometric designs in dark red against a creamy slip. This ware seems to be the oldest well-attested ceramic industry in Palestine; we may date it provisionally in the first half of the fifth millennium B.C.E.

Jericho IX was followed after a considerable interval by Jericho VIII; in this interval may be placed the Yarmukian of Sha'ar ha-Golan and the related culture of Wadi Rāba near the source of the Yarqon in the Coastal Plain. Jericho VIII has been treated as Chalcolithic ever since Garstang first discovered it. At that time it was believed to be post-Ghassulian. Now, however, the Wadi Rāba pottery has been found by J. Kaplan under stratified Ghassulian, so there can be no doubt that Jericho VIII does precede the Ghassulian, as maintained by the writer since 1948 on the basis of sequence dating.[25] It will, accordingly, be much simpler to treat Jericho VIII as late Neolithic rather than as early Chalcolithic. Subsequent denudation has destroyed almost all remains of their houses, the most distinctive feature of which was the shape of the sun-dried bricks then used; it is plano-convex, flat below and rounded above like a bun.

Neither of these two cultures is as interesting as the Yarmukian, first discovered by M. Stekelis in 1943.[26] The remains of this culture in the Yarmuḵ Valley below Lake Kinnereth may be dated roughly in the third quarter of the fifth millennium. Chopped straw was still used, the large amount of grit found in the ware coming chiefly from poor levigation. A favorite type of decoration was incised herring-bone bands, which were used singly, in pairs, and in geometrical grouping. Other types of incised decoration were also known. The stone industry was Tahunian, featuring deeply notched sickle-edges, arrow-heads, and especially many axes, hoes, and celts with well-ground cutting edges.

The most interesting group of objects discovered here by Stekelis consists of carved stone objects with sexual denotation. Among them are phalli and schematic female figures emphasizing the sexual organs, all of which presumably served as fertility charms. Curiously enough, this is the earliest Palestinian culture known to feature sexual symbols so prominently, though scattered precursors are known from Carmel and Jericho.

H. The Chalcolithic of Palestine

For practical purposes we may date the transition from Neolithic to Chalcolithic about 4000 B.C.E., which appears to separate the end of Jericho VIII from the precursors of late Ghassulian. At Jericho there was a complete gap during most of the fourth millennium, but many other sites help to fill the lacuna. By far the most interesting Chalcolithic culture is the Ghassulian, first discovered by Alexis Mallon at Teleilat el-Ghassul. From the beginning the writer insisted on dating this culture in the fourth millennium, but for many years there was a strong tendency among archaeologists and prehistorians to follow the excavator and date its end as late as the early second millennium. At one time, indeed, the writer was wholly alone in his early dating, which he based primarily on the fact that pottery of very similar type had been found by Turville-Petre, Dorothy Garrod, and Eann Macdonald both in stratigraphical priority to Early Bronze and in typological association with other Chalcolithic assemblages.[27] Now, in spite of occasional demurrers, the stratigraphical sequence is established firmly by E. L. Sukenik's discovery of a Ghassulian stratum underlying the Esdraelon period at ʻAfula in the Plain of Jezreel and more recently by J. Kaplan's excavation at Wadi Rāba, where a culture closely related to Jericho VIII turned up under a characteristic Ghassulian level. The view expressed in the thirties (and subsequently) that Ghassulian was an intrusion (from where?) into the Early Bronze of Palestine and that it disappeared without leaving a trace, has been effectively disproved by the discovery of many Ghassulian sites, ranging from Galilee to Beersheba, and from Transjordan to the Mediterranean.

The basic site for study of this important culture, which may have flourished between ca. 3800 and 3400 B.C.E., is Teleilat el-Ghassul itself. At that time (see above) erosion had not cut so deep into the little valleys which crossed the Ghor of the Jordan from the foot of the hills of Gilead, and there were many more springs to feed the perennial streams which flowed through them into the Jordan. It was, therefore, possible to cultivate the soil of the lateral valley by which stand the hillocks (*teleilat*), which still rise above the alluvium. Aside from quite inadequate soundings, only the two levels of the uppermost stratum have been excavated, leaving the three lower strata little known, though reportedly all Ghassulian in general character.

Ghassul was probably not fortified (unless very sketchily) and it ranks, therefore, as a village rather than as a town. The houses were quite well constructed of hand-moulded sun-dried bricks on a foundation of field stones. Some of the walls had been covered with fresco paintings, including an amazingly intricate polychrome painting of an eight-pointed star, a naturalistic bird, a presentation scene (only the bottom of which is preserved, and elaborate combinations of dragons (?) with geometric designs. When we bear in mind that Ghassul was only a large village, this fresco art seems completely different from anything we should expect. And yet this art does remind us in some important respects of the extraordinarily varied and sometimes very elaborate polychrome designs on the painted pottery of the Halafian age in northern Mesopotamia, the last of which may easily overlap the Ghassulian period.[28] At Ḥadera in the Plain of Sharon E. L. Sukenik discovered house-urn burials, with painted clay models of rectangular huts, which seem to have stood on piles — as one should expect of huts built in the swampy coastland plains.

Since 1952 excavations carried on in Chalcolithic sites of the Beer-sheba area by Jean Perrot and Moshe Dothan have yielded very interesting remains from an immediately post-Ghassulian culture with strong Ghassulian affinities. The sites of Bir Abu Matar, Khirbat al-Bayṭār, and Bir es-Safadi have yielded remains of three phases of occupation, all with such a homogeneous culture that its entire duration in this area can scarcely have been more than a century or two.[29] Most of the houses were subterranean pit dwellings, some of them remarkably complex. Local industries were well developed; even copper-smelting was represented. Interestingly enough, one of the graves excavated by Perrot contains Armenoid skulls, suggesting that there may have been an Anatolian component in the Ghassulian population, which seems to have been in part intrusive. Typical piriform mace-heads and other cultural elements suggest comparison with early Gerzean Egypt, and this is supported by a radiocarbon dating ca. 3325 ± 150 B.C.E., i.e., not long after the probable date of the final destruction of Teleilat el-Ghassul itself. It should be added that for all the similarities, there are striking differences between Ghassul IV and the Beer-sheba Chalcolithic. The latter employed painted ornament proportionately far more than did the former, with much less incised decoration. Handles also tend to be different. The spread of true Ghassulian over Palestine is now so well documented that we cannot explain these and other differences solely by geography; chronology must be the dominant factor. It is by no means impossible, however, that the Beer-sheba culture extended down into the following Esdraelon period.

For some time it was thought that the Esdraelon culture, first discovered in the Chalcolithic series of Megiddo and Beth-shean and then named by G. E. Wright,[30] was quite distinct from the Early Bronze cultures of the north. Now it has become clear that there was much overlapping, and that there was no abrupt change during the period between about 3300 and 2900 B.C.E.[31] Yet as the find-spots dominated by one or another feature have increased in number and geographical extension, it is certain that we must assume a certain amount of succession of types, even though details remain to be defined. In general, the grey-burnished bowls of the Esdraelon phase and the contemporary high loop-handles are earlier than the grain or band slip characteristic of Early Bronze I. The "Aeneolithic" tomb-groups of Tell al-Far'a (northeast of Nablus), excavated by R. de Vaux (cf. especially Tombs 11 and 12) are the best illustration of this pottery assemblage. With it the pottery of Miss Kenyon's Jericho tomb A 94 is in large part nearly identical; it is dated by radiocarbon about 3260 ± 110 B.C.E., i.e., between ca. 3370 and 3150.[32] The writer would date the Jericho group in or about the 32nd century and would consider it as a little more recent than the Tell al-Far'a tombs. The new date agrees fully with the synchronism already established between imported Syro-Palestinian vases from Ma'āda near Cairo, which belong to Middle Gerzean, and the Jericho-Far'a culture. All three groups belong to the 33rd–32nd centuries B.C.E.[33] By this time international trade relations were already well developed, and Palestinian culture was becoming part of the wider civilization of the ancient Levant. We stand at the threshold of the Early Bronze Age.

Mallaḥa (‘Enan) — Natufian burial in semi-contracted position. Level II — About 8000 B.C.E.
French Archaeological Mission in Israel (1956—1962).

Mallaḥa (‘Enan) — Incised pebble representing a human head. Natufian art, 8000 B.C.E.
French Archaeological Mission in Israel.

View of the tell of ancient Jericho from the West.
British School of Archaeology in Jerusalem.

Jericho — The great stone built tower of the earliest Neolithic defences, dating to ca. 7000 B.C.E.
British School of Archaeology in Jerusalem.

Jericho — A plastered portrait skull of the Neolithic period.
British School of Archaeology in Jerusalem.

Teleilat el-Ghassul — Fresco painting of bird.
Pontifical Biblical Institute, Jerusalem.

Aerial view of Abu Matar (the upper site) and Safadi (in the middle) near Beer-sheba.
French Archaeological Mission in Israel.

Safadi — An underground rectangular room, after the removal of the collapsed part of the roof. The pits are silos of two different periods.
French Archaeological Mission in Israel (1954—1960).

Safadi — A cache in an underground dwelling; an ivory figurine; an ivory ceremonial sickle; a sheath; a head; and basalt bowls.
French Archaeological Mission in Israel.

Safadi. An ivory figurine of a pregnant wom
French Archaeological Mission in Is

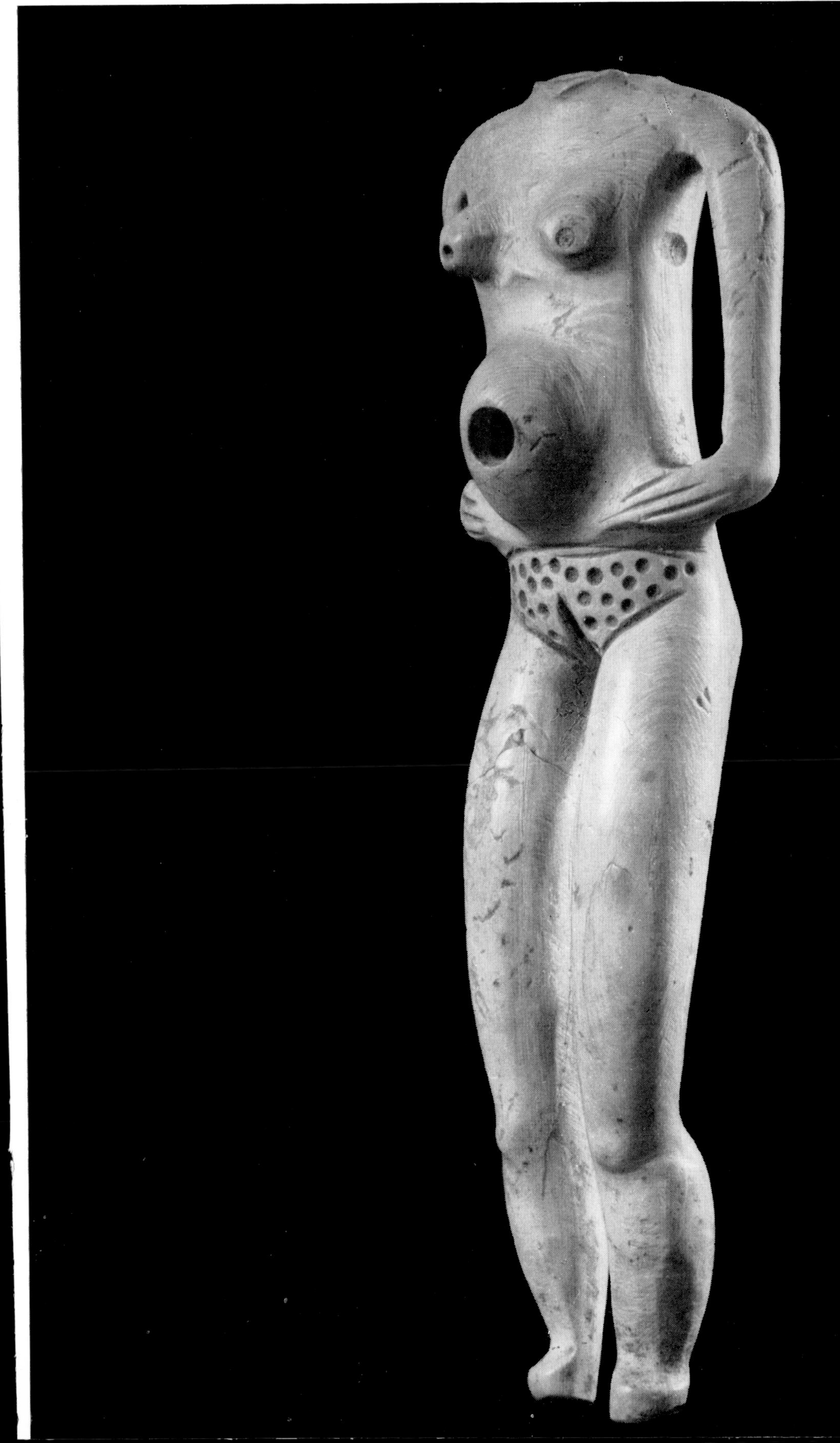

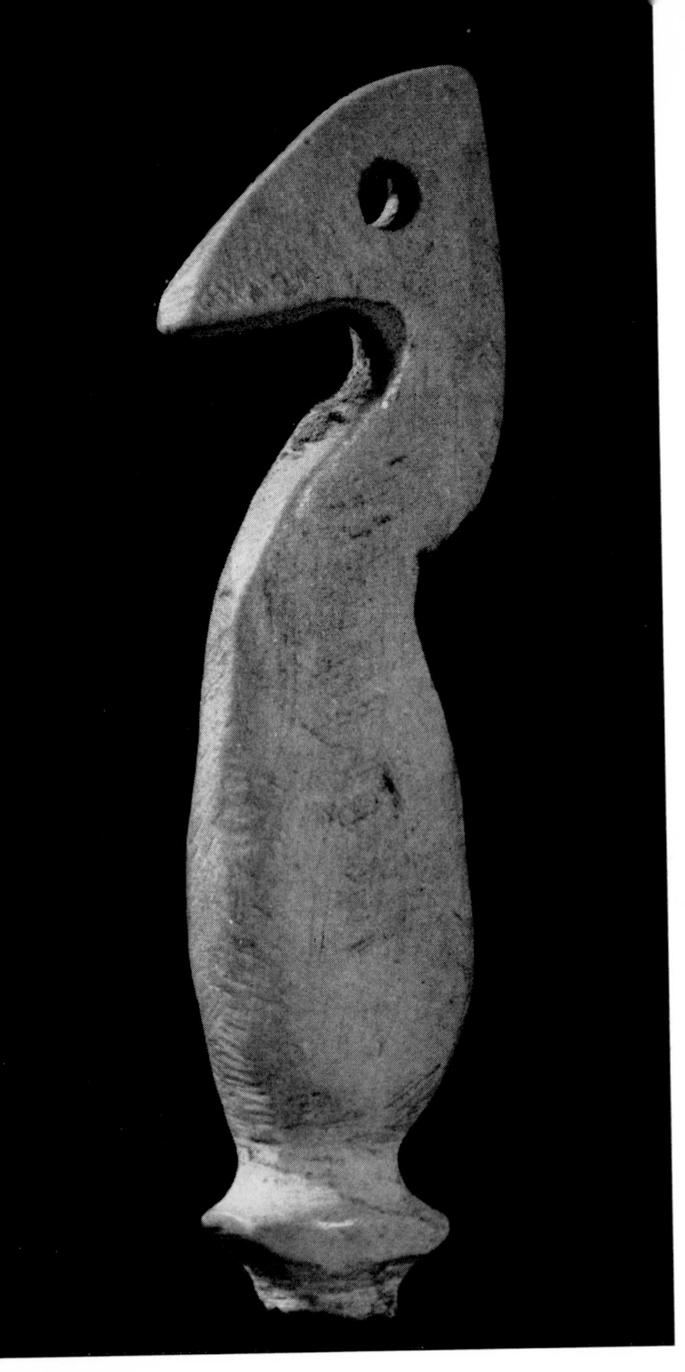

Abu Matar. Ornamental head of an ivory pin, representing a bird.
French Archaeological Mission in Israel (1952—1954).

Safadi. A copper a
French Archaeological Mission in Is

Abu Matar. Copper maceheads.
French Archaeological Mission in Israel.

B. THE LANDS TO THE NORTH

1. SYRIA — FROM THE LITANI TO THE EUPHRATES

by A. J. Brawer

A. Introductory Remarks

THE COUNTRIES fringing the northern end of the Arabian plateau, as well as the Sinai peninsula and Lower Egypt, are commonly known as the Fertile Crescent and also — though less commonly — as the Lands of the Bible. Besides Palestine, they include Syria and Mesopotamia — two countries with which the history of Israel was closely associated for many centuries. A general survey of both Syria and Mesopotamia from a geographic standpoint should therefore be included in the study of the background factors that affected the history of Israel in Biblical and post-Biblical times.

The country extending between the bend of the Euphrates near Tiphsah (Thapsacus), in the north-east, and the Taurus and Amanus mountains, in the north-west, to the northern borders of Palestine in the south, and from the Great Sea (the Mediterranean) in the west to the Syrian-Arabian desert in the east[1] — the country commonly known as Syria[2] — was more closely bound up with the history of Palestine than any other land. At the height of Israel's glory, during the period of David and Solomon, Syria was included in Israel's domain — an area which corresponded to the Biblical conception of the Promised Land.[3] In a later period, during the rule of the Seleucids, Palestine was included in the domain of Syria. Prior to that, however, in the times of the Babylonians and the Persians, Syria and Palestine formed one administrative unit, then known as the Province beyond the River (Euphrates). Except for periods when both countries were subjugated to the same foreign rule, or included together in a larger political domain, their history was marked by antagonisms and conflicts rather than by — if we may use a modern term — peaceful co-existence.

Both countries, as has been previously indicated, have, geographically, several features in common, yet they are also distinguished by dissimilarities and differences. The combination of characteristics peculiar to each country — height, climate, fertility, etc. — makes Syria as different from Palestine as any two countries could be within the framework of such a common geological history. Indeed, from the standpoint of geology as well as of morphology, Syria and Palestine constitute a single unit. Like Palestine, Syria, too — as pointed out — is composed of four longitudinal belts: the coastal plains, mountains, a rift valley (including lakes), and highlands. Again, like Palestine, it is divided by the rift valley into two main regions, a western and an eastern one; then, in further similarity to Palestine, west of the rift valley rise folded mountains, while east of it there are mainly plateaus; and an undulating, narrow coastal plain, which varies in width and is frequently interrupted by protrusions, separates the western mountains from the sea.

Comprising approximately 40,000 sq. miles — an area nearly twice as large as Palestine — Syria, however, differs little from Palestine in its maximum length and width. The distance between the northernmost and southernmost points of historical Syria was ca. 260 miles (as measured along the coastline), compared with the maximum length (as measured from Dan to Elath) of Palestine, 250 miles. The maximum width of Syria, measured from the Mediterranean to Palmyra, was 140 miles; that of Palestine, as measured from Caesarea to the eastern edge of the Jabal ad-Duruz, was 125 miles.

B. The Littoral

Extending from the southern end of the Ladder of Tyre up to the protrusion of the Amanus mountains into the sea, the Syrian coast stretches along a distance of some 260 miles, as the crow flies. The actual length of the coastline, however, with its profusion of bays and coves, exceeds 312 miles.

Unlike the sea action on the coast of Palestine, where the currents deposit sediments of the Nile, that on the Syrian coast is predominantly abrasive. This abrasion is not uniform. Masses of hard rock that withstood the action of the sea now constitute promontories that jut into the water. The road passes mainly along a strip of plain between the sea and the mountains, but here and there it is forced to ascend the promontories, and from these vantage points the traveler can view the stormy waves breaking upon the shore. One such site where the road transverses a promontory for a distance of seven miles (between Rosh ha-Niqra and Ra's al-Abyaḍ — *Promontorium album*) is the Ladder of Tyre. Passages across the mountains overlooking the sea were difficult and, in times of war, hazardous, and these hardships are attested to in inscriptions carved into the face of the rock (at the Lykus river [in Arabic, Nahr al-Kalb = Dog River], north of Beirut) by kings and warlords alike — from Ramses II in the 13th century B.C.E. to the French High Commissioner of Syria, Gouraud, in 1920.

On several of the bays and promontories, wherever shelter could be provided for small vessels, ports were built in ancient times. Tyre, "the crowning city" which originally was set "in the heart of the seas" (Ezek. 27:4), i.e. on an island near the coast, is now at the head of such a promontory. Sand deposited by the waves gradually narrowed the strait between the island and the coast, and Alexander the Great added the missing link by building a land bridge in the gap (332 B.C.E.).

At the southern edge of Tyre there was a tiny cove which sheltered the "Egyptian Harbor" of the city, while a similar cove to the north was the site of the "Sidonian harbor." Between Tyre and Sidon there are some coves and promontories, the most important of which is Zarephath, the home of the widow who gave the prophet Elijah nourishment in the years of famine (I Kings, 17:9).

Sidon is situated on a small promontory. Two islands enclose the city from the west and offer protection for the small cove to the north, where the northern port was situated, and for that to the south, where the Egyptian port was located. The ancient "ships of Tarsus" found refuge from ocean storms in the harbors of Tyre and Sidon.

The largest of the Syrian bays is that of Beirut — now the most important harbor of the Republic of Lebanon — whose southern shores are five miles long; to the north, however, the bay is open. The most beautiful of Syria's bays is that of Jawna (approx. 2.5 × 2.5 miles) which, surrounded as it is by hills, has the appearance of an amphitheater. Further to the north is the site of Gebal, the Byblos of the Greeks (today called Jabayl) — the shipyard of the Phoenicians, according to Ezekiel (27:9). It was situated on a promontory overlooking a small bay.

The largest and highest promontory between Beirut and Tripoli is that of Ra's ash-Shaqqa (in Greek: — θεοῦ πρόσωπον — The face of God), rising above a bay similar to that of Beirut. A triangular shaped alluvial plain projecting into the sea is the site of the three ancient cities known by the name of "Tripolis" ("three cities"), now Tarābulus ash-Shām, the second largest port of Lebanon. Between Tripoli and Latakia, an airline distance of 66 miles, are two large arc-like bays. The southern one is the Gulf of 'Akkār (16 miles long and 4.4 wide), opposite the northern end of which — 2.2 miles from the shore — lies the Biblical island of Arvad (800 × 500 yards in size). It is the only inhabited island near the Syrian coast, and the one spot in Syria where the maritime tradition of the Phoenicians has been maintained by the natives. The other bay is the Gulf of Jabla (25 × 2.5 miles), north of which, on a small tongue of land, is situated the city of Latakia (in Greek: λαοδίκεια), the Canaanite Rimita — "a mother (metropolis) in Canaan," according to one inscription. Six miles north of Latakia, on a tiny bay, is situated Ra's Shamrā, where the ruins of Ugarit (from the second millennium B.C.E.), unknown from ancient documents, were discovered in 1929.

The northernmost of Syria's bays is that of Antioch (35 × 5.5 miles), into which empties the Orontes, the largest of Syria's rivers. To the north of its mouth stood Seleucia Pieria, the harbor of Antioch. Sixteen miles inland on the banks of the Orontes was situated Antioch itself (today: Antakya), the capital of Syria for 937 years, i.e., from its foundation by Seleucus Nicator (300 B.C.E.) until the Arab conquest (637 C.E.). Besides the well known historical cities, there were along the shore, on the strips of the coastal plain, numerous villages which engaged in agriculture, fishing, and the gathering of murex — used in the production of purple dye. Phoinikia (Phoenicia), the Greek name for this region, was derived from the root of the word Φοῖνιζ which means purple.

C. The Coastal Plains

While the coastal plains of Palestine are generally lengthy and unbroken, those of Syria are short, narrow strips, separated by hills which project into the sea. Where large perennial brooks, descending from the mountains, cross these strips on their way to the sea, the coastal plains extend into the river valleys in the shape of an inverted funnel. The southernmost plain is that of Tyre which begins north of the Ladder and extends to 'Adlun (perhaps the Hellenistic Ornithopolis). More than a mile in width near Tyre, it provided sufficient agricultural basis for the original fishing village which existed here, but as Tyre developed into a large mercantile city, it was necessary to import food from abroad (cf. Ezek. 26 and 27). Sidon is situated in the center of another plain, now rich in citrus orchards, similar to those of the Sharon, and it would seem that the famous Jaffa-oranges originated in Sidon. Also Beirut and Tripoli benefit from a hinterland of small plains.

The largest of Syria's coastal plains is that of 'Akkār or Arqa (the Canaanite tribe 'Arqui, ערקי), which extends for seven miles in the gap between Lebanon and the al-'Alawiyye mountains. Its continuation to the east is the basaltic and subsequently alluvial plain of Homs. The latter reaches a height of more than 1,500 feet, but the slope is so gentle that the transition from the coast to the interior is hardly noticeable. To the north, the ʿAkkār plain becomes increasingly narrow, and 17 miles north of the Lebanon it is only a mere strip which is terminated near Banias by a basaltic flow. North of Banias begins the plain of Latakia, famous in antiquity for its olive groves and now known chiefly for its tobacco. From Latakia to the coastal plain of Antioch there are only very small strips of plain, as the greater part of the coastline is mountainous. The coastal plain of Antioch is connected by the Orontes Valley with the fertile alluvial plain of ʿAmqā in the interior, which was the agricultural hinterland of Antioch in the days of her greatness and glory.

D. The Western Mountains

From the coastal plains rise the western mountain-ranges of Syria. Their eastern slopes are not as steep as those of the Judean desert or the Arabah, but are nonetheless steeper than those of Samaria and Galilee. Owing to the abundance of precipitation, the erosion is here more marked. Since the composition of the strata is mostly calcareous as in Palestine, the same Karstic phenomena appear: numerous caves, subterranean water-basins feeding great springs and similar soil types.

The western mountain wall is broken near the middle by the plains of ʿAkkār and Homs. At the northern end, the Syrian mountains are separated from the Amanus and Taurus mountains by the valley of the Orontes and the plain of ʿAmqā. The chief roads from the Mediterranean coast to the valleys of the Tigris and Euphrates passed through these gaps.

The mountain range stretching from the plains of ʿAkkār and Homs to the largely gorge-like valley of the Qāsimiyya river — the continuation of the Litani (the old Litas) — is commonly called Lebanon. For 106 miles the axis of this range runs SSW-NNE. The southernmost ten miles are not distinguishable from the mountains of Upper Galilee, as the rising of the Lebanon begins only north of the Zahrānī river. The Lebanon becomes progressively wider and higher from south to north. At the line of Sidon, it is nearly 17 miles wide and 6,070 feet high (at the peak of Tūmāt Nihā) at the line of Tripoli, it is 28 miles wide and 10,138 feet high (at Qurnat as-Sawdāʾ). The only passes suitable for commercial traffic are those of Ẓahr al-Baydār, 4,500 feet above sea level, now used by the Beirut-Riyāq-Damascus railway, and the pass of Zaḥla-Maʿruj through which runs the railway line from Beirut to the Biqāʿ.

As far as its altitude is concerned, the Lebanon is divided into three zones. Of these, the most significant economically is the middle one. Blessed with extremely fertile soil and an abundance of water for irrigation, its slopes are terraced and intensively cultivated. Forests, too, abound in this zone and the last remnants of the renowned cedars of Lebanon are also to be found here. In ancient times this area supplied timber (cedars and cypress) for both Phoenicia and Egypt. Nearly all the Biblical passages glorifying the Lebanon refer to this zone (Hos. 14:7; Cant. 5:15; Isa. 60:13; Ps. 29:5).

Between the Lebanon and its northern continuation, the ʻAlawiyye mountain range, there is a gap of some seven miles consisting of the above mentioned coastal plain of ʻAkkar and its eastern continuation, the plain of Homs, covered by deep basalt layers with a surface of very fertile soil.

The axis of the ʻAlawiyye runs S-N, instead of following the SSW-NNE axis of the Lebanon. Together with its continuation, the ʻAqra (ancient Mons Cassius), up to the lower part of the Orontes valley, the ʻAlawiyye range is about 100 miles long. Its width varies between 16 and 28 miles, the narrowest part being southeast of Latakia. Its highest point in the north is Mt. Dariyus (4,700 ft.). The range as a whole is composed of calcareous rock with some basalt strips overlying them. Mount ʻAqra (5,800 ft.), descending abruptly to the coast, is a conspicuous landmark for sea travelers. Fault-lines divide the ʻAqra from the Taurus-Amanus and between these ranges lies the valley of the Orontes.

E. The Rift Valley

Not a continuous depression as in Palestine, the rift valley in Syria consists of several sections, separated from each other by ground swellings which affect the hydrography of the country. The southern section, i.e. the valley between the Lebanon and the Anti-Lebanon, is commonly called the Valley of Lebanon (from the Hebrew: *Biqʻat ha-Levanon*, now known by its Arabic name, al-Biqāʻ). The length of the Lebanon Valley corresponds to its mountainous enclosure; the width varies, but does not exceed eight miles. Its average altitude is 2,400 feet above sea level. North of Baalbek, a swelling rising to an altitude of 3,320 feet divides the rift valley into two basins, that of the Litani, which descends to the south, and that of the Orontes, which slopes to the north. The basin of the Litani has an area of 855 square miles, that of the Orontes, reaching to the northern edge of Syria, is more than 9,000 square miles. The geographical name Hollow Syria

(Κοίλη Συρία), the extension of whose application varied from 300 B.C.E. to 300 C.E., originally signified only the rift valley. The richest part of the valley is a centrally located area, 150 square miles of well-irrigated grain and fruit fields. It was once the heart of the kingdom of Khalkis. The Riblah oasis (on the road to Hamath) which was much frequented in antiquity, is now in ruins, but still retains its Biblical name. The *Handbook of Syria*, prepared by the Intelligence Division of the British Admiralty, informs us (p. 372): "In the neighbourhood of Riblah, altitude 1,740 ft., there is a sudden change to a tract of fine deep soil, well cultivated and abundantly watered, which continues for two or three miles. . . Here access is easy from every direction and this. . . makes the locality most suitable for military encampments." Evidently the intelligence service of Nebuchadnezzar, who established his military headquarters here in 586 B.C.E., was motivated by the same considerations. From here Nebuchadnezzar sent the captain of his guard, Nebuzaradan, to besiege Jerusalem (II Kings 25:20–21).

The continuation of the rift valley north of the Lebanon Valley is disrupted in the plain of Homs by basalt flows and by deep alluvial sediments. The ancient lake of Kadesh (6 × 3 miles) was artificially created by a dam. It received its final shape at the end of the 3rd century by the Emperor Diocletian. The lake collects the water of the Orontes and stores it for irrigation purposes. The water-shed between the Orontes and the Nahr al-Kabīr (the "large river") — the Hellenistic Eleutheros — is only slightly higher than 1,500 ft. above sea level. A tiny rift valley, comparable to the northern Jordan valley, is that of al-Ghāb — the ancient plain of Appamea (ca. 40 miles × 3–4 miles), abounding in grain and fruits. North of al-Ghāb lies the plain of 'Amqā or Antioch (25 × 25 miles), surrounding the shallow lake and swamps of 'Amqā (7 × 6 miles). The 'Amqā plain is well watered by the Orontes as well as by several brooks which flow into it from all sides. The lake empties on the west into the Orontes, whose valley — some 22 miles long — is a western continuation of this plain. Into this area flow numerous springs, the most famous of which are those of Daphna — in antiquity a site dedicated to Apollo and the summer resort of Antioch. Winds from the sea sweep inland between the Amanus and the 'Aqra mountains, thereby creating a natural wind-tunnel, which attracts the fresh sea breezes. The advantages of this site from the standpoint of climate and communication were the main cause of Antioch's having been rebuilt after it had been repeatedly destroyed by earthquakes. It remained an important city for over 1,500 years, up to the end of the Crusaders' rule.

F. The Eastern Highlands

The eastern enclosure of the rift valley to the south consists of the Hermon and its northern continuation, the Anti-Lebanon — the eastern counterpart of the Lebanon range. The name Anti-Lebanon is of Hellenistic origin; the Biblical name is doubtful, perhaps Amana (Cant. 4:7–8), and it is possible that in some Biblical texts, the Anti-Lebanon is conceived of as merely a part of the Lebanon (Deut. 1:7). Compared with the uniformity of the Lebanon, the structures of the Hermon and the Anti-Lebanon are complex. Mount Hermon (9,500 ft.) is clearly visible from all sides, being separated from the Anti-Lebanon by a break in the crest line which descends here to 4,500 ft., thus providing a natural pass from the coast to Damascus. Mount Hermon, being higher than the surrounding mountains, receives greater precipitation and therefore feeds many springs — among them the chief sources of the Jordan.

In its southern part, the Anti-Lebanon is divided by a longitudinal depression (16 miles long and 3–4 miles wide), beginning some 20 miles north-east of Damascus. The bottom of the depression, 1,200–1,500 ft. below the mountains on either side, is a fertile and well watered alluvial plain — the source of the Barada River (the Biblical Amanah or Avanah). Supported by some very abundant springs, it flows by Damascus where it provides water for irrigation. The river evaporates in the Meadow Lakes, approximately 18 miles east of the city.

On the eastern side of the Anti-Lebanon some lower ranges bifurcate to the north-east. One of them reaches Tadmor (Palmyra), the famous trading center (on the road from Damascus to the Euphrates) whose foundation is attributed to King Solomon (I Kings, 9:18). In the folded layers of this range accumulate the water of the springs which issue from a fault-line. This and other fault-lines, the sources of water and consequently of fertility for many places in eastern Syria, are also the cause of earthquakes, which are sometimes severe. The ruins of Palmyra, Heliopolis (Baalbek), and ancient Antioch are somber illustrations of the devastating effects of the Syrian earthquakes.

At the foot of the Qāsiyūn range (4,000 ft.) there is a very fertile depression (approximately 150 square miles in area), watered by the aforementioned Baradā River and its southern neighbor, the Nahr al-A'waj (the Biblical Pharpar). At the western edge of the plain is situated Damascus (2,264 ft.), one of the most famous cities of antiquity — the capital of Aram-Damesheq, known from its conflicts with Israel.

The Damascene plain, on the fringe of the desert, is a spacious orchard land which also provides excellent pasture for dairy cattle. Celebrated by Arabic poets as a paradise on earth, the plain did not equally impress the Biblical writers who must have compared it to Egypt ("the garden of the Lord," Gen. 13:10), or to Palestine's own plains, some of which, like that of Ginnosar, are comparable in fertility with that of Damascus. Aside from its significance as an agricultural center, Damascus was also an important junction of communications, as a number of major trade routes passed through the city: to Phoenicia and Palestine, to Arabia and the Gulf of Elath, to Babylonia and Assyria, to Aleppo and Antioch, and to Asia Minor.

Whereas the Lebanon continues northwards to the Taurus range with only two breaks in this extension, the northern continuation of the Anti-Lebanon (toward the Anti-Taurus) consists of scattered hilly ranges and plateaus of moderate altitude. Jabal ash-Shumariyye, north-east of Homs, and Jabal al-Arbain to the north of Homs, west of the Orontes, are the most southern of these elevations. Then follow Jabal Zawiya (opposite the 'Alawiyye), Jabal Rīhā, east of the Zawiya, and finally the most northern range —Jabal Sam'ān, north-west of Aleppo. All these mountains between the Anti-Lebanon and the Anti-Taurus do not present a real barrier to communication. They receive sufficient precipitation for agriculture and, while they are now considerably inhabited, they supported an even larger population in the past.

2. MESOPOTAMIA — THE LAND OF THE TWO RIVERS

by A. J. Brawer

THE SYRIAN-ARABIAN plateau, whose north-western fringes are bounded by Palestine and Syria, slopes eastward towards the Tigris-Euphrates valley and the Persian Gulf. The Tigris and Euphrates emerge from the mountains which formerly formed part of Armenia and now constitute south-eastern Turkey. In Biblical times these regions were known as the Land of Ararat.[1] The Euphrates, the longer of the two rivers, begins with the confluence of two streams, the Frat Su and the more southerly Murat Su. Receiving most of its water in the mountains, the Euphrates emerges near Carchemish (a mound opposite the town of Jarābulus) into the elevated plain known as Aram Naharaim, i.e. Aram of the two rivers. At Maskana, east of Ḥalab (Aleppo), it comes so close to the Mediterranean that only 95–100 miles separate it from the sea. Beyond ad-Dibsī (perhaps Biblical Tiphsah) the river turns south-east and forms the eastern border of the Great Syrian Desert,[2] while the bend itself constituted the north-eastern boundary of the Promised Land; to this bend the Bible refers whenever it mentions the Euphrates as frontier. Along more than half of its upper course to the Persian Gulf, the Euphrates flows through a valley cut by its own waters into soft, marly strata of later tertiary sediments, dozens of yards below the surface of the north Mesopotamian plain. Here, in the northern plain, the irrigable area is a mere belt, at the most a few thousand yards wide, while the plain above this belt remains arid. Only in the upper course of the river, near the highlands, is there sufficient rainfall to grow cereals.

Having left the mountains, the Euphrates is joined in Aram Naharaim by two perennial tributaries, the Nahr Balkh, on the banks of which the town of Haran was situated, and the River Khābūr (Habor)[3] in the Land of Gozan.[4] From its confluence with the Khābūr downwards, the Euphrates loses much of its water through evaporation and permeation; the Tigris, on the other hand, is continually swelled by tributaries from the mountains of Iran — the eastern Khābūr, the Greater and the Lesser Zāb and the Diyālā (near Baghdad). The alluvial materials of the Diyālā have forced the course of the Tigris westward.

In Aram Naharaim or Padan Aram, the north-central part of the country between the two rivers, the transition to desert is gradual. Northern Mesopotamia never enjoyed an abundant water supply. The well of Haran barely supplied the needs of the sheep-flocks of the town.[5] The steppe country south of Aram Naharaim provides pasture for camels and sheep, as well as for horses.

The Tigris valley is similar to that of the Euphrates, although—owing to its large perennial tributaries, which come down from the western mountains of Iran — the Tigris carries more water than the Euphrates. Moreover, the volume of water in the Tigris does not fluctuate so markedly from season to season as does that of the Euphrates. The region stretching along both sides of the upper Tigris and extending into the mountains is the site of ancient Assyria. East of it, in the highlands of Iran, was the land of Media.

Some miles north of Baghdad, the Tigris and Euphrates draw near to each other so that their flood plains merge. From here southwards was the area of ancient Babylonia. The further the rivers flow from the mountains, the finer and more fertile become the sediments they deposit. In Babylonia there is neither stone nor sand, and the rivers' beds are only slightly below the surface of the plain, thereby facilitating irrigation. Here both the Tigris and the Euphrates also fork into natural arms. The largest arm of the Euphrates forms about 40 miles south of Baghdad; that of the Tigris branches off near Kūt al-'Imāra and flows southward into the Euphrates which is here lower than the Tigris. In the Bible and the Talmud the arms and canals of the Euphrates and the Tigris are likewise called rivers.[6]

In their lower courses the Euphrates and the Tigris form large swamps and lakes. The spread of the Euphrates waters is especially wide. The blocking up of the canals by sediments and by sand blown in from the desert, and the destruction of the dykes caused the swamps to expand. Of Babylonia it was said: "I will also make it the possession for the bittern and pools of water."[7]

The water regime of the Euphrates and the Tigris differs from that of the Nile, and since the utilization of their waters requires greater effort, it is less beneficial to man. The Nile receives most of its water from summer monsoon rains and overflows in the middle of the summer. In the autumn the water recedes. By the time winter crops are sown the soil is sufficiently dry for plowing, yet moist enough for the seed to grow. The Tigris and Euphrates flood in April and May. Mean summer temperatures in Mesopotamia are 18°F higher than in Lower Egypt. This is the season when irrigation is required, but the water in the rivers is then at its lowest. The irrigation system and the flood precautions required in Mesopotamia are complicated and likely to be damaged by nature or by man more easily than the canal system of the Nile. Nonetheless, the irrigated area in Mesopotamia was in ancient times much larger than in Egypt.

From the confluence of the Tigris with the Euphrates, some 95 miles from the Persian Gulf, the united river bears the name of Shaṭṭ al-ʿArab. The opinion, prevalent for the last hundred years, that the Persian Gulf extended much further north in early historical times and that the area of the Shaṭṭ al-ʿArab was still submerged at the time of Sennacherib, has recently been refuted by archeological and geological research.[8]

The third "partner" in the great united river flowing to the Persian Gulf is the Kārūn which, like the Euphrates and the Tigris, is navigable. Its main tributary is the Biblical Ulai,[9] whose modern Persian name is Ab-i-Diz. An ancient road leads into the Iranian plateau and follows the valley of the Kārūn and the Ab-i-Diz. The Kārūn and its tributaries, flowing down the mountains with a wealth of water, have deposited fertile alluvial soil. On this soil, with the aid of irrigation, an agricultural community established the kingdom of Elam,[10] with its capital Susa (Shushan) on the Ulai river. In the region of the Kārūn River, some of the world's richest oil wells have been found in the 20th century. Oil, however, was already known in the Tigris-Euphrates plain in ancient times.

C. THE REGIONAL ENVIRONMENT

by E. A. Speiser

HISTORY IS BASICALLY the story of man meeting the challenge of his physical environment. In terms of civilization, the human and the physical factors are interdependent. The Near East as a whole presents a number of unique environmental features. It has also been the stage of a unique record in the history of mankind. It would be idle to speculate whether the same environment acting against different human groups, or the same groups interacting against a different environment, would still have produced results of comparable significance. But the Near East can demonstrate more abundantly than any other region on earth how close and lasting is the tie between man's history and his natural background.

The essential facts of the physical and economic geography of Palestine, Syria, and Mesopotamia have been given in the foregoing chapters. Later portions of this volume will touch briefly on the geographic features of Egypt. The purpose of the present chapter is to bring together, in passing, the several areas of the Near East under a single focus. Did the important physical differences within the region have notable historical and cultural consequences? And how does the Near East as a whole relate to the neighboring regions? The questions are thus partly strategic and partly cultural. The answers concern primarily local history. But insofar as the Near East has been a world center of gravity, they may have a bearing also on some matters of interest to world history.

The interplay of environment and history in the Near East can perhaps best be illustrated by juxtaposing Egypt and Mesopotamia. Lying as they do at opposite ends of the region, these two lands have much in common on the surface; yet the differences between them are more significant ultimately than the similarities. Each area is centered about a great river valley; each is blessed with fertile soil, but this cannot be activated without extensive irrigation. Both Egypt and Mesopotamia developed outstandingly successful irrigation economies, and went on to evolve great civilizations, the oldest in the annals of mankind. But although these civilizations advanced at approximately the same pace, and were never entirely out of touch with each other, they could hardly have been more distinct in basic content and orientation.[1] Was there anything in their respective environments to foreshadow such dissimilar results?

In the case of Egypt, it is safe to say that nowhere else has a great civilization been molded to such a degree by a single river. With practically no rainfall outside the northern part of the Delta, settled occupation is all but restricted to the reach of the river and the yearly flood of its silt-laden waters. Because the width of the valley is confined on both sides by high cliffs, the habitable part of the country is narrow and elongated in the extreme; the rest is forbidding desert land. Inside the valley the rhythm of life is governed by the changeless routine of the Nile. The economy of the land is subordinated to this routine. It is in the main a rural rather than industrial and trading economy. The peasant's eyes are attracted to the river and its bed far more than to the sky. It is thus the animals in and along the river, not the astral bodies, that affect most deeply his early religious beliefs and practices.

In general, then, the Egyptian environment may be described as conducive to stability and provincialism from the outset. Yet the cultural progress which stemmed from that same environment could also be a factor in the opposite direction. Expanding economy creates the need for materials unavailable locally, and thus paves the way for an exchange of goods and ideas. The resulting contacts, since the dawn of Egyptian history, have been mostly with neighboring Asia, where the older attractions included the mineral resources of Sinai, the land bridge to the Fertile Crescent, and the prized timber of Lebanon. But the contrary tendency toward isolationism has also left its mark. Although in many ways a part of the Near East, Egypt has never stopped being parochial and antiforeign in various other respects.

The valley of Mesopotamia, especially in its lower reaches, is no less river-dominated than Egypt; more so, in fact, since here the amount of available ground has depended directly on how much of it the waters have submerged or laid bare. Yet the whole character of the country is much different from Egypt's. Mesopotamia is not walled in by cliffs, and the steppe constitutes here only a minor and occasional barrier. The river cannot hold firm in the soft alluvium. The land mass itself is unstable and has been advancing, at least within historical times, at the expense of the Persian Gulf. Thus, in sharp contrast to the Egyptians, whose environment was stable and changeless, the Mesopotamians were forever confronted with changing and unpredictable manifestations of nature.

Contact with neighboring territories was never a serious problem. Thanks to the exceptional fertility of the soil, which could readily be implemented through irrigation, the land was a powerful economic magnet long before it became recognized as a great cultural attraction. It was wide open, hospitable, and accommodating, the kind of melting pot that could inspire tales about the Tower of Babel. The prevailing orientation was international, not isolationist as in Egypt.

It would be futile, of course, to speculate on how much these differences in natural background contributed to the known cleavage between these two centers in regard to the respective concepts of state. One might argue that the critical shortage of arable land in Egypt could not but lead to rigid regimentation under a deified ruler. There is no way to prove or disprove such a hypothesis, although it is reasonable to assume that such a view would tend to oversimplify the situation. No doubt, there were other significant factors in each instance. And it must be admitted that the sharply contrasted concept of state in Mesopotamia cannot be traced analogously to the local environment. It is probable, on the other hand, that the physical background of Mesopotamia had an important bearing on this important aspect of religion, among others: accustomed as he was to open spaces in which he pastured his sheep and his cattle, and being dependent on an agricultural economy which was guided largely by the seasons of the year, the Mesopotamian accorded much prominence in his religious beliefs and practices to the sky, the sun, the moon, and the stars. On this score, too, the contrast with Egypt could thus be ascribed to differences in physical background. But no such deductions should be mistaken for demonstrable facts.

The territory that connects the great valleys of Egypt and Mesopotamia is usually given the convenient designation of Syria-Palestine. It is an intermediate area in more ways than one. For the most part, this land link constitutes a raised bridge between two vast river systems, with one of the northern exits leading to Anatolia. The central hill country is paralleled by the sea on one side and the earth's greatest inland depression on the other. The whole area benefits from a relatively copious, though seasonal, rainfall, but it has only little space and limited resources for irrigation. The resulting dependence on rain has left its own tell-tale marks on various local religions, most of which diverged from Egypt and Mesopotamia alike, in making the storm god the chief of the pantheon.

The political and cultural history of the area has no less an intermediate bearing than its geography. It needs stressing, in this connection as well as in others, that the whole of the Near East was destined, by virtue of its location, communication routes, and natural resources, to be a strategic center of gravity from the beginning of history down to this day. It attracted early settlers who proceeded to develop advanced cultures. Cultural progress in turn brought more settlers and further advances, so that the Near East became also the cultural center of the Old World. Throughout its long historic career this region has thus remained the key to world power and prestige, and thereby the target of all rulers who would aspire to world power. And as the sensitive epicenter of that critical region, Palestine — in pre-Israelite times and ever since — has enjoyed or been embarrassed by unceasing world attention.

Small wonder, therefore, that Palestine was to witness a long procession of conquerors and would-be conquerors from near and far. Pre-classical Egypt sent its Thut-mose III and Ramses II, its Mer-ne-ptah and Shishak. From the opposite end of the region came Sennacherib and Esarhaddon, among many others. In this contest for high stakes local rulers rose occasionally to incidental, and perhaps unwelcome, prominence. Old Merodach-Baladan, who led his native Babylonia against the Assyrian giant, took time off to show diplomatic solicitude for the health of Hezekiah, far away in little Judah (Isa. 39:1). But when Josiah sought to intercept the Egyptian army led by Necho, his political and military miscalculation cost him his life (II Kings 23:29) in the battle of Megiddo — the Armageddon of later symbolic parlance. In all such power contests, the strategic land bridge was not an end in itself but merely a means to an end. And so it has been throughout the passing centuries and millenniums: under an Alexander and a Pompey, a Napoleon and an Allenby, down to the very present. On purely strategic grounds, environment has served the Promised Land both as a blessing and a curse.

But the land's promise, in the traditional sense of the phrase, was not confined to strategic considerations. As has been indicated in the opening chapter of this volume, it was a cultural thoroughfare as well as a busy route between two great civilizations and a landing area for travelers from across the Mediterranean. And as the cultural traffic quickened, keen and sensitive observers could take stock and ponder. Vast spiritual areas remained to be explored, beyond the economic and cultural values of the day. It was an opportunity that Israel saw and did not shrink from following. And the validity of Israel's findings was to be borne out by their ever widening recognition and acceptance. Herein lies perhaps the greatest single example of fruitful interaction between environment and the human element.

PART TWO: THE ETHNO-LINGUISTIC FACTOR

A. LINGUISTIC DATA

B. ETHNO-LINGUISTIC ELEMENTS

Editor's Note

Actors on the stage of history reveal themselves by their actions. Through much of the early historic record the main action unfolds in two parallel courses, those of Mesopotamia and Egypt. The careers of these societies will be traced in separate accounts constituting the main themes of the present volume.

But group actions, no less than those of individuals, can often be illuminated with the aid of backstage evidence about the actors. Where the distant past is concerned, such supplementary information derives largely from linguistic and ethnic data. Material of that kind, however, should not be allowed to obstruct the flow of the connected narrative. This is the reason why the pertinent background details have been relegated in large part to a special section. The section is divided into two parts.

The chief spokesmen for the two dominant political centers are the Akkadians and the Egyptians. Hence the required ethnic data about them could be woven into the connected accounts. Accordingly, the supporting material in their case is confined to linguistic facts about Akkadian and Egyptian. A general statement on Semitic linguistics provides a fitting introduction to the subject. These three chapters make up the first part of the present section.

The second part is given over to ethnic elements whose role, although discontinuous, was of outstanding significance nevertheless. Here the data are both ethnic and linguistic, sometimes rich and at other times meager, but seldom appropriate to the running narrative. They are consequently summarized at this point under the combined heading of "Ethno-linguistic Elements." The respective chapters deal with the Sumerians, the Hurrians and Hittites, and the Amorites and Canaanites. The introductory essay attempts a hypothetical reconstruction of the movements of the pro-ethnic Semites.

A. LINGUISTIC DATA

1. SEMITICS

by H. Polotsky

A. Comparative Study

THE RELATIONSHIP between the older Semitic languages is such that no modern professional training is needed to perceive it. As early as the Middle Ages the resemblance of Hebrew to Aramaic and to Arabic was obvious to Jewish exegetes and philologists. It was they who made the discovery that obscure words and passages in the Bible could sometimes be made to yield a plausible sense by giving the Hebrew words the meaning which similar sounding terms had in Arabic; they thus were the first practitioners of a method which underlies many a note on this or that obscure Hebrew word till the present day. On a rather higher level we find grammarians using Arabic for the elucidation of Hebrew morphology. And the highest stage is represented by scholars who systematically compared the structures of Hebrew and Arabic by establishing the functional equivalents.[1]

The early history of Semitic studies in the Christian world offers little of interest for our special purpose.[2] A substantial contribution to the rise of Semitic philology was made by a typical achievement of 17th century Christian scholarship, viz., the Polyglot Bibles of Paris and of London.[3] These large folios, which do honor to the skill of their printers, were intended to serve the double purpose of (a) providing materials for textual criticism and exegesis, and (b) assisting in the comparative, or at least parallel, study of the languages related to Hebrew.

The Polyglot Bibles or selections from them continued to serve this useful purpose well into the first half of the 19th century. The last, and most scholarly, publication of this nature appeared exactly 200 years after the London Polyglot. It was William Wright's *Book of Jonah* in Jewish Aramaic, Syriac, Ethiopic, and Arabic.[4] Explaining his purpose in compiling this book, Wright speaks in the Preface of the difficulties encountered by the student of theology in his Biblical studies, viz. the "indifferent" quality of the Authorized Version, and the frequent obscurity and apparent corruption of the Masoretic text: "the only means of getting over at least a part of these difficulties is the study of the other Semitic languages and the comparison of the Translations that exist in them, more especially the Aramaic and Arabic."[5]

Some kind of start in Comparative Semitic Linguistics could thus be made a good deal earlier than in Comparative Indo-European Linguistics, for example. Parallel grammars of Hebrew, Aramaic (Syriac), Arabic and sometimes Ethiopic, or grammars of Hebrew as illustrated by Arabic, were indeed composed fairly early, and were, in fact, a characteristic feature of 18th century Christian Hebrew scholarship, especially in Holland and Germany. Yet, when at last it was clearly realized that linguistic relationships had historical implications, and that their study had been the subject matter of a science which did not as yet exist, the upshot was that this new science arose mainly in application to the Indo-European languages, whereas Comparative Semitic Linguistics has a reputation, possibly unfounded, for backwardness and lack of scientific precision.

We have seen that the comparative study of the Semitic languages was originally undertaken as a help towards the better understanding of Hebrew and the Hebrew Bible. It was fundamentally the desire to equip themselves for that purpose which prompted scholars and libraries to assemble materials for the study of Arabic, Syriac, and Ethiopic. But as such materials became more plentiful, they began to attract the attention of scholars for their own sake; and it was found, perhaps with a feeling of relief, that if Hebrew was dependent on its sister-languages, those sister-languages could very well do without Hebrew.

Now it is precisely this dependence on its sister-languages that makes Hebrew eminently fitted for the role of a unifying factor, by which the Semitic field is held together. But obviously Hebrew can fulfil this function only so long as by general consent the study of the Bible and its language is accorded a dignity which other fields of learning wish to share. In the Christian world the Bible belongs to the province of religion and theology. Once the prestige of theology was shaken, an entirely different attitude towards Hebrew developed. Its very dependence on its sister-languages became a cause for contempt. The handmaids were only too glad to dethrone the queen. The greatest calamity that has befallen Hebrew is that in the divorce of Semitic studies from theology, Hebrew was assigned to the latter.[6] On the other hand, in emancipating themselves from their subservience to theology, Semitic studies lost their center, and failed to find a substitute.

The scientific unity of the Semitic field rests entirely on the unity of origin inferred from the interrelationship of the various Semitic languages. The only science which professedly deals with Semitic unity as such is therefore Comparative Semitic Linguistics in the strictest sense of the term.

If, on the other hand, we turn to those aspects of civilization which are traditionally the province of "philology," we find that the literatures written in the several Semitic languages tend either to be self-sufficient, or to have their connections outside the Semitic field. There is no unity here; "Semitic Philology" is an empty name corresponding to no reality and justified only by the needs of academic economy; it simply means as many single "Semitic Languages and Literatures" as the incumbent of the chair so named can manage.

In a field where both workers and academic posts are relatively few, there are practical reasons against carrying the distinction between linguistics and philology to the full length demanded by theoretical considerations. However, in Semitics the confusion is more pronounced than elsewhere, at any rate more than in the Indo-European field, not only in teaching but also in research. It is probably without parallel elsewhere that the same scholar is the author both of the standard Comparative Grammar of the Semitic Languages and of the standard History of Arabic Literature — and it does not matter in the present context whether either of these works conforms to the highest ideal of its kind. The fact that Comparative Semitic Linguistics has never achieved independent status is a very prominent feature of its entire history.

When, in the 18th century, scholars began to acquaint themselves with the Arabic manuscripts which European travelers and diplomatic agents had brought back to the libraries of Europe, they could not fail to realize that the Arabic language could claim a higher status than that of a purveyor of "tow for upholstering exegetical works,"[7] and that the Arabic Bible versions were poor stuff compared with the riches of original Arabic literature. Clearly, Arabic was worthy of study for its own sake and offered abundantly precisely those things that the incipient romantic movement was eagerly looking for in exotic literature. The biography of J. J. Reiske (1716–74)[8] suggests that some pioneers had to pay with personal hardship for their devotion to a field of learning which had not yet received the stamp of official academic recognition. But it did not take long before Arabic Language and Literature, an essentially philological rather than linguistic field of study, assumed the dominant position in Semitics.

The greater interest taken in Arabic literature naturally led to a nonpolemical interest in Islam and thus to an Islamic rather than Semitic conception of Arabic Language and Literature, as well as to its association with other Islamic languages and literatures, especially Persian and Turkish.[9] The ultimate outcome of this trend was the rise of Islamic Studies as a self-contained field of research and academic instruction, tending to be contemptuous not only of linguistics but also of philology, though on the other hand more or less openly allied with Current Affairs, and thus the most influential and most topical of "Oriental Studies."

In a less spectacular way, the Christian Semitic languages, of which Syriac is the most important representative, likewise followed their extra-Semitic connections. Culturally, Syriac belongs to the non-Semitic languages like Coptic, Armenian, and Georgian, not to mention Greek. To take an intelligent interest in Syriac literature, the student has to be thoroughly acquainted with early and medieval Christianity. If he is not, he will be unable to appreciate what is most valuable, though possibly of somewhat specialized interest, in Syriac literature. It was therefore inevitable that Christian Oriental studies, which naturally appeal most to Catholic scholars, should finally set up their own specialized journals and declare in rather aggressive terms their secession from the Semitic linguistic fold.[10]

Thus even before Comparative Semitic Linguistics had had time to consolidate, it was weakened by the powerful competition of particularist and centrifugal tendencies.

The 19th century saw the addition of several new members to the Semitic family. Of these none is comparable in point of antiquity and general importance to Akkadian, the recovery of which was made possible by the gradual decipherment of the cuneiform script. The revolutionary effect which this discovery has had upon Ancient Near Eastern studies is too well known to require more than a passing reference here. The contribution of Akkadian to Comparative Semitic Linguistics is less conspicuous; in so far as it has found its way into standard works of reference, it seems more prominent in lexicography than in grammar.

After an initial shock at the divergence of some of the grammatical features of Akkadian from what was believed to be the Semitic norm, some of the younger Semito-Assyriologists proclaimed already in the late seventies and early eighties in more or less restrained language that the time would come when Akkadian would set the pace for Semitic grammar. Yet at that time the study of Akkadian was insufficiently advanced for such pronouncements to be taken as more than propaganda. They were unable to shake the position held by Arabic, supposed to be the secure foundation of Semitic Linguistics, and for all practical purposes as near to Primitive Semitic as one could expect. A good deal of strictly philological work had to be done before the evidence of Akkadian could be made to bear upon Comparative Semitic Linguistics.

There is no lack of factors which tend to make of technical Akkadian philology (as distinct from Assyriology in general) just another watertight compartment within Semitics, engrossed in its own narrow problems and lacking all interest in anything outside the "cuneiform" world. There is certainly enough day-to-day work to keep the student of Akkadian busy. The extra-Semitic connections within the "cuneiform" world are at least as numerous as, and hardly less important than, the Semitic ones, and it may indeed be hard to show reason why the Akkadologist should not employ his energy on Sumerian or Hurrian rather than on general Semitics. Moreover, after the study of Akkadian had, in its early stages, received a good deal of substantial help from the other Semitic languages, the prejudiced interference of Comparative Semitics had, in some cases, undeniably stood in the way of understanding peculiar features of Akkadian. The consequence of this experience was a revulsion from comparativism and the conviction that the time had come for the study of Akkadian to stand on its own feet; if the results did not agree with the accepted notions of Comparative Semitics, so much the worse for the latter. There arose a school in the linguistic study of Akkadian which made a point of avoiding the misleading associations of traditional Semitic grammar. It deliberately turned to other branches of linguistics for categories and technical terms and used them as tools to describe and analyse Akkadian grammar in terms adequate to its own system.

In the nineteen-twenties anti-comparativist tendencies were fairly widespread and by no means peculiar to Assyriology. They found theoretical support in the ideas of F. de Saussure (himself an outstanding comparativist), which just then were beginning to be heard of. In fact, on few points in General Linguistics is there agreement as general as on the principle that synchronic analysis must have precedence over comparative studies. However, the precedence and possibly greater interest of synchronic analysis does not annul the claims of Comparative Linguistics. The very existence of related languages constitutes a problem the legitimacy of which can hardly be denied. The synchronic analysis of Akkadian would seem to have reached a stage where communion with General Semitics may become fruitful for both sides. Without such communion Comparative Semitic Linguistics is doomed.

B. Distribution

If we go back to the year 600 C.E., that is before the rise and spread of Islam, and if, for the moment, we disregard Abyssinia, the area of Semitic speech was then very much what it had been for nearly three millennia. What had changed considerably during that period was the actual aggregate of languages attested at any one time, and their distributiou within the area. A series of maps would show this more effectively than tedious verbal description and enumeration, were it not for the danger that the blanks which such maps would inevitably present for the older periods might be wrongly interpreted as ethnic and linguistic voids.

The manner of attestation differs widely in different periods. For ancient times it is so haphazard and so much at the mercy of accident that we cannot even be sure that our inventory of written laguages is complete. A piece of archaeological good luck may bring unforeseen surprises. Direct attestation, through texts written in a language, is not the only means by which we may gain actual knowledge of that language; nor is direct attestation a measure of its importance, either historical or linguistic. A language may, at a given time, be attested mainly by loan-words in a neighboring language (as, for example, the "Canaanite" loan-words in New Kingdom Egyptian, some of which were to survive even into Coptic), or by proper names, especially when proper names are of the "sentence-name" type and therefore allow a glimpse into verb morphology and certain principles of syntax, besides characteristic vocabulary; cf. the case of what is variously known as "East Canaanite" or "Amorite." Incidentally, according to one authoritative opinion,[11] it was from this language rather than from "Canaanite" in the narrower sense (Phoenician, Hebrew, etc.) that the Egyptians borrowed the loan-words just referred to.

Direct attestation is limited not only by the accidents of archaeological discovery, but also by an objective factor. Throughout the history of Semitics we find surprisingly many instances of superregional and even supernational common languages, *Verkehrssprachen*, which various linguistic groups employ in writing in preference to their own language. That Akkadian, the language of a Great Power, was at different periods and for various purposes written outside the Assyro-Babylonian area proper, is not astonishing. It is less clear how a language like Phoenician came to be used for royal inscriptions as far afield as Cilicia (Karatepe), where the vernacular was not even Semitic, and at Zenjirli, where Phoenician was gradually, within a century, replaced first by what may have been the vernacular ("Ya'udic")[12] and finally by Old Aramaic almost in its standard form. As for Aramaic itself, which seems to have been autochthonous somewhere in N. Mesopotamia, no satisfactory explanation seems to be available for its remarkable ascendancy in the Achaemenian Empire, where we find it used by members of different nationalities, in inscriptions and business documents as well as in literary texts from Upper Egypt to Afghanistan.

An especially interesting offshoot of this Official Aramaic ("*Reichsaramäisch*") is Nabataean, which was written, but hardly spoken, in an Arab kingdom that stretched along the fringes of the Arabian Desert. Nabataean illustrates yet another possibility of indirect attestation, namely the Arabisms — single words, occasional grammatical forms, and syntactic constructions — which betray the living Arabic substratum beneath the written Aramaic. These Arabisms are older than any directly attested Arabic.

Mesopotamian Aramaic displaced Akkadian and developed into the various so-called East Aramaic dialects, of which we have three medieval literary representatives. Syriac, originally the language of Edessa (now Urfa), became the language of Mesopotamian and Persian Christianity and has remained till the present day the liturgical language of the Jacobites ("Occidentals") and the Nestorians ("Orientals"),[13] as well as of the Maronites.[14] The ecclesiastical differences between the Jacobites and the Nestorians coincide with certain linguistic ones, mostly phonetic, which hardly show in the consonantal orthography; the Maronites go in this matter with the Jacobites. A near relative of Jacobite ("Western") Syriac survives today in Torani, the dialect of the Tur Abdin.[15] The exclusive status of Syriac as the only written language prevented the spoken Aramaic of "Assyria" (Mosul and its vicinity) from being used in writing; it survives, however, in the Neo-East-Aramaic ("Modern Syriac") dialects spoken today, or at least until very recently, by Christians as well as Jews from Mosul to Persian Azerbaijan.[16] On the other hand, the two varieties of Babylonian Aramaic which were employed in writing in the Middle Ages, viz. the language of the Babylonian Talmud and Mandaean, did not leave descendants.

Less clear than the development of East Aramaic is that of what used to be called West Aramaic.[17] The way in which it came to replace the Canaanite languages of Palestine and Lebanon (and other parts of Syria) is quite obscure. That it actually took root there, among Jews, Samaritans, and Christians, as a spoken, and not only as a written language, is shown by an abundance of evidence and put beyond doubt by the fact that vestiges of it still survive as a peasants' speech in three villages not far from Damascus.

Thus on the eve of the Islamic expansion the whole non-Arab Semitic area west and north of the Arabian Desert, i.e. Central and Northern Palestine, Lebanon-Syria, and Iraq, was Aramaic in speech.

The Islamic conquest carried Arabic over the whole Semitic area (with the exception of Abyssinia) and beyond, to Egypt and parts of the Sudan and East Africa, to North Africa as far as Morocco, and temporarily as far as Spain.

Alongside their everyday speech, split into numerous — but by all accounts mutually intelligible — tribal dialects, the conquerors possessed a supertribal common language, which they used on formal occasions, in speeches and in messages and in their highly developed traditional poetry; it was likewise more or less the language of their holy book. It was this common language which became, and has remained till the present day, Classical Arabic, [18] one of the great languages of the world. It is a language that combines artificiality and vigorous vitality in a most extraordinary manner. While vocabulary, phraseology, prepositions, and conjunctions admit of a certain latitude, the grammar proper — in particular the distinction of noun cases and verb moods — has remained, at least formally, exactly what it was 1200 years ago. The way in which Classical Arabic, often of a very strict observance, has been adapted to modern literary forms is a remarkable achievement of the last two generations.

While the written language of the whole Arab world is one — in fact, "High Arabic" is probably the most powerful instrument and symbol of Arab unity —, spoken Arabic falls into a great number of considerably differentiated dialects, which in extreme cases are mutually unintelligible.[19] A strong tradition and convention excludes the dialects from literary use, except for the lighter forms of literature. About the ancient dialects of Northern Arabia we have only occasional indications, scattered in the works of native lexicographers and grammarians. A recent attempt to interpret them in terms of dialect geography[20] has yielded remarkably plausible results: the geographical distribution of many linguistic features now becomes more intelligible than it had been so long as only Classical Arabic had been taken into account.

Archaeological discoveries going back to the beginning of the 19th century have acquainted us with the rich civilization of Ancient South Arabia. They brought to light many inscriptions in several dialects, of which the most important ones are Sabaean and Minaean. The immediate yield of these sources for Semitic linguistics is unfortunately somewhat limited both by the highly technical contents of most inscriptions and by the absence of an explicit vowel notation. Recent research in that area has already greatly enhanced our knowledge, and further investigation will no doubt supplement it.[21]

The linguistic position of the so-called Modern South Arabian languages, Mehrī, Soqoṭrī, etc., is not yet quite clear. For the bulk of our material the credit belongs to the South Arabian Expedition of the Vienna *Akademie der Wissenschaften* in 1898-9, especially to David Heinrich Müller and Alfred Jahn; the study of the "Mahra" languages has long been the domain of the Viennese school (Maximilian Bittner, Viktor Christian). It is much to be desired that improved records of these languages be obtained before it is too late.[22]

At some time before the beginning of the present era South Arabian conquerors carried their language and script to Abyssinia. "Ethiopic" (Geez) became the language of an extensive Christian literature and is still the language of the Abyssinian Church; it is even nowadays sometimes written—for instance, in a peculiar kind of poetry. Modern Abyssinian Semitic is represented by a rich variety of languages and dialects, such as Amharic, the official language of Ethiopia, Tigriňa and Tigré in the North (Eritrea), Harari and Gurage in the South. These languages have undergone the deep-reaching influence of several Cushitic substrata; their sentence-structure is unlike anything known elsewhere in the Semitic field. Ever since the days of Hiob Ludolf (1624-1704) the Semitic languages of Ethiopia have been fortunate in the men whom they attracted. August Dillmann's (1823—94) *Grammatik der äthiopischen Sprache*, which appeared more than 100 years ago (Leipzig, 1857) and has not yet been superseded;[23] his *Lexicon linguae aethiopicae* (Leipzig, 1865), and especially Franz Praetorius' (1847—1927) *Amharische Sprache* (Halle, 1879) are works of which Semitic linguistics can be proud. The field is inexhaustible and exceptionally fascinating.

The great differences in the transmission of the Semitic languages require a correspondingly great variety not only of approaches and of "techniques," but also of individual talent and specialized skill. There are the unwritten modern dialects, the description of which has to begin with procuring reliable phonetic records and continue with the running of the whole gamut of linguistic analysis from phonemics through syntax. From the orthodox linguist's point of view these are the most favorable cases — in fact, the only satisfactory languages to deal with. In literary languages the pure linguist finds it sometimes difficult to hold his own and may find himself forced to meet the traditional philologist on the latter's own ground.

How and by whom these different tasks have been grappled with and more or less successfully accomplished, is the subject matter of a History of Semitic Studies, an attractive subject, of which lack of space forbids us to attempt so much as a sketch. It is, however, impossible not to mention the name of Theodor Nöldeke (1836—1930), whom all Semitists, whatever their speciality and their allegiance, acknowledge as The Master.[24]

C. Classification and Internal Relationships

Having mentioned, in the preceding section, most Semitic languages worth mentioning, we are now expected to arrange them in groups, so as to indicate succinctly the internal relationships within the Semitic family. This is one of the most delicate operations which the linguist can be called upon to perform, and one the theoretical foundations of which are least certain. On consulting recent works on Semitic linguistics, it will be seen that few authors care to assume personal responsibility for the groupings which they set before their readers; they are careful to state that they merely report what is "usual" or "accepted." This is in fact the only reasonable attitude to be taken so long as there is nothing in the field of Semitics to match A. Meillet's antiquated classic *Les dialectes indo-européens*, not to mention more recent and more elaborate works such as W. Porzig's;[25] in the Indo-European field the problem is at least fully discussed, if not solved. Here we shall merely explain, without entering into discussions of theory, what is implied in the "usual" and "accepted" groupings.

We assume, rightly or wrongly, that so close a relationship as that which exists among the Semitic languages, presupposes with logical necessity a period in which the language "family" was one single tongue spoken by a compact society in a geographically continuous area. According to this assumption the existence of related languages cannot be conceived of except as the result of the breaking up of a primitive unity, involving geographical separation (but not necessarily migration) and the rise of several "dialects," which developed independently of each other and thus became different "languages," not necessarily spoken in contiguous areas.

This breaking-up process may repeat itself indefinitely; some scholars go pretty far in assuming intermediate stages of unity, while others prefer what has been called a "multilingual" approach. An argument in favor of the latter is the familiar experience that once a dialectological framework has been set up, it may prove too rigid for fresh discoveries. Newcomers will almost inevitably be looked upon as intruders. There is the temptation to leave the existing framework intact and to accommodate additions in such a way as to cause minimal disturbance. It is thus likely that new entities which have every claim to a central or even independent place are assigned a marginal and subordinate position. The only way to obviate this danger is not to regard with too much reverence even such well-established and time-honored sub-groups as "Canaanite."

It has been claimed that the logical cogency of the assumptions outlined above is not as great as used to be believed. There has been talk of other ways in which languages can acquire family-likeness. For the time being the old assumption provides at least a working-hypothesis, and in the present account it is used only as such. It must be emphasized that the notion of "primitive unity" has to be taken with a grain of salt; it is, in fact, as chimeric as would be that of the First Semite. The "unity" we think of is not absolute; the roots of the differences which were to become more and more pronounced must have existed already in the earliest period.

The internal classification of the Semitic languages presented a problem with the beginning of the inquiry into the relationship of Akkadian to the other languages. It was obvious that in terms of so central a feature as the verb system, Akkadian stood quite apart from the rest. The Akkadian system diverged strikingly from what was believed to be the typically Semitic two-tense system (*qatala-yaqtulu*), into which Hebrew was thought to have introduced certain specifically Hebraic complications, while Ethiopic showed a slight, purely formal, deviation (believed to be an internal innovation of Ethiopic) in its *yəqattəl* as against *yaqtulu*. The divergences between the two systems may be summed up as follows: the normal function of *qatala* (narrative past) is fulfilled in Akkadian by *iprus*, and that of *yaqtulu* ("Present") by *iparras;* Akkadian possesses moreover a form, the inflexion of which is similar to that of *qatala*, while its function is peculiar to Akkadian (the "Permansive" or Stative). Though puzzling at first, these divergences held out the hope that they would at last bring some life into Semitic grammar and shed light on the antecedents of its apparent uniformity.

It was Eb. Schrader and after him F. Hommel who concluded from these facts that Akkadian was a group by itself ("East Semitic") within the Semitic framework. Hommel insisted in particular on the insignificance of all the differences within the other languages ("West Semitic"): according to him, any subdivision within the Western group ("North-West, South-West")[26] was not only irrelevant and superfluous but misleading, because it obliterated, for instance, certain special points of similarity between Aramaic and Arabic.

In the course of time it was discovered that the two systems were not entirely independent of each other. Already in 1878 Paul Haupt recognized the identity of the Ethiopic Imperfect *yəqattəl* with the Akkadian *iparras*, its functional equivalent. Supposing that the divergence between the two systems was to be interpreted as an innovation on the part of the Western group, i.e. as a replacement of *iprus-iparras* by *qatala-yaqtulu*, Haupt's identification implied that Ethiopic had taken part in one of the two Western innovations, but not in the other; in other words, that it had branched off from the bulk of the Western languages, before these had had time to replace *iparras* by *yaqtulu*. This identification was widely accepted, and several scholars based on it the theory of an especially close connexion between Ethiopic and Akkadian, and by implication between South Arabians and Akkadians, representing together an older ethno-linguistic stratum. This view found expression, for instance, in A. Ungnad's *Grammatik des Akkadischen* (3rd ed.), where South Arabians and Akkadians are both seen to branch out from what he called "Ostsemiten" (Eastern Semites).

But Ethiopic *yəqattəl* is not the only instance of an overlapping between the two systems. It is possible to detect in "West Semitic" traces of a form corresponding to *iprus*. The Hebrew forms used after the *wa*—consecutivum were formerly described as shortened Imperfect, i. e. *yaqtulu*, forms. If we regard them as real "Jussive," i. e. *yaqtul*, forms, we are able to identify this (*wa-*) *yyaqtul* with *iprus*; the old narrative past would then be preserved under special syntagmatic conditions. Another survival of *iprus* could be identified in the Jussive used after the negative *lam* in Arabic: *lam yaqtul*, "he did not kill".

These survivals made it possible to think of reconstructing the way in which the Western system could have developed out of an older system, which is fairly faithfully preserved in Akkadian and which we may for all practical purposes identify with Proto-Semitic. Three questions have to be answered:—

(1) What is the origin of the Western "Perfect" *qatala*?

(2) Why was *iparras* abandoned?

(3) What is the origin of *yaqtulu* (replacing *iparras*)?

The first two questions can be answered without undue difficulty:

(1) The Western "Perfect" represents the form which appears in Akkadian as "Stative." The inflexion is practically the same. As for the meaning, it is a matter of experience that forms expressing a "state" frequently replace older narrative forms.

(2) *iparras*, or rather *yaCaCCa/i/uC*, was abandoned because it was

insufficiently differentiated from the "Intensive Stem," Preterit *uparris*, Present *uparras*. That the similarity of the two forms could lead to an alteration, is shown by Ethiopic, where the form of the "Intensive Stem" was altered.

No really convincing answer has yet been given to the third question.[27]

The basic assumption which underlies the entire reconstruction is the identity of Akkadian *iparras* and Ethiopic *yəqattəl*. The individualism of linguistic reasoning is well illustrated by the fact that this identity seems evident to some and utterly unproven to others. An important argument in favor of the identification is the circumstance that it rests on two separate features of external similarity, namely (1) the vowel after the first radical, and (2) the doubling of the second radical. By the presence of two such features the likelihood of mere chance is considerably reduced. The doubling of the second radical is a particularly valuable argument, precisely because outside the "Intensive" Stem it seems so absurd from the standpoint of Arabic, Aramaic and Hebrew, and so utterly contrary to the very principle of the system of "Stems." That this absurdity should have occurred independently both in Akkadian and Ethiopic — and, at the opposite end of the "Hamito-Semitic" (or, in J. H. Greenberg's nomenclature, the "Afro-Asiatic") area, in Berber[28] — is, in some people's judgment, so unlikely as to outweigh all possible arguments against the identity of the two forms, such as those recently brought forward by Marcel Cohen.[29]

2. AKKADIAN

by E. A. Speiser

Since the history of the Semitic inhabitants of Mesopotamia will be given its due share of attention in a later section of this volume (IIIA), the present chapter will concentrate on linguistic data to the exclusion of the ethnic.

The term "Akkadian" was used by the Babylonians themselves to designate the local Semitic language. Modern scholarship has extended this usage to cover all the pertinent dialects.[1] The term is based on the geographic name for northern Babylonia, or Akkad, as contrasted with southern Babylonia, or Sumer. And the district, in turn, was so named after the city of *Agade*,[2] which owed that significant prominence to the achievements of its celebrated local dynasty, founded by the original Sargon.[3] Before Sargon, then, the whole district and its Semitic speech must have been known by other names. What these may have been is still a matter for speculation.[4] In any case, the new designation, even though it derived from a hitherto obscure place, soon gained general acceptance. The language itself was destined to have an extraordinary career. It came to be the internationally accepted medium of law and diplomacy;[5] its written remains were to bulk large in more ways than one; and its recorded life span was to extend from about 2500 B.C.E.[6] to about 50 C.E. Today, Akkadian is by far the oldest known representative of Semitic, and the only member of that family to have left direct witnesses that reach back to the third millennium.

Beyond its direct historical testimony, moreover, Akkadian contributes also several useful hints in regard to the protohistory of Semitic. In its choice of the 3 p. pronouns with initial *š* (m. *šū*, f. *šī*),[7] Akkadian lines up with Minaean (*s*-) and Modern South Arabic (Mehrī and Soqoṭrī f. *s*-), as against the other languages which have corresponding pronouns with *h* (**hū*', **hī*', the latter originally **šī*').[8] The same correspondence holds true on the whole for the respective causative morphemes: *š*-/*s*- as against *h*- > '-.[9] What is more, causative morphemes with initial sibilant confront us also in Egyptian and Hamitic.

Aside from these broader correspondences, which Akkadian thus shares with some of the other Semitic languages and also, in certain instances, with Egyptian and Hamitic, there are others of more limited distribution, and hence perhaps more significant for that very reason. Thus Akkadian indicates the dative case of pronouns by means of *-š-*, and the accusative by *-t-*; the identical morphemes with the same functions have been established for the Agaw branch of Hamitic.[10] This juxtaposition is far too detailed to be ascribed to mere coincidence. No less suggestive is the correspondence of the Akkadian present *iparras* and the South Arabic imperfect indicative (cf. Eth. *yəqattəl*), two disyllabic stems which contrast with the prevailing monosyllabic type (e.g., **ya-qtul*). Here again we must assume a generic relationship that goes back to the Proto-Semitic stage.[11]

On the basis of the connections just cited, for which Akkadian is the key witness in each instance by reason of full documentation all the way from remote antiquity, one may reconstruct provisionally the following process. A proethnic Hamito-Semitic stage preceded the separation of the Semitic group in which the ancestors of Akkadian and South Arabic were in the forefront. They thus retained certain common features which later Semitic groups did not share. Eventually Akkadian separated from South Arabic, thereby retaining archaic details that were to set it apart from the rest of the Semitic family. To be sure, these are far-reaching conclusions founded on relatively slim evidence. Yet the nature of the evidence is such as to lend the reconstruction a substantial measure of probability. It is worth repeating that Akkadian, as the main witness in the case, testifies with authority to conditions of nearly five thousand years ago.

Separation from the common Semitic stock brought early exposure to foreign influences. The cultural environment of Mesopotamia meant that the chief counterinfluence would be Sumerian. This proved to be highly pervasive; it profoundly affected not only the phonology of Akkadian[a] and a large portion of its vocabulary, but also its morphology[b][12] and syntax.[c] By emerging, however, as the linguistic vehicle for the expanding civilization of Mesopotamia, Akkadian was itself destined to undergo enormous expansion. Its dialects came to include such more or less direct descendants as Old, Middle, Late, and Neo-Babylonian, as well as Old Assyrian — including the speech of the business colonies in Cappadocia —, Middle, and Neo-Assyrian. In addition, there sprang up numerous su-

[a] e.g., weakening and reduction of the laryngeals.

[b] e.g., the separative *t*-form, as in *wabālum* "to bring": *itbulum* "to take away."

[c] e.g., placing the predicate at the end of the clause.

perimposed dialects, literary media for the most part in districts with a different vernacular: Elam, Lullu, Northern Akkad, Arrapkha-Nuzi; the Akkadian dialects of the Bogazkoy and Amarna archives, and of such Syrian centers as Alalakh and Ugarit; the first-millennium dialects of Iran and Urartu; and the like.[13]

The chief historical consequences of these vicissitudes were thus twofold. On the one hand, by branching off early from the rest of the Semitic stock Akkadian was in a position to retain certain old features which the rest of the family either modified or abandoned later on. And on the other hand, the new environment exposed Akkadian to specific extraneous influences which did not affect its sister tongues. In the present context, the question that matters most is not so much the new characteristics that were acquired, as the inherited characteristics that were retained by Akkadian.

On this last count, one does not have to look for a significant illustration. It is in the area of the verbal system that Akkadian differs most markedly from the rest of Semitic. This difference alone has been deemed sufficient to inspire a classification wherein Akkadian, under the label of East Semitic, is set apart from all its relatives, bunched together as West Semitic. It can be shown, moreover, on internal grounds that Akkadian alone has kept in this instance an original feature of Primitive Semitic, one that appears to go back in turn to the Hamito-Semitic stage.

The sharp distinction between the prefix conjugation (West Semitic "imperfect") and the suffix conjugation (West Semitic "perfect") is observed in Akkadian not only morphologically but also, and consistently, in respect to function. The Akkadian prefix conjugation belongs to the verb proper. It marks the action as a one-time event in the past ("preterit"), or as something unaccomplished, durative, or the like ("present");[14] the preterit takes the form of *ipr-s*, the present that of *iparr-s*.[15] The suffix conjugation, on the other hand, is specialized for the predicate in a nominal sentence. It is used primarily to describe a quality or a state (hence the name "stative") and it can be applied to nouns as readily as to adjectives.[a] When a verbal root is thus conjugated, the meaning is stative with intransitives, but becomes passive with transitives.[b]

As against this clear-cut and objective division in Akkadian between action form: prefix conjugation on the one hand, and stative form: suffix

[a] *bēl-ē-ta* "you (m.s.) are/were/will be master"; *damq-ā-ta* (<**damiq-*) "you are fair"; *marṣ-ā-ta* (<**maruṣ-*) "you are sick."

[b] *balṭ-ā-ta* "you are well," but *maḫṣ-ā-ta* "you are/were struck."

conjugation on the other, West Semitic emphasizes the complicated and subjective distinctions of tense. It has retained, to be sure, the outward difference between prefix and suffix forms; but the corresponding cleavage between action-sentence and nominal sentence has been suppressed in favor of indicating the impact on the speaker. The West Semitic perfect has become the medium for narrating past events; and if a given root was transitive to begin with, it continues to be active in the perfect.[a] Accordingly, Akkadian has no need for a regular passive,[16] whereas West Semitic was obliged to introduce special passive forms. In short, West Semitic underwent a drastic and complex transformation in regard to its verbal system.[17]

That it is West Semitic which represents a departure from an earlier scheme, as preserved in Akkadian, and not the other way about, may be gathered from a number of considerations. The Akkadian system is self-consistent throughout: the stative remains inactive, regardless of the root, and it is neutral in regard to tense. The West Semitic perfect, although morphologically the same as the Akkadian stative, is active with transitive verbs and signifies the past tense.[18] Furthermore, the Akkadian stative has a close analogue in the so-called "old perfective" of Egyptian (also known as the "pseudo-participle").[19] This particular correspondence vouches for the high antiquity of both these forms and suggests a common ancestry in Hamito-Semitic. The formal agreement between South Arabic indicative and subjunctive imperfect and Akkadian present and preterit respectively points to the existence of the present in Proto-Semitic. Finally, various uses of the imperfect in West Semitic reflect an intimate connection with the Akkadian preterit not only in form but also in function; cf., e.g., the West Semitic jussive, the use of the imperfect in Hebrew poetry to signify a one-time occurrence in the past (cf. Job 3:3), and the employment of the imperfect with Hebrew *'āz* and Arabic *lam;* all these cases have a more or less direct affinity with the Akkadian precative, which is a preterit in form. The West Semitic verbal system as a whole proves thus to be a secondary development, whereas its Akkadian counterpart represents a prior stage common to Semitic in general.

In none of the instances cited above can there be any question of direct Akkadian influence on its sister languages. It is only because of the greater antiquity of the Akkadian material, and the conservative nature of much of the underlying linguistic structure, that many of the peculiarities of Akkadian have emerged as indicative of earlier Semitic conditions. There

[a] WS*'*akal* "he ate," as opposed to Akk. *akil* "it is/was/will be eaten."

are other cases, however, in which the possibility of outright Akkadian influence cannot be ruled out; and in still other instances, the indebtedness of a West Semitic language to Akkadian can be definitely established. One example for each of these two categories will have to suffice by way of illustration.

The Hebrew imperfect with "conversive *waw*" is a construction for which Akkadian may well have furnished the model; but one cannot disregard offhand the likelihood of an independent development, let alone an inner-Semitic process. At any rate, the Akkadian analogues are sufficiently suggestive to afford a new insight into one of the most puzzling usages of Biblical Hebrew.

It will be readily recalled that the Hebrew imperfect with "strong *waw*" is basically an idiom arising out of, or carrying further, some previous occurrence; and that it can be used after a variety of preceding forms or phrases, without a direct link to the preceding, and even at the beginning of books (Lev., Josh., Jud.).[20] The perfect consecutive would seem to be merely the logical extension, and reverse complement, of the idiom which developed with the imperfect.

Now it happens that Akkadian makes frequent idiomatic use of an essentially similar construction. A present form introduced by a connective *-ma* (normally "and") may be employed after statives, imperatives, or preterits to signify purpose.[a] Invariably, (a) the verbal form in the second clause is contrasted with that in the first; (b) there is a mediating *-ma*; and (c) the sequel has the force of a *that*-clause arising out of the preceding statement. The close connection with the idiom contained in the imperfect consecutive is immediately apparent. To be sure, Akkadian uses here the prefix form which we know as the present; but Hebrew had no similar choice of prefix forms, the imperfect being the only one at its disposal. The important thing is the formal contrast with the first clause, on which both languages insist. In the light of this comparison, the recessive accent in the Hebrew idiom under review may receive a simple explanation: for neither the present nor the preterit of Akkadian stressed the last syllable.

If we hesitate, nevertheless, to view the above illustration as conclusive proof of Akkadian influence in this case, it is mainly because we may be confronted with a related development in Ethiopic; in which case, all three phenomena could be independent of one another, or else constitute

[a] e.g., *N pāšu īpušam-ma iqabbi* "N opened his mouth to speak" (lit. "that he might speak"); *iṭḫē-ma bēlum qabluš Tiāmat ibarri* "the lord drew near to examine the inside of Tiamat."

so many separate manifestations of a tendency common to Semitic as a whole. As was indicated above, the imperfect of South Arabic distinguishes an indicative, which is morphologically identical with the Akkadian present, and a subjunctive which corresponds to the Akkadian preterit. But the prevailing function of the subjunctive, notably in Ethiopic, is to express the predicate of the *that*-clause.[a] The question arises therefore whether the so-called subjunctive was not originally a finite tense rather than a mood, which was first specialized for purposes of continuing the principal clause where the normal narrative tense was employed, and only gradually acquired the exclusive functions of a "subjunctive." At all events, this is a possibility that has to be left open for the present. And whether or not the conversive use of the Hebrew tenses is ultimately traceable to Akkadian inspiration, this particular literary feature of Biblical Hebrew can no longer be regarded as a Canaanite peculiarity.

For a clear case of West Semitic indebtedness to Akkadian morphology we have to go to Aramaic. It is well known that the causative of Aramaic may take one of three formatives: *h*-, '-, or *š*-. It would be a mistake, however, to deduce from this circumstance — as is still being done at times — that Aramaic had from the start the choice of three independent causative morphemes. We know from Biblical Aramaic that '- is but a later phonologic development from *h*-. And it has been frequently observed that the causatives with *š*- came to Aramaic with a small number of culture loan words from Akkadian,[21] these loans being restricted to the fields of law and religion. With this specialized group as a nucleus, later Aramaic dialects went on to extend this formation to a limited degree. But the indigenous causative marker in Aramaic was *h*-, just as *š*- was the native causative morpheme of Akkadian. A single borrowing from the same source, which found its way into Biblical Hebrew, is *sanwērīm* (Gen. 18:11).[22] The initial *s*- suggests Assyrian mediation. The basic Akkadian stem was *nwr* "light," and the augmented form with an original *š*- (**šunwuru*) would have to carry, as we now know, some kind of emphatic connotation. The correct translation of the borrowed Hebrew noun is "dazzling light" rather than just "blindness" — a translation, incidentally, which happens to be uniquely appropriate in that particular context.

It is evident, however, from what has just been said that *sanwērīm* is not entirely on a par with the derivative verbal *š*-forms (the so-called "Shafels") of Aramaic. Not only is the Hebrew instance a noun instead of a verb, but it also lacks an outright causative value. The difference is

[a] e.g., *yeḥneṣ hagara lasemeka* "that he build a city for Thy name."

more than superficial. There are several categories in Akkadian which employ the same *š*-morphemes in the causatives, yet have nothing semantically in common with Shafels. In turn, these atypical Akkadian classes with *š*- help to explain some equally unorthodox Hebrew groups with *h*-, groups which are formed like Hifils but are definitely non-causative in meaning. Once again, then, a peculiarity of Akkadian linguistics serves to illuminate apparent irregularities elsewhere in Semitic.

Briefly,[23] Semitic could employ the same given formative to signify not only causation but also other nuances. With adjectives and statives this element brings out the sense of "more, most, especially." This is true of the Arabic elative, where the morpheme is '-, the same as in the causative form of the verb. It is likewise true of Akkadian.[a] When the Akkadian elative is turned into a factitive verb, the emphasized value carries over.[b] The emphasis thus imparted is not limited to the elative or superlative grade. In Arabic it is extended to colors and lasting afflictions; e.g., *'aswad* "black," *'aḫras* "dumb." In Akkadian it may be applied to such states as stillness (e.g., *šuḫarrur* "became motionless"), passage of time (e.g., *ušalbar* "grows old," *ušamša* "works late"), and the like.

The combined evidence of Arabic and, more especially, of Akkadian — since it is Akkadian that helps to place the whole matter in its proper focus — provides at last the proper explanation for a variety of Hebrew forms which have hitherto been grouped with Hifils but could never be suitably explained as causatives. There need no longer be any mystery about color verbs like *hilbīn* "became white," terms for stillness such as *heḥrīsh*, *heḥshā*, *hiskīt*, or indication of time as in *hashkēm* and *ha'arēv*. Nor are the apparent doublets in which Qals and Hifils are used side by side as devoid of differences in meaning as they have been commonly thought to be. Whereas *yāqaẓ* means "woke up (with a start)," *hɛyqīsh* may have the special sense of "was awake"; and while *yāvɛsh* denotes "dry," *hōvīṣh* has the added force of "was desiccated" (cf. Joel 1:17, 20). These are not intransitive Hifils, which is a contradiction in terms. They are special constructions which happen to share the same morpheme with the Hifils. Their meaning carries usually some connotation that marks them as out of the ordinary, something that is emphatic or "elative." And it is the unambiguous evidence of Akkadian that has helped to restore to these Hebrew forms their correct grammatical and semantic bearing.

[a] cf. *šurbū* "supreme" alongside *rabū* "great"; *šupšuqu* "most difficult," alongside *pašqu* "difficult"; *šumruṣu* "sorely afflicted" alongside *marṣu* "sick."

[b] *šurbū* "supreme" > *ušrabbi* "made greatest/supreme"; and so, analogously, **šunwuru* "made brightest, dazzling."

Perhaps even more helpful to Semitic comparative linguistics is another Akkadian formation which has hitherto been regarded as unknown elsewhere in Semitic. It is the so-called *tan*-form of the verb, which may be applied to any given stem or conjugation.[24] Its function is to express repeated or continuous action, e.g., *aš-tan-appar* "I keep on writing," from *šaparu(m)* "to write." Outside the present stem, however, where the extra vowel protects the nasal, the *-n-* becomes assimilated to a following consonant.[a]

Since Hebrew has no formation corresponding to the Akkadian present, it could not preserve a *tan*-form intact, if it had started out with one. There would be no outward means of distinguishing such a form from a regular Hithpael. The end product of a hypothetical **hiq-tan-til* would be exactly the same as the result of an original Hithpael, i.e., *hitqattεl.* The sole criterion is the internal test of meaning. It is, nevertheless, a reliable test. There is a large residue of Hebrew *t*-forms in which the function of the infix can hardly be reflexive, middle, or reciprocal. What is more, such forms occur often, in the Qal or Piel, without a *t*-morpheme, although no change in meaning is immediately apparent. On closer examination, however, there emerges a definite and consistent distinction. And the number of such cases is large enough to eliminate any chance of coincidence. The atypical Hithpaels prove to be clearly durative in connotation. We have to content ourselves here with a few selected examples.

With a stem like *hit'abbεl,* a reflexive or reciprocal meaning is scarcely in order. The required sense is usually "to enter a period of mourning." This durative nuance is actually confirmed in the Bible more than once by a special added phrase, as in the following examples (the addition is shown in italics): Jacob "mourned his son *for many days*" (Gen. 37:34); David "mourned his son *all the days*" (II Sam. 13:37); "*how long* will you mourn for Saul?" (I Sam. 16:1). Particularly revealing in this connection are the numerous occurrences of *hithallεḵ,* where the normal force of *-t-* is obviously out of the question. Cf., e.g., *qūm hithallεḵ* (Gen. 13:17) and Akkadian *eli-ma itallak* (Gilgamesh XI 303), both "up, walk about"; "walks about outside upon his cane" (Exod. 21:19); and especially *way-yithallεḵ Ḥanōḵ et-ha'elōhīm* "and Enoch walked with God" (Gen. 5:22, 24), which Akkadian parallels significantly with *ilšu ittišu ittanallak* "his god will walk with him" (ZA 43, 98.31). The case for a Hebrew *tan*-form, hitherto mistaken for a genuine Hithpael, could not be made more convincingly. And the witness and interpreter of this elusive Hebrew formation

[a] e.g., *iktabbit* < **iktanbit* "kept weighing heavy."

is Akkadian, which is in a position to shed light on Semitic features that would otherwise remain unrecognized.

In conclusion, it goes without saying that approximations in vocabulary and phraseology between Akkadian and a given sister language are a matter of cultural conditions rather than linguistics. This applies particularly to the various loanwords and glosses as such. Thus West Semitic glosses are common, e.g., in Akkadian texts from Mari and Ugarit, and are especially prominent in the Amarna correspondence. Indeed, in the latter instance we have often samples of a Canaanite dialect forced into an Akkadian mold. On the other hand, as the common literary medium of the ancient Near East, Akkadian was sometimes the source of sundry literary phrases in other languages. More than one such correspondence is reflected in the Bible. An eloquent case in point is Isaiah 59:17 "And He put on righteousness as a coat of mail/ And a helmet of salvation upon His head." The secular Akkadian prototype occurs in the annals of Sennacherib (Oriental Institute Prism V 67—69): *attalbiša siriam ḫuliam simat ṣilti āpira rašuya* "I put on my coat of mail; the helmet, emblem of victory, I placed on my head." In a way, these two passages may be regarded as symbolical of the underlying linguistic relations. By reason of its greater antiquity, Akkadian can give us a valuable commentary on its relatives. But the younger members of the family have their own advances and contributions to report.

3. EGYPTIAN

by H. Polotsky

A. Introductory Remarks

FOUR KINDS of sources are available for the ethno-linguistic position of the ancient Egyptians:—

(1) Actual remains of Egyptian corpses. Owing to the art of mummification we have, at least for the historic period, not only skulls and bones, but also specimens of flesh, hair, and nails.

(2) Works of art of all periods, paintings, reliefs, and sculptures, representing Egyptian men and women. From the materials under (1) and (2) the physical anthropologist is expected to be able to determine the race, or races, of the Egyptians.

(3) Artefacts of every description. Archaeologists consider these, especially pottery, a sound basis for statements about the spread of cultures and, by implication, of their bearers.[1]

(4) The Egyptian language. What the linguist may have to say about the relationships of the Egyptian language, though irrelevant to the question of the ethnic relationships of the Egyptians themselves, is worth knowing in any case, and may be interesting to compare with the results derived from (1), (2), and (3).

It is hardly possible at the present time to give a unified account of the question by coordinating the findings of these separate branches of science and scholarship.[2] It is a regrettable fact that the assumptions and modes of reasoning accepted in each of them do not always carry equal weight with the specialist in any of the other two. Paradoxically, each of the three specialists involved is nevertheless likely to rely at least for a part of his arguments on what he imagines to be evidence from "another science which is imperfectly understood and therefore the more respected." A further difficulty arises from the unfortunate part which Noah's sons have come to play in ethno-linguistic nomenclature.

If we apply to the physical anthropologist, we may be certain to hear him sooner or later, in one form or another, use the term "Hamites" with reference to the Egyptians. Since in the Psalms "the land of Ham," either in parallelism with "Miẓraim" or alone, refers unambiguously to Egypt, the purely conventional term "Hamites" was originally coined to group together the Egyptians (and their language) with certain peoples (and languages) believed to be related to them. The statement that the Egyptians are "Hamites" is a mere tautology.

Some scholars acquainted with the results of African anthropology have used, none more brilliantly than the late Henri Frankfort (1897–1954),[3] modern "Hamitic" parallels to elucidate important aspects of ancient Egyptian civilization. Granted the validity of the analogies in question and of the interpretations drawn from them, the fact remains that Frankfort's "Hamites" and "half-Hamites" include such groups as the Nubians, the Shilluk, and the Masai, whose languages no competent linguist nowadays classes as Hamitic.[4] Yet Frankfort relies expressly on such supposed linguistic evidence in calling them "Hamites" and assuming a physical relationship between them and the ancient Egyptians.[5]

We conclude that the interests of the general reader will be better served if every specialist, for the time being, keeps strictly within the limits of his own competence. Even so, there will be more than enough that remains uncertain and speculative.

B. Egyptian and the Hamito-Semitic Languages

Egyptian displays similarities, both grammatical and lexical, to the Semitic languages as well as the Berber dialects — or languages — (Tuareg, Shilh, Kabyle, etc.), and to certain languages of East Africa included under the heading Cushitic:[6] Northern Cushitic is represented by Beḍawye (Beja); Central Cushitic consists of the Agaw dialects;[7] Eastern Cushitic includes Saho[8]-Afar, Somali, Galla and some minor languages; Western Cushitic, the least known of all, comprises Sidama and other groups.[9]

These similarities are such as can hardly be accounted for by the assumption of borrowing. Although it is not (and perhaps cannot be) established that even whole grammatical paradigms are immune in this respect, it is safer to assume that languages sharing fundamental morphological[10] elements, owe them to common origin rather than to borrowing.[11]

The Semitic languages thus constitute merely a "family" within a "stock" or "phylum," to which the name Hamito-Semitic has been given. This name inevitably suggests a dichotomy into two major groups, "Hamitic" comprising the African members of the stock. Yet it is clear that there exists no "Hamitic" family comparable to the Semitic family. "Hamitic" alone should either not be used at all, or only as a conventional and purely referential equivalent of "Egyptian, Berber, and Cushitic". The internal relationships within the stock are quite obscure. Of recent opinions we shall only mention the attempt to "explain" Egyptian as a set of linguistic strata, attributing the responsibility for each stratum to one of the surrounding groups: Berber ("Western Hamitic") from the West, Cushitic ("Southern Hamitic") from the South, and Semitic, acting as the superstratum, from the North-East.[12] The most sensible attitude is, to say the least, to refrain from premature stratigraphical theories and to accept as of equal standing the four main groups, Semitic, Egyptian, Berber and Cushitic,[13] — plus any group which further research may find it necessary to add, such as Chad-Hamitic (including Hausa).[14]

A conservative attitude is the more desirable since Comparative Hamito-Semitic Linguistics is still in its infancy and the prospects that it will ever grow to maturity are not very bright. A less gloomy outlook hardly seems justified in view of the nature of the material and the state of research. Apart from Egyptian, none of the African members of the stock is known from sources earlier than the 19th century.[15] As in other fields, this lack of time-depth can no doubt, and probably will one day, be remedied up to a point by the rigorous application of the comparative method, starting from smaller groups such as Agaw or Eastern Cushitic;[16] even so, a good deal of strictly descriptive work will have to be done first. For the time being, comparison with Egyptian can only be haphazard, and Egyptologists cannot reasonably be blamed for showing little eagerness to take a hand in a kind of research that promises them scant reward.[17]

C. The Study of Egyptian: A Survey

It is not at all certain that the unsatisfactory state of Comparative Hamito-Semitic Linguistics really need cause much sorrow to the student of Egyptian. Even if we knew much more about the genetic relationships of Egyptian than we can ever hope to know, our main task would still be to gain an insight into the distinctive system of the Egyptian language and to understand the transformations undergone by that system in the course of the three millennia during which we are able to follow its history. The attainment of the latter goal is wholly independent of Comparative Hamito-Semitics; and as to the former, comparativism can interfere just as much as it can help.

The problems of the Egyptian language are mirrored in the history of its exploration, of which we now shall give a brief account.

The language of Pharaonic Egypt entered the orbit of modern philology and linguistics in 1822, when the hieroglyphs, for centuries a mystery, were deciphered by Jean-François Champollion (1790–1832). The stages through which the work of decipherment had to pass, the vicissitudes of trial and error, the partial successes of other scholars, especially J. D. Akerblad (d. 1819) and Thomas Young (1773–1829) — all that against the background of Champollion's harassed life —, are all of absorbing scientific and human interest.[18]

A younger phase of the Egyptian language had been known to European scholars since the 17th century. The idea that Coptic, the language of the Christian Egyptians, was essentially the old language spelled in Greek characters goes back to Athanasius Kircher (1601–1680),[19] who is chiefly remembered for his fanciful interpretations of hieroglyphs, but has also more solid work to his credit. In Champollion's days this idea was endorsed by Étienne Quatremère (1782–1857), one of the most erudite Orientalists of all time, in his *Recherches sur la langue et la littérature de l'Égypte* (1808), which also contains a history of Coptic studies down to the discovery of the Rosetta Stone and the first attempts of Silvestre de Sacy and Akerblad.[20] Champollion was convinced of the identity of Coptic and the language of the hieroglyphs; he was himself an accomplished Coptic scholar, and it was doubtless to his thorough knowledge of Coptic that he owed that "feel" for the older language which enabled him to make so an astonishingly rapid progress in the years left him after the decipherment.

Coptic was studied with a view to the help it might afford in the recovery of Ancient Egyptian as well as on its own merits as the language of Christian Egypt. In the 18th century, when classical, oriental, and theological studies were held together by *Philologia Sacra*, this double aspect of Coptic would hardly have troubled anyone. Nowadays the place of Coptic has become somewhat problematic; there is a dangerous tendency towards a split into an Egyptological-linguistic and a theological-philological branch.

The heroic age of Egyptian philology lies outside the scope of the present chapter. Here it must suffice to mention the bare names of some of the men who laid the foundations: Emm. de Rougé (1811–72), Sam. Birch (1813–85), Fr. Chabas (1817–82), C. W. Goodwin (1817–78), Heinrich Brugsch (1827–94).[21]

The beginning of the modern period is associated with the name of Adolf Erman (1854–1937), who held the Chair of Egyptology at Berlin from 1884–1923. Together with his disciples Georg Steindorff (1861–1951) and Kurt Sethe (1869–1934) he represented what soon came to be known as the Berlin School.

Erman's first major work, the *Neuaegyptische Grammatik* (1880), was the first systematic description of one well-defined stage of Egyptian, while his treatment of syntax was something entirely new.[22] Yet it owes too much to the great pioneers of the preceding generation, especially to Chabas and Goodwin, to be viewed exclusively as the beginning of a new period. It was the *Aegyptische Grammatik* (1894), outwardly an elementary manual of the classical language, that marked the emergence of a new "school" with a "doctrine" and a "method" of its own. In the interval between these two books Erman had made a discovery of great importance and far-reaching implications (the Pseudo-Participle, see below) which played a great part in shaping the Berlin doctrine.

The rise of the Berlin School has to be seen against the background of that movement in linguistics which set in in the 'seventies, the best known representatives of which are the "Neogrammarians." The influence of specifically neogrammarian principles is best seen in the early work of Steindorff. By the nature of the hieroglyphic writing, the older stages of the language are not immediately amenable to the application of rigorous methods in phonology and morphology, as demanded by the new trend. It was entirely in keeping with neogrammarian tenets that Steindorff attacked the task from the Coptic side. To him we owe the discovery of some of the fundamental laws of Coptic phonology, on which all reconstruction of Egyptian phonology ultimately rests; in morphology he concentrated upon noun-formation, where Coptic could be seen to have been especially conservative.[23]

The crowning achievement of the Berlin School was Sethe's treatise, in two large autographed volumes (1899),[24] on the Egyptian verb, a marvel of industry, learning, and analytical power. For a generation it remained the last word on the subject, and it took some time to discover that even Sethe's armor was not wholly without chinks.

The characteristics of the Berlin School can thus be summed up under two heads: (a) its employment of neogrammarian methodology, which insisted upon phonology and phonetic laws as the necessary basis of morphology; (b) its ties with Semitic linguistics. The most far-reaching single tenet of the Berlin School was the contention that certain alphabetic hieroglyphs denoted not vowels, as they were represented in the then current transliteration, but consonants. The idea, for instance, that "a" and "ā" corresponded to Aleph and 'Ayin respectively, was not altogether new in itself.[25] It was rather the implications of this insight, fully expounded in the first volume of Sethe's work,[26] that seemed revolutionary and aroused at first a good deal of violent opposition. Recognition of the consonantal principle meant not merely acceptance of new symbols for transliteration, but also implied an entirely different conception of the root structure in Egyptian. The Egyptian root, and not only the "strong" one, appeared henceforth very much like the familiar three-consonantal root of the Semitic languages. If the analogy of Semitic was obvious in this fundamental matter, Erman's discovery of the Pseudo-Participle ("Old Perfective"), already referred to, meant a whole grammatical paradigm whose Semitic affinities were manifest. These successes understandably encouraged the belief that Semitic was as a matter of course to be looked to for general guidance and specific comparisons.

The work of the Berlin School was enlivened by a lifelong rivalry between Erman and his opposite number at Paris (and Cairo), Gaston Maspero (1846–1916). The controversies between the two schools are now a thing of the past, but it is interesting to recall that some of the sharpest differences of opinion referred precisely to the nature of the relationship of Egyptian to the Semitic languages and its bearing on the method to be employed in Egyptian grammar. What the Berlin School was most often criticized for was the tendency "to squeeze the Egyptian language into the framework of Semitic grammar."[27]

Although some diehards, to whom unfamiliar transliteration symbols and grammatical terms were distasteful, continued to combat the Berlin School as late as the 'twenties, its real struggle for recognition did not last long. Well before the First World War its teaching had ceased to be a local or national affair and had become, so far as the study of the language was concerned, modern Egyptology pure and simple.

After Sethe's *Verbum*, the most significant single contribution to Egyptian grammar was Battiscombe Gunn's (1883–1950) *Studies in Egyptian Syntax* (Paris, 1924). Although in general this book gives the impression of continuing the tradition of Erman and Sethe, its very first page contains a programmatic statement announcing a fundamental change of attitude: "I would here state my opinion for what it may be worth that during the last thirty years Egyptian philologists have stood too much under the influence of the Semitic categories of perfect and imperfect — the completed and the non-completed event. In happy contrast with the two or three tenses of the older Semitic languages, Egyptian possesses a great wealth of finite forms and constructions, only one of which goes back to the Semito-Egyptian stock, all the rest being native products." Gunn's book sets forth some of the unexpected discoveries to be obtained by internal analysis, proving the originality of Egyptian syntax, especially in the field of the verb.

Erman's *Aegyptische Grammatik* remained through three editions (^{2}1902, ^{3}1911) the authoritative handbook of the classical language. Of the 4th edition (1928) this was no longer quite true. In the meantime (1927) Sir Alan Gardiner's monumental *Egyptian Grammar* had appeared, where the description of both morphology and syntax, especially the latter, was enriched by many new observations, and was illustrated with a wealth of examples and references; a new edition, with many minor additions and corrections, appeared in 1950. Gustave Lefebvre's *Grammaire de l'égyptien classique* (Cairo, 1940, ²1955) is doctrinally as well as in range rather similar to Gardiner, though based on an independent study of the texts; it is esteemed for its clear and systematic presentation.

It is gratifying to note a recent revival of grammatical research. Of late, almost every year has seen the publication of a major work on Egyptian grammar, especially in the fields of Old Egyptian and of verbal morphology and syntax.[28]

D. Structural Peculiarities in Egyptian: Two Examples

This chapter would fail of its purpose, if it did not attempt to show by a concrete example or two how the Egyptian language actually works, especially from the standpoint of what it does with the Hamito-Semitic heritage and where it shows its originality. Such an attempt cannot be undertaken without bringing in technical details and quoting actual linguistic forms. Even so, it must be clear that the account here given is greatly simplified, though not, it is hoped, to the point where simplification becomes distortion.

The reader who does not choose to skip this section is advised to refer to C. T. Hodge's "Outline of Middle Egyptian Grammar," *SIL*, 12 (1954), 8–23, which will enable him to place each detail within the framework of the whole structure; Hodge's "Outline," the substance of which, as distinct from its modern externals, is rather conservative, may serve to represent the average grammatical theory now current.

1. The Pseudo-Participle

The form called Pseudo-Participle or Old Perfective is the show-piece of Comparative Hamito-Semitics. When the relatively straightforward narrative of the *Westcar Papyrus* enabled Erman in 1889 to piece together the paradigm of this form, he was immediately struck by the resemblance of its endings to those of the Semitic Perfect, although the function was not exactly the same. Further research revealed that the Akkadian "Permansive" (= Stative) offered an even better analogy in respect of both form and function. Finally it was discovered that the special inflexion which "verbs of quality" possess in certain Berber dialects, clearly represents the same paradigm, at least for the singular.[29]

		Egyptian	*Akkadian*	*Arabic*
Sg.	1st c.	*-kwỉ*	*-āku*	*-tu*
	2nd m.		*-āta*	*-ta*
		-tỉ		
	2nd f.		*-āti*	*-ti*
	3rd m.	*ỉ-/w*	------	*-a*
	3rd f.	*-tỉ*	*-at*	*-at*
Pl.	1st c.	*-win*	*-ānu*	*-nā*
	2nd m.		*-ātunu*	*-tum*
		-tỉwnỉ		
	2nd f.		*-ātina*	*-tunna*
	3rd m.	*-wỉ*	*-ū*	*-ū*
	3rd f.	*-tỉ*	*-ā*	*-na*

Of all these forms it is only the Akkadian ones which can be easily understood within the grammatical framework of Akkadian itself: the endings of the 1st and 2nd persons are the personal pronouns less the initial element *a*(*n*)-[30], the 3rd persons are the "predicative state" of nouns, substantive and adjective. This circumstance is significant and would certainly seem to lend support to a pan-Babylonian attitude towards "Hamito-Semitic," somewhat in the manner of F. Hommel. From the point of view of Egyptian the form makes the impression of a "transplanted growth languishing in an unfriendly soil," although this way of putting it (Gunn) is perhaps more picturesque than strictly exact. In any case, it is only the inflexion that can at all be said to have suffered from languor.[31] As regards syntax, the "transplanted growth" has struck remarkably strong roots. Egyptian syntax is quite unthinkable without the Pseudo-Participle.

Egyptologists have always encountered great difficulty in finding a name for this form. "Pseudo-Participle" is intended to convey that the form is not a participle, as some of its most characteristic uses might suggest: the name is, of course, open to the objection that a grammatical term ought not to tell us what a given form is not.[32] Gardiner's term Old Perfective has the defect of its excessive pre-historical bias. "Stative" would be adequately descriptive, so far as it goes: this term, which has been occasionally employed by Albright, has the advantage of agreeing with current Assyriological usage (in preference to "Permansive").

A term need not cover all uses. Thus the term "Stative" is not appropriate to certain survivals which, as such, are especially valuable to the comparativist because they seem to confirm a connexion not only with the Akkadian "Stative" but even with the West Semitic "Perfect," namely the active narrative use which is practically restricted to the 1st person singular and had become rare already in the 12th Dynasty. From the Egyptian point of view such employments are residual and marginal. The essentially Egyptian career of the Pseudo-Participle "drifts" in quite a different direction. Its history is characterized by a tendency to enter into complementary syntactic partnership with the phrase "on" (*ḥr*) plus Infinitive: they provide expressions for the resultative as against the progressive aspect.[33] It was presumably through its contrasting association with this particular prepositional phrase that the Pseudo-Participle acquired its surprising property of patterning with adverbial expressions generally. The following examples illustrate both a typical use of the Pseudo-Participle and its pattern congruences: -

gm.n.f sw sḏr[34] "he found him *lying*"
gm.n.f Rd-ḏdt ḥms. tỉ "he found R. (a woman's name) *sitting*"
gm.n.f sw ḥr prt "he found him *coming forth*"
gm.n sw wpwtỉw ḥr w3t "the messengers found him *on the road*"

In Late Egyptian verbal phrases, or phrasal tenses, compounded with the Infinitive[35] or the Pseudo-Participle become ever more numerous. At the same time both the Infinitive and the Pseudo-Participle gradually lose their power of being employed in the way illustrated by the Middle Egyptian examples quoted above; they require more and more the support of the "auxiliary" *ỉw(f.)*, cf.

ỉw.s gm Ḥr ỉw.f sḏr "she found Horus *lying*"

by the side of the more archaic

ỉw.f ḥr gm t3y.f ḥmt sḏr.tỉ "he found his wife *lying*"

This all but constant association with an inflected auxiliary rendered the inflexion of the Pseudo-Participle itself superfluous and led to its decline. In Coptic only one form survives, as a rule the 3rd masc. singular. Practically the whole conjugation now consists of a long series of phrasal tenses inflected with the help of "conjugational auxiliaries." The contrast between Infinitive and Qualitative (as the Pseudo-Participle is habitually called in Coptic grammar) remains a vital principle. The tenses fall into two classes, according as they take either the Infinitive alone (point tenses) or both the Infinitive and the Qualitative as well as adverbial expressions (durative tenses).[36] While this wealth is one of the main attractions that the study of Coptic has to offer, to those who are unversed in the language the apparatus may seem somewhat heavy. It is interesting to note the testimony of an outstanding Egypto-Semitist to the effect that these "remarkable composite structures" are "the despair of the Semitist who glances into a Coptic grammar."[37]

2. The Suffix-Conjugation

If the intra-Egyptian development of the Pseudo-Participle has carried it a long way from its Hamito-Semitic antecedents, it is very doubtful whether the so-called suffix-conjugation (type *sḏm.f*) has any Hamito-Semitic affiliations at all. If it has, it is so thoroughly egyptianized as to be practically indistinguishable from an original Egyptian formation.

Since Egyptian possesses a form transparently related to the Semitic "Perfect," the comparativist will naturally ask what has become of the "Imperfect," the more so as it is precisely the preformative-conjugation which serves as a sort of *Leitfossil* in Hamito-Semitic Linguistics; its absence in Egyptian would be decidedly disturbing. Since, on the other hand, some members of the Egyptian suffix-conjugation are used in a way reminiscent of the preformative-conjugation, it was not unnatural to suspect that the clue to the mystery of the missing Imperfect might be hidden in the *sḏm.f*. The obvious feature of dissimilarity between the two forms — preformatives on the Hamito-Semitic side *versus* suffixes in Egyptian — was of course no obstacle to comparativist ingenuity. The most ingenious attempt to explain away this "major disagreement" is the hypothesis that the *sḏm.f* was prehistorically a **f.sḏm*, the old Hamito-Semitic preformatives having been replaced by the Egyptian person-markers, which only in historic times became restricted to suffix position.[38]

The author of the hypothesis referred to goes on to suggest an idea which has also occurred to other comparativists who would perhaps hesitate to accept his solution of the preformative vs. suffix problem, viz. that it may be possible to correlate the bases underlying the different varieties of *sḏm.f* with the different forms of the Semitic preformative-conjugation. Thacker,[39] e.g., sets up the following correspondences:—

Perfective		("indicative narrative")	Akkad. *iprus*[40]
Imperfective	*sḏm.f*		Akkad. *iparras*[41]
Prospective		("jussive/optative")	Ethiop. *yəngər*

It remains to be seen whether this idea can be made to tally with the results of internal analysis on the Egyptian side. For, as it happens, many Egyptologists are fairly confident of being able to penetrate the structure of the suffix-conjugation strictly within Egyptian.

Any reader who will consult the sections on the *sḏm.f* forms in Gardiner's *Grammar* will be struck by the amount of space there devoted to the theory of these forms, especially to the problem of their origin. Quite apart from current predilections in linguistics, it is obvious that on this particular point description has been subordinated to rather speculative prehistory. It must be admitted, however, that the *sḏm.f* forms tempt glottogonic speculation to an exceptional degree. One gains the impression, possibly quite erroneous, that these forms came into existence only just before the dawn of history and that their origin is almost within our reach.

The main feature of the suffix-conjugation is implied in its name: the pronominal actor is expressed by the same suffixed person-markers as are used after substantives to express the "possessor," and after prepositions to express the complement:-[42]

sḏm.f "*he* hears"
sn.f "*his* brother"
n.f "to *him*".

Eighty-five years ago Friedrich Müller[43] concluded from this fact that Egyptian ("despite the excellence of its structure") had no real verb and that the base of *sḏm.f* was a nominal expression, since the actor was expressed by the possessive suffix. As Hugo Schuchardt[44] has pointed out, this argument, strictly speaking, cuts both ways: it could be argued with equal justification that Egyptian had no real noun, since the possessor was expressed by the actor suffix. The point which Schuchardt really intended to make was to warn against the misleading practice of rendering, in linguistic descriptions, single expressions by multiple meaning-equivalents, in this case the Egyptian person-marker 3rd m. sg., *-f*, by (1) "he" and (2) "his." Yet, in spite of Schuchardt's caveat, Müller was essentially right: the nominal character of the suffix-conjugation is confirmed in other ways; it is indeed one of the characteristic traits of Egyptian and has been rightly stressed as such by Gardiner.[45]

The base of the suffix-conjugation is either the bare stem (*sḏm.f*) or the stem enlarged by "tense-markers" (*sḏm.n.f*, *sḏm.ỉn.f*, etc.). For the purpose of the present discussion we shall restrict ourselves to the *sḏm.f* and the *sdm.n.f*, because these two formations have a feature in common which sets them apart from the other members of the suffix-conjugation.

This feature is the fact that both the *sḏm.f* and the *sḏm.n.f* possess two variants each, differing both in form and in function. In the one the stem is invariable, in the other it is capable of assuming nominal endings, among which the feminine ending *t* is the most conspicuous. The former is used predicatively; the latter is used attributively with an antecedent with which it agrees in gender and number (it can also be used substantivally, with "implied antecedent"): these are the so-called "relative forms,"[46] perhaps the most original and, from the Semitic point of view, the most unfamiliar feature of Egyptian conjugation.

Now it is a rule of Egyptian syntax that an adjective used as predicate must precede its subject and does not agree with it either in gender or number, as it would have to do if it were used attributively. It seems therefore a reasonable assumption that the base of the suffix-conjugation is a verbal adjective, a participle, obeying the rule of concord/non-concord, according to its syntactic function. As to the voice of this participle, it would seem that it must be passive, as only a passive participle seems capable of furnishing a base for the "relative form."

Applied to the *sḏm.f*, this would mean that in a sentence like *m3.k pr.k* "thou wilt see thy house," *pr.k* "thy house" is the subject of the predicative passive participle *m3*, to which is attached the possessive suffix expressing the actor.

Supposing that this was really the genesis of the *sḏm.f*, we are forced to admit that this cannot have been the way it structured for the historical Egyptians. First, we would have to assume, without support from the oldest texts, that the *sḏm.f* could not originally be formed from intransitive verbs: a passive participle followed by a possessor would not have been a predicative expression unless it was followed by a subject (expressing the undergoer). Secondly, the word-order in cases like *mr sw nṯr* "may God love him" does not agree with the theory that the relation of *nṯr* "God" to *mr* was that of a possessor; if such were the case, *nṯr* could hardly be separated from *mr* by the dependent pronoun *sw*, the subject of *mr*. In spite of these difficulties, the theory has been reported here at length, because thus far it is the only one that makes sense.

The *sḏm.n.f* seems to lend itself more easily to an explanation along these lines. The tense-marker *n* invites identification with the preposition *n*, which means "to"; one of its functions is to serve as a predicative expression for possession, i.e. what modern European languages express by the verb "to have." Assuming again the base to be a passive participle, the whole phrase would be an exact equivalent of the *habeo factum* type, to which modern European languages owe their *j'ai fait*, *ich habe getan*, *I have done;* these phrases were originally present perfects,[47] but have in many cases ousted older expressions for the narrative past. As Julius Wellhausen long ago pointed out to Sethe, an almost exact parallel for the formation thus assumed for Egyptian is provided by Syriac. Ancient Syriac created, by the side of the old "Perfect" *šqal*, which originally served both as a narrative past and as a present perfect, the phrase *šqi : l* (fem. *šqi :la :*, masc. pl. *šqi :li :n*) *leh* "taken (is) to him" = "he has taken (him, her, them)." In Modern Syriac *šqille*, *šqi :la :le*, *šqi :li :le* has become the narrative past, *šqal* having entirely disappeared, while a new present perfect has been formed with the help of the Perfect Participle (cf. note 32).

As in the case of the *sḏm.f*, the form has developed in a way which shows that the historical speakers of Egyptian cannot have "understood" it exactly as the theory will have it: the *n* is invariably attached to the verb-stem instead of invariably preceding the nominal actor, if the latter happens to be removed from the verb-stem. If the writer may be allowed to record his personal hunches, he would say that he feels much more sceptical about the prehistory of the *sḏm.f* than about that of the *sḏm.n.f*. In any case, it is abundantly clear that dogmatism is thoroughly out of place in these matters. The only belief of which the writer would be reluctant to be deprived is that the predicative and the attributive ("relative") *sḏm.f* and *sḏm.n.f* differ merely in syntactic function, not in morphological nature.

We may now return to the question whether it is possible to correlate the moods of the Semitic, or Hamito-Semitic, preformative-conjugation with the different forms of the *sḏm.f*. We have seen that the "imperfective *sḏm.f*" has been claimed as the Egyptian representative of the "Afro-Asiatic Present." Unhappily for this view, there are serious reasons for doubting the very existence of an "imperfective *sḏm.f*." The form to which this appellation has been applied is a non-predicative verb-form, in all likelihood morphologically related to the relative forms. It differs from them by denoting not the "undergoer" of the action but the action itself.[48]

Moreover, the syntactic properties of the "imperfective *sḏm f*" are not co-extensive with its only visible morphological characteristic: all reduplicating *sḏm.f* (*mrr.f*) forms are non-predicative,[49] but not all forms of the suffix-conjugation employed non-predicatively are *sḏm.f* forms with reduplication of the 2nd radical in weak verbs. There exist *sḏm.n.f* as well as non-reduplicating *sdm.f* (*mr.f*) forms, which occur in the same syntactic patterns with the same characteristically non-predicative function as the reduplicating *sḏm.f*; they are in every respect equivalent to the latter except as regards tense, the *sḏm.n.f.* referring to the past and the non-geminating *sḏm.f* to the future.

We must, then, conclude that the correlation of the reduplicating *sḏm.f* and the "Afro-Asiatic Present" (Akkadian *iparras*) rests on rather insecure foundations.

E. Some Features of the Egyptian Language

In older works the Egyptian language is often described as simple and primitive, and similar judgments linger on till the present day. As a result of the work of the last seventy years it can be stated quite confidently that this view is false; it merely reflects a primitive state of grammatical understanding.

Which phase of the language one prefers depends mainly on one's special field of interest. Naturally, the niceties of the later phases are more readily perceived owing to the analytical character of many of their constructions. F. Ll. Griffith,[50] for instance, thought that "the best stage of Egyptian speech" was Late ("Roman") Demotic, and there is much to be said for his choice, in spite of the abominable script in which Demotic is written. Coptic, although "here and there more exactly expressive than the best Demotic," is doubtlessly somewhat disfigured, in an Egyptologist's view, by its many Greek words, especially the Greek particles which it so freely employs, but the reproach of "clumsy pleonasm" is hardly justified. Late Egyptian is now better known than it was at the time when Griffith wrote, and its tense-system especially is now better understood: it is seen to lack hardly any of the merits of Demotic and to possess at least one of its own, viz. the clear distinction between a narrative past and a present perfect. But even Middle (and partly Old) Egyptian yields more and more of its morphological and syntactic secrets, and allows us to appreciate its "classical" quality. So far from being primitive and simple, Egyptian, in all its stages, reveals itself as possessing a rich and most sophisticated structure.

B. ETHNO-LINGUISTIC ELEMENTS

I. SEMITES

by E. A. Speiser

THE PRECEDING section includes a comprehensive survey of salient linguistic data about Semitic: progress in the study of the subject, nature of the material, problems of classification, and the like. It remains now to relate these and similar relevant details to the question of the people behind the languages, that is, to the ethno-linguistic aspect of the problem.

Inevitably, such a discussion must have recourse to arguments that are largely hypothetical. It cannot confine itself to historical "Semites," for these are already clearly differentiated into Akkadians, Amorites, Canaanites, Aramaeans, and the like, each with their own separate and distinctive careers. Our real objective in the present instance concerns the "Pro-ethnic" or "Primitive" Semites. And by definition, such targets cannot be arrived at by any direct mode of approach. They can only be reconstructed in theory, mainly from suitable linguistic facts, and to some extent also from the circumstantial evidence of location and environment. Where available controls are so few and indirect, methodology has to be especially rigorous. The potential value of such an inquiry, in lending perspective to the subsequent historic process, is immediately apparent. But the results should never be mistaken for more than just a working hypothesis.[1]

If Primitive Semites are thus destined to remain wholly and forever beyond the reach of history, can physical anthropology help make up the deficit at least in part? In other words, can the ancestors of the historic Semites be circumscribed as a race if not as a people? On this point, too, no positive answer can be expected. Scholars have long had reason to doubt the existence of a clearly differentiated Semitic race. These doubts have been strengthened with each new finding. To be sure, widely scattered skeletal remains show that much of Western Asia and Northern Africa was populated in early times by a physical type that was often classified as Mediterranean. But no correlation can be established between that particular racial type and members of any single linguistic family. For example, speakers of Sumerian, an isolated language with no genetic ties whatever to Semitic or Indo-European, were predominantly Mediterraneans in an anthropometric sense. On the other hand, Semitic is known to have been spoken by members of the Anatolian race in the north, and by other racial types in South Arabia and neighboring areas of Africa. Thus race and language were by no means coextensive in any age that is accessible to us. Actually, recorded history can take us back only five thousand years. Prehistoric settlements and linguistic paleontology increase this span by a few additional millenniums. All this is but a short time in terms of man's total estimated age. Yet scores of thousands of years earlier, say, 75,000 years ago or more, Mount Carmel caves housed two different racial types; and racial intermixture has been going on ever since. If pure races were ever present in a central region like the Near East, that period was too remote to be articulated by present scientific methods. And the concept of a pure Semitic type is an anachronism pure and simple.

It follows, therefore, that linguistic reconstruction is the only path that can lead us back to the earliest Semites, that is, the oldest ascertainable group using an ancestral form of the Semitic speech. Our present purpose, however, is to learn what we can about the speakers rather than the speech. This can be accomplished to a limited extent by selecting the proper linguistic data and interpreting them as geographic and historical milestones.

The outline of Primitive Semitic developments that is attempted below — with all due reservations — takes for granted the results that have been incorporated in the separate accounts on Semitics (IIA, 1), Akkadian (2), and Egyptian (3). It will be useful, moreover, in this connection to point to the experience accumulated in similar inquiries into Indo-European origins. Comparative Indo-Europeanists have long operated with a set of workable criteria of linguistic interrelationships. They found out decades ago that the decisive test is that of morphology; minute attention to phonological details can then lead to significant chronological formulations. On the other hand, vocabulary in itself is not a dependable witness, unless the given term is widely attested and has undergone in each instance the appropriate phonetic changes. In such cases terminological comparisons may yield unexpected dividends. The demonstration that a series of words relating to flora, fauna, and climate must have originated with Primitive Indo-European points necessarily to an area in which all such conditions prevailed when the as yet undivided group occupied it as its home.[2] In

Bound Syrian captive. Carved on the head of a ceremonial walking stick of Tut-ankh-Amon; found in the latter's tomb, ca. 1350 B. C. E.

Prisoners from Ramses III's foreign conquests; left to right: Libyan, Semite, Hittite, Philistine, Semite. Medinet Habu, Temple of Ramses III.
Oriental Institute, University of Chicago.

A fortress in Amor manned by Syrian lancers attacked by Ramses III. Medinet Habu, Temple of Ramses III.
Oriental Institute, University of Chicago.

Gudea, Ruler of Lagash.
The Louvre.

A Hittite prisoner (from Abu Simbel).

Hittite figure from Bogazkoy.
Hittite Museum, Ankara.

	A	B	C	D	E
	Original pictograph	*Pictograph in position of later cuneiform*	*Early Babylonian*	*Assyrian*	*Original or derived meaning*
1					bird
2					fish
3					donkey
4					ox
5					sun day
6					grain
7					orchard
8					to plow to till
9					boomerang to throw to throw down
10					to stand to go

Stages in the development of cuneiform script.
Photographs from J. H. Breasted, Ancient Times, 2nd ed. Boston 1935, fig. 86; compiled and drawn by Arne Poebel.
Oriental Institute, University of Chicago.

this instance, both India (Sanskrit) and Chinese Turkestan (Tocharian) were thus automatically eliminated from further consideration. It was also discovered that the tempo of linguistic change may vary substantially from language to language. Modern Lithuanian, for example, has proved to be in some ways far more archaic and conservative than ancient Hittite.

As applied to the problem before us, the environmental criteria — flora, fauna, and climate — turn out to be of little value. Indo-European languages extend from Scandinavia to India and thus cover several climatic zones. Historical Semitic, on the other hand, is limited to a single subtropical zone, and the recoverable Primitive Semitic vocabulary indicates no change in this respect. Common terms for "ass" or "sheep," for example, fail to locate the original Semites in any one particular area. And the fact that the words for "horse" and "camel" are not uniform merely serves to confirm the independently established conclusion that the animals in question came to the Semites in relatively late times. Linguistic paleontology can thus be of scarcely any assistance in tracing Semitic origins.

Not quite so negative is another possible line of inquiry: if Primitive Semitic itself should prove to be an offshoot of a larger linguistic stock, it might be easier to delimit the area in which the whole parent body could best be accommodated. To be sure, if one includes Indo-European as a potential relative of Semitic, all hope of tangible results must be given up from the very start. The comparison has been tried more than once, at times even by entirely responsible scholars.[3] With the means at our disposal, however, even the best of such attempts can be no more than an interesting intellectual and methodological exercise, subject to no factual controls. The oldest Semitic documents known to us are Akkadian texts of nearly 4500 years ago. Yet their language is close enough to modern Arabic or Hebrew to yield evidence of genetic relationship that is readily apparent. On this basis, the existing gap between Semitic and Indo-European — assuming that the two stocks were originally related — would presuppose separate careers lasting several times 4500 years. The separation would have to be put somewhere near 15,000 years ago or a distance hopelessly beyond the reach of linguistic science. Such structural similarities as exist between Semitic and Indo-European may be just as readily the result of coincidence as of common ultimate origin. No real evidence can today be adduced for either assumption.

In contrast, there are sound and solid grounds for subsuming Semitic under a larger stock that also includes Egyptian as well as the Cushitic and Berber languages. The evidence is varied and manifold. It comprises significant details of morphology — especially in the pronoun and the verb — aside from copious lexical material. The linguistic areas in question formed a geographic continuum, with Egypt as the bridge between Western Asia and the other pertinent regions of Africa. The Semitic and Egyptian material comes to us in great depth, thanks to the antiquity and time span of the respective records. And while the rest of the recorded African evidence is recent, its character is convincing none the less. The only obstacle to a completely satisfactory classification is lack of adequate historical knowledge of Cushitic and Berber. If we classify the African material as a whole, provisionally and for the sake of convenience, as Hamitic,[4] we can speak with reasonable confidence, though as yet only in general terms, of an early Hamito-Semitic stock from which the historically attested subdivisions, including Semitic and Egyptian, had branched off at a remote prehistoric stage.

Where was the home of the posited Hamito-Semitic parent body? The answer has to be theoretical of necessity. And theory calls for an area best capable of justifying the known distribution of Hamites as well as Semites. This immediately disposes of those older hypotheses that sought to locate the home of the Semites in Armenia or Mesopotamia, regions sharply off center as regards the Hamites — and now independently eliminated from consideration by the full weight of the vast archaeological evidence. Nor does the commonly favored derivation from Arabia stand up under closer scrutiny. This view would imply that the ancestors of the Hamites crossed over westwards into Africa, while successive branches of Semites migrated north into the Fertile Crescent. But was Arabia sufficiently hospitable as recently as, say, 10,000 years ago to have nourished a group large enough to account for the historical Hamites and Semites? At best, it would seem, Arabia could have served as a secondary center of dissemination for Semites alone; but it is more likely that the Semites were already differentiated to some extent by the time some of them had settled in, or were passing through, Arabia. If so, the home of the pro-ethnic Semites can best be localized somewhere in Northern Africa.[5]

This hypothetical reconstruction receives a measure of support from concrete linguistic data. Akkadian, which is the oldest recorded Semitic language, also features the largest body of grammatical correspondences between Semitic and given members of the African group. Among them are:

(1) the Akk. present *iparras* with geminated second radical : the "habitual" of Berber and related forms of Cushitic[6]

(2) the Akk. personal pronouns *šū* "he," *šī* "she," and causatives in *š* : Eg. *sw* "he," *sy* "she" (both from an older *ś*), and causatives in *ś* — with analogous forms elsewhere in Hamitic

(3) the Akk. stative ("permansive") *paris* : the Eg. "pseudo-participle," which corresponds to the Akk. stative in form and function

(4) the Akk. pronominal datives in *š* (*yā-ši*) and accusatives in *t* (*yā-ti*) : datives in *s* and accusatives in *t* in the Agaw branch of Cushitic

These are intimate correspondences that can only denote genetic relationships. And the ties involved embrace the whole African group under discussion. It follows that Akkadian inherited from the pro-ethnic Hamito-Semitic stock all the features just listed, and retained them after it had separated from that stock. The place where that separation occurred had to be somewhere close to the parent body's center of gravity, hence in all probability on the African rather than the Asiatic side of the Red Sea.

The split that has thus to be posited, however, must have comprised more elements than the future Akkadians alone; for otherwise one could not account for certain features which Akkadian shares with the rest of Semitic, but not with Hamitic. In other words, Proto-Semitic as a whole must already have constituted a separate group, with one segment of it branching off and moving towards Mesopotamia, while the rest advanced by slower stages eastward — or to the north, if the crossing to Arabia had occurred previously. In any case, the next segment to break away consisted of the ancestors of the South Arabic, or Southwest Semitic, family (Minaean, Sabaean, Ethiopic; and modern Mehrī, Soqoṭrī). This can be inferred in particular from two grammatical facts: (1) Ethiopic still has the form *yəqət[t]al (imperfect indicative),[7] which is formally the same as the Akkadian present *iparras* (and the related forms of Hamitic); (2) the sibilant pronominal forms and the corresponding causative in *s* are retained in Minaean, while Mehri uses *si* for "she" but *he* for the masculine. On the other hand, South Arabic agrees with Northwest Semitic (Canaanite, Aramaic, North Arabic) in employing an active perfect, *qatal*, as opposed to the Akkadian stative, and hence passival, *paris*.

The last-named feature, always difficult to interpret, is especially troublesome for any hypothetical timetable of Semitic migrations. If the active perfect was developed before the separation of Southwest Semitic, why is it that Northwest Semitic has no pronouns with *š/s-*, and so far also no form **ya-qattal* (Akk. *iparras*)? Moreover, on that assumption we should have to date back the development of an active perfect — and with it the emergence of a passive *yuqtal* — to a period not long after the departure of the proto-Akkadians. Yet the earliest sign of the *qatal-yuqtal* process turns up very much later, namely, in the Old Babylonian material from Alalakh. It would appear, therefore, that the active *qatal* was introduced into Southwest Semitic under the influence of North Arabic, or the like.

In the foregoing sketch the attempt was made to bring to bear the best available linguistic data, meager though they are, on the problem of the prehistoric Semites. The hypothetical nature of the conclusions thus arrived at has been stressed repeatedly. What we are left with is a handful of geographical and chronological hints, which can claim, nevertheless, a modest measure of probability. The common home of the parent body in question toward which the clues appear to point is North Africa. The oldest constituent in this group was in all likelihood ancestral to Egyptian, Berber, and Cushitic, or in short Hamitic — for want of a more convenient term; together with the ancestors of the Semites they constituted the pro-ethnic Hamito-Semitic family. Its Semitic offshoot migrated to Asia in successive stages, the first of which was to produce the Akkadians, followed by Southwest Semites, and eventually by several groups of Northwest Semites.

In these circumstances it was not unnatural that the first Semitic segment to break away should have traveled farthest from the original home. By the same token, however, the Akkadians stand apart from the rest of the Semites, while yet retaining the clearest traces of underlying Hamito-Semitic conditions. Both these seemingly contradictory features receive their logical explanation from one and the same event.

The early separation of the Akkadians from the Proto-Semitic stock helps to explain, finally, one aspect of sharp sociological cleavage between Akkadians and other Semites. In Hebrew, the term for "individual" is *'īsh;* and the corresponding word for a nuclear family unit is *'am*, or rather its plural *'ammīm*, derived from a more specific kinship term for "paternal uncle." Both these words have cognates, and corresponding applications, in other West Semitic languages. Significantly enough, however, neither term is found in Akkadian. There the word for "man" is *awīlu*(*m*), originally an appellative; and its group correlative is not a term for "family," but instead *ālu*(*m*) "city," or *mātu*(*m*) "country." To put it differently, Mesopotamian society was built around the socio-political concepts of city and state in which the single member functioned primarily as a citizen rather than an individual. In the West Semitic world, the basic group was the family made up of individuals.

In other words, Mesopotamian society, which had gone through several phases of intensive cultural progress prior to the arrival of the Akkadians, had become urbanized by the time the Semites appeared on the scene; and Akkadian terminology reflects this state of affairs. The Western Semites, on the other hand, continued as nomads, whose mode of life places a premium on the individual and his blood relatives. This is why adoption, which often disregards consanguineous relationships, became such an outstanding feature of Mesopotamian society, but is not once clearly attested in the Bible. In contrast, the levirate, which seeks to maintain the family line, is upheld in the Bible but is absent from Mesopotamia proper.[8] Thus early exposure to foreign influences and the impact of a long-established civilization tended to draw the Akkadians away from their inherited customs and institutions; whereas the original non-urban environment of the Hebrews and their closest relatives left them with an appreciation of the nomadic ideal long after their change-over to a settled mode of existence. The background in each case had an appreciable effect on actual history.

2. SUMERIANS

by S. N. Kramer

SUMERIAN IS the name given to the people and language of ancient Sumer, the land later known as Babylonia. The word "Sumer" is first found on inscriptions dating from about 2500 B.C.E., but was no doubt in use much earlier. The Sumerians probably settled in Sumer toward the end of the fourth millennium B.C.E., but what they and their language were then called is unknown. In their new land the Sumerians found an earlier population consisting of two major linguistic groups. The one spoke a Semitic tongue. The other spoke a still unnamed language which has left its traces in such names as Tigris and Euphrates, in the names of the more important Sumerian cities and in such culturally significant words as those for farmer and herdsman, plow and furrow, palm and date, smith and metal worker, carpenter and basket-maker, weaver and leather worker, potter, mason and perhaps even merchant. Sumerian, therefore, contains numerous loan-words from these two languages.

Sumerian is an agglutinative tongue, not an inflected one like Indo-European or Semitic. Its roots, by and large, are invariable. Its basic grammatical unit is the word-complex rather than the individual word. Its grammatical particles tend to retain their independent structure rather than become inextricably attached to the word-roots. In structure, therefore, Sumerian resembles no little such agglutinative languages as Turkish and Hungarian. In vocabulary, grammar and syntax, however, Sumerian still stands apart and alone, and seems to be unrelated to any other language, living or dead.

Sumerian has six vowels[a] and fifteen consonants.[b] Its roots are monosyllabic in large part, though there are a considerable number of polysyllabic words. Reduplication of roots is used to indicate plurality of objects or actions. Substantives frequently consist of compound words: *lu-gal* "king" (big man), *dub-sar* "scribe" (tablet-writer), *di-ku* "judge"

[a] Three open vowels, *a, e, ô* and three corresponding closed vowels, *ā, ē, ū*.

[b] *b, p, d, t, g* (hard), *k, z, s, sh, ch* (like in the Scotch "*loch*"), *r, l, m, n* and *g* (like the *ng* in English "*lung*").

(judgment-determiner). Abstracts are formed with the help of *nam* (English "-ship"): *lu-gal* "king," *nam-lu-gal* "kingship." The substantives have no grammatical gender. Instead, they are divided into two categories: animate and inanimate. Animals belong to the inanimate category, grammatically speaking.

The Sumerian sentence consists of (1) a series of substantive complexes related to the predicate either as subject, indirect object, dimensional object, or direct object; (2) the grammatical particles expressing these relationships; and (3) the predicate, consisting of the verbal root preceded by a thematic particle and a series of infixes recapitulating the relationship between it and the substantive complexes. The substantive complex may consist of a noun alone, or of a noun and all its modifiers, such as adjectives, genitives, relative clauses and possessive pronouns. The relationship particles always come at the end of the entire substantive complex, and are therefore known as postpositions.

Sumerian is rather poor in adjectives, and often uses genitival expressions instead. Copulas and conjunctions are rarely used; the relevant words, complexes and clauses are usually arranged asyndetically. There is no relative pronoun in Sumerian: a nominalizing particle is used at the end of the clauses instead. Relative clauses, moreover, are used to a limited extent only; their place is often taken by a passive participle which is identical with the infinitive in form.

In addition to the main Sumerian dialect, which was probably known as *Emegir*, "the princely tongue," there were several others which were less important. One of these, the *Emesal*, was used primarily in speeches made by female deities, women, or eunuchs.

Sumerian has been found inscribed on tens of thousands of clay tablets, cones, prisms and cylinders. More than ninety per cent of these are administrative, economic and legal documents: inventories of all types and sizes, promissory notes and receipts, deeds of sale, marriage contracts, wills, and court decisions. These tablets contain hundreds of names of persons, deities, places and products; they provide the major source material for the study of Sumerian society and its economy. Many of these documents are dated by the scribes in accordance with some significant yearly event, and are therefore invaluable as historical sources.

Close to a thousand Sumerian inscriptions found primarily on statues, steles, vases, bricks, door-sockets, and foundation deposits, are votive in character. These are written in "high" prose, and their contents are all-important for the study of Sumerian history and religion.

More than five thousand tablets and fragments are inscribed with

Sumerian literary and religious works: myths and epic tales, hymns, lamentations, and historiographic documents, essays large and small, precepts and proverbs. The Sumerians probably first began to write down their literary works at the turn of the second half of the third millennium B.C.E. Their literary output increased with the centuries and became prolific towards the end of the third millennium, when the Sumerian academy known as the *Edubba* ("House of Tablets") had developed into an important center of learning. Sumerian literary activity continued unabated throughout the first half of the second millennium B.C.E., in spite of the fact that the Sumerian language was gradually being replaced by the Semitic Akkadian as the spoken tongue of Sumer. In the *Edubbas* which functioned throughout this post-Sumerian period, the earlier literary works were zealously studied, copied, redacted, and imitated.

The large majority of the Sumerian literary works are written in poetic form. The use of meter and rhyme was unknown, but practically all other poetic devices and techniques were utilized with considerable skill, imagination, and poetic effect: repetition and parallelism, metaphor and simile, chorus and refrain. Sumerian narrative poetry abounds in static epithets, lengthy repetitions, recurrent formulae, leisurely descriptions, and long speeches. By and large the Sumerian writers show little feeling for closely-knit plot structure; their narratives tend to ramble on rather disconnectedly and monotonously, with but little variation in emphasis and tone. Above all, the Sumerians, quite unlike the Semitic Akkadians, lacked a sense of climax; they did not seem to appreciate the effectiveness of bringing their narratives to a climactic head. The myths and epic tales, for example, show little intensification of emotion and suspense as the story progresses, and often the last episode is no more moving or stirring than the first. Nor is there any attempt at characterization and psychological delineation. The gods and heroes of the Sumerian narratives are broad types rather than recognizable flesh-and-blood individuals.

Some twenty Sumerian myths are now available either wholly or in large part. In addition there are a number of "disputation" compositions such as "Summer and Winter," "Cattle and Grain," "Bird and Fish," "Silver and Copper," etc., which contain no little mythological material. In general, the Sumerian myths revolve about the birth of the gods, and their deeds and exploits: the creation of the universe, the creation of man, the establishment of the world order, the acquisition of the divine laws and regulations, the struggle with the forces of the Nether World, the dying god and his resurrection, the unsuccessful attempts to destroy mankind by flood and plague. Only two of these myths have as yet turned up in almost identical form in Akkadian literature: "Inanna's Descent to the Nether World" and the "Flood" story. Two others ("The Deeds and Exploits of Ninurta," and "The Return of Ninurta to Nippur") have been found in bilingual form, that is, the Sumerian text is accompanied by an Akkadian translation. There is little doubt, however, that the Akkadian mythographers borrowed most of their mythological motifs from Sumerian sources, though these may not be readily traceable at the moment.

The Sumerian epic tales revolve about the three heroes Enmerkar, Lugal-banda, and Gilgamesh. One of the Enmerkar-Lugal-banda poems has actually turned up with a verbatim Akkadian translation. But it was Gilgamesh, the supreme hero of Sumerian story and legend, who most inspired the Akkadian poets. They took over the relatively brief, episodic and disconnected Sumerian Gilgamesh tales, and wove them into a long, unified and deeply moving epic, whose hero was a brave, adventurous, but tragic figure, symbolizing man's unceasing drive for fame, glory and immortality. If Gilgamesh, as is well known, became the hero par excellence of the ancient world, it was due as much to the Akkadian poets as to their Sumerian predecessors.

Hymnography was a carefully cultivated, highly sophisticated art in Sumer, an art which the Akkadians took over almost *in toto*, and to which they added very little. Scores of Sumerian hymns, varying in length from less than fifty to close to four hundred lines, have come down to us, and there is every reason to believe that this is but a fraction of the hymns composed in Sumer throughout the centuries. There were *divine* hymns, often in the form of a glorifying address by the poet to the deity. There were numerous and diverse *royal* hymns, most of them extravagantly self-laudatory: the king himself is purported to have uttered grandiloquent and vain-sounding paeans of self-glorification without shame or inhibition. Quite different in character were the numerous royal hymnal prayers in which paeans of praise to the gods are interspersed with blessings and prayers for the kings. Finally, there were quite a number of hymns dedicated to all the more important temples of Sumer and Akkad; one of the most noteworthy is that inscribed on the long-known Gudea cylinders, which consists of more than 1300 lines of text, and celebrates the rebuilding of the Eninnu temple in Lagash. Sumerian hymnography had developed into so complex a literary art, that it was subdivided into numerous categories by the ancient poets themselves. There were "harmony(?)hymns" and "musical hymns," "spell(?)-hymns," "hymns of heroship," and "hymns of shepherdship for Inanna" (that is hymns concerned with the god Dumuzi); there were hymns accompanied by the lyre, the drum, and other musical instruments. Not infrequently the hymns are broken up into sections or stanzas, and some make use of a one to four line antiphon or choral refrain.

Sumerian lamentations are primarily of two kinds: those bewailing the destruction of Sumerian cities and city-states, and those lamenting the death of the divine Dumuzi, or one of his counterparts. Examples of both types have been found with Akkadian translations, and as far as is known, the Akkadians themselves added little if anything to this literary genre.

The longest Sumerian "historiographic" composition as yet known is "The Curse of Agade," which attempts to explain in theological terms the catastrophic destruction of that city by the barbaric people known as Guti. Another historiographic document revolves about the defeat of these same Guti by the Sumerian "liberator" Utuhegal. A third, and rather brief, "historiographic" piece concerns the successive restorations of the *Tummal*, an important shrine in the city of Nippur. There are also indications that there had existed a series of legendary tales clustering about Sargon the Great. None of these documents has as yet turned up in Akkadian translations, but there is little doubt that Akkadian historiography was profoundly influenced by its Sumerian prototype.

One of the most illuminating types of Sumerian literary documents — and almost entirely unknown until quite recently — is the group of Sumerian "wisdom" compositions, consisting of essays large and small, and collections of precepts and proverbs. The essays deal almost entirely with the Sumerian academy, the *Edubba*, and its faculty and students. One essay revolves about daily school life. Another consists largely of a bitter harangue by a disappointed scribe to his ungrateful and disobedient son. Two essays are in the form of disputations between individuals connected with the *Edubba* in one way or another. Three Sumerian collections of precepts are now known and at least ten collections of proverbs including all types of maxims, sayings, apothegms, and even short Aesop-like fables. Akkadian translations of some of the Sumerian essays and proverbs have been known for some time, and Akkadian "wisdom" literature contains much of the older Sumerian material, remoulded and redacted to accord with Akkadian style, taste, and temper.

The Sumerian literary documents are particularly revealing for the psychological analysis of Sumerian conduct and behavior; they shed no little light on the ethnic traits and characteristics of the Sumerian people, their ideas and ideals, their values and goals, their drives and motives — in short, all the psychological factors underlying Sumerian character and personality. Thus, to begin with that which is basic and fundamental in all cultures, life itself, the Sumerian documents reveal that love of life pervades Sumerian civilization in all its forms and aspects: social, political, economic, and religious. On their numerous votive objects which the Sumerians dedicated to one god or another, they state frankly and expressly that they do so for their own life or for the life of those close to them, or both. The royal hymnal prayers practically all contain a special plea for "long life" for the king. The vain and pathetic quest for eternal life is a favorite theme of the Mesopotamian epic. Indeed it was immortality that, according to the Sumerian belief, most distinguished the gods from man, who is doomed to remain ever mortal. Thus when the Sumerian Noah, Ziusudra, a favorite of the gods, was saved from the flood which had wiped out all mankind, the supreme gift bestowed on him was immortality "like a god." While all peoples and cultures tend to cherish life, the Sumerians drive to cling to it was due in part to their theological convictions. Though not with absolute consistency, the Sumerians believed that at death the emasculated spirit descended to the Nether World, dark and dreary, where "life" at best was but a dismal, wretched reflection of life on earth. There was no heart-lifting, soul-soothing hope of a life in Paradise even for the righteous and deserving; only the ghastly, ghostly world below. In death, therefore, there was nothing to look forward to; life alone was of value in spite of its uncertainties, disappointments, anxieties, and pain.

Closely allied to the love of life was the value put on material prosperity and well-being. The Sumerians prized highly wealth and possessions, rich harvests, well-stocked granaries, folds and stalls filled with cattle large and small, successful hunting on the plain, and good fishing in the sea. The kings constantly boast in their hymns of bringing prosperity and well-being to the land and its people. The disputation texts, such as "Summer and Winter," "Cattle and Grain," are replete with passages exalting the products of farming and cattle-raising. In the lamentations the poets constantly and in no uncertain terms bemoan the loss of material possessions. To take only one example, from a lamentation over the destruction of Ur:

> My possessions like heavy locusts on the move have been carried off,
> O my possessions, I will say.

> My possessions, who comes from the lands below, to the lands below has carried off,
> O my possessions, I will say.
>
> My possessions, who comes from the lands above, to the lands above has carried off,
> O my possessions, I will say.
>
> My precious metal, stone, and lapis lazuli have been scattered about,
> O my possessions, I will say.

The Sumerian proverbs contain many a jibe at the weakness, ineffectualness and wretchedness of the poor, such as:

> When a poor man dies, do not try to revive him.
> Wealth is hard to come by, but poverty is always with us.
> The poor have no power.
> How lowly is the poor man. The edge of the oven is his mill; his ripped garment stays unmended; what he has lost remains unsought for.

The pursuit of wealth and possessions was motivated to no little extent by the longing for security which was in itself a most precious ideal and value. This longing was no doubt a reflection of, and a reaction against, the fears and anxieties which beset the Sumerian all his life. From birth to death he had cause to fear on occasions his parents, his teachers, his friends, his fellow-citizens, his superiors, his rulers, the foreign enemy, the violence of nature, vicious monsters and terrifying demons, sickness and disease, death and oblivion. "To make the people dwell in security" is one of the proud boasts of the Sumerian rulers. No wonder that one of the most desirable features of man's "Golden Age" was, according to the Sumerian thinkers, freedom from fear, or as one poet put it:

> Once upon a time, there was no snake, there was no scorpion,
> There was no hyena, there was no lion,
> There was no wild dog, no wolf,
> There was no fear, no terror,
> Man had no rival.

Turning to the Sumerian cultural institutions, we find that a happy family life was a longed-for ideal and an all-pervading value. The family was the basic unit of Sumerian society and its members were knit closely together by mutual respect and responsibility, as well as love. Love played a larger role in Sumerian life than is usually attributed to it. There was the passionate sensuous love between the sexes, the love between husband and wife, between parents and children, between the various members of the family, between friends and intimates. On a more exalted and sublimated level, there was love among gods, kings, and people, as well as the love of the good, the right, and the just. In the case of the family, there is some evidence to show that love, at times, played a role both before and after marriage, though by and large marriage in ancient Sumer was a practical arrangement, in which the carefully weighed shekel counted more than love's hot desire. Normally, too, Sumerian parents loved and cared for their children, children loved and heeded their parents, and the relationship between brothers and sisters was warm, intimate, and tender.

Like the love of family, patriotism, the love of country and particularly love of one's city, was a supreme value. Love of the city-state naturally came first in time and was never altogether superseded by the love of Sumer as a whole. The inhabitants of a city were known as its "sons" and considered to be a closely-related integrated unit, that took pride in its city, god, and ruler and was ever ready to take up arms in its behalf. Just when Sumer began to think of itself as a political unit and entity is uncertain. Probably it was sometime before 2500 B.C.E., which was the approximate time when we find the world *lugal* ("king") coming into vogue. In the course of the centuries, as is well known, the institution of kingship came to be considered as heaven-sent and of fundamental importance for civilization. The love of the people for their city and state makes itself particularly manifest in the bitter, heart-breaking lamentations in which the Sumerian poets bewail the destruction of both the city and the state.

On the religious side, the Sumerians laid great store on the building and upkeep of their temples, and the careful and constant observance of the cult, in line with their theological conviction that the gods had created man for one purpose only, that is, to serve them and supply them unceasingly with food and shelter. Presumably, therefore, the relationship between god and man corresponded to that between master and slave. But religious attitudes and practices rarely accord with theological theory altogether, and the love of god for man, on the pattern of love between parents and children as well as between wife and husband, is found frequently in the Sumerian documents.

In the area of ethics and morals, the documents reveal that the Sumerians cherished and valued goodness and truth, law and order, justice and freedom, wisdom and learning, courage and loyalty, in short, all of man's most desirable virtues and qualities. Even mercy and compassion were treasured and observed, at least in the breach, to judge from the numerous references to the special protective treatment accorded to widows, orphans and refugees, as well as the poor and oppressed. The step-by-step evolution of these ethical values is as difficult to trace for the ancient Sumerian culture as it is for our own. At least in part, they must have grown out of the extension of the love motive from the individual and his immediate family to the community at large, and even to humanity as a whole. For the Sumerians, the "blackheads" as they came to be known, realized quite clearly that they were only part of a larger humanity which inhabited the four *ubda's*, the four regions into which they divided the world as a whole. In fact, as has only recently been pointed out, the Sumerian word for "mankind," *namlulu*, came to designate in Sumerian, not only humans in the collective sense, but, like the English word "humanity," all conduct and behavior characteristic of humanity and worthy of it. Thus, for example, in an essay which may be entitled "A Scribe and His Perverse Son," the father upbraids his son, not only for shocking ingratitude and for failing to follow in his footsteps and become a scribe, but for actions not worthy of his humanity. One passage, for example, reads:

> Because of your clamorings, yes, because of your clamorings, I was angry with you. Because you do not look to your humanity, my heart was carried off by an evil wind. Your grumblings have put an end to me, you have brought me to the point of death.

Or, to take another passage:

> I, night and day, am I tortured because of you. Night and day you waste in pleasure. You have accumulated much wealth, have expanded far and wide, have become fat, big, broad, powerful, and puffed up. But your kin wait expectantly for your misfortune, and will rejoice at it because you looked not to your humanity.

Yet, in spite of their lofty ideals and ethics, the probabilities are that the Sumerians would never have come as far, or achieved as much, either materially or spiritually, had it not been for one very special psychological drive which motivated much of their behavior, and deeply colored their way of life: the ambitious, competitive, aggressive, and seemingly far from ethical urge for preëminence and prestige, for victory and success. This will to superiority, this driving ambition for victory over a rival, is most vividly illustrated by the poetic essays which the ancient scribes themselves categorized as "contests" or "disputations." The major ingredient of these literary debates consists of a bitter argument between two rivals, in the course of which each of the opponents talks up his own importance in glowing terms without shame or inhibition, and talks down his opponent with sneers, jibes, and humiliating insults. At least seven of these uninhibited quarrelsome literary debates have come down to us, and their very popularity indicates that they reflect a behavioral pattern well known to the Sumerians, and favored and approved by them.

The competitive drive for superiority and prestige played a particularly large role in Sumerian formal education, which entailed many years of school attendance and study. Together with the whip and the cane, it was consciously utilized by both parents and teachers to make students exert themselves to the utmost, and master the complicated, but far from exciting, curriculum in order to become successful scribes and learned professors. Here, for example, is a passage taken from a school essay in which a teacher reassures, in flowing language, an ambitious and aspiring student whose father had just lavished upon him a number of gifts:

> Young man, because you did not neglect my word, did not forsake it, you will reach the pinnacle of the scribal art, you will become perfect in it. (Five lines omitted). You will be the leader of your brothers, the chief of your friends; you will rank as the highest of the schoolmen.

In another school essay, two worthies, by the names of Enki-mansi and Girni-ishag, belabor each other with such insulting and vituperative name-calling as "dolt," "numbskull," "pest," "illiterate," "clever-fool (i.e., sophomore)," "bungler," and "windbag." This particular essay ends in a sentence which seems to justify a rather startling, but not unilluminating, conjecture concerning another important feature of Sumerian culture, the extraordinary emphasis on law and legality, the strong penchant for legal documents and law-codes, which has long been recognized as an all-pervading characteristic of Sumerian economic and social life. This sentence reads: "In the dispute between Enki-mansi and Girni-ishag, the *ummia* (the professor) gives the verdict." The Sumerian word here used for "verdict" is the same that designates verdicts at court-trials, and one cannot hold back the thought that the extraordinary value which the

Sumerians attached to law and legal control stemmed not so much from lofty moral and ethical conviction, as from the contentious and aggressive behavioral pattern which characterized their culture.

Turning to the political scene, there are now available two poems celebrating the victory of Enmerkar, the ruler of Uruk, over a presumptuous rival who ruled over the city-state of Aratta. To judge from their contents, it was the driving ambition of each of these rulers to break down the morale of his rival in a kind of "war of nerves." The two tales are replete with taunts, threats, challenges, and contests. Finally it is Enmerkar who emerges as victor and to whom, according to one of these poems, the lord of Aratta offers abject submission in these rather revealing words:

> You are the beloved of Inanna, you alone are exalted,
> Inanna has truly chosen you for her holy lap,
> From the lower (lands) to the upper (lands) you are the lord,
> I am only second to you,
> From the (moment of) conception, I was not to be your equal,
> you are the big brother,
> I cannot compare with you ever.

Quite revealing, too, for the Sumerian yearning for victory, prestige, and glory on the political front are the numerous self-laudatory royal hymns, in which the Sumerian king recites his own virtues and achievements unblushingly and uninhibitedly in quite hyperbolic and extravagant language.

It is thus fairly obvious that the drive for superiority and prestige deeply colored the Sumerian outlook on life, and played an important role in their education, politics, and economics. All of which suggests the tentative hypothesis that, not unlike the strong emphasis on competition and success in modern American culture, the aggressive penchant for rivalry and the ambitious drive for preëminence provided no little of the psychological motivation which sparked and sustained the material and cultural advances for which the Sumerians are not unjustly noted: irrigation expansion, technological invention, monumental building, and the development of a system of writing and education.

3. HURRIANS AND HITTITES

by E. A. Speiser

Although Hurrians and Hittites represent two separate and distinct ethno-linguistic groups, they have much in common with each other. In Eastern Anatolia and Northern Syria they came in contact geographically, and their historical careers converged and interlocked through much of the second millennium B.C.E. The cultural interrelations of these two groups were exceptionally close, in that the Hittites came to be indebted to the Hurrians in such matters as writing, literature, religion, and art;[1] small wonder, therefore, that Hittite records show a considerable proportion of Hurrian loanwords. All these would be details of purely local interest if it were not for the fact that both the Hurrians and the Hittites played prominent parts on the international stage. In one way or another they were factors in the history of the ancient Near East as a whole, and they were also to leave their mark on the classical world. There are frequent, if largely enigmatic, allusions to both in the Bible. The Hittite language, moreover, is the oldest recorded representative of the Indo-European family.[2]

It thus follows that a comprehensive statement about the Hurrians and the Hittites alike — their distinctive as well as their common features — must not be omitted from any up-to-date introduction to Biblical history. Within the scope, however, of the present volume such a statement has to be limited, of necessity, to barest essentials. It should contain the briefest possible historical summary; and since the respective languages prove to be significant in more ways than one, room must be made for a minimal description of Hurrian and Hittite. Finally, and most important of all, one cannot avoid the complex task of seeking to clarify the scattered Biblical references to the two groups in question. The material will be presented, accordingly, under three headings: (a) Hurrians; (b) Hittites; and (c) Hurrians and Hittites in the Bible.

A. Hurrians

The original home of the Hurrians[3] has to be sought in the mountains of Armenia, from where they spread to the neighboring areas of Eastern

Anatolia, Northern Syria, and Central Mesopotamia. The oldest known records in their own language go back to the period of the Dynasty of Akkad,[4] in the second half of the third millennium. Early in the next millennium they are attested in Babylonia, in the kingdom of Mari, and in various Syrian centers, particularly Alalakh. A subsequent migration deposited large Hurrian settlements throughout much of the Near East. By the middle of the second millennium they are encountered as far east as Nuzi and as far south as Central Palestine, notably at Taanach.[5] Hurrian personal names abound throughout, and Hurrian glosses and even connected texts turn up in such places as Ugarit, Tunip, Alalakh, and Boghazkoy.

This large-scale expansion of the Hurrians did not have, by and large, corresponding political results. In Southern Mesopotamia, the newcomers submitted to established local authority. Elsewhere, they founded a number of city-states which enjoyed only limited, and usually short-lived, prominence. It is possible, but by no means certain, that the success of the Hyksos in Egypt was due in some part to Hurrian participation. Only in Central Mesopotamia did the Hurrians succeed in establishing a semblance of an empire. This was the empire of Mitanni which extended, ca. 1400 B.C.E., from Alalakh in the west to Nuzi and Arrapkha in the east, and served to maintain the balance of power in the Amarna age. Before long, however, Mitanni succumbed to the onslaught of the resurgent Hittites, while its eastern sectors were gradually taken over by the Assyrians. The political role of the Hurrians was thus of ephemeral consequence at best. Indeed, the brief upsurge of Mitanni itself was due in large measure to Aryan — that is, eastern Indo-European — leadership.

In the cultural sphere, on the other hand, the Hurrians proved to be a far more significant factor.[6] To begin with, they came early under the influence of the dynamic Sumero-Akkadian civilization and showed themselves to be eager and able pupils. What they thus learned, in such fields as writing, literature, religion, law, and science, was then blended with native Hurrian traditions. The combined product could subsequently be transmitted to other groups with whom the far-flung Hurrians had occasion to come in contact. The principal beneficiaries of this cultural chain reaction were the Hittites. It is through the Hurrians that the Hittites became acquainted with the cuneiform script and its multiple traditions; through them they acquired the Akkadian version of the Gilgamesh Epic as well as numerous works of Hurrian literature. Eventually, some of these importations were transmitted by the Hittites to their closest European neighbors. Among the other lands to be influenced by Hurrians were

Syria and Canaan. Biblical civilization received impulses of such Hurrian influences through one of two channels. One can be traced back to the Patriarchs, whose early home in the district of Haran lay in the very heart of Hurrian cultural activity. The other channel was the eastern Mediterranean coastland, which was dotted with Hurrian communities by the middle of the second millennium B.C.E.; for details see below under (c).

What are the means that enable us today to pick up the trail of the Hurrians with any degree of certainty? One important method of identification is provided by material remains. Hurrian sculptures and pottery are usually sufficiently distinctive to leave little, if any, room for doubt. Then there are certain geographic and gentilic terms which constitute dependable witnesses of Hurrian presence. Thus the ethnic name *Šubarû* ("Subarian") and the geographic name *Subartu*[7] come to refer to Hurrian people and centers, especially in Assyrian usage. Similarly, the term *Mitanni* is now known to apply to a state whose dominant population were Hurrians and whose official language was Hurrian. Of still greater significance is the native stem on which our designation "Hurrian(s)" is based. This stem appears as *Ḫurri* in Akkadian documents (e.g., from Bogazkoy and Alalakh), in Hittite texts, and in Mitannian correspondence;[8] as *ḫry* in Ugaritic; as **Ḫuru*[9] in Egyptian; it is found, furthermore, in some of the occurrences of the Biblical name *Ḥōrî*, and especially in *Xorraîoi* of the Septuagint. The unusually wide distribution of this term is itself an excellent index of Hurrian expansion.

It is, however, Hurrian personal names and the glosses and texts in that language that furnish the most reliable proof of Hurrian infiltration. Gentilics and geographic terms can be misapplied; but personal names, technical terms, and connected sentences or complete documents in a given language are concrete and inescapable evidence. When large numbers of the population of, say, Nuzi, Alalakh, or Taanach bear Hurrian names; when Hurrian texts appear in Mari, Ugarit, or Bogazkoy; when Sumero-Hurrian vocabularies and Akkado-Hurrian bilinguals have turned up in Ugarit — when this happens, the direct association of Hurrians with all these areas becomes an indisputable fact.

Positive identification of all such linguistic remains was not possible, of course, until sufficient progress had been made in the recovery of the Hurrian language.[10] For a variety of reasons — the relative paucity of the material, the fragmentary nature of the extant texts, and the uncommon structure of the speech itself — our understanding of Hurrian is as yet far from adequate. Nevertheless, the many doubts that remain to be resolved concern details rather than general characteristics; and the validity of our attainments to date has been confirmed in a most gratifying manner by the recently discovered Akkado-Hurrian bilingual from Ugarit.[11]

Hurrian has no connection whatever with either Semitic or Indo-European. Furthermore, no generic relationship exists between Hurrian and Sumerian, Elamite, or any of the other languages of ancient Anatolia. The only demonstrable ancient relative of Hurrian was Urartian, the pre-Indo-European language of Armenia, from which region the Hurrians are known to have fanned out to many areas of the Near East. Modern structural parallels to Hurrian can be adduced from among some of the Caucasic languages, but the available evidence is insufficient to speak as yet with confidence of an actual relationship between ancient Hurro-Urartian and any branch of modern Caucasic. Hurrian employed a great profusion of suffixes, whereas prefixes were absent altogether. The verb shows a passival orientation: to express the concept "the lord sent a messenger," Hurrian has to resort to "the messenger was sent by the lord." The syntax of the transitive verb is entirely different from that of the intransitive verb. It may be added in passing that Hurrian proved hospitable to a great many loanwords, particularly from Akkadian — independent proof that the Hurrians owed much to the dynamic civilization of historic Mesopotamia.

B. Hittites

The term "Hittites" is used today in several different and conflicting meanings. The confusion is due in part to historical developments in ancient Anatolia, where the bearers of that name were centered; and in part to the notice in the Table of Nations (Gen. 10:15), according to which Heth was the brother of Sidon son of Canaan. The facts in the case are many and complex. In the present context, however, only the main points need to be brought out to clarify the situation in respect to terminology.

We find thus in Anatolia an ancient land name *Ḫatti*, whose "Hattic" people spoke "Hattic" and had their capital at *Ḫattuša* (modern Bogazkoy). Now when Hatti was overrun by a foreign people, apparently some time at the turn of the third millennium, the conquerors retained the old geographic names for the country and its capital, but imposed on the area their own Indo-European language, which had no connection whatever with Hattic. But the modern decipherers of this new language can hardly be blamed for calling it "Hittite," especially in view of the Biblical references. Yet in addition to this Indo-European Hittite, whose records have been preserved in the cuneiform script, there was still a third language, distinct from Hattic but related to Hittite, which employed a hieroglyphic script. It was used sparingly as a literary medium before 1200 B.C.E., but supplanted cuneiform Hittite thereafter; its records have come down to us from Northern Syria as well as Anatolia.

It follows that the term "Hittite" has connections with three separate linguistic units: old Anatolian Hattic, cuneiform Hittite, and hieroglyphic Hittite. Each of these represents also a distinct ethnic group. Accordingly, when the Bible speaks of Hittites, the question arises as to which of the above three entities is involved in any given instance. We shall see presently that all three may have figured at one time or another within the total span of Biblical history.

First, however, a brief statement is in order in regard to Hittite history in general. There is not much to be said about the autochthonous Hattians, since the evidence about them is both too fragmentary and remote for our present purposes; except only that there exists the theoretical possibility that some Hattians, or their relatives, may have settled in Canaan in pre-Semitic times, so that traces of their presence could have survived down to the early historical period. When it comes to the Indo-European Hittites and their relatives, we know of an Old Hittite Kingdom during the second quarter of the second millennium B.C.E. One of its rulers, Mursilis I, sacked Babylon in the seventeenth century and put an end to its celebrated First Dynasty (of which Hammurabi had been an illustrious representative). The middle centuries of the second millennium were characterized by the Dark Age,[12] brought on in all likelihood by Indo-Aryans. One of the results of that great upheaval was the emergence of Mitanni. The fourteenth century witnessed a Hittite revival under the New Kingdom and the consequent partition of Mitanni. Soon it is Egypt, under Ramses II, and the Hittites who contend for supremacy in Western Asia. But the battle of Kadesh (1291) resulted in a stalemate which was formalized in the Hittite-Egyptian treaty of 1276.

After the catastrophic invasion by the "Sea Peoples" (c. 1200), Hittite historical tradition breaks off. The literary slack is taken up to some extent by hieroglyphic Hittite, which enjoys a new lease on life now that its cuneiform rival has fallen into disuse. Speakers of this language maintain limited principalities in Cilicia and Northern Syria. Assyrian records continue to refer to them as Hattians. Eventually, their territories come under Assyrian domination.

As has already been stressed earlier in this account, the Indo-European Hittites were permeated throughout by the culture of the Hurrians, although they eventually established their political mastery over the latter. It is exactly the same kind of interplay that is encountered elsewhere between the Assyrians and Babylonians, or the Romans and Greeks. Some of its cultural results, moreover, were to be reflected in due time in classical sources, notably in portions of Hesiod's Theogony.[13]

A few comments, in passing, about the languages in question. Anatolian Hattic confronts us as yet as an isolated medium, with no demonstrable affinity to any of the other languages that are known from the ancient Near East. Nor can it be linked with Hurrian, although the two areas were contiguous over a long stretch of time: whereas Hurrian specializes in suffixes, Hattic is characteristically partial to prefixes. Intrusive Hittite, on the other hand, belongs to the westerly, or *centum*, branch of Indo-European, in marked contrast to Indo-Aryan which is also attested in cuneiform records. The only thing that can, or needs to be, said for the present about hieroglyphic Hittite is that it represents another Indo-European language which must not be confused with the Hittite of the cuneiform inscriptions. It is interesting to note that, although hieroglyphic Hittite continued in use well into the first millennium, speakers of that medium had arrived on the scene much earlier, indeed by the end of the third millennium. There is thus a great deal that remains to be found out about the Anatolian gateway to the ancient Near East.

C. Hurrians and Hittites in the Bible

The Biblical gentilic term *Ḥōrî* was long regarded as referring to one of the less important peoples of early Palestine, too insignificant to be included in the standard lists of the pre-Israelite nations. It required the insight and acumen of Eduard Meyer[14] to show that the Horites had been seriously underrated. They were not confined to pre-Edomite Seir, as the Masoretic text indicates. For the Septuagint version, by speaking of Horites instead of Hivites in Genesis 34:2 (Shechem) and Joshua 9:7 (Gibeon), locates Horites in Central Palestine. Accordingly, reported Hivite settlements in Lebanon (Jud. 3:3) and at the foot of Mt. Hermon (Josh. 11:3) must also have belonged to Horites.

The subsequent discovery of the prominent part played by the Hurrians throughout the ancient Near East lent vivid color to Meyer's deductions. Cuneiform sources record Hurrian personal names at Taanach and Shechem, the same area where the Bible locates Hivites-Horites; indeed, it is in connection with actual Canaan that the Hebrew text interchanges "the Hivite" (Gen. 36:2) with "the Horite" (vs. 20). Since the Hebrew form *Ḫōri* would be the only possible transcription of cuneiform *Ḫurri*, and since the Septuagint spelling *Xorraîoi* proves the point directly, nothing seemed to oppose the outright equation of Horites with Hurrians.[15] Moreover, the Biblical Jebusites, too, proved to be Hurrians in disguise. They were of foreign stock (Jud. 19:12), a description borne out by the Jebusite personal name *Awarnah* (II Sam. 24:16, *Kᵉthib*). A 14th century ruler of Jerusalem, or Jebus, bore a name containing the attested Hurrian element *Ḫepa*.[16] Thus Jebusites and Hivites alike — two of the featured pre-Israelite nations — were merely subdivisions of the wide-spread Hurrian group. All in all, therefore, the Horites must once have been even more prominent than Meyer had deduced.

The above conclusion, however, must now be modified in one significant respect. The required change detracts nothing from the position of the local Hurrians in early Biblical times; but it does affect the automatic identification of Hurrians with Horites. In the first place, the Horite names as listed in Genesis 36:20–30 are transparently Semitic for the most part; the Hurrians, on the other hand, were demonstrably non-Semitic, as is also true of the Jebusites as well as the uncircumcised Hivites (Gen. 34:14ff.). And in the second place, there is no archaeological evidence whatever for a Hurrian settlement in Edom or Transjordan. It follows, therefore, that the Biblical term *Ḫōri* — much in the same manner as Cush — must have been used at one time in two distinct and unrelated meanings. One, apparently of strictly local origin, was to designate the Semitic predecessors of the Edomites. The other, based on the heterogeneous *Ḫurri*, was the comprehensive term for Hurrians. The discrepancy between the two could not have been lost on later Biblical tradition. Whereas the Septuagint still speaks of Horites (in the sense of their non-Semitic namesakes) outside Edom, the Masoretic text came to restrict the Horites to Seir,[17] while substituting for the other element the local variant designation Hivites.

Hurrian cultural echoes in the Bible are many and varied. Some of these are extra-territorial and date back to the period when the Patriarchs lived in intimate contact with Hurrians in the area of Haran. That was the time when early Hebrew society incorporated numerous Hurrian customs and usages. Our best source for tracing such influences is furnished by the Nuzi texts — records of an outlying Hurrian community which was, nevertheless, typical of Hurrian society throughout. Thanks to Nuzi parallels, virtually all the patriarchal narratives appear now in a new and authentic light. The three recorded instances of the wife-sister motif (Gen. 12:10–20; 20; 26:1–

11), the rivalry between Sarah and Hagar (Gen. 16:1–6), Isaac's reversal of the order of his sons' birthrights (Gen. 27), Rachel's removal of Laban's housegods (Gen. 31:19, 30) — these and many other details now receive their correct explanation from Hurrian sources.

The Hurrians were active also as cultural intermediaries between Mesopotamia and the Bible. Much of the material utilized in the first eleven chapters, or the Primeval History,[18] of Genesis was ultimately of Mesopotamian origin. This was a normal result of the Hebrews' arrival from that quarter; and it was likewise natural that the Bible should present such borrowings critically and in the spirit of its own central theme. Yet some of this imported matter did not come straight from Southern Mesopotamia but rather from a secondary center of dissemination. Thus the names of the Patriarchs before the Flood are different from the names of the corresponding antediluvian rulers of Sumer. Just so, Noah has nothing in common onomastically with Sumerian Ziusudra or Akkadian Utnapishtim; and the ark does not land on Mt. Niṣir but in the country of Ararat. The latter, however, points to the original home of the Hurrians, and a name quite similar to Noah occurs in the Flood passage of the Hurrian version of the Gilgamesh Epic. All of this indicates strongly that it was the Hurrians through whom the prehistoric traditions of Mesopotamia came to be relayed to the Bible.

There are certain linguistic traces of the actual presence of Hurrians in Canaan proper. The most interesting of these by far is the so-called process of spirantization. In common with Phoenician and Aramaic, Hebrew changes its stops *b g d k p t*, in certain given positions, to corresponding spirants. This pattern is foreign to general Semitic, but indigenous with Hurrian. Since spirantization occurs precisely where Semitic and Hurrian were in intimate contact, but is absent elsewhere, and since the process can now be synchronized with the period of greatest Hurrian expansion, it is evident that the practice was taken over by Northwest Semitic from Hurrian.

The problem of the Hittites in the Bible is far more complex. To begin with, there is the question as to which type of Hittites may be involved in any given Biblical passage: Hattians, Indo-European Hittites of the cuneiform records, or hieroglyphic Hittites. Furthermore, there are some clear instances in which the term "Hittites" is used broadly for Hurrian elements. The "Hittite mother" of Jerusalem in Ezekiel's metaphorical usage (16:3, 45) is an obvious reference to the early settlement of the Jebusites, who were a Hurrian sub-group, as we have seen. Elsewhere, however, we find "Hittites" plainly distinguished from Hurrians (e.g.,

Gen. 36:2; Exod. 23:28). Lastly, in the Table of Nations Heth is a son of Canaan (Gen. 10:15).

It is thus apparent that the term "Hittites" in the Bible was flexible and had various connotations. In the Table of Nations it seems to be used comprehensively of the non-Semitic population of Canaan alongside the Semitic Sidonians or Phoenicians. This accords in large measure with Assyrian references to Hattiland after the upheaval of 1200 B.C.E., and explains at the same time the subsuming of Heth under Canaan. On the same basis, other writers might equate a particular non-Semitic element with Hittites; Ezekiel did just that in the case of the Jebusites.

Was the term ever applied more specifically in the Bible? The answer will depend in the first place on the date of the given passage. If the designation of Uriah as a Hittite (II Sam. 11:3 ff.) is meant to be precise, his ethnic group can be equated only with "hieroglyphic" Hittites. Yet the plene writing of this name with *-w-*, which was scarcely used as a vowel in Davidic times, might well point to an actual *ewri-*, the common Hurrian term for "lord" and a frequent component in Hurrian personal names.

For the Indo-European Hittites of the cuneiform texts one would have to go back to the period before the Judges. Even then, however, Palestine would be too far to the south of Hittite penetration. Nor do any relevant personal names come into consideration. The situation changes, however, when we go back to the patriarchal age. This time we find named individuals designated as Hittites, such as Ephron son of Zohar (Gen. 23:8), Beeri, and Elon (Gen. 26:34; 36:2). Chronologically, these could have been Anatolian Hittites or Hattians. But the names can be analyzed as Semitic; moreover, a substantial settlement of Anatolians in the south of Palestine does not appear plausible. It can thus be said that while the extra-Biblical Hittites have ceased to be a mystery, some of the Biblical uses of that ethnic term are still as much of a puzzle as ever.

4. AMORITES AND CANAANITES

by E. A. Speiser

OLD ETHNO-GEOGRAPHIC names usually depend for their proper explanation on the abundance of significant references. This does not hold true, however, of Biblical "Canaanite" and "Amorite." In their case, the number and variety of notices does more to confuse the issue than to clarify it.[1] For the usage is far from uniform. The connotation is at times general, at other times seemingly specific. In some occurrences the two terms appear to relate to one and the same subject; but in others they are distinctive and contrasted. Moreover, the ethnic listing of Canaanites and Amorites in the Bible, notably in the Table of Nations (Gen. 10:6, 15 f.), is sharply at variance with modern linguistic classification. In these circumstances, it has proved to be virtually impossible to arrive at self-consistent definitions of these two terms.

Fortunately, notices of both Canaanites and Amorites are not limited to the Bible. Both names appear, in one form or another, in various extra-Biblical sources. Indeed, the outside material shows that the two elements in question constituted far greater magnitudes than one would deduce from the Biblical evidence alone. These extraneous sources, and particularly the extensive cuneiform references, place the whole problem in an entirely different perspective. Yet they fail to add up to a clear-cut solution of the issue before us. While some of the difficulties in regard to the Canaanites are substantially reduced as a result, the problem of the Amorites becomes still more complicated. In any case, a constructive approach to the question as a whole must start out with an evaluation of the extra-Biblical evidence. The summary that follows will be presented, accordingly, under these headings: a. Extra-Biblical witnesses — (1) Canaanites; (2) Amorites; (3) Canaanites and Amorites compared; b. Canaanites and Amorites in the Bible.

The discussion will be devoted of necessity to matters of terminology, location, languages, and ethnology — in that order. How much ethnic history is taken into consideration will depend in large measure on the results yielded by the other data. For one cannot deal with the history of a given unit unless it can first be established that the subject was a tangible entity.

A. Extra-biblical Witnesses

(1) *Canaanites*. The oldest known forms of this term carry a geographic meaning. They come from the city of Alalakh, the capital of the land of Mukish, in northern Syria. The statue of the local ruler Idrimi (ca. 1500 B.C.E.) is inscribed with a text which mentions "the land of Canaan" (*ma-at Ki-in-a-nim*KI, lines 18, 19).[2] Clay tablets from the same site (AT[3] 48.5; 154.24; 181.9) show the same spelling, which is significant because the writing *-in-a-*, as opposed to the expected *-i-na-*, is a local convention (just as in the syllabic texts from Ugarit) to indicate the presence of a medial *ʿayin*. Amarna texts record eleven occurrences of a land-name *Kinaḫḫi*, *Kinahni/na*, as against a single gentilic *Ki-na-ḫa-ay-u* "Canaanite."[4] The forms with *-n-* reflect consonantal *knʿn*; those without *-n-* involve the Hurrian derivational suffix *-ḫi*. A geographic connotation underlies also the Nuzi adjective *Kinaḫḫu*, which designated a type of purple wool imported from *Kinaḫḫi*.[5] What is especially interesting in this connection is the fact that the name "Canaan" was sufficiently entrenched as a concrete geographic concept to be used as a trade label no later than the fifteenth century. There is further the Egyptian land name *p' Kn'n* and the Phoenician *knʿn*, the latter being applied to Phoenicia itself.[6] The corresponding gentilics, including Ugaritic *knʿny*, are found as a rule less frequently in the same sources.[7]

The pertinent material, moreover, permits us to recover the approximate boundaries of Canaan proper. From the vantage point of Alalakh, the area in question lay to the south. Its eastern borders, to judge from various other data, ran between the Lebanon and the Anti-Lebanon. In other words, the term Canaan covered principally the maritime region which the Greeks knew as Phoenicia. As such, the name was shared by a number of political units along the Syrian coast. How far to the south this usage extended is not altogether clear. But Egyptian references apply the name more broadly to the Egyptian provinces of Asia.[8]

Based on this primary geographic connotation of Canaan, the derived adjective could be employed in one of several ways. "Canaanite" might be applied as a gentilic to the dominant population of the region, or any of its component areas, e.g., Phoenicia or portions of Palestine. It could also be used of any local group regardless of ethnic affiliation. Or it might serve in a linguistic sense, to designate the principal speech of the land, and hence by extension any or all of the related dialects. In this sense, the term is once found in the Bible (Isa. 19:18); and it has been taken over by modern scholarship to classify Phoenician, Hebrew, Moabite, and the like. Nor have the two other uses been ignored, as we shall see later on.

In these circumstances, there can be no such thing as a comprehensive history of the Canaanites. One can deal only with the individual histories of the several component groups, depending on the particular application of the term. Thus an important recent study substituted "Canaanites," properly enough, for Phoenicians.[9] And when the time is at hand to write an account of the adjacent areas of pre-Israelite Palestine, their inhabitants could be described with equal propriety as "Southern Canaanites." Such flexibility is entirely consistent with the underlying geographic connotation of the term in question. And it is the same feature that accounts for the various Biblical uses of this name. But before these uses can be reviewed, it is necessary to sample the extra-Biblical material that bears on the Amorites.

(2) *Amorites.* The problem in this instance is vastly more complex than that of the Canaanites. The material is incomparably more abundant; the area involved extends all the way to Sumer; and the time span reaches back well into the third millennium. The enlarged scope carries with it a corresponding increase in difficulties.

The main body of our references stems from Southern Mesopotamia.[10] The earliest of these, which date from the latter half of the third millennium, bear the form of MAR.TU. This is used to designate both a given land or region, and a type of function or occupation. It is worthy of notice that a number of such Martu have personal names that are clearly Sumerian or Akkadian. It is only under the Third Dynasty of Ur (at the turn of the third millennium), and especially during the succeeding Old Babylonian stages, that the names become markedly West Semitic.[11] Simultaneously, Martu is equated with, and largely displaced by, *Amurru(m)* in the sense of a region, and Amurrû as an ethnic and occupational label.

We have as yet no way of deciding whether Martu and Amurru were originally independent terms, graphic equivalents, or linguistic cognates. All we can be sure of is that by Old Babylonian times the two could be, and often were, interchanged.[12] Their eventual equation does not guarantee original identity. In any case, however, both Martu and Amurru come to designate "west" in Babylonian as well as Assyrian usage.

Without digressing here into undue detail, it will prove simplest to assume, as a working hypothesis, that the two forms Martu and Amurru were unrelated to begin with. Martu started out in Lower Mesopotamia as an early geographic concept, which signified "west" in relation to Sumer. On that basis, any locality in that general direction could be characterized as Martu. The same would apply also to various western ethnic groups. And if such groups had become known for particular habits or occupations — say, nomads or itinerant workers or mercenaries — these, too, would come to be identified in time as Martu. On this assumption, the presence of Sumerian, Akkadian, and other elements among early Martu names would receive a perfectly logical explanation.

The term Amurru, on the other hand, has to be ascribed to an extra-Mesopotamian source. The relevant forms, in phonetic spelling, are not restricted to Babylonian and Assyrian sources. We find them in Cappadocian, Hittite, and Syrian archives, in the Amarna Letters, in Ugaritic, in Egyptian, and in Hebrew. We hear of Amurritic or Amorite groups and individuals, and also of a political state called Amurru. In short, this was necessarily a native name. It could not have been modeled after an Akkadian word for "west." As seen from Lower Mesopotamia, the people and the land so designated were western, to be sure. But Amurru was certainly not to the west of Hattusa, or Alalakh, or Ugarit, or the centers named in the Amarna correspondence. Nor were the Amorites "westerners" to Egyptian or Biblical writers. Whatever the name may have meant at first, and whether its origin was geographic, social, or ethnic, it must have been native with the "Amorites" themselves. Incidentally, in Biblical usage at least, the term functions exclusively as a gentilic: as opposed to the frequent mention of "the land of Canaan," there is no such thing as a Biblical land of *Amor, but only "land of the Amorites."

In the light of the facts just cited, the ultimate equation of Martu with Amurru in Akkadian usage presents no difficulties whatever. Local Martu had developed the directional sense of "west." In the course of time, but no later than the period of Ur III, the western neighbors of Sumer and Akkad came to be known, on as yet unspecified internal grounds, as Amorites. The two names, one Mesopotamian and the other extra-Mesopotamian, thus became interchangeable. And before very long, the foreign *Amurru* was to rival, and eventually replace, the local *Martu* in the sense of "west," the process being aided considerably by the increasing prominence of Amorites in the evolving history of Mesopotamia.

As a new factor in Mesopotamian affairs, the Amorites can be identified in part by the growing use of the labels *Amurru* and *Amurrû*. In much larger part, however, they make known their appearance by the distinctive character of their personal names. A brief linguistic statement on the subject will be given in the next section. For the moment it will suffice to say that the Amorite names bear the unmistakable stamp of West Semitic, contrasting plainly with local Akkadian, or East Semitic, onomastic usage.

Traced in this manner, the newcomers from the west[13] can be seen to play a part in the collapse of the Ur III empire. Amorite dynasties spring up in Larsa and Eshnunna, and soon thereafter in Babylon — whose First

Dynasty, which included Hammurabi, came to be known as the Amorite Dynasty — as well as in Ashur. Outlying Mari had naturally been an Amorite center long before that. When the first waves of these invaders had been duly assimilated to the traditional civilization of Mesopotamia, and had made their own contribution to it, fresh waves continued to pose a constant administrative problem. The Old Babylonian state had several officials charged with various Amorite affairs, and Mari featured a *ṭupšar Amurri*, or approximately "Amorite Secretary."

Naturally enough, Amorite witnesses increase as one moves westward from Mesopotamia to Syria. The various Syrian dynasts of the Old Babylonian age, as they are known to us from Mari, early Alalakh, and other records, show a vast preponderance of Amorite names. After the middle of the second millennium the situation undergoes a change, in that the Hurrians are now in the ascendant. There ensues thus a period of Hurro-Amorite symbiosis.[14] The state of Amurru itself starts out with Amorite rulers (cf. Abd-Aširti and Aziru of the Amarna Letters), but these give way to Hurrian kings, or at least kings with Hurrian names (notably Tuppi-Tešub, and Pente-šina).

Mention of the state of Amurru brings up the question of its location. On this point our data are regrettably vague. That state's ruler Abd-Aširti is shown by the Amarna Letters as being active in the latitude of Byblos. Hittite treaties with Aziru and Pente-šina locate the northern boundaries of Amurru within the political reach of Anatolia. Alalakh texts enable us to recognize Amorites to the south and east of that center; but it should be stressed that Amorite-occupied territory does not coincide by any means with a specific state of Amurru. At all events, the state of Amurru must have been based largely on the Anti-Lebanon, paralleling Phoenician holdings along their eastern borders, and extending southwards to Damascus and beyond. But the Syrian steppe lands in general must long have constituted the favorite stamping grounds of the Amorites. It is here, apparently, that the Amorites became experts in the breeding and care of horses, to judge from references in the Old Babylonian texts from Alalakh.[15] And it was from the same quarter that they must have directed their repeated thrusts against Mesopotamia.

(3) *Canaanites and Amorites compared.* Since we have no references to Canaanites prior to 1500 B.C.E., there is no suitable basis for an earlier comparison between them and the Amorites. For the 15th-13th centuries, on the other hand, there is the cumulative evidence from a number of sources, and more particularly from the texts of Level IV of Alalakh, the Amarna Letters, and the syllabic as well as the alphabetic material from Ugarit.

What this evidence shows in the first place is that Canaan and Amurru were distinctive geographic entities. Canaan occupied the coastlands of Phoenicia and Palestine. Its extent was relatively fixed and not readily capable of expansion. Indeed, the name Canaan itself was in all probability a geographic term to start with. Amurru, for its part, formed the inland neighbor of Canaan. But its eastern borders were fluid. What is more, the name traveled with the people, and its origin was in all likelihood ethnic or sociological rather than geographic. If the Amorites are difficult to pin down, it is mainly because their settlements were largely unstable. Interestingly enough, old Mesopotamian sources describe the Amorites as lacking the arts of civilization — in other words, as nomads. The Canaanites, by contrast, appear as prevailingly urban.

Our other means of comparison are linguistic. This is a technical and delicate process, chiefly because Canaanite and Amorite represented at worst two closely related dialects of West Semitic. Another inherent problem is of a chronological nature. Granted that it is best to separate for the time being the mid-second millennium sources of Canaanite, Ugaritic, and Amorite respectively;[16] but would the same separation be in order if we had comparable older material from the 18th century or the 20th? This is one of the points that make the whole issue uncertain and controversial.

Nevertheless, if we leave Ugaritic aside as not germane to our present problem, there still remain sundry details which favor a distinction between Canaanite and Amorite. Even as far back as the Old Babylonian period at Alalakh, the local term for "sun" was *saps*,[17] in partial agreement with Ugaritic *špš*,[18] but in contrast to common Canaanite **šamš*. From the same time, too, we have the personal name *Iš-ma-a-da* (Alalakh, for Canaanite *yišma'-?) as compared with Amorite *Yasmaḫ-Addu* (/*yašma'*-, Mari), and Akkadian *Išme-*. Amorite *s*: Canaanite *š* might be another significant point of interdialectical difference.

Be this as it may, the geographic distinction between Canaan and Amurru is not subject to dispute. Just so, the Phoenician coast as a whole withstood Hurrian pressure much better than neighboring Syria. Contemporary Akkadian documents from Ugarit and Alalakh — two relatively close centers — are a good case in point. Whereas West Semitic remains the principal speech of Ugarit, and Semites continue there in the majority, 15th century Alalakh becomes overwhelmingly Hurrian;[19] similarly, Semitic rulers of Amurru are superseded by Hurrian kings. Does all this reflect a difference in tempo between urban and semi-nomadic societies, the sown and the desert, or — in other words — Canaanites and Amorites? The evidence, to be sure, is far from conclusive. Yet the indications, slight though they may be, are consistent with the assumption that Canaanites and Amorites differed from one another not only in geographic distribution, and apparently in their respective dialects, but also in their modes of life.

B. Canaanites and Amorites in the Bible

The results that have just been summarized have an obvious bearing on the combined Biblical material relating to Canaanites and Amorites. It is now amply and independently established that the two terms had separate and distinctive connotations from the start. This accords with some of the Biblical references, but would seem to conflict with others. It remains, therefore, to evaluate the pertinent occurrences in the Bible[20] in the light of the data obtained thus far.[21]

The Table of Nations lists Canaan as the father of Sidon and Heth (Gen. 10:15). This reflects the same geographic principle of classification that is apparent in the Table of Nations as a whole. Sidon stood for Phoenicia (cf. I Kings 5:20; 16:31), and the Phoenicians themselves referred to their land as Canaan. And Heth in this context represents the "hieroglyphic" Hittites of Northern Syria (see above, pp. 158 ff.). That the grouping was basically geographic is confirmed by the further mention of Arkites, Arvadites, and Hamathites (Gen. 10:17–18); note also the association of Jebusites and Hivites — these being subdivisions of Hurrians — and of Amorites (vss. 16–17). In other words, we have here city-states and peoples found in Canaan and adjoining areas, but all subsumed under Canaan, and subordinated to Sidon (Phoenicia) as Canaan's "first-born" (vs. 15). The whole group yields an appropriate regional unit; it would be incompatible on an ethnic or linguistic basis. And we have seen that the primary sense of "Canaan" in extra-Biblical sources was likewise geographic.

The usage thus attested proves to be significant also in another connection. Some critics, puzzled by the interchangeable employment of "Canaanite" and "Amorite" elsewhere in the Bible, sought to solve the problem by asserting that the former term was habitual with source "J," and the latter with source "E." Yet passages commonly assigned to "E" often use "Canaan" as a land name (e.g., Gen. 42:13, 29, 32; 45:17, 25). It thus follows that the geographic application of the term cannot be limited to any particular source.

Accordingly, the appellation "Canaan" derived from "Canaanite," could and did develop in several directions. It could refer to the inhabitants of Phoenicia, its townspeople and its traders (cf. Isa. 23:1–12); hence also, by extension, to dwellers in the maritime centers to the south and corresponding settlements in the Jordan Valley (Num. 13:29; Josh. 5:1). Alternatively,

"Canaanites" could designate the population of the onetime Egyptian province of Canaan, without regard to a particular district of the given ethnic element; for this broader sense cf., e.g., Genesis 12:6. Where rough subdivisions were desired, the account might read "Canaanites and Perizzites" (Gen. 13:7; 34:30; cf. Jud. 1:4, 5), or "the Hivites, the Canaanites, and the Hittites" (Exod. 23:28). This amounts to much the same thing as Semites and non-Semites in the modern sense. For purposes of further distinction we are given the standard lists of pre-Israelite nations, consisting of six, seven, or even ten (Gen. 15:19–20). In these detailed groupings the Canaanites revert to the sense of Phoenicians and their close relatives. It may be noted in passing that the Philistines are never included in such lists, for the sound historical reason that their date does not go back to pre-Israelite times. In other words, the lists may be stereotyped, but they rest on reliable traditions.

Where and how do Amorites fit into this picture? It will be recalled that this term, unlike "Canaanites," was in all probability ethnic in origin; that the extra-Biblical Amorites were at home to the east of Canaanite territory;[22] and that, as seen from still farther east, the Amorites were Western Semites in our sense. All these points have a bearing on the Biblical uses of the term.

One early account places individual Amorites at Mamre, or Hebron (Gen. 14:13); but the whole of the Promised Land could be described to Abraham as occupied by Amorites (Gen. 15:16). Elsewhere, five prominent Palestinian cities (Jerusalem, Hebron, Jarmuth, Lachish, and Eglon) are explicitly identified as Amorite (Josh. 10:5). On the other hand, Numbers 13:29 narrows down the usage as follows: "The Amalekites dwell in the land of the Negev; the Hittites, the Jebusites, and the Amorites dwell in the hill country; and the Canaanites dwell by the sea, and along the Jordan." Thus, in common with "Canaanite," the term "Amorite" was employed both generally and specifically. Where the two were contrasted, the former was applied to old and stable settlements along the coast, and the latter to the more fluid occupations in the inland mountain districts.

But it is the area east of the Jordan rift that was most consistently linked to Amorites. Between the Arnon and the Jabbok lay the kingdom of Sihon the Amorite which, back in the 13th century, impinged on Ammonite and Moabite territories (Num. 21:21–31; Jud. 11:19–22). Farther north stretched the Amorite kingdom of Og (Deut. 3:1–8; 4:47), which reached to Mt. Hermon. As applied to these two states, the Biblical term "Amorite" coincides with the southern sections of extra-Biblical "Amurru," which embraced, as we have seen, the area of Damascus and districts farther south.[23]

PART THREE: THE CULTURAL FACTOR

A. MESOPOTAMIA — EVOLUTION OF AN INTEGRATED CIVILIZATION

B. EGYPT — THE KINGDOM OF THE "TWO LANDS"

A. MESOPOTAMIA — EVOLUTION OF AN INTEGRATED CIVILIZATION

by E. A. Speiser

1. PRELUDE TO HISTORY

A. General Remarks

MESOPOTAMIA was a primary factor in the emergence of world history. Biblical origins, moreover, have close ties with Mesopotamia, some direct and others indirect. When the Patriarchs migrated to Palestine from the Central Euphrates valley, they could not but carry with them various social and cultural usages of their native land. Subsequent contacts played their part in reviving and maintaining the original ties. Aside from this direct process, there was also the intermediate route by which Mesopotamian influences reached Palestinian soil — in the normal chain reaction of cultural diffusion. It is thus in more ways than one that an understanding of the Mesopotamian civilization is basic to a full appreciation of the Biblical experience.

It should be stressed at the outset that what is involved here is a cultural and not a historical account. The story of a civilization, to be sure, is likewise history, but only in a strictly specialized sense. Political events and dynastic successions, the impact of personalities and the details of chronology — these and many similar features of overall history recede into the background when the main topic is a civilization as such. The hero of the story, so to speak, is not an individual, or a group of individuals, but society in quest of a way of life. In the case of Mesopotamia, this quest was to prove on the whole singularly successful at home and highly significant abroad. In some respects, however, the results turned out to be negative, to judge from the perspective afforded by some twenty-five centuries during which Mesopotamian civilization held sway. Indeed, these drawbacks may be viewed in retrospect as the essential, if not the sole, reasons for the ultimate decline of that civilization. By that time, however, Mesopotamian society had established a record of immensely fruitful achievement at home, and had contributed vital elements to several societies abroad, elements whose force has not worn off altogether in some notable instances to this very day. All in all, therefore, the Mesopotamian quest — which is the central topic of the present account — constitutes one of the truly pioneering experiences of mankind.[1]

B. Physical Environment

All history involves a human factor set against a specific physical background. A brief sketch of the Mesopotamian environment is hence in order at this point. As its classical name implies, Mesopotamia should be literally a land between rivers, in this instance the Euphrates and the Tigris.[1a] Actual usage, however, has seldom been in complete agreement with the etymology. On the one hand, the area is usually understood to have extended well beyond the inner valley, to the left of the Tigris and to the right of the Euphrates. And on the other hand, the term Mesopotamia is not applied to the upper reaches of the two rivers, in the recesses of the Armenian highlands. Since neither nature nor usage has here marked out clearly defined boundaries, it may suffice to posit, as a rough working definition, that the area of historic Mesopotamia coincides by and large with the extent of present-day Iraq.

The twin rivers which jointly constitute the dominant physical feature of the land have also been a primary factor in the historical career of Mesopotamia. The Euphrates finds itself within a hundred miles of the Mediterranean before a sharp change in its course takes it, in common with the Tigris, to the far more remote Persian Gulf. The valley becomes thus in effect a broad channel between the lands of the Eastern Mediterranean and the northwest reaches of the Indian Ocean; not merely a land between rivers but a link between continents. The northerly semicircle of mountains, moreover, stretching from Syria and Anatolia to Iran, sets up an automatic gravitation towards the heart of the valley. With the evolution of an agricultural economy, the celebrated fertility of the lowland basin became an added source of attraction, particularly in the silt-laden sector of Lower Mesopotamia.

The geological history of the Mesopotamian plains has recently been subjected to a fresh study, with wholly unexpected results.[2] It had been universally assumed that the area at the head of the Persian Gulf — including ancient Sumer — was the cumulative product of sedimentation left by the Euphrates, the Tigris, and the Kārūn. The land area, it was held, has been expanding steadily, although at a very slow pace, at the expense of the sea. We are now told, however, that the traditional view is both oversimplified and inaccurate. Not very long ago — as geological stages are reckoned — the reverse process may have taken place. Waters from the

Gulf appear to have submerged a large coastland area, to be driven back at length by the alluvium. It was essentially a question of balance between sedimentation and subsidence of the Gulf bottom. A sudden rise in the sea level could have precipitated enormous floods. In short, much older land, possibly supporting many settlements, may well lie buried beneath the relatively recent alluvial deposit.

It may be questioned, however, whether these new conclusions have a direct bearing on the present subject. The process involved cannot have been recent enough to make a substantial difference. At the dawn of history, geographic conditions in the valley appear to have been much the same as traditionally estimated. By that time, Lower Mesopotamia had already become an alluvial area, much of it transformed into marshland for months on end. The river beds were shallow and changeable. The land area was advancing, however imperceptibly, in an easterly direction. In the course of time, the twin rivers converged — or reunited, as the case may be — to be soon joined by a third stream, the Kārūn. The settlements that archaeology has uncovered lay all upstream, well to the west of the upper confluence. If their inhabitants ever had a tradition of worlds submerged, they neglected to transmit it in a manner that posterity could evaluate. It is conceivable, of course, that the several accounts of the Great Flood, as handed down to us by literature, may hark back to a catastrophic inundation of pre-alluvial lands. This is perhaps the most attractive vista that the new hypothesis has opened up. But the literary accounts in question now fall under the heading of legend, although they may yet turn out to be an actual echo of prehistory.

In any case, the immediate background of Lower Mesopotamia is alluvial. This circumstance was to affect the history of the land in several ways. Traceable human occupation of the lower valley is here more recent than in the higher portions, the relative antiquity of the settlements increasing as one draws closer to the highland zone. The respective areas — ancient Sumer in the one instance, and Akkad and Assyria in the other — differ, furthermore, in vegetation and in the ethnic and social characteristics of their populations. Above all, alluvial lands are notoriously deficient in mineral resources, thus necessitating imports of many vital materials. This affects in turn the overall economy and places a premium on international trade.

In summary, the Mesopotamian environment as a whole may be described as consistently catalytic. The land was open and accessible, a grand thoroughfare and a potent magnet in its own right. But it required unceasing activity, in channeling the energy of its turbulent streams and in far-flung trading enterprises. It was, in other words, an environment conducive to a dynamic civilization.

C. The Protohistoric Period

The conventional scheme of classifying man's remoter past, especially in preliterate times, is to name each stage after that material which was the chief source of its tools and weapons. In accordance with this technological yardstick, there was first the Old Stone or Paleolithic age, whose span is beyond computation. Then came the New Stone or Neolithic interval, relatively brief by comparison, yet varying in absolute length from region to region; in some areas it ended some 6000 years ago, whereas in others it survived several millenniums longer. The Neolithic period was followed by the hybrid Stone-Copper or Chalcolithic age, and this gave way in turn to Bronze and Iron, each with its several subdivisions.

Such a technological classification, however, can scarcely serve as a proper index to the nature of each given period. The criteria are superficial and generally non-distinctive. Iron, for instance, never succeeded in wholly eliminating stone or copper from daily use. The system, moreover, tends to emphasize external features at the expense of the inner content; a necessary evil, no doubt, when one deals with the oldest stages, but increasingly pointless as the later phases are reached. And although such a scheme may still have its uses in an archaeological account, it is of little merit in a comprehensive cultural outline.[3]

It was to be expected, therefore, that modern study would seek to develop a more pertinent scheme based on valid internal criteria.[4] The system that has recently gained favor starts out with the food-gathering stage, inevitably of very great length. This period was brought to a close at long last by the introduction of agriculture, which came with the discovery of the causal link between planting and growth, sowing and reaping.[5]

No continuous study of any given society can start farther back than the earliest traceable village settlements. Now the fullest evidence on that all-important juncture comes from the northern border areas of Mesopotamia, so that early Mesopotamian society furnishes today the clearest illustration of societal beginnings anywhere. The logical starting point is the agricultural revolution which underlies the first settlements. The next major juncture is the urban revolution, which coincides — as will be brought out in the next section — with the emergence of the historic age. The interval between these two major milestones, the agricultural and the urban, was the prelude to history, not only in time but also, and more particularly so, in substance;

it brought about the conditions without which history could not have set in. The natural designation for the interval between the two junctures is, accordingly, protohistory. In the present context, at any rate, such a designation would not seem to need any further explanation.

Why southwestern Asia in general, and parts of Mesopotamia in particular, should thus have been the home of the first known village settlements — if not indeed of the first such settlements ever known — remains uncertain. Our familiarity with the dawn of protohistory, or the transition from food-gathering to incipient agriculture, is as yet too recent to permit a confident answer to this question. It is quite possible, nevertheless, that the occurrence in this region of the wild ancestors of the principal cereals had been the decisive factor in locating here the unplanned laboratory that led eventually to the agricultural revolution. Any such suggestion, however, cannot for the present be much more than guesswork. But the whole subject is being studied intensively by competent specialists, and a positive answer may be forthcoming in the near future.[6]

It is noteworthy that the earliest village settlements are found not in the broad valleys but in the nearby hill country. This fact is surely not to be ascribed to mere coincidence. The late food-gatherers lived in caves. When these were abandoned for pioneer villages, the new centers would be founded close to the previous homes rather than far out in the flatlands. The move to the valleys was evidently a slow and gradual process, favored by the superior promise of the fertile plains but requiring, none the less, much adjustment to the new conditions. It is not surprising, therefore, that the first phase of Mesopotamian protohistory should be highlighted in the foothills of Kurdistan, to the east of the Tigris. The next phase spreads to the central valley, whereas the occupation of the alluvial area of Lower Mesopotamia does not take place on any large scale until the third and most advanced phase has been reached. All these developments follow a logical — one might even say predictable — order. What is far less apparent, and could by no means be called predictable, is the reason why history proper was to emerge particularly in Lower Mesopotamia. This complex problem will be investigated later on. Our immediate task is a brief outline of the pertinent data of Mesopotamian protohistory.

The overall picture that can now be pieced together is based on a mass of detail gathered from many sites and processed by various teams of archaeologists. The individual sites are so many stratified samples of successive occupations. Their deposits reflect sometimes a single culture in several progressive phases, and sometimes several distinctive cultures one after another. The same culture is often represented on a number of sites, so that occasional gaps in one can be filled in from the combined evidence from elsewhere. The total result is an orderly sequence, complete on nearly all major counts, which runs throughout the length of the protohistoric age, from the first appearance of the village communities to the rise of the urban centers. Innumerable stray pieces from a vast puzzle have gradually been rearranged in their proper pattern.

To be sure, Mesopotamia is not the only portion of southwestern Asia to shed light on the dramatic interlude between the agricultural and the urban revolutions. Nor is the testimony from each area substantially the same throughout, for interregional differences increase as time goes on. The Mesopotamian evidence, however, is the fullest that has yet been unearthed. What is far more important, it is in this area that history proper is first seen to emerge. The mainstream of human advance, so to speak, had been channeled temporarily through this sector. For an appreciable period of time, and at a highly significant juncture in human affairs, Mesopotamia is to occupy the center of the stage.

A comprehensive survey can only touch upon the highlights and must ignore many details. As regards chronology, round figures will have to suffice. In the present instance the period in question may be placed conservatively between 5000 and 3000 B.C.E. Thanks to the new technique of radioactive carbon dating, we are no longer limited to relative dates alone when it comes to deposits that are not within the range of written records. The lower limit of the protohistoric stage in Mesopotamia was established some three decades ago by working back from datable texts. The upper limit is our unexpected dividend from recent carbon readings. For the key site of Jarmo, which will be taken up presently, three carbon tests yield the average figure of ca. 4700 B.C.E. with a margin of error of ca. 350 years either way.[7] Allowing for a brief phase or two antecedent to Jarmo, we arrive thus at the round figure of 5000 B.C.E. as a reasonable starting time of the protohistoric interval.

The period itself can best be described in terms of several characteristic sites.[8] These include Jarmo, Hassuna, Gawra, and Halaf — all in the north — Samarra in the central part, and Obeid and Eridu in the south.[9] Some of these places, e.g., Halaf and Obeid, are so-called type sites; their remains furnished identifying "culture" labels for related finds from elsewhere. Other sites, notably Gawra, while not necessarily type sites,[10] are significant because of the overall bearing of their total evidence. Each is thus in one way or another a milestone along the main route of Mesopotamian protohistory.

At Jarmo, which is situated in the Kurdish hills between Kirkuk and Sulaimaniya, the lower levels cannot be very far in time from the earliest settlements in the wake of the agricultural revolution.[11] The houses are as yet of stamped clay — so-called *pisé* — a stage preceding moulded bricks. Pottery does not appear until the upper third of the deposit, the result of a vital discovery that had been made in the meantime on some other site at a comparable level of development. That the process of cultural diffusion had already set in is shown by another body of Jarmo finds: a considerable obsidian industry, the material for which had to be imported from great distances. Such trade could not but serve at the same time as a channel for cultural interchanges.

The next step on the protohistoric scale is reflected at Hassuna, a few miles to the south of Mosul.[12] The typical Hassuna ware from the lower levels has its analogues at various other sites, which proves that this culture had the capacity to expand. Still more significant is the fact that Hassuna witnesses for the first time the convergence and overlap of heterogeneous cultures. The upper strata yielded painted pottery of two distinct styles, one named after Samarra — north of Baghdad — and the other after Halaf, in the Khābūr valley. Both types were found in conjunction with the local Hassuna ware. The Samarra pottery is notable chiefly for its strikingly painted decoration, which tends to favor whirl-like movement.[13] The Halaf designs are often polychrome and the motifs include geometric patterns of great intricacy.[14] The Halaf ware, moreover, is unusually well fired, thanks to the use of a closed kiln and the resulting benefits of controlled temperatures.

Hassuna is thus the earliest known example of a cultural merging on a large scale. Samarran pottery[15] shows connections with the Iranian region to the east. The Halafian culture is no less notable for its contacts with the west.[16] In line with these expanding geographical horizons there is also marked progress in the content and refinements of daily living. Halafian architecture utilizes not only the rectilinear design but also the circular form, the so-called *tholos*.[17] Stone and sunbaked brick have replaced *pisé* as building materials. Religious growth is attested by the rising number of shrines, not to mention the apparent religio-magical bearing of some of the painted decorations and the all but ubiquitous amulets and "mother goddess" figurines. Stamp seals make their appearance, one of the earliest datable examples coming from a Halafian level at Gawra.[18]

Tepe Gawra, situated some fifteen miles north of Mosul, yielded a total of twenty-six occupational levels. All but the upper six (Levels VI-I) antedate the historical period, although only the first fourteen (XXVI-

XIII) are strictly protohistoric, the remainder (XII-VII) falling within the period of transition from protohistory to history.[19] In common with Hassuna, Gawra is a good example of cultural overlapping, this time one phase later. For in this instance the Halafian deposits do not link up with the previous stage, but shade off instead into the one that immediately followed, commonly known as Obeid. The prevailing eclecticism of the period is well illustrated in the lower Obeid levels at Gawra, where typical Obeid temples, which were to reappear at a later age (Gawra VIII), alternate with characteristic Halafian *tholoi*. And an intimate link between the north and the south is shown for the first time by the close correspondence of a temple in Gawra XIII with one at Eridu (VII), a major religious center of Lower Mesopotamia.[20]

The southern analogue just cited, backed, among other things, by corresponding parallels in pottery, is the first substantial proof we have that the south was now ready to play its part on the Mesopotamian stage. Whatever the underlying geological conditions may have been, the archaeological evidence before us is clear and unambiguous: the north had already passed through the Jarmo and Hassuna phases, and evidently also most of the Halaf stage, before the south could become a factor in its own right. This fact is of more than merely local significance, for it has a bearing in turn on our understanding of the urban revolution and the historic process which followed.

Meanwhile, however, the Obeid culture held sway over the largest area yet covered by any protohistoric phase. Its remains are encountered all the way from Iran to Syria. New heights are attained in the delicacy of the ceramic shapes and the artistic impact of their decoration. Religion stimulates the growth of architecture — as is strikingly demonstrated at Gawra and Eridu — and it enjoys in ever increasing measure the auxiliary services of painting, sculpture and seal-engraving. Copper has begun to figure as a medium for tools and weapons, and hence as a new factor in peace and war. Music, wrested from bone pipes, injects a new element into daily life.[21]

It follows, that the Obeid culture managed to overrun and supplant its various predecessors in Mesopotamia and the adjacent regions. Its original home appears to have been Iran, but this particular question is not material to our present inquiry. What matters is that a period of cultural symbiosis with the older cultures — as evidenced so strikingly at Gawra — preceded the Obeidian dominance over Mesopotamia. We cannot tell whether the attendant political changes were major or minor, peaceful or violent. Very likely, actual conditions varied considerably from place to place. The cultural results, in any event, point to basic cooperation and gradual evolution rather than sharp conflicts and sudden change. This is a pattern that is due to become typical of the subsequent career of Mesopotamia.

Thus far there have been many references to "cultures,"[22] but none whatever to people. Yet the residual impact of any society will remain faint at best unless some contact can be established with the underlying human element. Did the Halafian phase really originate on the very site that bears the present Arabic name by which the mound is known?[23] If so, who were its oldest inhabitants? What was their language, their social structure, their political organization? Similarly, did the Obeid culture with its unprecedented sweep over vast portions of southwestern Asia receive its initial impetus from the small site near Ur which goes by the modern and modest name of *Tell al-ʻUbayd* "The Mound of the Little Servant"? The relative chronology of the Obeid spread alone would be enough to refute such an assumption. Yet we keep on using "Obeidian" and "Obeidians" as though these variants were derived from the original term. We do so solely because protohistoric languages and peoples are beyond our direct reach, an unavoidable consequence of preliterate conditions.

This is not to assert that in dealing with the older cultures we are wholly restricted to their material products. Contemporary burials, for example, allow certain inferences as to the physical type or types involved. But this kind of evidence is as yet meager and far from conclusive. At best, it suggests that the basic population of the region belonged to the so-called Mediterranean type.[23a] Does this indicate that, say, the Hassunians and the Halafians and the Obeidians were all physically related? It is possible, of cuorse, but by no means certain. Let us grant, for the sake of argument, that the Obeid culture spread originally from Iran. This would not imply of itself that the bearers of that culture came to Mesopotamia in numbers large enough to alter the physical character of the local population, if there was any anthropometric difference to begin with. And with whom would we then identify the deviating minorities? Clearly, the skeletal material remains inarticulate in so far as the ethnic background of Mesopotamia is concerned.

Available human representations in several forms of art are even less conclusive on this score. The slender clay figurines from the south, with curiously stylized heads, may be compared with engraved figures on the stamp seals from Gawra and with some of the painted representations on the contemporary pottery.[24] If we allow that the artists had already gained sufficient mastery over their respective media to render their human subjects with reasonable accuracy — which is altogether probable — the most that we can derive from this source is a belief that the favorite models were all roughly of the same graceful type. This is hardly a basis for anthropometric correlations, not to mention ethnic or linguistic deductions.

Under these circumstances, there would seem to be only one field that offers some hope of tackling the problem with any prospect of success: the field of so-called linguistic paleontology. Starting with the earliest analyzable written data, one can attempt to separate the existing linguistic strands and, working back, to distinguish the native from the intrusive. For after contemporary borrowings have been ascertained and discarded, one is left with an older residue which has to be ascribed to the linguistic substratum — always granted that such a substratum could be presupposed.

The oldest written documents from Mesopotamia are composed in the Sumerian language. They soon come to include sundry loan-words from the Akkadian, the eventual dominant speech of Mesopotamia. Occasional intrusions from other known, or partially known tongues, such as West Semitic, Hurrian, and Elamite, can likewise be recognized if and when they occur. When all such material has been eliminated, we are still left with a substantial amount of linguistic matter that falls into no known classification. Some of this residue, moreover, points back to a time prior to the earliest written records, as will be presently shown. This, then, is the residue that can be assigned to one or more of the protohistoric populations of the land. If the effort has been successful, the substratum or substrata, as the case might be, will turn out to be not only non-Sumerian but necessarily also pre-Sumerian.

More than a quarter of a century ago the present writer used the approach just described to isolate a considerable body of place names. These names comprise some of the oldest and best known centers of Sumer, among them Uruk, Ur(im), Kish, Shuruppak, Lagash, and the like.[25] They include also, it may be added, the two main rivers, *Purattu* (Euphrates) and *Idiqlat/Ḫiddeqel* (Tigris). In none of these terms is there anything resembling Sumerian elements and structure. And the places and rivers which they designate have precisely the prominence that would safeguard their traditional forms from replacement in the wake of ethnic or political changes.

Since then, an independent study has demonstrated, with marked insight and originality, the strong likelihood of a linguistic substratum within Sumerian itself, as distinct from mere geographic terms found in the land of Sumer.[26] The results are particularly significant in terms of the principal professions and occupations. The basic vocabulary for such classes as farmer, gardener, shepherd, cook, weaver, smith, and carpenter, among others, is credited to the pre-Sumerians. To the Sumerians, on the other hand, have been traced many of the terms applied to sailing, jewelry, sculpture, glyptics, land measurement, writing, education, and law. If these conclusions stand up — and they bid fair to do so in a great majority of the instances cited — Mesopotamian scholarship should have at its disposal an extremely valuable new tool. Aside from shedding further light on the immediate ethnic and linguistic problems, this method and its results will have furnished a new insight into underlying social and economic conditions, by uncovering the skills which the newcomers brought with them as against the crafts that had been developed by the natives.

In passing, we may cite one pair of examples in order to show concretely how far-reaching the implications can be. The terms *nangar* "carpenter" and *guza* "chair" have long been familiar from old Sumerian texts. Both can now be assigned to the protohistoric period with excellent reason, in that they fail to follow the established linguistic norms of Sumerian. In other words, these two terms go back to an older stage, one that had produced, as we have seen, a high material culture in which carpentry must have played a prominent part. The Sumerians appear to have taken over from their predecessors not only the handicraft itself but also, as so often happens in such cases, the pertinent terminology. The Akkadians, for their part, borrowed the same pair of words from the Sumerian as *naggāru* and *kussû* respectively; other Semitic languages, including Hebrew, acquired them in turn from the Akkadians (in Hebrew: *naggār*, *kissē'*). It would be difficult indeed to find more telling proof of the vitality and continuity of a civilization which has thus persisted in some instances since remote protohistoric times down to our own day, and has influenced in the course of its long career not just the successive populations of Mesopotamia but much of the rest of the Near East as well.[27] In some respects, moreover, that influence was to extend, as we shall see, beyond the limits of southwestern Asia into Europe and Western Civilization.

D. Transition

The Protohistoric period, as defined and described in the preceding section, was the interval between two major revolutions, the agricultural and the urban. Fundamental changes which came about with the advent of agriculture are immediately apparent. The emergence of the city, on the other hand, is not equally obvious as a revolutionary factor in human progress. Nor was the process of a kind that was bound to take place independently in several regions at the same time. The transformation required a number of favoring circumstances. Once it had been achieved, however, in a given area, it would normally be expected to spread to neighboring regions and thus signal the dawn of a new era. Since this achievement can be seen unfolding in Lower Mesopotamia, and since all indications point to its actual origin in that part of the world, a closer glance at the facts and conditions involved is now in order.

The use of the term "revolution" in this connection should not be taken to imply sudden change. Rural communities cannot be transformed overnight into urban-dominated societies, particularly when such a step happens to be a pioneering venture in the advance of mankind. The transition requires time, no matter how startling it may appear to be in retrospect. In the present instance, the critical interlude in question, as manifested in Lower Mesopotamia, extends from the end of the Obeid phase to the beginning of the Early Dynastic period — the first historical stage to be documented by written records. Archaeologically, the whole amounts to a series of stratified occupations in depth and several centuries in time.

The current name for this interlude is the "Protoliterate Period."[28] Yet this is much like placing the cart before the horse. To be sure, writing is an absolute prerequisite for history. Its introduction, however, was not the sort of event that could be readily anticipated. Besides, literacy is but one of a number of significant factors in the whole process. For these and other reasons it would seem to be least prejudicial, and at the same time more truly descriptive, to designate this juncture simply as one of "Transition."

Perhaps the simplest way to gain an insight into this "hinge of history" is to contrast conditions before and after. By the end of the Obeid period we are already confronted with a many-sided economy. Although agriculture, with emmer wheat and barley as the principal crops and the sickle as the main tool, was the dominant pursuit, other occupations had also attained great prominence in the meantime. Stock-breeding had come into its own, the production of textiles was progressing steadily, and new skills had been developed in the manufacture of a great variety of stone objects. The potter's craft, aided by the invention of the wheel, had been raised to great heights of technical and artistic proficiency. Architecture, which could now operate with systematically fashioned bricks, showed imagination in design and a progressive mastery of functional and decorative detail. Metallurgy was gradually overtaking the traditional stone industry. Finally, trade had been a far from negligible factor ever since the inchoate Jarmo phase.

Yet all the settlements known to us from the several pertinent sequences[29] were essentially village centers. Their economy and social structure were strictly on a rural scale. The only field in which a higher level of organization and cooperation has been brought to light is that of religion, for a group of temples such as that at Gawra XIII can be understood only as a central acropolis serving the needs of a number of villages.[30] Yet even in this instance the community of interests that can be inferred would seem to have been rather loose and one-sided.

With the beginning of the Early Dynastic period, on the other hand, the picture changes considerably. There is an immediately noticeable difference in the size of settlements and public buildings such as temples. Agriculture is now a joint communal enterprise which calls for constant tending of its elaborate irrigation networks. Metallurgy, as a means of obtaining any desired shape by smelting and recasting the ores, had long supplanted stone as the vital source of tools and weapons. It had also placed a premium on international trade — for the all-important mines were widely scattered — thus greatly increasing the radius and complexity of the essential caravan routes. All this called for efficient organization and management, the heart of the system being the temple. A complicated legal machinery had to be evolved to regulate the expanding social and economic structure. Stamp seals had given way to cylinder seals which served as a means of personal as well as group attestation. Above all, transactions and events could now be recorded in writing, a medium of enormous potential, yet one that required at the same time a vast degree of application and ingenuity. Writing, in turn, stimulated progress in other forms of intellectual and scientific endeavor.[31]

It will be seen at a glance that the changes involved were not only quantitative but also, and more especially, qualitative. The new age differed from the Obeid phase at its best not so much in the size of the component units as in the content and orientation of the respective societies. It was, in a word, historic as opposed to prehistoric; not alone because the present could now leave an articulate record for posterity, but also because its own awareness of what was happening had meanwhile undergone a profound change. Man had become conscious of the fact that the present was but a link between the past and the future. In sum, historic civilization had at last arrived in the wake of a series of protohistoric cultures.

Since the introduction of history in Lower Mesopotamia marks at the same time man's first experience of that process anywhere, it is only natural that we should wish to go beyond the mere statement that the event had taken place. One is bound to wonder how this was accomplished, and why, and by whom. Unfortunately, there is not much that one can do about it, other than to wonder and speculate. To be sure, we have before us an impressive body of pertinent material, and the amount is growing all the time. It is, however, one of the corollaries of the protohistoric period that it is, by definition, preliterate. Hence the human element behind it remains anonymous and for our purposes largely inarticulate. What has come down to us may be rearranged into more than one pattern. No one is in a position to assert with complete confidence that he has found the final answer to the puzzle. The ultimate test in these circumstances must be the familiar test of any working hypothesis: how many of the basic questions entailed does the same single answer succeed in solving? The whole issue thus resolves itself into a choice of probabilities.

It is clear, at any rate, that the decisive changes which brought on the historic age are first witnessed in the course of the transitional interlude. They all take place in the south, to spread gradually to what came to be known later as Northern Babylonia and Assyria. Among the major centers of that time which have been unearthed to date are Uruk and Ur in the far south, Kish and Jemdet Naser further up the valley, and some sites in the Diyālā region, so named after one of the main tributaries of the Tigris. The most important specific changes may be listed as follows:

In pottery, the Obeid ware with its typical monochrome decoration had disappeared. In its place we find first the highly burnished but otherwise undecorated Uruk ware, and later on the Jemdet Naser type of pottery with distinctive polychrome designs. It should be stressed in this connection that the break in continuity which is implicit in these ceramic developments in the south is either wholly absent farther north or else barely perceptible. In old centers like Gawra, e.g., painted designs continue in fashion together with some of the inherited motifs.

In architecture, the prevailing temple design can be traced back to the protohistoric shrines at Eridu, which in turn link up with one of the styles featured at Gawra.[32] The south had made its selection: it adopted neither the Halafian *tholos* nor the "long-room" design — which is found as early as Gawra XVII, not to mention Gawra VIII and the historic Assyrian style[33] — but picked instead the "broad-room" scheme once and for all. Something new, however, has been added. Every major temple is now erected not on level ground but on an artificial elevation of varying height,[34] chiefly the *ziggurrat*[35] of the written sources. The form of the temple itself is thus one that had long been familiar in the land. But the underlying concept is altogether different, as will be shown later in the section on Mesopotamian religion.[36]

In art, the outstanding innovation is the cylinder seal, as has already been indicated. Stamp seals had been in use since the remote Halafian age, and they were not to be given up altogether in other regions of the Near East. In Lower Mesopotamia, however, beginning with the transitional period, the cylinder alone is encountered, to spread from there to other sections of the land and to many outlying regions — an advance emissary, so to speak, of the expanding Mesopotamian civilization. It is more than coincidence, therefore, that the eventual decline of this civilization, in the first millennium B.C.E., brings with it the return of the long-displaced stamp seal. The cylinder is thus a matchless witness of both the length and the reach of the historic civilization of Mesopotamia.

Of far deeper significance, however, not only locally but to mankind as a whole, is the appearance of writing.[37] The reasons for viewing the advent of writing as a truly epochal development are not far to seek. Writing did more than make history; it made history possible. It transformed the oral statement into a lasting and fully articulate record. The immediate results, it is true, seem relatively modest: economic transactions have the benefit of added precision and security, being now protected from the failings of human memory. But more substantial and expansive dividends are soon to follow. Writing is aimed primarily at the future. It is not surprising, therefore, that in due time rulers address themselves to coming generations with reports and promises, pleas and warnings.[38] For its part, posterity is placed in a position to reconstruct and evaluate the experience of the past on an ever increasing scale. As a means of communication writing has never been matched and is never likely to be. Modern inventions have conquered space; writing conquered time.

The advent of this revolutionary medium, however, does not tell us of itself how this fact was accomplished. Nor are we as yet in a position to retrace the antecedent steps in every detail with sufficient confidence. Some points are clear, but others leave room for speculation. At all events, it has long seemed to the present writer that the total available evidence adds up to an intelligible and self-consistent pattern.[39] Perhaps the most valuable lead of all is the inherent probability of an intimate connection between writing and the cylinder seal. Engraved with a variety of designs, the cylinders were used as distinctive markers of their respective owners. This custom, in turn, was but a specialized extension of an old and widespread usage whereby detachable parts of a person, or sundry items of his dress, could be employed as valid substitutes for the whole person.[40] In their turn, given designs on seals came to stand for temples, cities, gods, and the like, all for purposes of identification; in other words, the designs acquired the function of graphs. The process was gradually extended to represent humans, animals, plants, and objects in general.

The next step was perhaps the most important of all: aside from suggesting a specific being or object, the graph stood also for the underlying word. The symbol for "star," for example, suggested "sky" and "sky-god," and was given whatever sound the respective word had in the language in question. The gap between symbol and sound had thus been bridged. A significant further step was to divorce altogether the symbol from its underlying picture, by using signs not only for concrete words but also for abstract syllables that happened to sound alike (homophones), much in the manner of our rebus. Say that the word for "arrow" was *ti*. An arrow was easy to draw and the drawing would be read *ti*. Suppose, however, that in the same language "life" was also *ti*. But how is one to draw "life"? Our pioneers solved the problem — for these examples are taken from actual use — by sketching the symbol for arrow, which would be sounded *ti*, but could not be mistaken in the context for anything other than the homonymous term for "life." Eventually, special means were devised — the so-called determinatives — for designating such categories as personal names, cities, deities, and the like, so as to guard against ambiguities and facilitate the handling of what was after all a highly complicated code. It required several centuries before the new medium could achieve sufficient flexibility to handle all manner of texts with relative freedom.[41]

It should be clear in retrospect that writing was by no means the result of a conscious and preconceived plan — a brilliant projection of some nameless benefactor of mankind. It was rather the unexpected byproduct of a combination of peculiar circumstances. One cannot foresee the uses of such a medium until it is actually at hand. The process had to be well on its way before man was first able to sense its potential. But once that understanding had dawned, the idea — if not the precise form — would quickly spread to other advanced regions which maintained contact with the originating center. All the evidence we possess points to just such a process of dissemination at about the turn of the fourth millennium.[42] At that, more than a millennium was to elapse before the invention of the alphabet, this time somewhere along the eastern shores of the Mediterranean.

According to the view here advocated, the home of the first script — its original and sole source — was Mesopotamia, more specifically Lower Mesopotamia. Only there is the cylinder seal fully established at the time in question. It can scarcely be mere coincidence that a number of the symbols known from the earliest written tablets available — those from Uruk — recur on contemporary cylinder seals. Equally significant perhaps is the abiding need for personal identification by means of these seals which is a constant feature of Mesopotamian society from earliest times on, a need made clear, e.g., by such widely differing sources as the Laws of Eshnunna and the account of Herodotus. This custom was a factor, as we have seen, in bridging the gap between picture and sound, through the link between designs and names. In addition, nearly the entire process of the evolution of writing is attested for us by stratified evidence: plain cylinders with no designs upon them; carved seals covered with representational symbols; clay tablets with many of the same symbols appearing as words; the gradual simplification of the signs and their reduction in number; the interchange of homophones which led to a syllabic orthography; the determinatives and phonetic supplements; and lastly, the emergence of a full-fledged system.[43]

The only other scripts of comparable antiquity are those of Elam and of Egypt. The proto-Elamite writing is much too scantily attested, and consequently obscure, for proper evaluation. On the surface it shows some tangible similarities with the early Mesopotamian forms. Since the two lands were neighbors and in close contact with each other, there is the inherent probability that their respective scripts were genetically related. But it is most unlikely that their common home should be sought in Elam. For one thing, the local variety enjoyed little success and was soon superseded by its western analogue. For another, there can be little doubt, as will be pointed out presently, that the Mesopotamian writing was originally designed for the use of Sumerian, so that monogenesis in this instance would imply borrowing from, and not by, Mesopotamia. In that event, what was borrowed was the basic idea rather than the detailed system.[44]

The problem posed by Egyptian writing is at once more challenging, important, and complex. The outstanding facts are that the Egyptian system is similar in structure to the Mesopotamian, but differs from it in the form of the signs. It is highly significant in this connection that Egypt's material culture and society lacked the very ingredients that proved to be factors in the development of writing in Lower Mesopotamia. Nor is the Egyptian system, as we know it, ushered in by a chain of evolutionary steps; it confronts us instead virtually full-grown.[45] All this would seem to add up to strong presumptive evidence that the basic idea of writing was carried to Egypt from Mesopotamia, particularly since actual contacts between the two respective civilizations are independently attested for the very period under discussion.[46] For the implementation of this idea Egypt would then have resorted to indigenous artistic forms. The alternative would be to assume that both Egypt and Mesopotamia enjoyed for some two thousand years parallel progress at a high cultural level but without any sign of literacy; and that each center suddenly evolved independent scripts at almost exactly the same time, yet with many striking and intricate similarities. It is difficult indeed to accept so much sustained coincidence, difficult, that is, for all practical purposes.

There remains then the perplexing question as to the ultimate authorship of the pioneering system of writing. On this score the evidence is still fragmentary and tenuous. Yet even in this instance some suggestive details are at hand. To the present writer, in any case, the following hypothesis[47] has long seemed to yield the most consistent results. Nothing that has turned up in the meantime, either in the field or in the technical literature on the subject, appears to have undermined this view. On the contrary, additional material has lent it further strength and won for it new adherents. Nevertheless, it is only fair and prudent to restate it here with all due reservations.

Although the oldest texts have been read only in part, there can be little doubt that their language is Sumerian. They contain well-known Sumerian terms and introduce unmistakably Sumerian deities. Moreover, there is not the slightest indication that this early writing was only being reused by the Sumerians after it had been designed originally for some other language. Secondhand employment of this kind cannot but leave tangible traces of the previous user, to judge from such pertinent parallels as the Akkadian, Hittite, and Greek systems. Nothing of this nature is apparent in the primitive tablets from Uruk and elsewhere.

It was observed earlier that linguistic paleontology points to the presence in Mesopotamia, in the period which we have defined as transitional, of two distinct linguistic elements, one Sumerian and the other pre-Sumerian. Names of principal places and of the two main rivers were shown to be pre-Sumerian. On the other hand, the terms for significant professions and occupations proved to derive from both sources. Among the Sumerian terms, however, were those which refer to writing and glyptics. This need not be important in itself, let alone conclusive. Yet in conjunction with the other evidence — the Sumerian language of the oldest texts; the relation between written symbols and designs on the cylinder seals; the other innovations of the transitional age; the gradual evolution of writing within that age — the whole adds up to two justified assumptions: (1) that the Sumerians arrived in Lower Mesopotamia in the course of the period under review; and (2) that it had to be the Sumerians who were the main factor behind the discovery of writing. With this as a start, it is now proper to make one further deduction: since the assured Sumerian culture terms include the basic vocabulary for sailing, education, and law, and since these pursuits are prominent in the land from the beginning of recorded history, it is reasonable to credit their development to Sumerian initiative. Conceivably, too, the adeptness of the Sumerians at sailing might have a bearing on the route by which they had arrived at the head of the Persian Gulf. For we shall see presently that the usual thesis of an overland route poses certain difficulties.

It would thus follow that on arriving in Lower Mesopotamia the Sumerians entered into close cultural contacts with the native population. They took over much that had been previously accomplished; but beyond that they contributed significant innovations of their own. The question is whether there are any physical indications, as distinct from cultural, to suggest independently a mixture of populations — granted, of course, that the respective types differed physically from the start. To this there is as yet no clear-cut answer. Once again, therefore, we are reduced to probabilities.

The skeletal evidence from the Obeid burials, which is prior to the transitional phase, shows as we have seen that the dominant physical type in most of southwestern Asia was at that time the so-called Mediterranean.[48] The later testimony of the early historical levels continues to reflect a preponderance of Mediterraneans, a notably longheaded group. But this result happens to be in sharp conflict with the evidence of the Sumerian sculptures which would seem to place that people in the roundheaded class — always allowing that the artists had rendered such details with sufficient verisimilitude. Yet the large number of sculptures featuring a brachycephalic type — many of them of high merit — should dispose us to believe that the representations were by and large dependable. We are led, accordingly, to the conclusion that, following the arrival of the Sumerians, the roundheaded newcomers contrasted with the longheaded natives. It also follows, however, that the intrusive Sumerians were not numerous enough to alter significantly the anthropometric situation as a whole. Nevertheless, their increasing political and social prominence could not but result in the predominance of roundheads among the sculptured portraits, for it would be precisely the leading class in the population who made up the bulk of the artists' subjects. No other explanation accounts so uniformly for the difference between the representational and the skeletal remains.[49]

In line with the argument just presented is one further bit of independent evidence. The human type of the Obeid period, as reflected — however broadly — on the stamp seals, in clay figurines, and in painted pottery designs, would appear on the whole to have been graceful and slender.[50] On the other hand, the demonstrably Sumerian sculptures of the early historical age point to a squat and heavy-set type. Once again, then, a distinction is indicated between the indigenous population and the newcomers.

We come, lastly, to an argument of yet another sort. One could call it an argument from location and survival. The Obeid culture is known to have covered vast areas extending from the Indian Ocean to the Mediterranean. If the Sumerians were indeed Obeiders, then we should have to posit, first, a drastic shrinkage of their one-time territory and reduction of their holdings to a small sector at the head of the Persian Gulf, to be followed centuries later by a political resurgence of the Sumerians and reconquest of much of their old realm. And second, all the other known occupants of the original Obeid domain — the Elamites, the Gutians, the Lullu, the Hurrians, and the various Semitic groups — would have to be viewed as intruders. Moreover, the separate indications of a pre-Sumerian linguistic substratum would have to be completely ignored. Yet where the Obeid culture can be studied in depth, as at Gawra, there is nothing about it that could be construed as a forerunner of the Sumerian civilization. Native forms continue there without an appreciable break. And the local languages live on, e.g., Hurrian through its Urartian relative of the first millennium B.C.E., and Elamite in a direct line of descent down to the tenth century C.E. Sumerian alone remains entirely isolated. Furthermore, when the historic Sumerian civilization has definitely penetrated the north, the contrast between it and the antecedent cultures is sharp and clear. None of these problems, however, need arise once it has been posited that the Sumerians arrived in post-Obeid times, probably by sea,[51] to settle initially in Lower Mesopotamia, thus setting in motion a chain of events which in due time led up to history.

Just what qualities the Sumerians may have possessed to make them such an outstanding catalytic factor is next to impossible to determine. Their society, at any rate, was adaptable and eclectic to a high degree, distinctive in its total character but incorporating many borrowed features alongside their own. Sumerian architecture, for example, is a modification of a local style, one of several encountered in Mesopotamia in protohistoric times. The indigenous crafts flourish after the arrival of the newcomers. Nothing new in the field of pottery can be ascribed with confidence to the Sumerians. On the other hand, the transitional age and its successors are distinguished by such new features as the ziggurat, the cylinder seal, writing, various new skills, and the rise of urban centers and an urban economy. Normal processes of evolution might be credited perhaps with some of these changes, but hardly with all of them.

It may well have been this ability of the Sumerians to select and blend diverse cultural products that had much to do with the dawning of a truly new era. For thereafter the accent is clearly on cultural cooperation as opposed to isolation and exclusiveness. The Sumerians appear to have been predisposed to such a course. Indeed, if language may be said to mirror in some ways the temperament of its originators, the language of the Sumerians would tend to reflect a soberly methodical approach to things; for it is an unusually orderly and neatly balanced instrument in which very little is left to chance. Correspondingly, the Sumerians themselves could aptly be described as a nation of bookkeepers. Very likely, there were other significant features about the Sumerians which are too elusive for later ages to apprehend. The safest approach to any advanced society of the past is through its religion and government rather than through material achievements. In retrospect, it is religion and government that emerge as the true core of the historic civilization of Mesopotamia. The Sumerians must have had a prominent share in both. But the exact details remain unknown, and probably will never be known. Today we are immeasurably closer to an understanding of the critical interlude in human affairs which resulted in the dawn of history than was thought possible a few decades ago. Yet much of that vital process still remains essentially a mystery.

2. THE HISTORICAL FRAMEWORK

A. Echoes in Myths and Legends

ALTHOUGH political history is not the main concern of the present account, its salient features need to be sketched here in broad outline, as a general setting for the cultural events. Only the major themes can be indicated; none can be developed in full. The recorded history of Mesopotamia covers some two millenniums, and literary echoes of protohistoric happenings increase this total by several centuries. Primary historical sources — original inscriptions, chronicles, annals — are at first few and fragmentary, but they soon hit their stride until, by the first millennium B.C.E., they swell to formidable proportions. Secondary material — building records, administrative and economic accounts, letters, legends, omens, and the like — make up another vast collection.[1] Peripheral areas, such as Elam, Mari, Syria, and Anatolia, have added their share of sources, an increase that can be disconcerting as well as welcome. In these circumstances, an adequate statement of the main facts of Mesopotamian history would require today a series of volumes. The present survey has to content itself with a single chapter. Each section thus has to take the place of a monograph already available; or, in more than one instance, it has to anticipate a book or an article yet to be written.

Direct historical material begins to appear by the middle of the third millennium, even by the lowest possible chronology.[2] The principal sources consist of inscriptions of the First Dynasty of Ur and the early princes of Lagash. We possess, however, other indirect epigraphic evidence which bears on still earlier times. It is imbedded in various myths and legends, or reflected in a historiographic work known as the Sumerian King List.[3] Such sources, of course, can be utilized only with the greatest caution, yet they should not be ignored outright. In this particular instance, the records are composed in Sumerian and offer thus no more than given Sumerian beliefs and speculations in regard to the remote past. In the hands of the Akkadians or the Hurrians, for example, the same pastime would produce different slants, as we know from actual samples; and the opening chapters of Genesis furnish yet another example of the same approach — a blend of native and borrowed motifs molded according to the local pattern. No such reconstruction, however, can be safely discarded; least of all the Sumerian version, which deals, to be sure, with the early history of Mesopotamia, but affects incidentally the dawn of world history as well.

On this basis, then, we obtain for the oldest stage a series of primeval kings who ruled a succession of city states before the Great Flood. Like their Biblical counterparts, but to a far greater degree, these Mesopotamian rulers were credited with reigns of fabulous length. Following the Flood, the first world capital was the city of Kish. Next came Uruk, a center celebrated both for its heroes and its shrines. Recent archaeological dis coveries bear eloquent testimony to the fact that the enduring fame of Uruk — the Erech of the Bible — rested indeed on very solid foundations.

The outstanding figure of the First Dynasty of Kish was Etana,[4] whom the King List describes, in one of its rare annotations, as a shepherd who "consolidated all the lands."[5] To later Mesopotamian ages, and through them to our own image of the past, Etana was to become the hero of a highly spectacular tale. Yet the atypical gloss in the King List, and the preamble to the epic itself — which will concern us in a later chapter[6] — combine to suggest that this hero owed his place in the legend to some memorable achievement in reality.

For its part, the First Dynasty of Uruk can boast several figures who merited special glosses in the King List. They are all grouped together and appear thus to represent the same general and evidently significant period. The group comprises Mes-kiag-gasher, Enmerkar, Lugal-banda, Dumuzi (Tamuz), and Gilgamesh.[7] The first of these is singled out for some unspecified exploits at sea, a tantalizing hint in view of the previously mentioned probability that the Sumerians came to Lower Mesopotamia by the sea route. The others are all principals in their own cycles of epics and legends, the most famous of which by far is the Akkadian Epic of Gilgamesh. Enmerkar, moreover, is credited with the building of the city of Uruk. Since that city is known to go back to protohistoric times, this statement — if at all valid — must refer to the establishment of Uruk's political might.

At all events, it would now be sheer recklessness to assert that all such indications are beyond historical salvage. The Gilgamesh Epic, to be sure, is in its Akkadian formulation a work of great literature pure and simple, perhaps one of the greatest of all time.[8] Yet its raw material was taken over from a whole series of Sumerian compositions. Their very variety and prominence would tend to show that the central figure had once been real eonugh, and that it was the magnitude of his exploits in the first instance that made of him eventually an outstanding favorite of legend. For actual proof that such things could happen we need look no farther than the example of Sargon of Akkad, who became a hero of fiction precisely because he was one of the giants of history.

To come back to Gilgamesh, there is one particular poem about him which may serve as a good case in point. This composition, which is significant also on other counts, as we shall stress in describing the Mesopotamian concept of government, dwells on the serious conflict between Gilgamesh and Agga,[9] the rival ruler of Kish, who is likewise included in the King List. Since this is strictly a secular piece, it is all the more likely to contain a historical kernel. The poem, then, would seem to hark back to some factual event of more than passing importance. When it is recalled that the Gilgamesh of the King List is the last of five rulers of the First Dynasty of Uruk to be given special mention in an otherwise bare enumeration, it becomes clear that this must have been an exceptionally eventful age. Apparently, Uruk had emerged as a serious challenger to the supremacy of Kish. For some time the issue must have remained in the balance. The contest between Gilgamesh and Agga brought matters to a head. The outcome cannot be judged from the poem before us, but it is implicit in the statement of the King List that kingship passed from Kish to Uruk.

In the light of the foregoing argument, we may hazard one further suggestion. All the kings of the First Dynasty of Uruk bear good Sumerian names.[10] Those of early Kish, on the other hand, appear mixed in origin, some of the names being Semitic, some Sumerian, and the remainder obscure. If it is granted that the Sumerians were relatively late arrivals in Lower Mesopotamia and needed time to consolidate their position, then the contest between Agga and Gilgamesh acquires a fresh perspective. Kish had made itself the master of a large area in which native elements mingled freely with the newcomers. In Uruk, on the other hand, it was the Sumerians who had emerged as the dominant element. Uruk's victory over Kish would thus mark not just the emergence of still another city but, beyond and above that, the establishment of Sumerian supremacy in the area as a whole. An event of such magnitude would surely have carried enough impact to account for the unique place of Gilgamesh in the cultural pattern of Mesopotamia, an accomplishment that owed so much to Sumerian leadership and initiative.

B. The Early Dynastic Period

The next and now unmistakably historic phase is known as the Early Dynastic. Its best written witnesses come from Ur and Lagash, although the prestige of the older centers has not worn off by any means. Political and social activities are centered about a number of autonomous cities, with one or another of these moving temporarily to the fore. The shifting fortunes of the various city states can now be followed for the first time in substantial detail. The cloak of anonymity has lifted. We know by name the cities and their gods, the kings and the temples, the allies and the opponents. And we get also from the written sources concrete data on the economy of the land, which can then be checked and supplemented with the help of material finds — one of our dividends from the numerous archaeological campaigns that bear on this period.

For a span of some two centuries the limelight rests on the two rival city states of Lagash and Umma. In part, to be sure, this is due to the accidents of discovery: the Lagash records for that time happen to be unusually explicit and detailed. Yet even on an absolute basis one would have to view Lagash and Umma as prominent and representative centers. The former was in many ways the political extension of Kish, and the latter seems to have had an analogous relation to Uruk. The pattern set by the previous phase is thus continued by and large, although new centers must also be reckoned with, notably Ur. The dominant note, however, in a cultural as well as a socio-political sense, is one of underlying continuity.

We have a particular wealth of detail about the contemporary dynasty of Lagash. Founded by Ur-Nanshe, it reached the peak of its achievement under Eannatum I and Entemena. The combined evidence affords a balanced picture of political developments and socio-economic conditions. Outstanding works of art throw added light on the progress and prosperity experienced under that dynasty. And a note of intimacy is lent by a relief which portrays the members of Ur-Nanshe's family, each clearly identified by name. History had become fully articulate in the course of a few centuries.

Yet the traditional challenge of Umma could never be held in check for long stretches of time. It runs through the whole of the Early Dynastic age as a recurring refrain; and in the end it leads to the emergence of Umma as a focal center in all of Sumer. By then Lagash had come to be ruled by one Urukagina, who was deeply concerned about social and legal reforms aimed at curbing the oppressive power of the priests and officials.[11] The local tensions at Lagash were just the opportunity for which Lugalzagesi, the king of Umma, had been waiting. The victory which he scored over Lagash was for him the first in a series of resolute steps that soon made him the most formidable power in Sumer. To underscore the extent of his success, Lugalzagesi transferred his capital, significantly enough, to the ancient dynastic center of Uruk.

This bold move was bound to revive the major regional rivalries within the country as a whole. The prestige of Kish was once again at stake. And, as happens so often in times of grave crises, a great challenge produced a fitting leader. The cause of Kish was taken up by a protagonist whose fame was to exceed even that of the now legendary Gilgamesh, and was to produce in turn a brand new cycle of legends. The man of the moment was Sargon of Akkad. His epochal achievements properly mark a new era in the history of Mesopotamia.

In passing, a brief comment is in order on the non-political aspects of the Early Dynastic period. As was indicated above, our written evidence is supplemented by a flow of material remains from various sites. Included among these centers, in addition to Ur and Lagash, are such cities as Nippur, whose chief god Enlil had become the head of the Sumerian pantheon; and the orbit of Sumerian civilization is extended to the Diyālā area, where the sites of Eshnunna (modern Tell Asmar) and Tutub (modern Khafajah), among others, have furnished a rich yield in architecture, sculpture, metal objects, pottery, and glyptics. Good organization and provident planning had enabled the Sumerian city states to raise their standard of living from a level of subsistence to one of occasional luxury. Although the economy was carefully regulated, ample scope was left for private enterprise. The craftsmen had made notable strides in the production of textiles, and they were unexcelled in the manufacture of jewellery and various metal objects. Production, after coping with the local demands, left substantial surpluses for export, in manufactured goods and such foodstuffs as grain and dates. These were traded for precious and base metals, stones, woods, and spices.[12]

Mesopotamian society had thus found a working solution to one of the two major problems that all civilizations must face and solve: the problem of insuring, through industry and administration, a more abundant life. It still lacked, however, an effective answer to another and no less urgent problem, one which concerns the relation of society to nature. A desperate attempt to fill this need may be reflected in the burial rites to which the "royal" tombs of Ur bear such impressive and awesome testimony. In a heroic but futile effort to achieve a harmonious balance between society and nature, the enormous treasure and the human hopes that were sacrificed in the mass burial pits at Ur — on behalf of a better life — only served to add to the cruel toll of death.

C. The Akkad Period

The abrupt termination of Lugalzagesi's meteoric career[13] put an end also to Uruk's current hopes of reviving its ancient glories. In conformance with a pattern by now some five centuries old, it was to be expected that the victorious opposition should be focused on Kish. The basic alignments had not changed, evidently, since the semi-legendary times of Gilgamesh and Agga. Yet a fundamental transformation was under way nevertheless. A long era was coming to a close at long last, and a new age was about to set in.

In a shift of such magnitude, the decisive events were likely to be of corresponding proportions. From our present vantage-point — at a distance of more than forty-two centuries[14] — it is scarcely possible to judge details. Was it chance and circumstance that produced the right leadership, or did the initiative stem from leaders who molded conditions to their own liking? Very likely, the two factors intermingled. In any case, to succeeding generations the new era was the personal achievement of two towering figures: Sargon of Akkad and his grandson Naram-Sin. And modern historians have honored this tradition by applying to the same era the label "Sargonid age," or alternatively "Akkad period."

The beginning seemed familiar enough. Proceeding from his own city of Akkad — Sumerian Agade — Sargon was still within the traditional framework when he shifted operations to Kish, the time-honored regional center in the northern part of the land. But his very regnal name is of more than routine significance. For *Šarrum-kên*, our Sargon, means the "king is legitimate," hardly a name to have been given him at birth. It asserts, indeed protests, too much, enough in fact to brand its bearer as a usurper. A telling parallel is to be found more than sixteen centuries later, when another famous bearer of the same name, Sargon II of Assyria,[15] likewise came to power by a process that was far from orthodox. More noteworthy in the present connection is the fact that the original Sargon was the first ruler in the post-legendary history of Mesopotamia to bear a manifestly non-Sumerian name. His main rival in the south, e.g., still adhered to accepted Sumerian usage by calling himself *Lugal-zage-si*, the first element being the Sumerian term for "king." Sargon's name is typically Semitic. And the specific language to which this name belongs was henceforth to be known as "the language of Akkad," our "Akkadian," just as the land in question was to be designated as "Akkad." Both these appellations derive from the name of a hitherto obscure town which Sargon's deeds alone brought into such striking prominence.

It is thus evident that Sargon's rise coincided with the emergence of a Semitic element as the leading ethnic factor in Lower Mesopotamia. But it would be a mistake to conclude from this that the Semites whom Sargon led had just arrived in the country. Lugalzagesi himself had composed his inscriptions in Semitic as well as Sumerian, and there are also other scattered signs of prior Semitic participation. The Akkadians — by whatever name they may have been known prior to the appearance of Sargon — must have been established, accordingly, for a considerable period of time. The area of Kish, as was suggested above, had been occupied since time immemorial by a population that was neither Sumerian nor — from all indications — Semitic. The ultimate prominence of the Akkadians could thus have been foreshadowed either by a recent influx of related elements or by the gradual ascendancy of a long-settled minority. At any rate, the local developments cannot be viewed along purely ethnic lines. The civilization was composite; it was essentially Mesopotamian, rather than Sumerian, Semitic, or aboriginal. At the same time, however, opposition to a state or confederacy of states dominated by the Sumerians was more likely to originate in Kish than in such southern centers as Uruk, Ur, or Eridu. The overriding factor was cultural; yet ethnic and linguistic divisions had not been overcome altogether.

But more was involved in the Sargonid accession than the traditional see-saw between Kish and Uruk. A drastic change was taking place in the whole political structure. Instead of two combinations of city states, gravitating towards their respective poles in the north and south, we now find an integrated unit which comprised both Sumer and Akkad. This unit was never to give up its cultural solidarity, even though political separatism might reappear in due time. And the strength of the unified state is reflected, aside from sweeping political and social measures, in the fresh spirit and renewed vigor of such significant art forms as sculpture and glyptics.

More revolutionary still, the newly united state becomes the heir of an empire extending from Iran to Asia Minor and thus recovering the range of the old Obeid culture. The original inscriptions of the Sargonid rulers state this achievement progressively and in matter-of-fact terms. Nor are these claims just so many idle boasts. They have been confirmed independently by the most trustworthy witnesses of all — the very hostile territories that the inscriptions list as conquered.[16] Thus Susa, the capital of Elam, has yielded monuments and texts of Sargon and his successors; and the Akkadian language became under that dynasty the legal and administrative medium of Elam. Naram-Sin has left us not only the celebrated victory stele that portrays his campaign in the mountains of Kurdistan, but also an inscription in Nineveh and another stele as far out as Diarbekir. In the light of such eloquent material there can be little reason for doubting Naram-Sin's assertion that he had marched all the way to Anatolia. Even Naram-Sin's daughters left inscribed objects which the excavators of Mari have unearthed.

The impact of the Sargonids on the contemporary scene can also be gauged from the following fact. Sargon and Naram-Sin came to enjoy a place in literature that must have exceeded their position in history. Legendary elaborations of their exploits, some of them achieved in spite of enormous difficulties, have survived not alone in Akkadian and Sumerian, but in Elamite, Hurrian, and Hittite as well. This bears eloquent witness to the fact that these rulers had become truly cosmopolitan figures as opposed to mere parochial heroes. Through these rulers history itself acquired an international standing.

Enlarged horizons open the way to greater opportunities, but they increase by the same token the area of inherent risks. The vast Sargonid empire, as a pioneering venture in government and politics, was obviously too extended to maintain itself for many generations. It exposed, moreover, the original seat of its power to counterattacks from far-away regions, places that had been sealed off hitherto by distance and darkness. And so the Sargonid expansion proved to be in the end more notable for its enduring civilizing achievements than for its political and military results. And the instruments of civilization which Sargon and Naram-Sin had carried with them left their mark, inevitably, on the subjected territories, and made these in turn a target for barbarian groups still farther afield. Thus it came about that towards the end of Naram-Sin's reign, about a century after Sargon's accession, the Sargonid empire was itself the victim of attacks by immense hordes of barbarians. This awesome irruption was to be recalled in legend, literature, and omens for nearly two thousand years to come. The sources ascribe this scourge to all but inhuman agents who bear the collective name of *Ummān-manda*.[17] Today there can be little doubt that behind these vague and incoherent accounts is concealed a blurred recollection of some actual event of frightening magnitude. It is perhaps not too venturesome to assume that we may have here an echo of distant stirrings which ultimately drove the "Hittites" and their associates into the orbit of the ancient Near East.

When the dust had finally settled, inner Mesopotamia was politically back where it had started from. The collapse of Akkad, however, was to posterity no less stunning a phenomenon than its spectacular rise. The upheaval is adduced time and again with all due solemnity. And just as the earlier successes of the Sargonids had been attributed in large part to divine favors, so too the eventual decline could not but be ascribed to the gods' displeasure. Mesopotamian sources identify the agents of this punishment as the Guti, an obscure people settled in the mountain districts to the east. Modern scholarship has followed suit with surprising docility. Yet the full evidence fails to bear out this interpretation. There is nothing in what we know about the Guti that would add up to a force capable of facing and humbling the mature civilization of Sumer and Akkad. What is more, the Guti themselves are included among the helpless victims of the Ummān-manda. It would seem, therefore, that the aftermath of the catastrophic invasion from distant lands had left the country so weakened as to make it a relatively easy mark for the unruly neighbors in the mountains nearby. The Guti reaped the benefits; but in their case sequence came to be mistaken for consequence.[18]

Nevertheless, even though their political structure collapsed, the incidental accomplishments of the Sargonids were not to be undone. The new horizons which the great conquests had opened up could not again be shrunk to their former limits. And the forces of Mesopotamian civilization that had thus been released were now spread wide and beyond recall. The parent culture was to be henceforward an ever-growing international factor.

D. The Neo-Sumerian Revival and the Role of the Amorites

Following the collapse of the Dynasty of Akkad, Mesopotamian affairs may be said to have reverted to type. The grandiose design of empire had to give way to more modest and practical schemes. To be sure, the autonomous city state had become outmoded. But the authority of its successors seldom embraced large areas with more than a handful of urban centers. Only on two occasions are we faced with regional states of substantial size. One such occasion marked the revival of Sumerian domination under the Third Dynasty of Ur. The other was the culmination of a long process highlighted by the appearance of a new ethnic group, the Amorites or Western Semites. The outstanding figure of this second phase is Hammurabi of Babylon, who flourished nearly half a millennium after the eclipse of the Sargonids.

Since the impetus for the Sargonid expansion had come from Kish, and the venture had been spearheaded by Semites, then—if familiar precedents were still valid — any effective local reaction should have originated in the south and been led by Sumerians. Both these premises turn out to be correct. The traditional pattern, to be sure, had been upset seriously in the meantime; but it still retained enough cohesiveness for one final manifestation. Indeed, the required leadership was furnished once again by Uruk. After sporadic skirmishes with the Gutian overlords, this ancient center succeeded in dealing them a decisive blow under the sole king of its Fifth Dynasty, one Utuhegal. But Uruk was soon supplanted by Ur, where the Sumerian revival attained its greatest heights, as well as its melancholy end, all within the short space of little more than a century. The absolute dates for this juncture are still a matter of dispute among modern scholars. All will concede, however, that this last flicker of Sumerian political authority coincided with the turn of the third millennium.

One does not have to probe deep below the surface to discover that this Neo-Sumerian phase did not carry with it a sense of abiding confidence. It certainly lacked the manifold exuberance of the early Sargonid times. The period of the new dynasty of Ur, the Third, was essentially one of compromise and consolidation. The compromise is reflected in the political organization. The realm of the Third Dynasty of Ur, it is true, gives the appearance of an integrated unit, more like the Sargonid structure than the earlier loosely confederated or wholly independent city states. Yet although governors of outlying provinces — including Assyria and Elam — were responsible directly to the ruling monarch, some of the old Sumerian centers nearby must have enjoyed a considerable measure of local autonomy. For only thus can one account for the evident freedom of Gudea of Lagash, who flourished, in all likelihood, during the early stages of the Ur period.[19] His extensive building activities, his far-flung trading enterprises, the general prosperity of his district which he administered under the modest title of *ensi* "toparch, governor," and the quality and tone of his literary output[20] — none of this suggests the least interference on the part of the sovereign king. In the cultural field there would seem to have been a tendency to take stock and put the results in writing, as though in anticipation of troubled times ahead. An outstanding example of this is the previously cited Sumerian King List, which appears to have been composed under Utuhegal.[21] More significant still is the first known compilation of laws, inscribed with the name of Ur-Nammu, the founder of the Ur Dynasty. This was to be followed by various others, the most celebrated of all being the Code of Hammurabi, some three centuries later.

There are also other indications that the Sumerians of this age were not fully secure in their role as the politically dominant element. The Sargonid upheaval had been spearheaded, as we saw, by Semites. This fact was underlined by the increasing use of Akkadian in the records of that age.

But added pressure on the part of the Akkadian element is now clearly mirrored by the names of the later rulers of Ur III, which are manifestly Akkadian. The ethnic situation was further complicated by infiltration of other elements. Records of this period disclose personal names that can be traced to Subarians and Hurrians, two independent groups concentrated along the northern peripheries.[22] There is, moreover, a steady trickle of West Semitic names which is soon to swell into a substantial flow. Against the background of such internal pressures, it could only be a matter of time before some resolute outsider put an end to the rule of Ur, and with it to Sumerian political authority, once and for all. The crushing defeat which the Elamites and their allies inflicted on Ibbi-Sin, the last king of that dynasty, was to be recalled in the omen literature time and again as a symbol of signal disaster.

Following the fall of Ur, the land of Sumer and Akkad broke up into a number of smaller states. Chief of these were Larsa in the far south, Isin in the center, and Eshnunna in the north, east of the Tigris. All three were at one time or another subject to Elamite sufferance. Indeed, the last two kings of the Larsa dynasty were sons of the Elamite Kudur-Mabuk.

The authority of Elam, however, was by no means a hindrance to native cultural progress. Mesopotamian civilization had by now acquired the resources for maintaining itself in the face of political adversity. In fact, it was even able to dominate the victors as well. This is immediately apparent from the Akkadian names Warad-Sin and Rim-Sin under which Kudur-Mabuk's sons reigned at Larsa. But our evidence goes still further. Eshnunna comes up with its own collection of laws — by now a characteristic Mesopotamian feature — which were written in Akkadian and date from shortly after the dethronement of Ibbi-Sin.[23] Lipit-Ishtar of Larsa does likewise, except that his compilation is couched in Sumerian,[24] the language of a people that had been eliminated as a political factor nearly a century earlier, but whose cultural influence remained distinctly alive and productive.

Such cultural manifestations, however, were not altogether part of a process that took the participants unawares. The Mesopotamians of that age were acutely conscious of their stake in the inherited culture and intent on preserving this heritage. They were mindful, moreover, of the fact that the basic medium in which this culture had found expression was the Sumerian language. And since this was now in effect a dead language, steps were taken to provide the necessary means whereby posterity would be able to know its structure and vocabulary and understand its written content. It is to this laborious and far-sighted endeavor that we owe today the various grammatical and lexical texts, the lists and compendia of all kinds, the collections of legal phrases, and the works of literature proper that have been unearthed in many centers of this particular intermediate age and of the Old Babylonian period which followed. Fifteen centuries later, Ashurbanipal could boast with snobbish pride that he had studied "the difficult tablets in the obscure Sumerian." The manuals which he had at his disposal were the very same works that have guided modern scholarship in the process of penetrating the language and its contents. The foresight of the old scholars — enlightened beneficiaries of the cultural contribution of the Sumerians — was thus to yield dividends far beyond any reasonable expectation. It is a tribute to their enterprise in the first instance, but above that also to the underlying civilization which was the ultimate source of their devotion.

By then, however, the Akkadian element, which must have played a major part in the conservation of Sumerian cultural treasures, was not the most forceful ethnic group in the land. This distinction belongs to new arrivals whom local sources designate as the *Amurrû*, while modern studies apply to them the Biblical cognate "Amorites." The name describes them as coming from the west, for Amurru in its geographical sense was used in Akkadian as one of the terms for "west." In all probability, the starting point of their migration was somewhere along the Mediterranean coast, although some nomadic groups among them may well have drifted in from the desert in the south. Mesopotamian literature delights in describing the Amorites — generally under the form *Mar. tu* — as barbarians who had neither houses nor agriculture, and lived on raw meat. Whether such censure was inspired in part by uneasiness, we have no way of knowing. There can be little doubt, however, that the settled Mesopotamians had ample cause to be apprehensive of the nomadic Amorites. For it was not long before the underprivileged marauders became a highly significant new element in the land.

In picking up the Amorite trail, we are not entirely dependent on records in which this appellation is used explicitly. Much concrete information can be derived from a substantial body of new proper names which are employed for persons and places. This distinctive onomastic material must be correlated on the whole with the Amorites, even though the correspondence is not absolute: not all Amorites had such names, nor can all the individuals so named be accommodated under the Amorite label as applied by the Mesopotamians. For our present purposes, these are but minor differences of detail. Nor is the question of the precise relationship between Amorite and Canaanite of immediate concern in this context.[25] It will suffice to state that the linguistic remains in question are of West Semitic origin, and that the Western Semites concerned may be conveniently identified as Amorites. What is significant is the fact that Amorites begin to confront us in the Sargonid period, their numbers increasing in Ur III, until they were prominent enough to supply the leading dynasties of the subsequent historical stage. This is true of Larsa and Eshnunna, and still more so of Babylon, Mari, and Ashur.

Since the discovery of the Mari archives,[26] in particular, our information about the Amorites has gained much in substance and clarity. Thanks to its location in the Middle Euphrates area, Mari was a natural intermediary between the coastlands of the Mediterranean and Mesopotamia. The local population must have been Amorite since early historic times. Under strong Mesopotamian influence, Mari was ever in a process of adjustment and assimilation to the norms of Sumer and Akkad; yet the pull in the opposite direction could not have been negligible. Thus at the time under review, shortly before the conquests of Hammurabi, Mari writes in Akkadian and acts in many other ways as an exponent of the culture for which her eastern neighbors were famous; but at the same time, this basically Amorite state has its problems with as yet unsettled Amorite tribes, which are referred to collectively as Ben-Semalites and Benjaminites (*Dumu-Sim'āl u Dumu-Yamīn*). There are special "Secretaries of Amorite Affairs" (*tupšar Amurrê*) who were delegated to deal with these fractious elements.[27] Very likely, the position called for a knowledge of the tribal customs and especially of the tribal dialects, in addition to the official Akkadian. A peace pact among these tribes sometimes called for the ceremonial slaying of an ass, the pertinent phrase being *qatālum ḫayaram bin atānim*,[28] which is still echoed in the Biblical *'īro . . . bnī 'atōnō* (Gen. 49:11); and Benjaminites were active in the districts of Harran and Nahur.[29] Theirs was indeed a West Semitic world; and Mari was in many ways a window facing west.

The Amorites of Mesopotamia proper must have been much like the settled Amorites of Mari. They had given up their nomadic ways and become Mesopotamians to all intents and purposes. But they seemed to retain the spirit and initiative of their nomadic ancestors, at least for a generation or two, to judge from the prominence which they achieved within a short time in all of the states concerned. Nor did they give up soon their distinguishing personal traits. For it would be difficult to read through a batch of letters from Mari without being struck by their difference in tone from a similar group of typical Mesopotamian documents. We shall come back to this point presently.

There is a celebrated Mesopotamian dynasty which has long been known to scholarship as the Dynasty of Amurru. Its focal place was a hitherto obscure city on the Lower Euphrates which bore the name — perhaps secondarily reinterpreted[30] — of *Bāb-ilim* "Gate of God." The founder of the dynasty was a man with the transparently Amorite name of Sumu-abum, who came to power at a time when the kingdoms of Isin and Larsa had already been established for some one hundred and thirty years. It required another century before Babylon was ready to make its own bid for supremacy in the whole of Sumer and Akkad. By then the incumbent ruler of Babylon could have had few if any of the outward characteristics of his remote nomadic ancestors. He was wholeheartedly Akkadian in speech and Mesopotamian in culture. His name was to become one of the most illustrious in the long history of the land, so much so that both the dialect and the period involved have come to be known as Old Babylonian, in tribute to the city which he had made pre-eminent. And Babylon's chief god Marduk similarly came to shine with reflected glory.

Memorable periods in history are often highlighted by clusters of outstanding personalities. Nearly six centuries earlier we saw one such group in the persons of Urukagina, Lugalzagesi, and Sargon of Akkad. More than seven centuries later, another great trio, consisting of Samuel, Saul, and David, was to illuminate and dramatize their age in far off Palestine. At the present juncture we find yet another outstanding triad in the persons of Rim-Sin of Larsa, Shamshi-Addu of Assyria, and Hammurabi[31] of Babylon. In each instance, the exceptional qualities of the given individual serve to place the other two in that much sharper relief. And in each instance, too, the last one to emerge triumphant also happens to be the one who was to make the deepest impression on history.

The first of the present triad to appear on the scene was Rim-Sin of Larsa. Since his reign lasted 61 years, and he followed his brother who had held the throne for a dozen years, Rim-Sin must have been an old man by the time he reached the end of his long trail. If in his case "fullness of years" was not synonymous with "contentment," as it is in the familiar Biblical phrase, the fault can hardly have been his. From all that we can tell about him, Rim-Sin was a wise, benevolent, and unassuming ruler, not unlike his father Kudur-Mabuk. He did put an end to the rival kingdom of Isin, but its capital was magnanimously spared, contrary to the usual practice. A long era of peace and prosperity was now in prospect. If there was a cloud on the horizon, it could scarcely threaten from the direction of Babylon, whose king, the father of Hammurabi, had joined Rim-Sin in his war on Isin. Conceivably, the upsurge of Assyria, now headed by a resolute usurper, may have given Larsa some cause for concern. But Ashur's drive pointed away from Larsa, towards the west and north, so that Rim-Sin had good reason to feel untroubled and secure.

The contemporary ruler of Ashur was, like so many others of his day, a man of Amorite origin. His name was Shamshi-Addu and his native city Terqa lay a short distance up the river from Mari. After his father had been deposed by his Mari neighbor, Shamshi-Addu fled to Babylonia. From that base of operations he was able to advance before long to the land of Assyria, where his efforts were crowned eventually by the capture of the old capital city of Ashur and the establishment of his own dynasty.

Assyria had been relatively slow in coming under the spell of the civilization of Lower Mesopotamia. Local traditions trace Assyrian history back to a remote period when the rulers "lived in tents."[32] But the earliest valid synchronisms of Ashur are with the Sargonids, at which time some of the recorded Assyrian royal names appear to be Gutian, or perhaps Subarian in the broad sense of the term. Later on Ashur was ruled by a governor subject to one of the kings of the Third Dynasty of Ur. Since the south was too solid for foreign adventurers to tackle, Assyrian energies had to find an outlet elsewhere. By the turn of the third millennium, Ashur enjoyed a considerable measure of prosperity, aided by its flourishing business colonies in Cappadocia. Ashur differed thus from the south in political, economic, and cultural respects. It had its own calendar. The language of Assyria, to be sure, was a dialect of Akkadian, yet it departed substantially from contemporary Babylonian, as can be seen from the Cappadocian texts and the early historical records of Ashur. This difference was to become more pronounced in later times.

As soon as his position in Assyria was secure, Shamshi-Addu lost little time in settling accounts with Mari, which had driven his father out of Terqa and brought about his own flight to Babylonia. Henceforward Mari was administered by Shamshi-Addu's younger son, who acted as his father's viceroy and bore the good Amorite name of Yasmah-Addu. The older son exercised similar authority over the eastern districts of Assyria. All this occurred within the lifetime of Rim-Sin, whose long reign at Larsa preceded that of Shamshi-Addu in Assyria by eight years and was to exceed it by twenty. On the other hand, at Shamshi-Addu's death Hammurabi was but in the eleventh year of his own long reign. The period during which all three kings were contemporaries was thus limited to a little less than a decade. From the standpoint of Babylon, the success of Ashur could only be welcomed, inasmuch as it detracted to that extent from Larsa's initial superiority. And had not Babylon given Shamshi-Addu asylum in the first place? Since his subsequent drive pointed away from the south, it doubtless had Babylon's blessing — at least initially — if not its active support.

Long friendship on the part of Babylon may perhaps help to explain Shamshi-Addu's own staunchly pro-Babylonian policy. This was particularly in evidence where cultural matters were concerned. His patron deity was the Sumerian god Enlil. What is more significant — and was to prove far more enduring — the language which Shamshi-Addu used in his official inscriptions was not Assyrian but Babylonian. This innovation established a precedent that was followed by a great many generations. Henceforth, except only for a relatively brief interruption, the Babylonian dialect was to remain the cultural medium of Assyria, in historical documents and in literary works, through all of Assyria's history.[33]

It may be said, then, that Shamshi-Addu was an Amorite by birth but a devoted Babylonian by adoption. Yet acquired characteristics are notoriously superficial. In Shamshi-Addu's case, at any rate, there is one outstanding trait that cannot be paralleled on a comparable scale in the known records from Mesopotamia proper. The explanation may perhaps be found in Shamshi-Addu's Amorite antecedents.

An outstanding authority on comparative Semitic linguistics observed years ago that there is a striking difference in spirit between Hebrew and Akkadian. Akkadian is notable for its measured precision which enables it to express complex social and legal concepts with accuracy and objectivity. Hebrew, on the other hand, is appreciably more vivid and subjective — an admirable medium for prophets and poets.[34] The linguistic background of Shamshi-Addu's ancestors was certainly closer to Hebrew than to Akkadian. His letters have now revealed a personality that would seem to point in the same direction. In contrast, Hammurabi's correspondence conforms just as markedly to the genius of Akkadian.

To be sure, Hammurabi himself was of Amorite origin, as his name alone is sufficient to demonstrate. But his forefathers had sat on the throne of Babylon for over a century. There had been ample time to assimilate and strike new roots.[35] Hammurabi's handling of Akkadian — without detracting from the credit to scribes who worked under his direction — was to become classical and paradigmatic. All in all, then, Hammurabi was a thorough Mesopotamian; Shamshi-Addu, apparently, was not, or not to quite the same extent. It is this disparity in degree that would seem to be sufficient to account for the manifest differences in the two as regards temperament and personality. Of course, all this, if correctly evaluated, could simply be a matter of the personal equation. One cannot be sure after all these centuries — thirty seven at a minimum. What is manifest, in any case, is the striking personal contrast between these two great contemporaries.

The letters of Shamshi-Addu which have turned up in the Mari archives reveal him not only as a resolute and efficient ruler but also as a devoted father, stern yet deeply concerned about the progress and performance of his sons. He is ever the solicitous head of the family, the vivid patriarchal figure. He fumes and scolds and cajoles; he can make his point by citing an earthy proverb or by injecting a touch of sarcasm; but he also understands the morale value of an occasional word of praise. "As for you," he writes to his pleasure-loving younger son Yasmah-Addu, "how long must we go on coddling you? Is there no hair on your cheek? Are you a child and not an adult? Why don't you heed the example of your brother who commands vast armies? [At least,] take charge of your palace and your household!"[36] For his part, Yasmah-Addu feels safe enough to talk back, with all due respect but also with evident impunity. None of this would seem out of keeping if applied to David and his family. What is noteworthy about such a comparison is not so much the similarity in character as the fact that there was in both instances the interest to depict it.

The strong family spirit of the new Assyrian dynasty survived the death of its founder. When crusty old Shamshi-Addu was dead, his older son and successor Ishme-Dagan addressed to his younger brother in Mari a message remarkable for its tenderness and protective sentiment.[37] But with the father gone, the force that held his realm together was quickly dissipated. Within a few months Mari reverted to the control of its former dynasty. Zimri-lim, the surviving son of the king whom Shamshi-Addu had deposed, returned from his asylum in Aleppo and was speedily restored to the throne of his ancestors. He proceeded to make of his palace a showpiece that was widely admired in his lifetime,[38] and was destined to be a source of rare delight to modern archaeologists. Ishme-Dagan managed to retain a foothold in Assyria for the rest of his life. But it must have been a kingdom sharply reduced in area and authority. Between Mari — newly freed and invigorated — in the south, and troublesome neighbors to the west, there was little room for a carefree Assyria. Above all, Hammurabi had begun to assert himself after a decade of quiet preparation. We know that Ishme-Dagan outlived Hammurabi by about a dozen years. But we are informed also that Hammurabi's authority extended eventually to Ashur and Nineveh. It follows that for the better part of his reign Ishme-Dagan could function only as a vassal of Babylon or as a fugitive in some of the less accessible districts of his kingdom. He was certainly no match for the Babylonian.

Until the appearance of the Mari archives, Hammurabi was known to moderns chiefly as an outstanding legislator, administrator, and builder. His military and political successes had to be inferred largely from such laconic sources as date formulae. The Mari letters shed much new light on these hitherto shadowy aspects of Hammurabi's career. One cannot but be impressed by his methodical ways, the shrewdness of his policies, and the skillful timing of his moves. In the single-minded pursuit of his plan to make himself the undisputed overlord of the whole of Mesopotamia, Hammurabi proceeded cautiously step by step, and it required nearly all the forty-three years of his reign to achieve his main objective. He made alliances with neighbors whom he intended all along to destroy in the end. By putting first things first, he was able to pick off his opponents one by one. Because of his coldly calculated pace, he was able to lull more than one of his ultimate victims into a false sense of security.

The Mari letters turn the spotlight not so much on things accomplished as on events in the making. Couriers were kept busy carrying vital news from one capital to another. Intelligence agents worked overtime, but their facts and judgment were no more foolproof in those days than they often are today. We do get a glimpse, however, of the size and intricacy of the preparations involved, and a feeling of the excitement that prevailed on the eve of a major event, for instance, the critical encounter between Hammurabi and Rim-Sin.[39] And it is only in retrospect that the result appears to have been a foregone conclusion. To the contemporaries, the balance of power seemed fairly stable, and estimates of the eventual outcome could be influenced by one's wish as much as anything else. For whether by design or because of his personality, Hammurabi did not impress his peers as an outstanding success in his major military undertakings.

A much-cited passage in a letter to Zimri-lim, written by one of his provincial governors, is an excellent case in point: "There is no king who is all-powerful on his own. Ten or fifteen kings may march behind Hammurabi the Babylonian; just so after Rim-Sin of Larsa; similarly after Ibalpiel of Eshnunna; similarly, too, after Amutpiel of Qatanum. Perhaps twenty kings march behind Yarim-lim of Yamhad (Aleppo)."[40] This is a fine example of the political philosophy of the time. But it is no less valuable as an index of the standing which Hammurabi enjoyed among his contemporaries. Evidently, he was not thought of as being head and shoulders above the others; if anything, he seemed to rate a notch below the ruler of Aleppo. Nor is there anything in Hammurabi's own statements to suggest an impressive and vibrant personality. His words are routine and matter-of-fact.

The results, however, are something else again. Ashur, Eshnunna, and Larsa were dealt with inexorably one by one. It may be that Zimri-lim expected to the very end to be treated by Hammurabi as a friend and ally. If so, he was due for a rude awakening.[41] Mari's turn came at long last. If it had not been for the eloquence of his archives and the mute but compelling testimony of his great palace, the role of Zimri-lim would have been put down by modern students as insignificant. We know now that such was by no means the case. But we know, too, that Hammurabi's personality did not communicate itself vividly, either to his contemporaries or — through his records — to posterity. He was methodical, single-minded, and exacting down to the smallest detail. But it is only by the sum of his achievements that we are able to gauge his own brand of greatness.

E. The Age of Upheavals

Ever since the beginning of Mesopotamian history proper, the center of gravity had been shifting in a northwest direction, up the river valley. Sumer had blended with Akkad, and the two jointly gave way eventually to Babylonia. Meanwhile, a secondary center had been building up slowly in Assyria, farther up the valley. As geographic horizons expanded, the number of participants grew proportionately. Sumerians and Akkadians were followed by Amorites and Assyrians, with Elamites, Gutians, and Hurrians turning up now and then in minor roles. Yet the larger number of actors did not entail a break in the prevailing continuity in culture. The whole process may thus be described as one of basic cultural uniformity against a background of ethnic and political diversity. Both these aspects, the unity as well as the change, were to be brought into sharper relief in the centuries that followed the age of Hammurabi. The period involved covers roughly the middle quarters of the second millennium B.C.E.

The first significant new ethnic factor at this juncture was a people from the mountains of Western Iran, known as the *Kaššû* in Babylonian, *Kuššû* in the records from Nuzi,[42] and *Kūsh* in the Bible.[43] These Kassites or Cossaeans began to infiltrate into the northern peripheries of Babylonia under Hammurabi's son and successor Samsuiluna, and they soon gained a foothold in Hana, not far from Mari. The Babylonian empire was gradually losing ground. It had to tolerate, in addition to the Kassite foothold, the establishment of an independent state at the head of the Persian Gulf, under the so-called Sealand Dynasty. The decisive blow, however, did not come until about a century and a half after Hammurabi, when the troops of Mursilis I, king of the faraway Hittites, sacked Babylon and left it desolate. In the wake of this disaster, the Kassites were able to move in and establish themselves as masters of the land for a very long time to come.

There is in this chain of events an immediately apparent analogy to the developments that attended the waning years of the Dynasty of Akkad, some six centuries earlier. In both instances, the general pattern was substantially the same: a devastating irruption from the direction of Anatolia; the collapse of a celebrated Mesopotamian dynasty; and the ensuing rule by a hitherto obscure people from the nearby mountains to the northeast. But closer study proves such comparisons to be superficial and misleading. The Gutian hold on Sumer and Akkad had been shortlived and largely nominal; and the invaders had left no tangible impression on the culture of the conquered land. The Kassites, on the other hand, were to remain in control of Babylonia for a period which native sources compute at 576 years, and which in any case could not have been much less than half a millennium; and the Kassite occupation was to leave distinctive cultural traces.

On further inquiry, moreover, it becomes evident that Mursilis' march on Babylon had little in common politically with the earlier hit-and-run raid of the Ummān-manda hordes. The Hittite king was an able and responsible head of a great civilized state. His campaign against Babylonia, therefore, must be viewed as a duly calculated step. Babylon had been for centuries the leading power in Western Asia. An attack upon it from as far as Anatolia could be little less than a major move in the game of interregional power politics. It follows that Mursilis must have allowed in advance for the part that the Kassites were to play in such a struggle.[44] It is thus most unlikely that the Kassites acted in this instance as a fully independent agent.

There are, besides, added reasons for concluding that the Kassite upheaval in Babylonia was but a part of a much more complex pattern. For this event has to be seen in connection with a series of other drastic changes which profoundly affected the ethnic and political picture of the Near East as a whole, and remained effective for centuries to come. These changes include the following, among others: the Hyksos domination of Egypt; the so-called "Dark Age," which lasted from 1600 to 1500 as a reasonable minimum,[45] and was experienced in Hittite territories, Syria, Assyria, and Babylonia; the emergence of the kingdom of Mitanni as a balancing factor during the "Amarna period"; and the ultimate resurgence of Assyria, in the wake of the decline of Mitanni, after 1400. This is not to imply, of course, that all these events — spread as they are over many lands and several centuries — were directly interrelated. All that can be reasonably inferred is an underlying common denominator. Many details point to such a conclusion, although the chain of evidence still lacks some important links. But even a rough analysis of the pertinent facts would take us too far afield. There is room here only for the broadest kind of outline.

The Hyksos domination of Egypt, between the 18th and the 16th centuries, followed the invasion of that country by Asiatics who had come from the direction of Palestine and Syria.[46] The invaders were an ethnically composite group, consisting of Semites in the main, but including apparently Hurrian and Indo-Aryan elements, if not others as well. Their success seems to have been due primarily to the use of horse-drawn chariots employed on a large scale; in other words, it was the result of a technological revolution with which the old civilizations were at first unable to cope. It is as yet not clear where this particular method of warfare was first developed and perfected. Transcaspia, or perhaps Transcaucasia, may have served as the testing ground. Driven by factors that can only be guessed at today, the dreaded forces found their way in time to the Fertile Crescent — among other as yet undisclosed regions, no doubt — dislodging and sweeping ahead of them various settled groups in their path. Among those affected were evidently Kassites and Hurrians, and later on also Semitic and perhaps Anatolian elements along the eastern shores of the Mediterranean. The Hyksos phase in Egypt and the Kassite invasion of Babylonia would thus constitute two separate reverberations of the same ultimate drive. Since the process thus set in motion was not to spend itself for many decades, or even centuries, its respective reflexes throughout the Near East need not have been closely synchronized.

It follows that the originators of this upheaval cannot be sought among the previous settlers in the region. This automatically exempts the Hurrians, although they have been often adduced in this connection. There are Hurrian records from Mesopotamia which go back to the time of the Dynasty of Akkad.[47] Personal names from Mari, Chagar Bazar, and Alalakh testify to a sizable Hurrian population in those districts in Old Babylonian times. What is more, the Dark Age — a sure indication that the invaders had struck — sets in at Alalakh after the Old Babylonian level (VII) with its large quota of Hurrian names, and lasts through two unliterate strata, till the start of Level IV in the 15th century. Nor can the Kassites be held directly responsible. For, on the one hand, their presence is witnessed in Babylonia shortly after the reign of Hammurabi, hence too soon for the local decline which was precipitated by Mursilis' attack; and on the other hand, there is no trace of Kassites[48] in Palestine, which the Hyksos had to cross on their march into Egypt, and which they are known to have used later as their avenue of retreat. Thus the fact that both the Hurrians and the Kassites show a marked increase in numbers, after the Dark Age had run its course, can only mean that each had received reinforcements in the wake of the invading hordes.

The only newcomers to be found on the scene after the dust had settled are the Indo-Aryans. Men bearing Indo-Aryan names confront us as members of the Mitanni dynasty and turn up also in sundry cities of Syria and Palestine.[49] Theophorous elements from the same quarter crop up among the later Kassite names, and Hittite treaties cite among the deities invoked some of the leading figures in the Indo-Aryan pantheon. And significantly enough, the technical vocabulary of chariot-racing, as practiced in Mitanni, contains transparently "Vedic" numerals. There can thus be no doubt that the Indo-Aryans had become a prominent factor in Western Asia; in all probability, they constituted an offshoot of the large-scale migration which was to usher in eventually the Vedic era in India. A movement of such magnitude, especially when powered by a new means of communication and warfare, could well account for the chain of upheavals in the Near East that began with the Hyksos. Whether the horse-drawn chariot originated with the Aryans themselves, or had been taken over from some other society,[50] is unknown and for our present purposes immaterial. In any event, one need not look any farther for the group that was responsible for the Dark Age.

To play a leading part, however, is not the same thing as having the whole play to oneself. Since the Indo-Aryans had to come from a considerable distance, and since the Near East was off their main route, it is unlikely that they appeared there in large numbers. They must have managed, therefore, to impose their will on various local elements and organize and lead them for their own purpose. All this would seem to follow logically from the relative paucity of Indo-Aryan names after the Near East had returned to its literate ways, in the 15th century. Babylonia remains in Kassite hands. And the initially formidable kingdom of Mitanni, although ruled by kings with Indo-Aryan credentials, now uses Hurrian as its state language and designates its inhabitants as Hurrians.[51] Even the aristocracy of that period, called *maryanni/a*, shows a preponderance of Hurrians, to judge from the evidence of the Alalakh tablets.[52] Accordingly, one of the main results of the Dark Age was the emergence of the Hurrians as a group that was now dominant in Syria, and thickly settled in some previously non-Hurrian districts, such as Arrapkha and Nuzi, east of the Tigris.[53] What is more, Assyria itself, which was flanked by Hurrian districts, was now at best a vassal of Hurrian-dominated Mitanni. Thus by the middle of the second millennium most of Mesopotamia was under non-Semitic rule, but the rulers were no longer Indo-Aryans in speech and culture. Assyria was controlled by Hurrians, and Kassites ruled Babylonia.

In retrospect, Mitanni may be viewed as an effective stop-gap in more ways than one. Politically, it marked the limit of Egypt's expansion, which had reached Northern Syria on the rebound from the indignity of Hyksos occupation; the new state compensated for the weakness of Hittite Anatolia and Kassite Babylonia. And culturally, Mitanni served to overcome the vacuum left by the Dark Age, by re-establishing a link with the past, through the adoption of the cuneiform script and the elevation to power of the Hurrians, who had local ties of long standing.

It is not altogether surprising, therefore, that after a relatively brief period of political equilibrium the scales are tipped once again, in favor of the traditional pattern. The Egyptian empire, weakened by internal schisms, is unable to maintain an effective hold on its Asiatic dependencies, a situation which is exploited to the utmost by roving units of the Habiru.[54] Mitanni finds itself powerless to withstand the challenge of the New Hittite kingdom. The once vigorous Kassites appear to have succumbed gradually to the enervating influence of their new surroundings. The new order is in retreat. But the only center to show any real vigor, in so far as historic Mesopotamia is concerned, is Ashur.

Assyria was quick to take advantage of the progressive disintegration of Mitanni. Centuries earlier, while the Kassites were establishing themselves at Hana — well before their advance on Babylon — the rule of Ashur had been taken over by a certain Adasi. Although to us he is little more than a shadowy figure, and the Assyrian lists designate him as "the son of a nobody," his descendants — either real or alleged — were to remain at the helm of the Assyrian state for over a thousand years. But the opportunity to capitalize on the decline of Mitanni did not come until the 14th century, whereupon a succession of Assyrian kings proceeded to carry out campaigns of conquests to the east and the north, while in the west they joined in effect the Hittites in partitioning Mitannian territories.

The renascence of Assyria may be said to mark the return of Mesopotamia as a whole — in the sense in which this term is here employed — to local control. As the international balance, which had typified the Amarna age, collapsed, and the Egyptian tide receded, regional realignments became unavoidable. The upshot in Mesopotamia was the emergence of a pattern in regard to Assyro-Babylonian relations which was to remain the norm until the last days of Assyria.

Under the rule of the Kassites, Babylonia was never able to achieve genuine political significance. In the Amarna period, for instance, Babylonian letters to the Pharaoh reflect an unmistakable subservience.[55] Yet one should beware of laying the blame for such degrading behavior on the Kassite masters of the country, for by that time the ruling class must have become thoroughly assimilated, except for the traditional names of the kings; and even these came to be replaced by native Akkadian forms. The fact is that the Babylonian state as a whole had sunk to a parochial role. But its traditional culture was every bit as cosmopolitan as it had ever been; indeed, the passing centuries only served to endow it with added prestige and effectiveness.

Assyria, on the other hand, was rapidly developing into the polar opposite of Babylonia. The energy and enterprise of a series of able rulers bore fruit in the form of a steadily expanding and progressively stronger state structure. But in the cultural field, Assyria was acutely aware of its solid ties with the south. In religion and ritual, law and government, literature and the arts — in these and many other aspects of societal life the influence of Lower Mesopotamia was always a potent factor. This is not to imply, of course, that Assyria was little more than the cultural shadow of Babylonia. Assyria had its own dialect and, for the most part, its own calendar; its laws reflected a divergent underlying philosophy; it was gradually evolving independent artistic and literary forms; and its military organization was obviously more than a match, as time went on, for its southern or any other neighbors. Yet the fact remains that the overall culture of Assyria bore a strong southern imprint; and the ruling classes retained a snobbish preference for the Babylonian dialect as opposed to the Assyrian vernacular. Thus, as was to happen many centuries later in the case of Rome vs. Greece, the blend of political might and cultural inferiority was to lead to serious psychological tensions.

These tensions found poignant expression in the dramatic career of Tukulti-Ninurta I, whose rule in Ashur covered most of the latter half of the thirteenth century. Ambitious and restless, he refuses to rest content with his early victories over the Hittites in the west, and in the foothill regions to the north. It is the pride and prestige of Babylon that most bother his peace of mind. Diplomatic negotiations produce only further tensions. The fratricidal war that ensues is destined to set a pattern which will survive more than six centuries till the very last days of Assyria.

After inflicting a crushing defeat on his Babylonian arch-rival, Tukulti-Ninurta not only occupies his capital but goes so far as to desecrate its main temple by dragging off to Ashur the statue of the chief god Marduk.

This sacrilege must have outraged the pious in Ashur as much as the vanquished in Babylon. But the headstrong conqueror brushes aside all scruples and adds to his other titles that of "king of Sumer and Akkad." Was this meant to suggest that the fabulous Sargon had at last found a fitting successor, after a lapse of a thousand years?

Suggestively enough, at any rate, the conqueror's domestic policies take on at this stage an increasingly pro-Babylonian slant.[56] This about-face was bound to arouse strong opposition on the part of the vested interests at Ashur. But defiant to the end, Tukulti-Ninurta turns his back on the traditional center and builds himself a new capital on the opposite bank of the Tigris. Eventually, a revolt led by his own son catches up with the king in his magnificent but lonely retreat, and brings his turbulent career to a violent end.

To many of his contemporaries, the murder of Tukulti-Ninurta must have appeared as just retribution for his sacrilegious acts in Babylon. Assyrian kings were to heed the implied warning for almost six centuries. The only one to disregard it at long last was proud and willful Sennacherib. And the frightening parallel of his death, in turn, was surely not lost on the Mesopotamian world in the year 681 B.C.E.

To this day, the impact of Tukulti-Ninurta's dynamic personality can be sensed from his building remains in Ashur, the stark evidence of his shortlived capital across the river, and the echoes of his various pursuits as reflected in the historical documents of Assyria. Aside from all these, we have still another, and far more eloquent, witness. An epic of great poetic appeal, composed evidently within the hero's lifetime, depicts Tukulti-Ninurta's struggle with Babylon in vivid detail.[57] There is nothing quite like it among the literary heritage of Mesopotamia. Its closest analogues are to be found in some of the poetic passages in the Bible. It would seem thus that Tukulti-Ninurta left a deeper mark on his own and succeeding generations than is generally realized.

There is indeed the inherent probability that the name of this king came to be reflected in the figure of a proverbial, but otherwise obscure, Biblical hero, the legendary Nimrod. As sketchily outlined in Genesis 10, this hero has been the subject of the liveliest sort of speculation for more than a score of centuries. Yet the best that modern scholarship could do with Nimrod has been to adduce for comparison the Mesopotamian war god Ninurta. But Nimrod's background and activities are clearly those of a mortal. His principal royal centers (*rēshīt mamlaḵtō*, Gen. 10:10) in Sumer are given as Babylon, Erech, and Akkad, thus showing a more than average knowledge of sound historical detail; and his progress in Assyria is said to take in not only Nineveh but also Calach, the latter place again reflecting more than routine information. We have just seen how much weight Tukulti-Ninurta attached to his title of "king of Sumer and Akkad."[58] As for Assyria, his own inscriptions refer to his building projects in Nineveh; and Calach, which was founded by his father Shalmaneser I, surely did not fail to attract his son's attention. Furthermore, Nimrod is listed in Genesis 10:8 as the son of Cush, which in this context can only be a reference to the Kassites;[59] and Micah 5:5 identifies Nimrod directly with Ashur. Finally, longer Akkadian names often tend to be abbreviated, as we know from many actual examples. This process would naturally be intensified on foreign soil, as is again attested by independent Biblical evidence.[60] On either count, *Tukulti-Ninurta* could be sloughed to *Ninurta* > *Nimurta* > *Nimrod*. Elsewhere, the same name appears to have yielded — by an analogous process—the classical designation *Ninos*, as has been independently suggested. And the further equation of Ninos and Nimrod is given both in Hellenistic and Rabbinical sources.[61] To be sure, we lack direct proof to support the above suggestion. Yet the Biblical statement about Nimrod fits so closely into the historical, geographical, and cultural context of Tukulti-Ninurta's career as to lend the proposed identification a very considerable measure of probability.

Be this as it may, the period of Tukulti-Ninurta I marks the definite emergence of Assyria as the undisputed military and political superior of Babylonia for a long time to come. It also sets the stage for further cultural symbiosis and increased psychological tensions, twin factors that were to prevail throughout the remainder of Assyrian history.

F. End of the Trail

The history of Mesopotamia after 1200 B.C.E. does not fall properly within the scope of this outline. The period in question is contemporaneous in its entirety with the historic Biblical age — to which the present volume is to serve as an introduction — and will hence be examined in due detail in conjunction with those events. It is a period, moreover, for which ample native sources have long been available, so that its contents have received an abundant amount of analysis and descriptive treatment. But this survey could not be permitted to end abruptly in midstream. For the sake of proper balance, therefore, and in order to round out the overall picture, a brief general statement is required concerning the main events that led up first to the peak, and soon thereafter to the headlong decline of the political might of Mesopotamia, towards the middle of the first millennium.

The independent cultural developments within the same period will be touched upon in the following chapter.

The time about 1200 B.C.E. constitutes another epochal juncture in the history of the pre-classical world, one in which the Near East was deeply involved, but other regions were likewise affected. Modern historical literature, influenced in this instance by the Egyptian view of things, has come to list the whole episode under the heading of the "Sea Peoples," a picturesque and not altogether inaccurate designation. The fact is that massive migrations by land and sea, proceeding perhaps from areas around the Black Sea, put an end to the Hittite domination of eastern Anatolia, exposed Egypt to critical danger, and deposited the Philistines in a land which was henceforth to bear witness to that event in its derived name of Palestine. If we look for the main factor behind this great upheaval, we cannot go far wrong if we trace it to the coming of iron. The Bible has preserved vivid recollections of this potent and new technological factor, in peace and war, in such passages as Judges 4:3 and I Samuel 13:19–22. Sweeping changes on such a scale were bound to have their repercussions also in the other portions of the Near East. One is not surprised, therefore, to note that both Babylonia and Assyria show at that time clear evidence of a temporary political decline. This circumstance is capitalized in the east by the Elamites, and in the west by a new and ever restive nomadic element, the Aramaeans. The Elamite ruler Shutruk-Nahunte invades Babylonia, sometime before the middle of the 12th century, and despoils its major centers of such priceless treasures as Naram-Sin's "Stele of Victory" and Hammurabi's famous law code stele, among many others. All were to be eventually recaptured in Susa by the far-reaching arm of archaeology. But the two Mesopotamian states are soon on the rebound. Babylonia puts an end at last to the unprecedentedly long reign of the Kassites, and proceeds to enjoy much success and prosperity under a vigorous local ruler, Nebuchadrezzar I (third quarter of the 12th century). Assyria, too, quickly regains its stride under a great new leader, Tiglath-pileser I. His name, in common with that of his Babylonian contemporary, was to be used again by other kings, in tribute to the achievements of the past and as a good omen for the future.

For a landlocked land like Assyria, bent as it was on expansion, there was little prospect of peace and security from any point of the compass. To the south, Babylon was ever a source of irritation in more ways than one. To the west, the elusive Aramaeans had to be dealt with in a virtually unending series of wearisome campaigns; and beyond the Aramaean territories lay the established states of the eastern coastlands of the Mediterranean.

To the north loomed the forbidding mountain fastnesses of Urartu. And the east, beyond the districts of the Lullu and the Guti, posed a constant threat on the part of the Elamites, and eventually the Medes and the Persians. It is readily apparent, therefore, why for a period of nearly four centuries — from the start of the reign of Tiglath-pileser I to the end of that of Tiglath-pileser III — Assyria could seldom enjoy a spell of genuine respite.

Much has been written about the various aspects of Assyrian life. Religion and literature, law and business, art and architecture — these and other facets on Assyrian society have received their due share of attention as reflected in special monographs. Assyrian sculpture in particular exercises to this day a powerful appeal, thanks especially to the boldness and vigor of its designs and the extreme sensitivity in its handling of animals. Comparatively little, however, has been done in the field of Assyria's military economy, although it was this area of endeavor above all others that had most to do with the mechanism of Assyrian expansion. A campaign in the mountainous districts of Armenia or Media, where massive fortresses barred the way to attackers weary from months of marching, must have required painstaking planning and organization as well as prodigious resources in manpower and supplies. The siege of such strongholds as Damascus and Tyre, or Samaria and Jerusalem, could not but be a costly undertaking. Nevertheless, the long string of Assyrian victories continued for centuries, unlike the awesome but ephemeral successes of the Ummān-manda or the Indo-Aryans in the past. All this argues for a sound prior tradition of administrative and military experience.

We now have sundry textual hints that such was indeed the case. Already in the days of Shamshi-Addu the military census was a solemn enough undertaking to be given the ritual designation *tebibtu* "purification."[62] One of the byproducts was the replacing "of the missing and the dead."[63] Later, under Mitanni, the Nuzi texts abound in lists of chariots and arms, horses and attendants, which the landowners were obliged to furnish to the proper authorities, and which had to pass rigid muster before being accepted;[64] we have seen that Mitanni paved the way for the rise of the Assyrian empire. Still later, at the height of the Middle Assyrian era, similar documents from Shibaniba (Tell Billa) allow some insight into frontier organization under Shalmaneser I, the father of Tukulti-Ninurta I.[65] The military tradition was thus carefully nurtured throughout the second millennium, and bore increasing dividends in the first. But it constituted a steady drain on the local economy, which booty and tribute could not entirely offset. The brunt of the suffering, of course, had to be borne by the vanquished. Yet the home front of the victors did not escape unscathed.

To return to our outline of salient events, there are several rulers within the span now under review whose names have long been familiar from Biblical sources and from native records. None, however, is as important to us from one particular point of view as Adad-Nirari II. For his reign was epoch-making in the literal sense of the term. Although we know little else about him that is noteworthy, the fact that the Assyrians began with this king a new eponym canon is sufficient to make his accession an event of great significance to the history of the Near East as a whole. It is this canon that enables us for the first time to establish a reliable absolute chronology for Assyria and thereby, thanks to certain synchronisms, not infrequently also for other areas of the Near East, including Israel and Judah. Precisely because the previous reigns are not covered by eponym lists of sufficient length and dependability, their dating remains uncertain and is subject to a margin of error which increases as we move farther into the past. Such decisive phases as those of Sargon of Akkad or Hammurabi have given rise to widely divergent chronological speculations, so much so that any semblance of absolute dating has been scrupulously avoided thus far in the present account. The canon of Adad-Nirari II frees us at last from undue dependence on relative chronology, and the consequent use of round figures; and his reign — to initiate the revised procedure — can be set down as covering the years 910-899.

In common with the later Athenians, the Assyrians listed regnal years since time immemorial, not after some special event — as was the case in Babylonia — but according to annually designated officials of the state, each serving one *līmu* or "eponymy." The eponym canon that began with the accession of Adad-Nirari II happens to cover an unbroken span of over a quarter millennium. What is more, this long sequence can be fixed astronomically, thanks to an eclipse of the sun which was duly recorded under one of the eponyms, and is dated exactly to June 15, 763. By working up and down from this fixed date, it is relatively simple to assign absolute dates to the other entries in the canon. Thus, through the priceless gift of literacy, a phenomenon that struck terror in the hearts of contemporaries was destined to be put by posterity to great positive service.

Three other kings of this half of the Neo-Assyrian period merit special mention even in the present sketchy outline. One is Ashurnasirpal II (884–859), who seemed to delight in recording his acts of mass violence against his defeated opponents. This policy may have been aimed at future foes as a potent warning. But it could also have stemmed in part from a striving to apply to the letter the various curses which Assyrian treaties reserve for violators, and which somehow required implementation. In any case, Ashurnasirpal is by no means the only Assyrian ruler to boast of his brutality. As regards domestic policies, and perhaps in line with the northward shift of the political center of gravity, the capital was moved to Calach (modern Nimrud), where cavalier excavations in the past century uncovered immense museum treasures, but ignored the inherent scientific evidence that modern archaeology has since learned to wrest from ancient sites. The outstanding sculptures of this period, which feature battle reliefs and hunting scenes, display a forcefulness of design combined with an economy of formulas.[66]

Shalmaneser III (859–824) was the first Assyrian ruler to come into direct contact with Israel as a result of Ashur's steady expansion towards the Mediterranean. His principal target was Damascus; but that city's Aramaean master had among his confederates "Ahab the Israelite," who is said to have furnished 2,000 chariots and 10,000 foot soldiers.[67] The famous Black Obelisk of Shalmaneser contains a panel which depicts the tribute of Jehu "the son of Omri."[68] Another rich pictorial record of Shalmaneser's campaigns was carved on the bronze plating of the palace gates in Imgur-Enlil (modern Balawat, near Nineveh).

Assyria had thus come a long way since its initial resurgence following the collapse of Mitanni. Essentially, however, it was still a bulging state rather than an integrated empire. The man whose deeds and policies brought about the transition from state to empire was Tiglath-pileser III (746–727), perhaps the ablest ruler and most original spirit in the long line of Adasi, which for a millennium exercised control over Assyria. His military triumphs include the defeat of Urartu, the capture of the stubborn fortress of Arpad (cf. II Kings 18:34 and Isa. 10:9), and the final subjugation of Damascus (732). It was in this last instance that Tiglath-pileser had the assistance of Ahaz, who had been hard pressed by an Israelite-Aramaean alliance, "these two tails of smoking firebrands" in the prophet's unforgettable phrase (Isa. 7:4).

Perhaps the most effective single policy in Tiglath-pileser's prominent career as empire builder was his treatment of conquered territories. Hitherto the Assyrians had sought to forestall rebellion by mass executions and deportations, which were calculated to turn the survivors into docile vassals. Tiglath-pileser's procedure was more far-sighted; he instituted a systematic interchange of frontier populations from one end of his domain to the other, while annexing the subdued districts as outright provinces of Assyria. Transplanted communities had less opportunity for uprisings than entrenched native groups. The Aramaeans, for example, who had been causing Assyria untold grief for many centuries, were now uprooted and dispersed — a circumstance which soon helped to spread their language as a common medium throughout the sprawling empire, but effectively neutralized at the same time their former military potential.

The best evidence, however, of Tiglath-pileser's constructive statesmanship is provided by Babylonia. None of the preceding Assyrian kings had been able to deal successfully with the complex and perennial southern problem. Harsh policies were certain to boomerang sooner or later, as was tragically demonstrated in the case of Tukulti-Ninurta I. Tiglath-pileser's approach was entirely different. He proceeded against Babylonia methodically and in judiciously spaced stages. And when Babylon's own turn came, he was at pains to respect the religious and psychological sensibilities of its governing classes. Instead of antagonizing them by annexing Babylonia as just another Assyrian province, Tiglath-pileser gained their cooperation by personally ascending the local throne under the inoffensive name of Pulu. By this novel device of a personal union he succeeded in flattering local pride while holding the opposition at bay.

The wisdom and foresight of Tiglath-pileser may not have been immediately apparent to all concerned. But these qualities stand out clearly in retrospect, in sharp contrast to the policies of his several successors.

The concluding phase is highlighted in Assyria by the successive reigns of Sargon II, Sennacherib, Esarhaddon, and Ashurbanipal. Yet the dominant personality of this era was a woman who had a singular effect on the careers of the last three of these far-famed rulers. In Babylonia, the protagonist is Nebuchadrezzar II, the most celebrated member of a new Chaldaean dynasty. But Mesopotamia's history can no longer be confined to its immediate geographic environment. The Valley of the Two Rivers is now more than ever but a link in a larger interregional configuration.

By a curious quirk of historical geography, the contemporary Near East as a whole yields a strikingly analogous pattern in terms of two parallel tiers of states. From west to east, the northern tier is highlighted by Israel, Assyria, and Media; this is matched in the south by Judah, Babylonia, and Persia respectively. Presently, like so many straws in the path of a mighty wind, Israel is cut off by Assyria, which in turn is swept away under pressure from Media; and Judah succumbs to Babylon, which is then displaced by Persia. Much of this correspondence, of course, is fortuitous. Yet the sweep of events and their consistent direction indicate that another epoch in world affairs is imminent. Some twenty-odd centuries of Mesopotamian

Tepe Gawra. General view of the acropolis of stratum XIII looking north.
The University Museum, Philadelphia.

El Obeid epoch (fourth millenium). Female figurine with human body and reptilian head, wearing crown, from Ur.
The University Museum, Philadelphia.

Inscription of Enhegal, king of Lagash, cut on stone tablet.
The University Museum, Philadelphia.

Statue of a priest from Khafaje.

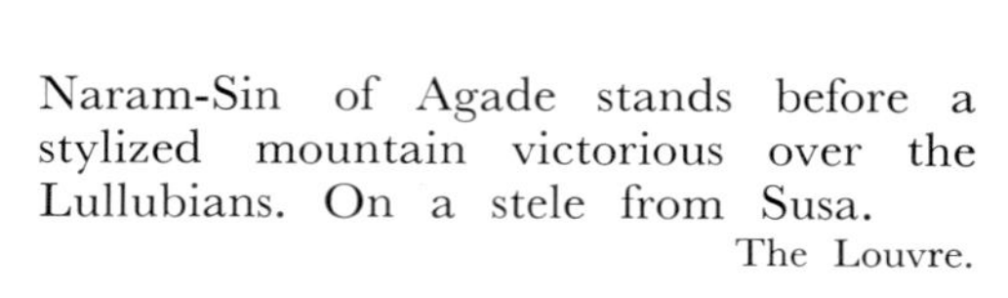

Naram-Sin of Agade stands before a stylized mountain victorious over the Lullubians. On a stele from Susa.
The Louvre.

King's Grave. Plaque of shell inlay from the end of the sound-box of Ur lyre.
The University Museum, Philadelphia.

Standard from Ur; "Peace panel" depicting celebration of a victory with music and feasting.
The British Museum.

Standard from Ur; "War panel" depicting the triumph of the king over his enemies.
The British Museum.

The Ziggurrat at Ur. N. E. Face, Southern angle, platform and central staircase.
The University Museum, Philadelphia.

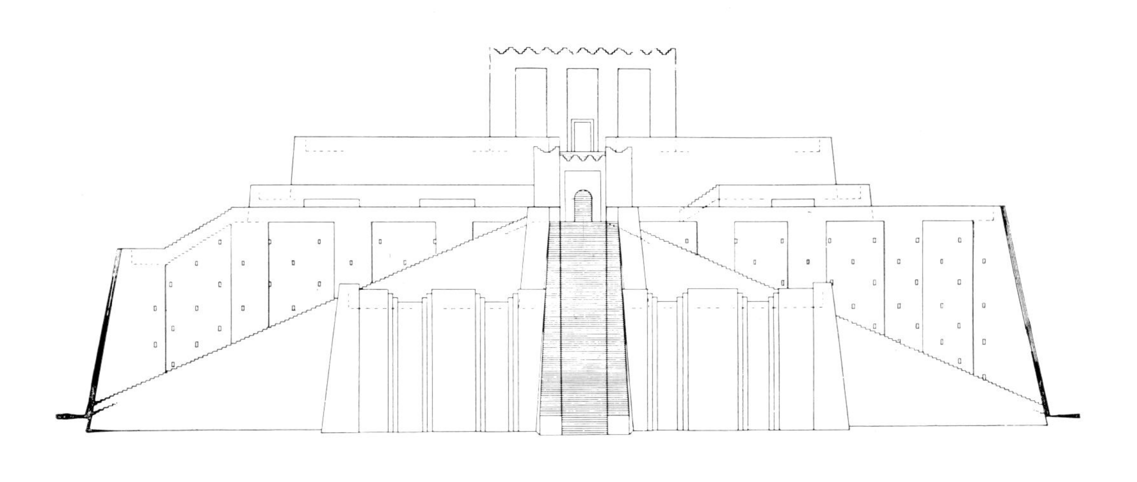

The Ziggurrat at Ur. N. E. Elevation. Reconstruction.
The University Museum, Philadelphia.

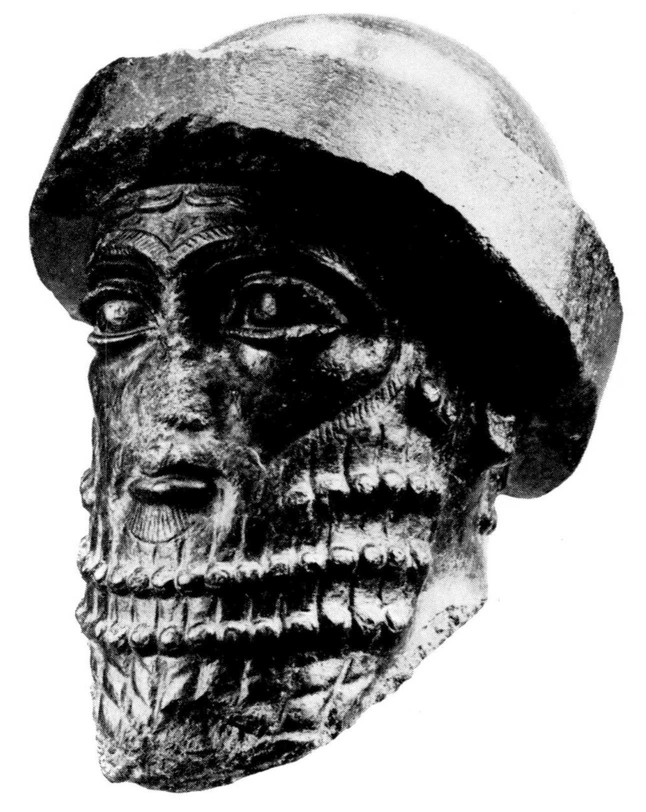

Head of a King, possibly Hammurabi.
The Louvre.

The Stele of Hammurabi inscribed with laws.
The Louvre.

Ashurnasirpal II hunting lions.
The Mansell Collection, London.

Dying Lion (9 Cent. B.C.E.).
The Mansell Collection, London.

Shalmaneser III receives tribute from "Jehu, son of Omri"; the latter is upon his hands and knees; detail from Shalmaneser's obelisk.
The British Museum.

Obelisk of Shalmaneser III
The British Museum.

Gold helmet of Mes-Kalam-dug, King(?) of Ur, from a royal tomb at Ur.
The University Museum, Philadelphia.

Man riding a bull; terra cotta plaque from Ishchali; beginning of second mill. B.C.E.

Clay chariot from Gawra.
Photograph, The University Museum, Phi

Tell Agrab, ca. 2800 B.C.E. Right side view of small copper war chariot drawn by four asses.
Oriental Institute, University of Chicago.

A harpist; terra cotta plaque
Ishchali; beginnig of second mill. B
Oriental Institute, University of Chi

self-rule are drawing to a close, and the Iranian phase of Near Eastern history is about to set in.

To return to Assyria, a few years after the death of Tiglath-pileser III the throne was seized by Sargon II (722–705). Although of royal blood,[69] he did not enjoy an undisputed right to succession, a fact which is underscored by the aggressive bearing of his regnal name *Šarrukên* "The king is legitimate." We had an identical instance of protesting too much in the case of his illustrious namesake Sargon of Akkad, back in the third millennium. The reign of the present Sargon got off to what must have been in Assyrian eyes an auspicious start: Samaria was captured after a long siege, which the previous king had begun; and the kingdom of Israel ceased to be. There followed a long line of military triumphs, in Media, Urartu, and Anatolia, in Syria and even on the island of Cyprus. Yet none of these successes could quiet Sargon's restless spirit. Driven by inner urges which are beyond our means to trace, this haunted ruler, so very like Tukulti-Ninurta I of half a millennium earlier, built himself a magnificent new capital a dozen miles north of Nineveh, and named it, similarly again, *Dūr-Šarrukên* "Sargonsburg." But even this resplendent retreat could not distract the monarch for long. Estranged from his favorite son Sennacherib, whom he had made co-regent, Sargon sought surcease in more strenuous exertions in faraway and inhospitable Media, where he met his death at last on some unknown battlefield. And according to Assyrian beliefs, death without benefit of the prescribed burial rites was the very antithesis of eternal rest.

Sennacherib (705–681) inherited his father's drive, and much of his restlessness, but his mode of self-expression was different in many ways. Unable to tolerate the slightest challenge to his supremacy, whether real or imaginary, Sennacherib must have decided early in his reign on a campaign against Egypt, the only traditionally prominent power that had yet to feel the direct impact of Assyrian arms. To this end he first had to obtain control of Palestine, and this brought him eventually into conflict with Hezekiah, king of unyielding little Judah. A frightful pestilence, however — a veritable act of God — took an awesome toll of Assyrian forces in 701, and their leader was compelled to give up the siege of Jerusalem, with only booty to show for all his toil and losses. A far more irksome blow to his pride was the refusal of Babylon — always a thorn in Assyria's side — aided and abetted by Elam, to pay him the homage that he deemed his due. In a punitive campaign against the south, in 689, Sennacherib vented his fury against the proud capital by razing it to the ground, after having desecrated its shrines with a thoroughness that exceeded even the savage efforts of Tukulti-Ninurta I. When the death of the vindictive conqueror followed a few years later, at the hands of his own flesh and blood,[70] there could not have been many educated members of his entourage who were unawed by the striking correspondence between the career of their master and that of his Middle-Assyrian predecessor, both in the sequence of events and in their tragic climax.

Unlike his father, whose prodigious building activities failed to give him lasting satisfaction, Sennacherib found much pleasure, as well as scope for his genuine technological bent, in ambitious and imaginative engineering enterprises. Among these may be listed the construction of a great aqueduct in the hill country near Jerwan, which assured his new capital at Nineveh of a steady water supply from thirty miles away; the erection of great palaces and temples in that same capital; and the building of ships for a naval engagement with Elam. In his personal life, too, Sennacherib proved to be a bold innovator. His favorite wife was a woman of foreign ancestry, as is clear from her dual Canaanite-Akkadian name of *Naqịyā-Zakūtu*, or approximately "Pure, Freed."[71] It would be tempting to see in this mésalliance the true reason for Sennacherib's ultimate estrangement from his father, but there is no evidence for such an assumption, suggestive though it may be. On the other hand, there is good reason for the view that Sennacherib's own violent death, to which both the Bible and the Babylonian Chronicle bear independent witness, was precipitated by advance arrangements for his succession. The eventual heir to the throne was Naqiya's son Esarhaddon. There were several anxious weeks during which Esarhaddon (681–669) had to battle for his right to the throne and — as he tells it — punish the murderers of his father. Curiously enough, the Assyrian sources never mention the assassins by name. This circumstance, among others, has led some modern students to conclude that Esarhaddon himself may have had a hand in his father's murder,[72] and was compelled immediately thereafter to withdraw temporarily from public life so as not to face public opinion.[73] As yet, there is no decisive evidence either to confirm or to reject such assumptions. It is, however, an established fact that the Queen Mother remained the major power behind her son's reign.

From what we know positively, Esarhaddon was neither as vindictive as his father nor as impulsive. In military matters, he placed much reliance on a group of experienced generals who had been brought up in the hard school of Sennacherib. Their greatest achievement was the conquest of Egypt, in 671, which for the first time in history brought the world's two oldest centers of civilization under single rule. In Babylonia, Esarhaddon strove to undo some of the harm that his father had caused. By helping to rebuild the ancient capital he managed to gain the cooperation of the local priesthood.

In the final analysis, Esarhaddon lacked both the temperament and the physical stamina for authoritarian behavior. His health was chronically poor, and there was also much sickness in his immediate family, except for the seemingly imperishable Naqiya. Two total eclipses of the moon in the single year 671 spread panic in the land, and desperate remedies were resorted to, including the ritual murder of a substitute king.[74] Nevertheless, soon afterwards an uprising in Egypt appeared to lend substance to the ill omens. The ailing king deemed it his duty to follow his armies in a punitive expedition against the rebels, but death overtook him before he could reach the Egyptian border.[75]

According to the law of the land, the oldest son was to receive a double and preferential share of his dead father's estate; the younger brothers had to be content with single portions of what was left. Yet this law, which surely played a part in the matter of royal succession, was disregarded on the death of Esarhaddon. The older surviving heir, Shamash-shum-ukin, was obliged to accept the throne of Babylon, while the younger, Ashurbanipal (660–630?), became the head of the whole Assyrian empire. In this violation of accepted norms, old Naqiya again played a decisive part. She had taken the necessary steps while her son was still alive; and when the moment came, she left no doubt in anybody's mind — as we can tell from a vivid account that luckily has come down to us — that she was in no mood to brook any opposition. And her will prevailed.[76]

In choosing Ashurbanipal, Naqiya had clearly picked the abler of the two brothers. To that extent, at least, her judgment was to be vindicated. Yet her decision entailed two consequences that could not be foreseen. One was the aggravation of latent hostilities between the sister countries of Babylonia and Assyria, and between the two brothers who took over their rule. This much could be foretold in advance, but Naqiya evidently discounted the inherent risks. It is unlikely, however, that even she anticipated the ruinous war in which Babylon would be starved into submission, its hapless ruler perishing in the ruins of his charred palace (648).

The other consequence was still more difficult to compute in advance. It derived from the circumstance that Ashurbanipal, as one of the younger princes, had been destined originally for the priesthood. This called for rigorous training in various disciplines, including languages, literature, divination, and the like. When fate, assisted by an imperious grandmother, had diverted his career from spiritual to secular channels, Ashurbanipal went on to capitalize on his intellectual investment in a number of ways. Yet he always retained a genuine appreciation of learning. This lifelong interest bore rich fruit in the form of the marvelous library which he assembled in Nineveh. His experts combed the best collections in the various centers of Mesopotamia, procuring, copying, or simply appropriating whatever seemed at all worthwhile.[77] Ashurbanipal, of course, could have no inkling at the time that the days of Assyria were numbered. Nor could he possibly foresee that his library would survive the destruction of Nineveh, to serve, two and a half millenniums later, as an excellent guide to the intellectual and spiritual treasures that had accumulated during the preceding twenty-five centuries, and had come to be embodied in the clay records left in the ruins of his capital.

The prolonged war with Babylon was bound to distract Ashurbanipal's attention from distant Egypt, which soon regained its independence. But nearby Elam, which had incited and backed Babylon's revolt, had to be taught a lesson once and for all. As matters turned out before long, Ashurbanipal was all too successful in carrying out this resolve. Elam was crushed, in 639, so thoroughly that it was eliminated forever as a political factor. But the power vacuum thus created was soon to be filled by other and far more dangerous antagonists. It was only a matter of decades before the Medes visited the fate of Elam on Assyria itself.

For some as yet obscure reason, a strange and ominous silence engulfs the concluding years of Ashurbanipal's reign. We cannot determine the exact year of his death; and it is pure guesswork whether he died from natural or other causes. For some time past, disquieting rumblings had been reaching Assyria from the northeast quarter, the echoes of vast stirrings among intrusive bands of Cimmerians and Scyths, Medes and Persians. The Medes were now ready for their major move on the stage of world history. Encouraged by a resurgent Babylonia, which meanwhile had come under the forceful leadership of the Chaldaean chieftain Nabopalassar (626–605), the new masters of Iran gradually forced the Assyrians to fall back upon their own capital. When Nineveh's end came, in 612, its destruction was so complete that within two centuries Xenophon's Greeks did not even know that they had been in sight of the remains of a recently mighty world capital.

Thus, within forty years, Assyria had toppled from the very pinnacle of power, as mistress of Western Asia and Egypt, to the depths of utter destruction and oblivion. Yet a mighty and well organized empire cannot fall overnight unless it had been exposed to commensurate forces, from without or within, or both. The full answer may well lie hidden under the cloak of silence that still covers the last decade of Ashurbanipal's reign. At the present rate of archaeological discoveries, this lost decade may yet be illuminated before very long.

For approximately two generations we witness a new balance of power. Media controls the north, from Iran to Anatolia, with former Assyria now included in this sprawling domain. Chaldaean Babylonia, under Nebuchadrezzar II (605–562) — the Nebuchadnezzar of understandably prejudiced Biblical memory [78] — is left in charge of the southern belt, all the way to the Mediterranean. But Babylon's hold on this vast area does not go unchallenged. The major claimant is Egypt, which hitherto had been alternating its support between Assyria and Babylonia, depending on which was weaker. The Egyptian policy is now to foment, from a relatively safe distance, rebel moves in Syria and Palestine, spearheaded by Tyre and Judah. Such moves, however, are foredoomed to failure. Among all those who witnessed the might of Nebuchadrezzar's hosts, there could not have been many who sensed, with the prophets, that the Babylonian giant had feet of clay, after all. But the realists were to be confounded, and the visionaries confirmed, within a few decades. In 539, Cyrus II (the Great), whose Persian forces had in the meantime wrested control from the Medes, opened a new chapter in world history by capturing Babylon, and with it not only the political but also the immense cultural heritage of the world's oldest civilization.

The prize that thus fell to Cyrus had been greatly enhanced under the long and prosperous reign of Nebuchadrezzar. Small wonder, then, that contemporary Babylonians had to reach all the way back to Hammurabi for a suitable parallel. It was, to be sure, only a fool's paradise. Yet the fame and prestige of Babylon — in contrast to Ashur's and Nineveh's — were now immune from political disasters. Even after the Persian phase had been superseded by the Hellenistic era, Alexander dreamed of making Babylon the capital of his new world empire. Like the fictional project of the Tower of Babel, this plan, too, came to an ironic end.

Mesopotamia's place, however, in world history is not wholly circumscribed by the political fortunes of the land. The local culture had always been a separate factor to some extent, immensely beneficial to the state, yet capable of pursuing an independent course. Thus Mesopotamian civilization reached out beyond its original geographic boundaries under the Sargonids, in the third millennium, and particularly in the second millennium when the land itself was largely under the control of outsiders. It is not surprising, therefore, that the indigenous cultural product did not die out with the fall of Nineveh and Babylon, toward the middle of the first millennium. Yet radical changes in environment will have their effect. What survived of the Mesopotamian influences abroad while Babylonia and Assyria were still flourishing, or at home after both had disappeared as sovereign states, was not so much the integrated and historic Mesopotamian civilization as certain specific features of it — disembodied elements, as it were, in new surroundings and combinations.

It remains, then, to discuss first the role of the native culture in the historic career of Mesopotamia, and next the independent manifestations of that culture beyond the geographical and chronological limits of the states that served as its background.

3. THE CULTURAL COMPONENT

A. History and Civilization

IN THE FOREGOING survey of Mesopotamian history the accent was largely on change. Nor was such emphasis out of place. The changes observed were by no means the normal byproduct of growth. They were in the main the outcome of ethnic movements which from time to time caused major displacements among the leading actors on the stage. The physical environment of Mesopotamia, to which attention was drawn at the start, had much to do, no doubt, with the course and tempo of events.

Yet frequent shifts in the ethnopolitical alignment do not of themselves afford an adequate insight into the historic career of Mesopotamia. As was indicated in passing on more than one occasion, the cultural conditions reflect a surprising degree of uniformity, despite an unstable ethnic pattern and a fitful political picture. Throughout the recorded history of the land, Mesopotamian civilization remained essentially a constant and steadying factor. What is more, it found some of its staunchest adherents among the converts along its route, notably in Assyria.

We have thus before us on the cultural side of the question the uncommon phenomenon of unity through change, and of ultimate harmony through underlying disparity. It is a phenomenon that merits closer investigation, for the problems involved are pertinent not only to the place and period under review, but to other civilizations and ages, not excluding our own. This is not the time, however, to attempt such an inquiry in appropriate detail. Within the present limitations of space and exposition, we can only take up, in broad outline, some of the main features.

It may not be amiss at this point to stress anew that the basic unity of Mesopotamian civilization is an actual fact and not just scholarly speculation. Such a re-affirmation is especially in order since a recent and widely acclaimed "Study of History" would distinguish the "Sumeric" and the "Babylonic" civilizations as two separate entities. The contrary evidence in this instance happens to be unusually rich, extensive, and pervasive.[1] It is best epitomized perhaps in a statement by a competent royal witness whose own consuming interest in the matter was to result in an imperishable anthology of the cultural achievements of Mesopotamia. In describing his education as a young prince, Ashurbanipal takes obvious pride in saying: "I read the involved texts in Sumerian and in the obscure Akkadian, so difficult to understand. And I took up the . . . stone records from before the Flood."[2] So speaks an Assyrian king of the mid-seventh century, one whose reign was marred by the bitterest kind of fratricidal struggle with Babylonia. Yet he never lost sight of the fact that the two countries shared the same culture. It need hardly be added that the great library which Ashurbanipal assembled contains innumerable illustrations of that one fundamental fact.

Nor is Ashurbanipal's enlightened tribute an isolated or atypical example. Similar recognition of the underlying cultural factor was already apparent under the Dynasty of Akkad — sixteen centuries earlier — and indeed even before that, when official inscriptions began to use Sumerian and Akkadian side by side. This was not merely a concession to the existing ethnic and linguistic dichotomy, but rather another reflection of the fact that the two unrelated languages concerned were joint carriers of the same cultural heritage. The resulting linguistic symbiosis is probably unmatched in the annals of mankind either in duration or in the degree of its intimacy. It was not simply a question of writing and orthography. The Sumerian language itself came to insinuate itself into the fabric of Akkadian — in phonology, morphology, and syntax, and in countless modes of expression. Bilingualism struck root and flourished precisely because it was in the service of a single civilization. The prodigious and successful labors of the Old Babylonian schools to preserve the Sumerian legacy for posterity are but another indication of the essential cultural unity of Mesopotamia.

It is impossible here to do justice to the rest of the available evidence; a few additional samples will have to suffice. Thus literary motifs and personalities that were featured in Sumer and Akkad in the third millennium maintain their hold on second-millennium Babylonia and first-millennium Assyria. Traditional hymns and prayers, rituals and omens, fables and proverbs — these and many others enjoy, in virtually unaltered form, the same wide usage through all the periods and areas involved. This does not mean, of course, that each age and district subsisted only on what tradition had managed to preserve. Distinctive new contributions are never lacking. But the inherited matter, so far from being discarded, is treated with ever increasing appreciation and reverence. Such an approach might be understandable in the south, where a Nebuchadrezzar would have good grounds for harking back to the golden age of Hammurabi. The tendency, however, to fall back on the common cultural core — one which Assyria shared with Babylonia — is no less in evidence in the north. Once again, Ashurbanipal is our shining example, although there are many others like him. One of his antiquarian agents, on a collecting mission to the south, was told to procure "rituals, prayers, inscriptions on stone, and whatever else may be good for my kingship," as well as "any tablet or ritual . . . that is good for my palace."[3] To a royal student of history the past was significant because it could help the present to face the future. But the past in this case had become a strictly cultural concept. And culturally, the roots of historic Assyria were felt to reach deep down into southern soil.

In the face of so much common interest, one might ask why the existing differences remained so acute and constant. It is in order, therefore, to emphasize that the divisive factors were by no means negligible. To concentrate only on Babylonia and Assyria — as the two antagonists of longest record — their two lands differed in physical environment and local economy, in details of dress, laws, and customs, in art and architecture, in dialect, and in national temperament. What is remarkable, then, is not that political division and animosity persisted, but that cultural unity survived in spite of these obstacles. In Assyria, at any rate, the civilization that was shared with Babylonia was taken for granted as the common heritage of Mesopotamia.

Why is it, then, that among the interested students there are still some who are unaware of the fundamental unity of the historic civilization of Mesopotamia? It would seem that the current notions as to what makes a distinctive civilization are urgently in need of revision. "Material remains in themselves are not the decisive criteria of ancient civilizations that they are usually believed to be. However great may be the difference between the pyramids and the ziggurrats, and however spectacular, the principal features of the parent cultures reach deeper and loom larger."[4] The really decisive criteria prove to be societal: religion, government, law. Even the material content, if not the form, will often be found to reflect the influence of the overriding societal factor, notably so in architecture and art. How, then, did that factor manifest itself in the career of ancient Mesopotamia?

B. Religion

It may safely be taken for granted that all major civilizations must eventually come to terms with two issues above all others: the relation of the individual to society; and the alignment of society with nature.[5] The one is the essence of government; the other is the foundation of religion. Because Mesopotamia's own approach to the religious issue had a very special bearing on the local concept of state, it will be dealt with first.

As was indicated in the foregoing section, the civilization of Mesopotamia maintained exceptional unity in spite of a variety of participants. Assyria was keenly aware of its cultural kinship with Babylonia, and Babylonia in turn looked back with reverence on its heritage from Sumer and Akkad. It follows that the dominant religious beliefs of the land must have arisen early in its history. Our first direct written evidence cannot, of course, antedate the pioneering period of Sumer, but certain typical features of the religion of Mesopotamia are already apparent in the oldest texts. For still earlier periods recourse must be had to conjectural reconstruction. It is inherently possible that in their spiritual system the Sumerians incorporated elements which had come down from their predecessors, just as they did in various phases of their material culture.[6] This time, however, they would seem to have been less eclectic. The principal deities of the Sumerian pantheon bear names that are transparently Sumerian. The world in which they move is part of one and the same consistent pattern. In all probability, therefore, the religion of historic Mesopotamia was in its essentials an original Sumerian contribution.

It must suffice here to name only the leading deities. There was thus the top male triad consisting of *An*, "Sky, Heaven," *Enlil*, apparently "Lord of the Atmosphere" in name, but in function a mountain god as well, and *Enki* (Akkadian Ea), god of the netherworld and the deep. The female associate of these three was sometimes *Ninḫursag* "Lady of the Cosmic Mountain," and at other times *Inanna* "Mistress of Heaven."

With the shift in political authority from the Sumerians to the Akkadians, there occurred in due time a corresponding change in religious emphasis to the male triad of *Šamaš*, the sun god, *Sîn*, the moon god, and *Adad*, the storm god; and the appertaining goddess emerged as *Ištar*, the counterpart of Inanna. Yet the old Sumerian hierarchy is by no means ignored. Enlil is still formidable; he might be replaced, for local reasons, by a *Marduk* in Babylonia or an *Aššur* in synonymous Assyria, but the change is primarily one of name rather than function. Above all, Ea continues as patron of wisdom — which was also one of Enki's attributes — and as mankind's tried and trusted friend in the community of the gods.

In regard to cosmology and theogony, the orthodox tradition, as embodied in the canonical Creation Epic *Enūma Eliš* "When on High" (after the initial words of the poem), recalls a period of acute crisis when the fate of the world was in the balance. But the emergency ended with the victory of Enlil — elsewhere of Marduk or Ashur — over the forces of Chaos headed by *Tiāmat*, goddess of the seas. Thereafter all was peaceful and serene in the cosmic realm. This blissful state, however, is a theological dogma carried by the prevailing orthodox version. Fragments of more or less apocryphal and apparently earlier accounts give hints of rivalries and violence following the defeat of Tiamat, whereby Enlil deposed his father An and was in turn challenged by his own descendants.

The motif of primeval strife, which orthodoxy thus chose to center about Tiamat, but to which it gave wider distribution, becomes one of the basic features of the Mesopotamian world view. This contest was never resolved for all time. It is echoed annually in the dramatic struggle between winter and spring — or death and life — and reaches its climax with the turn of the New Year.[7] The event is commemorated on a note of abject despair followed by joyous release of pent-up emotions. Such spring rites, of course, have their analogues all over the world. In Mesopotamia, however, they were endowed with singular gravity, in that the period in question was one of critical decision on which hung the destiny of the cosmos for the ensuing year. It was then that the fate of everybody was recorded and sealed. The sense of acutest anxiety that was bound up with these proceedings colored the Mesopotamian's whole philosophy of life:

> The Anunnaki, the great gods, foregather;
> Mammetum, maker of fate, with them the fate decrees:
> Death and life they determine.
> But of death, its days are not revealed.[8]

These beliefs were so pervasive as to leave an indelible impression on the cultural affiliates of Mesopotamia. Even though the Jewish New Year, for example, came to be celebrated in autumn as opposed to spring, the Mishnah[9] and the traditional prayers[10] still reflect in sentiment and phraseology their acute awareness of destinies to be recorded and sealed, in common with Mesopotamian beliefs and practices.

What aggravated the sense of danger at the turn of the New Year was the accepted fact that the gods themselves were in the dark to the last moment as to what lay ahead. And the reason why they were undecided and unsure was that none of the gods, not even the head of the pantheon, was truly omnipotent.[11] For ultimate authority was vested not in any given individual deity but in the community of the gods as a whole. To be valid and effective, all major decisions had to be passed upon by the full assembly. Thus the grant of immortality to the Flood hero Ut(a)napishtim required the approval of the plenary body; by the same token, lack of such sanction would prevent Gilgamesh from escaping his mortal destiny.[12] Even a Marduk could not take command in the crucial struggle against Tiamat, and earn the right to top rank in the event of victory, until the divine assembly had ratified the plan.[13] To be sure, in that instance the gods were lulled into acquiescence by a surfeit of food and drink, thanks to the scheming of Ea. But the tactical details by which the vacant post of chief god was filled are incidental. The significant fact remains that group approval was imperative. Although the very existence of the cosmos was at stake, the authority that was wanted in such a dire emergency could not be usurped, or the process of parliamentary rule suspended. Unilateral solutions were out of the question.

If group action, then, on the part of the gods was an article of the Mesopotamians' faith, what principles guided such action? A positive and consistent answer to this question would be difficult to find in all the vast literature that has come down to us. It will be freely granted that over a span of more than two millenniums, which this literature encompasses, individual thinkers were certain to rise here and there above the level of popular belief. But the general tenor of religious opinion and practice was little affected by the passage of time. The traditional framework remains normative to the end. Now, traditionally, the gods of Mesopotamia were motivated, as a rule, by a sense of what is right and just. Yet they were also inscrutable and unpredictable; they could be arbitrary and capricious, vindictive and malevolent. The passing centuries failed to purge them of these all too human traits. In short, the cosmos of the Mesopotamians lacked the support and comfort of ethical and moral principles. For all that mortals knew, the actions of the gods might be due to whim as much as anything else.

In these circumstances, one hoped for the best, but had to be prepared for the worst. To be sure, piety and good deeds were always helpful in minimizing the chances of misfortune. "If one rejects sin, his god will always walk with him,"[14] says an ethical omen. Just the same, exemplary personal conduct was not enough in itself. In a capricious cosmos, form might be every bit as important as content. And form meant ritual. Since there were countless grounds on which the gods might take offense, there was virtually no end to possible ritualistic safeguards. The ever more complex task of averting the gods' anger had to be entrusted to various classes of priests. The priests in turn prescribed increasingly more laborious observance. All this took an ever mounting toll of the individual's time, energy, and resources.

It is easy enough to see in retrospect that a greater emphasis on ethical content might have checked this process before it assumed the proportions of a cancerous growth. But such a shift in religious orientation would have required a drastically new approach as well as a sharp break with established tradition. And so the necessary step was never taken. Instead, the accent on external trappings grew stronger all the time. We can see from the official correspondence of the Neo-Assyrian period that ritualism had become a dead weight at the very time that Assyria was emerging as the leading world power. Beyond doubt, it would be a gross injustice to all the known facts to ascribe the fall of the Assyrian empire to any single factor; the result was conditioned by a number of causes. Nevertheless, it cannot be too hazardous to conclude that the internal spiritual vacuum helped to undermine the political structure and precipitate its eventual collapse.

There is much in the foregoing statement that is schematic and oversimplified. The religious life of an old and mature civilization cannot be capsulated in a few paragraphs. The total impression may thus be unduly onesided. It is in order, therefore, to point out for the sake of better balance that the Mesopotamian had strived from the start to decipher the will of heaven, even though in the end he found himself no closer to that goal than he had been in the beginning. He did succeed, however, in passing on to posterity a concrete and impressive symbol of his abiding quest: the temple tower or ziggurrat (Akkadian *siqqurratum*). On its artificial mound representing the cosmic mountain, stood a temple designed as a shrine on high to welcome the gods in their contacts with the world of mortals. The whole was conceived as a link between heaven and earth — a lofty affirmation of man's hope for a nobler future.

To this day, remains of isolated ziggurrats stand as eloquent witnesses of the Mesopotamians' earnest efforts to attain harmony with the forces of nature. The truncated cones at Borsippa and Dur-Kurigalzu are still among the tallest monuments in Iraq. In ancient times, similar temple towers rose up throughout the land, wherever in fact Mesopotamian civilization had struck firm root. Stratigraphically, the ziggurrat goes back to the earliest occupations that can be confidently assigned to the Sumerians. It is not likely, however, to antedate the Sumerians, inasmuch as the oldest known protohistoric temples in the land lack the lofty base. In other words, the specific concept of a visual bond between heaven and earth could well have been a Sumerian innovation. It was a concept, obviously, that could lend itself to abuses and thus draw the ridicule that is implicit in the Biblical account of the Tower of Babel.[15] The underlying idea, nevertheless, was one of humble hope rather than overweening pride. As such, it played a prominent part in sustaining Mesopotamian civilization through its long and fruitful career.

c. Government

The symbolic link between heaven and earth, as expressed by the ziggurat, had its practical counterpart in the field of government. The Sumerians' need for symmetry and balance — which is reflected also in the contrapuntal structure of the Sumerian sentence — led, among other things, to a concept of state on earth that was the exact replica of government in heaven. Accordingly, no mortal ruler could command absolute power, since even the head of the pantheon was not truly omnipotent. The authority of the king was thus circumscribed by two factors: his domain, like the celestial state itself, was subject to the principle of government by assembly; and his own mandate stemmed from the gods, so that he was responsible to them for his every move.

There is a variety of evidence for the normative role of the assembly — Sumerian *ukkin*, Akkadian *puḫrum* — in the socio-political structure of Mesopotamia. Corporate authority had to be the final authority among men, exactly as among gods. The Flood hero Utnapishtim cannot leave his doomed city, even at the request of the god Ea, until he had given a plausible excuse to his senate;[16] neither can Gilgamesh embark on his expedition against the dragon Huwawa without the consent of his council, however reluctantly it might be granted.[17] More important, because echoing actual if remote history, is the campaign of Gilgamesh against Agga of Kish; the protagonist obtains this time the solemn sanction of two assemblies, one of his warriors and the other of his elders.[18] The foundation of the state was thus consultative government. Mankind, we are told in the preamble to the Epic of Etana, was in a state of barbarism until "consultation" — Akkadian *mitlukum*, from the common Semitic root *mlk* — had been sent to earth from heaven.[19]

The above instances have been cited precisely because they are legendary or semi-legendary in nature. For by that very token they furnish intimate proof that in the consciousness of the Mesopotamians the overriding authority of the assembly reached deep down to remote prehistoric days. The practice, needless to add, was not confined to the dim past. It was a concrete feature of the historical age, which is why it was extended to the heroes of myths and legends in the first place. Nor was assembly approval a mere formality. We know this from the sober testimony of the omens, which can reflect history in stark and independent fashion. And this is why their statement, "the assembly has failed to reach an agreement" is both reliable and revealing.[20] Hung juries are not made up of mere yes-men.

If government by assembly was as much a safeguard against despotism in practice as it would seem to be in theory, there are two far-reaching tests which should show us conclusively whether such was actually the case in Mesopotamia. One is bound up with the question of the divine nature of the king; for a deified ruler implies an authoritarian type of government. The other touchstone is law; absolute royal power is not compatible with the independent authority of an impersonal legal system. It is necessary, therefore, to attain a measure of clarity on these two highly significant issues.

Perhaps no single problem relating to the history of Mesopotamia — with the possible exception of chronology — has led to such sharply divided opinions as the question whether the local king was regarded as divine. Yet a closer look at the total picture can yield only one answer. On the surface, some Mesopotamian rulers have the determinative for god prefixed to their names and affect certain other prerogatives of divinity. This practice, however, is limited and sporadic.[20a] It is met with under Naram-Sin of Akkad and his successor, the rulers of the Third Dynasty of Ur, and the kings of the transitional period prior to the First Dynasty of Babylon. But it is never encountered under Sargon of Akkad, or Hammurabi, the two greatest rulers of the south, or under any of the kings of Assyria, powerful though many of these turned out to be. The concept of a deified ruler is such an intimate component of the underlying civilization that it either belongs throughout, as in Egypt, or not at all, in which case it betrays itself as alien. Furthermore, such a practice, if genuine, should command universal acceptance and pervade all important phases of the society that evolved it. In Egypt, for instance, the divinity of the king was reflected prominently in art and architecture, in historical and literary works, and — negatively — in the absence of an impersonal code of laws.[21] None of this obtains in Mesopotamia. On the contrary, some of the very kings whose names carried the divine label in their lifetime, are soon held up as the image of ill-fated rulers by omens and threnodies. Such is notably the case with Naram-Sin, whose empire was ravaged by the Ummān-manda, and with Ibbi-Sin, who was overthrown by the Elamites.[22]

The typical Mesopotamian king was at pains to stress the difference between himself and his gods. Old Assyrian monarchs were content with the modest title of *iššakku* "toparch, governor," on the premise that only the gods were sovereign.[23] And Babylonian kings, in the course of the commemoration of the New Year, allowed priests to smite their cheeks, box their ears, and divest them of the insignia of their kingship, in order to emphasize the unworthiness of the incumbent.[24] Such a procedure would have been as shocking to an Egyptian as the concept of a divine pharaoh must have been repugnant to a Mesopotamian. Thus the sporadic and superficial deification of a limited number of rulers in Sumer and Akkad cannot be regarded by any means as a true reflex of the local culture. When it is recalled, moreover, that this usage is encountered during unsettled times, it cannot be too venturesome to conclude that the trappings of divine kingship were resorted to in Mesopotamia, in scattered instances and without any enduring effects, in an effort to bolster waning or threatened authority. But the idea was soon rejected as alien to the native culture in nature and in spirit.

In its bearing on the character of government in Mesopotamia, the argument from law has enough force and substance to be conclusive by itself; for legal systems mirror and implement the underlying concepts of state. Law and government are thus interrelated. While all advanced governments must have their laws, the status of the law in each instance will depend very largely on the type of government that the parent society has evolved.[25]

The Mesopotamian king was not the source of the law but only its agent; unlike the authoritarian ruler, he was not the master of the system but its servant. He was bound by the provisions of the law fully as much as his humblest subject; indeed more so, for he was accountable to the gods for eventual enactment. The Akkadian phrase that describes law in general is *kittum u mēšarum*, roughly Hebrew *'ᵉmeṯ wəẓedeq*, our "truth and justice." Now *kittum* stands for universal and immutable truths, the source of which was divine, not human. On the other hand, *mēšarum* is the process whereby law is made to function equitably. One of the king's principal duties was to institute *mēšarum*, by supervising, adjusting, or amending the current laws. When necessary, revised compilations were made, thus resulting in new "codes." Hammurabi did just that, and Lipit-Ishtar before him, and one of the kings of Eshnunna; so did also Ur-Nammu, and apparently Urukagina. Each time the compiler strives to carry out the divinely ordained *kittum*. The basic distinction between *kittum* and *mēšarum* is observed carefully by Hammurabi, who refers to himself as "the just king (*šar mēšarim*) to whom Shamash committed the sum of truths (*kinātim*, pl. of *kittum*)."[26] But total law was impersonal and above the crown. The king was only its duly appointed trustee. Legal practice did not lag far behind theory. The truth of this statement is borne out by the tens of thousands of juridical documents that have come down to us from all parts and periods of Mesopotamia, not to dwell at this time on the various cultural dependents of that land. The legal tradition was obviously a prime factor in the cultural life of the land. And the abiding appeal of the law was due, in the final analysis, to its proved ability to protect the basic rights of the individual and to serve as a buffer against absolutism.

Thus government by assembly and the overriding authority of the law are two separate facets of one and the same societal system. The passing centuries might bring successive changes; they might even witness contrary tendencies under this or that over-ambitious chief of state. In the long run, however, tradition would always prevail. As against the capricious cosmos and the inscrutable gods, there was always the *kittum* to afford a measure of security, as well as the *mēšarum* embodied in law and government.

Mesopotamian civilization had solved the major issue of the individual's relation to society in a manner beneficial to the many as opposed to the few. The same cannot be said, however, of the twin problem of society's relation to nature. There remained the task to bring these results — the positive as well as the negative — into some kind of equilibrium. The effort to arrive at such a balance is best reflected in the native literature. It is, therefore, to Mesopotamian literature that we shall turn next for a few representative samples.

D. Echoes in Literature

The written output of Mesopotamia is beyond doubt more bulky and unwieldy than any other to reach us from antiquity. The nature of the writing material, and the tens of centuries during which this imperishable medium was in use, are not the only or even the main reasons. The result is due primarily to the Mesopotamians' inveterate habit of recording practically everything. Theirs was indeed a civilization of bookkeepers in more ways than one.

The total output, nevertheless, is a good index of prevailing interests. The large number of texts devoted to business, administrative, and juridical matters speaks for itself, and the same is true of the documents that are concerned with rituals. In addition, however, to these routine and expected categories, there are many others, still routine though not as readily predictable. All of them come in one way or another under the heading of applied science: lexical and grammatical manuals, lists of various entries in the fields of natural sciences and industry, mathematical and astronomical texts, omens, and the like. As time passes, historical records become more frequent and detailed. Letters, both official and private, provide an excellent running commentary on everyday events.

Aside from these functional groups, there are others which deserve to be classified under literature proper. Their theme is for the most part religious, but the treatment is clearly literary. Here belong the compositions which the moderns designate as myths; but it is doubtful whether their originators thought of them in mythological terms. In this group, too, we find epics, religious poems such as hymns and prayers, secular poems, and several forms of wisdom literature.

This vast material cannot but shed welcome light on what were the favorite preoccupations of the Mesopotamians, from early Sumerian down to late Assyrian and Babylonian times. There is surprisingly little, however, that bears directly on the question of general philosophy of life. What we do have, though — especially in wisdom works — concerns largely, and naturally enough, man in his relation to the cosmos. Inevitably, both the society and the universe reflect native Mesopotamian concepts.

The keynote is struck by the theme of the Righteous Sufferer which we know from three major recensions,[27] the earliest of these dating from Old Babylonian times. In other words, the Job motif crops up throughout most of Mesopotamian history. It dwells on two points, above all others. One is that the blameless may be exposed to suffering, but this is because the divine plans are inscrutable.[28] The other point is that the truly meritorious need never despair of ultimate salvation; the trials of the sufferer only serve to emphasize the miracle of ultimate deliverance.[29] In short, the answer to the problem of a workable balance between society and the cosmos, as seen by the religious philosopher, was continued piety and acceptance of fate:

> "Wherever the earth reaches, the heavens extend,
> The sun shines, flames burst forth,
> Waters flow, the wind blows —
> Those whose clay (bodies) Aruru has formed,
> Endowed with life and the power of motion,
> All of mankind, to Marduk give praise!"[30]

There were those, however, who balked against such surrender. They refused to accept the pious maxims and, above all, they rebelled against the stark finality of death. Their cry reaches far beyond their own age and society, beyond cultural and national boundaries, to become the universal voice of mankind itself. This is the central theme of the Epic of Gilgamesh, one of the great literary masterpieces of all time.

The nameless genius who created this outstanding literary monument, sometime before the Old Babylonian age, out of sundry traditions about the old Sumerian hero Gilgamesh, made his protagonist start out as a carefree demigod to whom nothing was sacred. But the hazards of life dispel his conceit and endow him with human feelings and anxieties. At the height of his personal triumph he discovers the meaning and the fear of death. Now thoroughly humanized, yet passionately intent on averting his mortal destiny, Gilgamesh sets out to find a remedy. In the course of this epic journey, which takes him to the farthest confines of space, he learns at last some facts about life which wisdom alone can present in their true perspective:

> "In the House of Dust which I entered,
> Reside High Priest and acolyte,
> Reside incantatory and ecstatic,
> Reside the ranking priests of the great gods.
> Etana is there, and Sumuqan,
> And Ereshkigal, Queen of the nether world.
> Belit-seri, scribe of the nether world, kneels before her.
> She holds [a tablet] and reads to her from it."[31]

All dignitaries and heroes suffer the same fate and go to the same place. And the scribe of the nether world is ever ready to add new names to her list. It is futile, therefore, to hope for a different fate. Nothing on earth lasts for ever:

> "Do we build houses for ever, or seal contracts for ever?
> Do brothers divide shares for all time?
> Does (even) hatred persist in [the land] for ever?
> Does a river always rise to bring floods?
> The dragon-fly [drops] its shell
> That it might but glance at the face of the sun!
> Since the days of yore there has been no [permanence];
> Those who lie dead, how alike they are!
> Do they not compose a picture of death,
> The commoner and the noble, once they have met [their fate]?"[32]

The wise thing, then, is not so much to affirm that all is just and purposeful, as to bow to the inevitable but enjoy the good things of life while one may:

> "Gilgamesh, whither rovest thou?
> The life thou pursuest thou shalt not find.
> When the gods created mankind,
> Death for mankind they set aside,
> Life in their own hands retaining.
> Thou, Gilgamesh, let full be thy belly,
> Make thou merry by day and by night.

Hold a feast each day,
And dance and play day and night!
Let thy garments be sparkling fresh,
Thy head be washed; bathe in pure water.
Pay heed to the little one that holds on to thy hand.
Let thy spouse delight in thy bosom,
As is [a woman's] role."[33]

But Gilgamesh had come too far to turn back now. After suffering the utmost in exertion and danger, he is admitted at long last to Utnapishtim's retreat, where he is told the story of the Great Flood, followed by the crushing news that no celestial assembly would grant immortality to another human. The best that a mortal could hope for was the boon of rejuvenation.[34] Yet even that consolation is not to be his, for on his return journey a snake steals the precious plant with the power to restore one's youth. Here is supreme irony — and supreme though sad wisdom. The hero is now reconciled to the constructive task of heading a great city state.

The epic speaks thus for mankind as a whole, but it also symbolizes the achievements and the shortcomings of Mesopotamian civilization. Society had come a long way in its quest for a good life. The cosmos, however, remained forbidding and unfathomable. It was probably not the solution that man hoped for, but it had to do. No other society had traveled as far in seeking to solve the larger issues of life and destiny. Mesopotamia's neighbors appreciated the value of that collective experience and were willing to learn from it. They took over the Epic of Gilgamesh. And they became devoted followers of the great civilization which had found in that epic such a masterly and poignant expression.

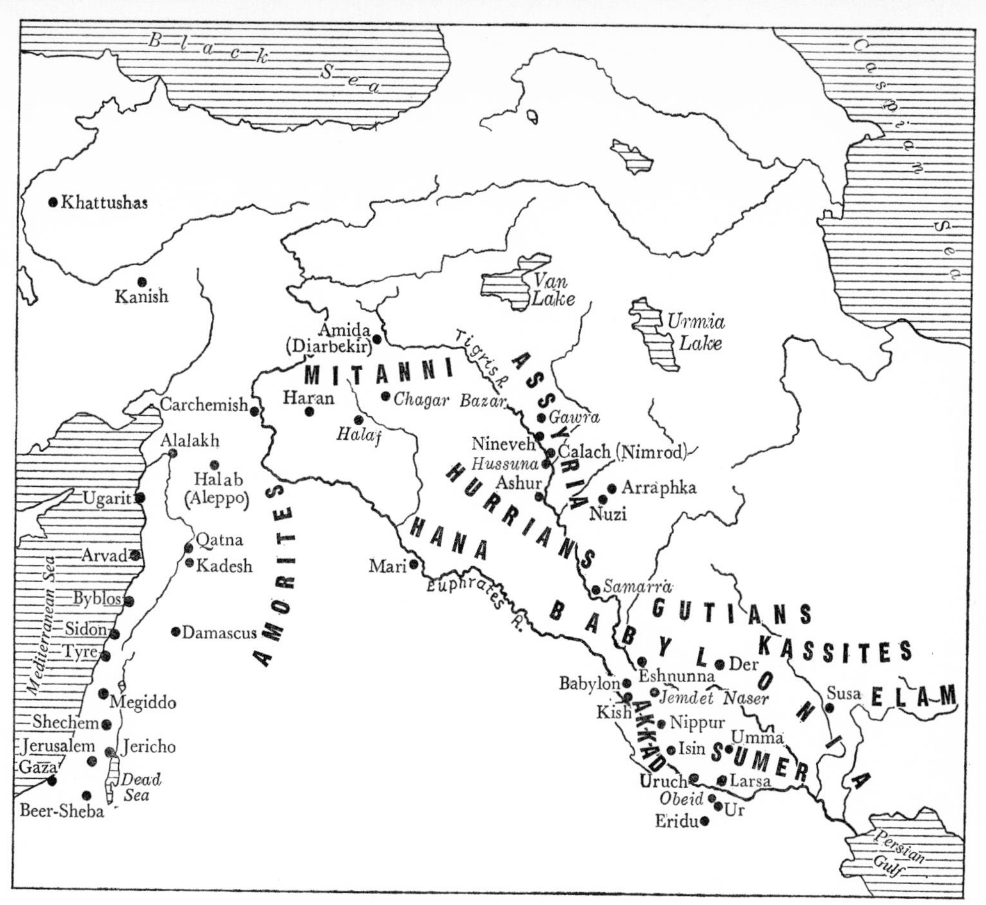

States and Peoples of Ancient Mesopotamia

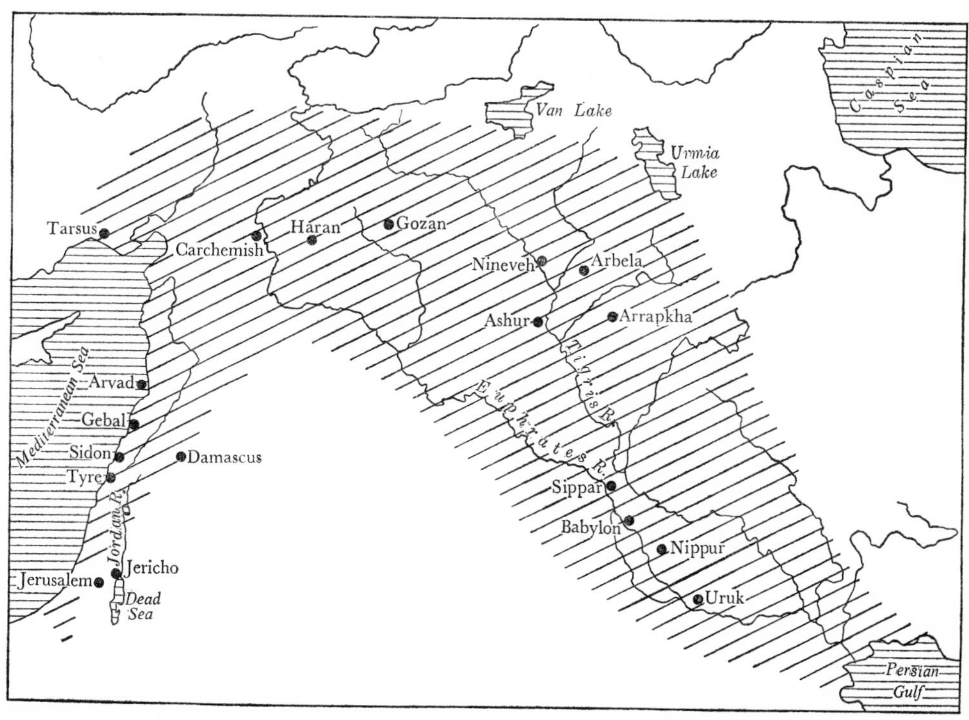

Assyrian Empire in the 8th century B. C. E.

4. THE EXPANDING ORBIT OF MESOPOTAMIAN CIVILIZATION

THE ULTIMATE TEST of a system lies, of course, in its application. We know that Mesopotamia enjoyed an independent historic career until the middle of the first millennium B.C.E. or, in other words, through half of the recorded history of mankind. And we have seen that during the whole of that long stretch Mesopotamian history and culture were closely interrelated. Indeed, the history we have followed proved eventually to be cosmopolitan rather than parochial — or Mesopotamian as opposed to Sumero-Akkadian, Babylonian, or Assyrian — thanks primarily to the underlying cultural component. On this basis, among others, Mesopotamian civilization emerges as an influence of exceptional magnitude; it was dynamic, pervasive, and enduring. It remains only, in conclusion, to examine this factor, not so much for its basic content — since that has already been summarized — as for its mode of operation. Is it at all possible to glimpse the manner whereby Mesopotamian civilization achieved results on so broad a scale?

The proposed examination may be pursued under three separate headings: (a) Internal consequences; (b) Mesopotamia and the neighboring regions; and (c) Mesopotamia and the world of the Bible; a summary retrospect (d) will bring this whole tale to a conclusion. The present account can attempt only rough outlines of these topics; none of the themes can be developed in proper detail within the space that remains at our disposal. But the usefulness of even such a general summary should be apparent. And because the period involved was so long and the area so large, and because the leading actors played such important roles on the world stage, the over-all results may have some bearing on mankind's early history as a whole.

A. Internal Consequences

It was emphasized repeatedly in the preceding pages that Mesopotamia's major cultural contributions pertained to society in the narrower sense of the term. They were especially outstanding in the domain of government, and of law as the agent and the reflex of government. Intimately associated with both these subjects was writing, in that it gave permanent expression to the traditional concepts of law and government. What is more, the emergence of writing may itself be viewed as a byproduct of these two basic manifestations of society. For it was the place of the individual in the normative Sumerian scheme of things, and the need for safeguarding his rights through the use of the cylinder seal, that can best account for the evolution of the script in the first instance.[1] The resulting combination, in turn, set up a cultural chain reaction with an ever widening range. It was clearly a set-up conducive to balanced cultural activity.

In its pioneer form, writing represented a complex and cumbersome system. By the very nature of its origin in concrete pictographs, the parent script was an elaborate medium which comprised thousands of items. It was essentially a code designed to convert the given graphs into specific words which could then be sounded in appropriate fashion. Such a code, however, could not be used without a proper key. Of necessity, that key had to take the form of lists arranged in some practical order for ready reference. The lists in question were thus in effect so many analytical catalogues of symbols grouped together according to their appearance. And since each symbol was at the start a reflection of something specific in the material world, their catalogues amounted to systematic arrangements of related objects.[2]

We find thus, virtually from the start, listings of birds, fishes, domestic and wild animals, plants, and the like. Once initiated, these compilations set up a tradition that is to be maintained throughout the duration of the script itself. From the outset they presuppose careful observation and imply organization and analysis of the data at hand.[3] And while their original purpose was incidental to the practice of writing, the passing centuries lead to the independent study of the subject matter involved and bring with them substantial revision and expansion. In short, we have here the beginnings of a number of systematic disciplines, such as zoology,[4] and botany.[5] The study is soon extended to other topics, including mineralogy and chemistry on the one hand,[6] and various industries[7] and crafts on the other.

This is not to suggest that writing alone was responsible for the emergence of all, or even most, of these disciplines. The methodical ways of the Sumerians and their successors, which were manifested also in other fields, were bound to result in an increasing preoccupation with "science." But the initial impetus of the classified lists that were begun as aids to writing cannot be discounted. And the writing habit, in turn, which was so characteristic of Mesopotamia, was a prime factor in the further cultivation of the older disciplines and the development of new ones. The rise of mathematics as an exact science, and the subsequent emergence of astronomy — two subjects in which Mesopotamia had no peer[8] — were but two of the many other instances of this happy form of chain reaction. In sum, the cultural climate of Mesopotamia was conducive to balanced progress on a broad front. Pharmacology flourished alongside botany; case law led to jurisprudence; and chronicles of past events shaded off into incipient historiosophy.

Nowhere, however, did the cultural environment have a greater effect on scientific progress than in the field of language and philology. Because the Sumerians, as was indicated earlier, had been a prime factor in molding the cultural history of Mesopotamia, the Sumerian language became the medium whereby much of the living cultural tradition was communicated to succeeding generations. Since this was rightly felt to be a vital process, it was deemed imperative that the medium be kept alive even after its speakers had disappeared from the scene. And so the Akkadian successors took every conceivable precaution to maintain a working knowledge of Sumerian. Their efforts were successful to an astonishing degree, considering their remote date. Not only did the later users of Akkadian have at their command the means for learning all the Sumerian that they needed; modern scholarship, too, was to find the same aids indispensable to the recovery of that isolated language and the rich cultural treasures for which it served as a vehicle.

The end products of those ancient scholarly labors were pedagogical. The subject to which they were dedicated was Sumero-Akkadian philology. The discipline employed for the purpose — a discipline that had to be introduced, developed, and perfected — was linguistic analysis. But the ultimate inspiration behind all such activities was cultural. And the final result is an achievement that was not be equaled, let alone exceeded, for at least a millennium and a half, not until the time of Pāṇini and his school of Sanskrit grammarians.

In the present context one need do no more than mention in passing the many extant syllabaries, lexical texts, or the longer Sumero-Akkadian bilinguals. This material gives careful and systematic instruction on such points as orthography, pronunciation, meaning, and dialectal peculiarities. It is remarkably detailed, immensely helpful, but represents by no means the peak of the contemporary linguistic achievement. That distinction belongs unquestionably to the works which deal directly with grammar. Here we find the subject matter analyzed according to parts of speech, number, and gender. The subtlest niceties in the structure of the Sumerian verb are recognized, brought out, and duly interpreted. And the special terminology that has been created for the purpose reflects the acuteness of the underlying analysis. It can label, for example, such fine distinctions as those between the present form and the imperfective root on the one hand, and the preterit form and the perfective root on the other. And the far-reaching differences between the Sumerian and Akkadian verbs — so disparate in their ultimate orientation — are scrupulously observed.[9] The Mesopotamian linguists of the nineteenth century B.C.E. were fully a match for their colleagues of the nineteenth century C.E.

One way of gauging the importance of a given scientific contribution is by tracing its influence on later ages and other cultures. Mesopotamia passes this particular test with flying colors. The Old Babylonian grammatical texts have their lineal descendants in Neo-Babylonian times.[10] And the pertinent terminology finds its way to much later grammatical works in other languages. Thus the Sumerian pair of contrasted linguistic terms *an. ta* "from above" and *ki. ta* "from below" is reproduced exactly in the Aramaic pair *mil'eil* and *milra'* as applied to the needs of Hebrew grammar. The fact that these Sumerian terms were used respectively for "prefix" and "suffix" has no bearing in this connection, since the pertinent Aramaic pair was not restricted to the accent, but was put to other uses as well.[11] Even more suggestive is the Akkadian pair *ḫamtu* "preterit, perfective," lit. "rapid (pronunciation)," and *marû* "present, imperfective," lit. "slow (pronunciation)."[11a] Syriac reflects this in its *marhəṭānā* "accelerator," which points to the lack of a vowel, and *məhaggəyānā*, a term denoting deliberate pace and hence, in grammatical context, the insertion of a secondary vowel.

This argument from adoption by other cultures is not limited to the linguistic contribution of Mesopotamia. It can be extended to such fields as law and religion, as well as various natural sciences. When it comes to the other Semitic languages, care must be exercised, of course, to distinguish between cognates and demonstrable loans. For the most part, however, it is easy enough to eliminate all doubt. For instance, if a term that is found in some Semitic language outside of Akkadian can be shown to be ultimately of Sumerian origin, it had to be imported from Mesopotamia. Such a case, e.g., is postbiblical *šwalyā* "apprentice," Akk. *šamallû*, from Sum. *šaman. lá*. To cite another example, the Shafel form of the verb is atypical in Aramaic but normal in Akkadian. When it is further realized that in Aramaic such forms are specialized for legal and religious terminology, or two fields in which Mesopotamian influence is known to have been considerable, the Aramaic indebtedness to Akkadian in this particular regard is safely established. A still better case in point is Heb. *sefer* "book." The term cannot be proto-Semitic, for writing was not introduced until the dawn of history, or in relatively late times. The corresponding Akk. term is *šipru* "message." The proper Hebrew cognate should show an initial *š*-. But the actual term has *s*-, as is to be expected in certain types of borrowings from Akkadian. All of this accords perfectly with the fact that writing itself was one of the distinctive contributions of Mesopotamian civilization.

Nor are such borrowings restricted to the immediate neighbors of Mesopotamia or the direct relatives of Akkadian. They can be found farther afield, not only in Greek but even in the Western languages. This applies especially to the field of botany. The relevant examples include "cassia" cuneiform *kasû*, "chicory" *kukru*, "cumin" *kamūnu*, "crocus" *kurkānu*, "hysop" *zūpu*, "myrrh" *murru*, "nard" *lardu*, and "saffron" *azupirānu*, among others. In the domain of minerals we find such terms as "jasper" *yašpû* and "naphta" *napṭu*. There are others in metrology, jurisprudence, and the like.[12] Many of these Western borrowings used to be traced to Arabic. They are now known to have been transmitted through cuneiform sources. But this is no warrant in itself that the ultimate source was Akkadian, or even Sumerian. A number of the words just cited, and many others like them, lack clear Akkadian or Sumerian credentials. They may go back in turn to one or another of the lesser Mesopotamian groups, or to some elements from outside Mesopotamia. Some indeed could well be pre-Sumerian.

What all of this means in the final analysis is that the scientific activity of Mesopotamia, stimulated and facilitated by the local cultural environment, was not parochial in scope by any means. Rather it was broad enough to reach out in space and in time. The same cannot be said, at least not to the same extent, of Mesopotamia's contemporaries. If there is an intimate correlation between culture and achievement, the balanced progress that has just been outlined is an indirect tribute to the basic strength of the civilization of Mesopotamia as viewed from within. We shall see presently that the view from without points to a similar conclusion.

B. Mesopotamia and the Neighboring Regions

There is a continuous flow of evidence that bears on Meospotamia's relations with the outside world. Some of this evidence consists of material remains, but it is the written sources that provide the fullest and most dependable testimony. These sources come from a number of lands which jointly form a northerly semicircle extending from Iran to the Mediterranean. The time span involved is equally impressive; for our sources reach back to the Sargonid period, in the third millennium, and continue down to the Hellenistic age, two thousand years later. It is abundantly clear, moreover, that in all these interrelations Mesopotamia was for the most part the dispensing center whereas its neighbors were usually the recipients. Political factors alone cannot account for this situation. The Mediterranean districts, for example, show no trace of Mesopotamian authority during the second millennium; and after the fall of Nineveh and Babylon all of Mesopotamia came under the political dominance of Iran. In other words, it was the cultural factor first and foremost that caused Mesopotamia to continue as the focal center throughout the long period under review.

This conclusion can be confirmed at a glance, before one even tries to probe beneath the surface. For virtually all the relevant inscriptions are written in cuneiform. So significant is this medium that the term "cuneiform civilization" has occasionally been employed to pay it due heed; yet this does little more than call attention to what is but an incidental manifestation. The full evidence goes much deeper. It involves the use of the cylinder seal, the widespread employment of Akkadian as an international language, and — more important still — the infiltration of Mesopotamian concepts of law, government, and religion. Mesopotamian civilization as a whole was thus prominently engaged beyond its native boundaries.

The cylinder seal, like the script to which it may have been generically related, is a transferable commodity. Its adoption, to be sure, is a sign of influence from a particular quarter; but the influence need not be more than superficial. It is a different matter, however, when a country has co-opted a foreign language. For such an act involves not only form but content. And this is exactly what happened wherever Akkadian was imported: the loan was tied up with other cultural borrowings.

To give first a review of the areas affected, Iran uses Akkadian, with its appropriate cuneiform accompaniment, already back in the third millennium. And as late as the time of Darius, nearly a score of centuries later, the Bagistana inscription carries a Babylonian version, alongside the Elamite and the Old Persian; all three texts are inscribed in cuneiform. The Hurrians, for their part, had likewise been converted to literacy by the time of the Sargonids. From the start, it would appear, they used the cuneiform script not only for their own distinctive language,[13] but also for Akkadian.[14] Both these practices continue into the second millennium, as is voluminously demonstrated by the correspondence of Tushratta, king of Mitanni. Through the Hurrians the cuneiform syllabary was transmitted to the Hittites,[15] who applied this loan primarily to their intrusive language, without ignoring Akkadian, however, for diplomatic and other purposes. Alalakh had resorted to Akkadian already in the Old Babylonian period, and resumed the practice under the new order which followed the Dark Age. Ugarit, for all its dedication to its own language and its novel alphabet, found ample scope for Akkadian — written in the traditional syllabary — in legal, economic, and diplomatic matters. Even conservative Egypt could not bypass Akkadian as the accepted international medium of communication in the Amarna age. And secluded Urartu, the sturdy opponent of Neo-Assyrian rulers, displayed no such opposition to cuneiform as applied either to its native tongue alone, or to Akkadian-Urartian bilinguals. So pervasive an influence — in space, time, and degree — of a language and its script, is unique in all history. It should be remembered that when Latin was at the height of its popularity abroad, it had long ceased to be a living language used by a political or cultural rival. French never approached the life span of Akkadian, and English would still have a long way to go in order to match it.

What, then, were the main reasons for this unprecedented popularity of Akkadian and its traditional mode of writing? It was indicated earlier that culture and not politics must furnish the answer. But to deduce that a given culture was dynamic and attractive is not the same thing as to point out the sources of its power and magnetism. In the present instance, the full explanation would probably turn out to rest on several factors. But we are not as yet in a position to make such fine distinctions. There is one factor, however, which stands out even now. How decisive it may have been ultimately is a different matter entirely; nor is such a question of direct concern in the present context.

In any case, the fact that emerges on further probing is that the spread of cuneiform and of Akkadian coincides by and large with a marked attention to the law in many of the adoptive lands. What we are confronted with is a package deal, so to speak, embracing script, language, and law, all imported from, or influenced by, Mesopotamia.[16] The law is not necessarily, or prevailingly, Mesopotamian in content; but it is markedly Mesopotamian in form and, above all, in its status within the given society. A few details must suffice to illustrate this point.

As the oldest historical representative of Iran, Elam was in a favored position to reflect the influence of Mesopotamian law in considerable detail. It is not surprising, therefore, to discover that the legal document had come to be at home in Susa.[17] Significantly enough, its language was Akkadian and its provisions followed Babylonian norms. In the Hurrian territories we face, at least after the middle of the second millennium, a feudal system that was markedly at variance with the Mesopotamian concept of state. Nevertheless, the legal documents from Arrapkha and Nuzi often show the closest kind of adherence to Babylonian practices.[18] Records from the Old Babylonian level in the Syrian center of Alalakh reflect analogously attested legal usages of contemporary Babylonia. And Anatolia, for its part, pays its own tribute to Lower Mesopotamia in the form of the Hittite Code.

In these circumstances, the question has to be posed whether it was not the appeal of Mesopotamian law, in the first instance, that promoted the widespread use of Akkadian as the language of that law, rather than the other way around. For one can account readily for the diffusion of a script; but the acceptance of a foreign language is a different matter altogether, unless that language be the vehicle for an important cultural feature which other societies wish to adopt. There is, of course, no definite proof for such an assumption; but the weight of probability would seem to be strongly in its favor; the example of Latin, as the vehicle of Roman law, among other things, may serve as a pertinent illustration. Having thus gained acceptance on legal grounds, Akkadian could then be extended to international diplomacy, thereby acquiring still greater vogue.

There is no question, at any rate, that Mesopotamian legal forms, and not infrequently also the legal content that went with them, became significant elements in the fabric of the adoptive cultures. Since law and government are closely interrelated, the regions that were attracted to the law of Mesopotamia could not well have subscribed to a radically different concept of state. Adherence to a system of law that was impersonally conceived would not be compatible with belief in a deified ruler; it precluded, at least in principle, autocracy in government. It follows hence that, however much the respective states of the Iranians and the Hurrians, the Syrians and the Hittites, may have differed in detail from one another, or each in turn from those of Mesopotamia, they all had a great deal in common as a group and were thus jointly the opposite of Egypt. Small wonder, therefore, that the assembly, which was such a significant institution in Mesopotamia, plays a comparable role in Hittite society, whose *pankus* — the local analogue of the Akkadian *puḫrum* — had jurisdiction over the king and the royal house.[19] And even a Cyrus applies to himself the traditional phraseology of Mesopotamian royalty. He is "king of totality, great king, mighty king, king of Babylon, king of Sumer and Akkad, king of the four quarters," as well as "the enduring seed of royalty, whose rule Bel and Nabu loved and whose kingship they desired."[20] So speaks the conqueror of Babylon who was, nevertheless, both indirectly and directly, a disciple of Mesopotamian civilization, a civilization which had found a universally valid solution of the problem of the individual's relation to society.

Cultural influences, however, once they have reached the level of law and government, are not likely to be dammed up at that level. The flow is bound to contain other features. Even in hostile Egypt, where only the Akkadian language had penetrated, as the common diplomatic medium of the Amarna age, copies of Akkadian epics turn up among the state archives. In friendlier surroundings, such secondary imports from Mesopotamia may be expected to appear in greater volume and variety. This expectation is borne out convincingly, as will be seen from the following sampling, which will be limited to the Hurrians for the sake of convenience and economy of space.

In the cultural structure of Mesopotamia the religious factor played its own deeply significant role. In view of their other intimate ties with Mesopotamia, it would be strange if the Hurrians proved to be wholly immune to religious influences from that quarter. Extant witnesses of Hurrian literature shed light on this question. They show that the Hurrian gods reflected a hierarchy that was closely modeled after the Sumerian pantheon. The Hurrian Kumarbi was in many respects the counterpart of the Mesopotamian Enlil. What is more, some of Kumarbi's associates were transferred bodily from Mesopotamia, in name as well as rank. More significant still, the savage family battles in which the leading Hurrian gods were involved prove to have striking antecedents in Akkadian religious lore. Obviously, therefore, the Hurrians must have reshaped their original theogony in accordance with borrowed Mesopotamian traditions.[21]

Now the Hurrian epic work in which these doings were recorded has come down to us, so far, only in its Hittite version. We have here the same line of cultural transmission that had previously carried to the Hittites the Hurrian form of the cuneiform syllabary and, no doubt, other similar goods as well. But the line does not stop with the Hittites. For the hybrid sequence of Anu, Kumarbi, and Teshub — which is headed by the Mesopotamian sky-god — reappears in Greek sources, in the same turbulent context, as Uranos, Kronos, and Zeus.[22] The identical cycle was also known to the Phoenicians,[23] and an echo of it appears to have reached the Bible in the form of the episode of the Fallen Giants, Genesis 6:1–4.[24] Here is truly a parade example of an extensive cultural chain reaction.

In the realm of primitive historiography, the Sumerian King List began its account with a sequence of dynastic centers from which the world was ruled successively. The Hurrians have left us a similar account in their own language.[25] The places and the dynasties are different, but the motif of shifting world rule remains much the same.

In the field of strictly secular literature, the Hurrians, once again seconded by the Hittites, pay their tribute to the Gilgamesh Epic in the form of independent translations. No such direct dependence is traceable to the Greeks. Yet the various points of contact that have been found or are alleged to exist between the Odyssey and the Gilgamesh Epic, and the very form of the epic as such, would seem to indicate that the Greeks did not remain untouched by the literary achievements of Mesopotamia. In fact, there is at least one Greek fable which is all but a literal translation of an Akkadian original.[26]

The foregoing sketch should suffice to bring out the dynamic character of Mesopotamian civilization, and perhaps indicate some of the channels through which the results were communicated to the world outside. There still remains, however, one important source which is ideally qualified both to reflect and to test certain specific influences which emanated from Mesopotamia. That source is the Bible.

C. Mesopotamia and the World of the Bible

Any treatment of Mesopotamia in relation to the Bible is bound to carry with it a considerable measure of risk. The comparison may lead to such one-sided appraisals as Friedrich Delitzsch's *Babel und Bibel*, in which an otherwise competent scholar allowed pan-Babylonianism to run rampant. Equally out of focus, however, is the position of those who would deny Mesopotamia any substantial influence on Israel and the Bible. Neither extreme can be backed today by anything resembling a valid argument. But even a balanced inquiry into this subject is not in itself a guarantee of smooth progress. Further advance is today more complex and difficult precisely because recent discoveries have added a vast amount of new material which must be taken into account.

The Bible did not arise in a vacuum. Its birthplace was a land which had local cultural traditions and which, moreover, constituted a bridge between two great centers of civilization. It is inevitable, therefore, that the Bible should reflect an underlying cultural debt to older sources, both domestic and foreign. These borrowings were integrated with the distinctive contribution of Israel, the whole to be transformed into a new and unique design for living, a design that has proved to have universal validity. But it is only by isolating first the inherited and borrowed elements that we can gain a true appreciation of the final contribution of the Bible; the independent achievement is thus brought out in clearer relief.

Now the outside sources should be traceable theoretically both to Egypt and Mesopotamia, with the former predominating because of geographic location. Yet this premise is borne out only in part; for Israel's contacts with Mesopotamia were far more intimate, on the cultural side, than they ever were with Egypt. The Bible itself supplies the reason for this apparent paradox. Abraham, we are told at the very beginning of the patriarchal narrative (Gen. 11), started out from Ur of the Chaldaeans, stopping for a time at Harran on his way to the Promised Land. All subsequent connections of the Patriarchs were with Harran. This general formulation may leave some room for doubt, on historical and textual grounds, about the initial stage at Ur. But the statement as a whole is fully in accord with the independent cultural evidence.

Most of the important outside influences as reflected in the Bible come indeed from the direction of Mesopotamia. Not all of these, however, were Mesopotamian in the narrower sense of the term. Some originated in the area of ancient Sumer, for which Biblical Ur is a good enough substitute. Others point to the Middle Euphrates area, say, Harran; today one has to add Mari to this category. Still others reached Israel from the neighboring lands in the north. In a broader sense, of course, it was the dynamic character of the native civilization of Mesopotamia that was responsible, as was indicated earlier, for much of the cultural ferment throughout the Fertile Crescent. But we must distinguish, wherever possible, between direct and indirect influences, and between primary and secondary centers of dissemination. As a cultural concept, Mesopotamia in no longer coextensive with Sumer, Babylonia, and Assyria. On this count, then, as well as on others, the pan-Babylonian school has been guilty of a serious oversimplification of the actual facts in the case.

The present sketch, however, is not the proper place to go into the matter in such fine detail. We must content ourselves with the bare indication that the distinctions just described are not to be ignored; and that aside from influences emanating from Mesopotamia proper, Israel was the recipient of others from the same general quarter, which might or might not go back, in turn, to Mesopotamia itself. Our main task here is to outline the extent of Israel's indebtedness to the traditional civilization of Mesopotamia. When it comes to the secondary influences, and to those that cannot be linked up at all with Lower Mesopotamia, one or two representative instances will have to suffice.

The story of the Flood is a clear example of a Mesopotamian theme that was transmitted to the Bible at second hand. As we have known ever since that memorable occasion on December 3, 1872, when a great scholar by the name of George Smith caused a sensation in England with his paper on "The Chaldean Account of the Deluge," showing that the Biblical record of the Flood was based on cuneiform sources. It follows very closely the dramatic accounts as given in Tablet XI of the Gilgamesh Epic. But the correspondence is not complete. One major difference involves the name of the protagonist, who is called Utnapishtim in the Akkadian version, but Noah in the Biblical formulation. Similarly, the name of the mountain on which the ark landed is Mt. Niṣir in the one, and Ararat in the other. Obviously, therefore, the Bible based its account on some secondary recension, one in which both the hero and the scene had been changed. The change in locale is especially significant, in that it points to some region far to the northwest of Babylonia. When it is recalled that there was a Hurrian version of the epic, and that the home of the Hurrians must be sought in the general direction of Ararat, the assumption lies near at hand that the Hebrews got their account of the Flood through Hurrian mediation. That ancient Palestine was no stranger to the direct Akkadian version as well, has recently been demonstrated by the discovery of a fragment of the Gilgamesh Epic in Megiddo. The actual recension, however, which the Bible incorporated had been modified in transit.

We come next to selected examples of a different kind. They come from centers in which Mesopotamian civilization was a manifest and prominent factor; yet in the instances at issue there is no sign of indebtedness to traditional Mesopotamia. What the Bible took over in such cases would seem to have originated in given cultural colonies of Mesopotamia rather than with the dominant civilization itself.

Our first example of this type comes from Mari. It is of exceptional importance, since it pertains ultimately to the institution of prophecy. Several records from Amorite centers in Mari testify to the activities of certain individuals who could speak up to the authorities on matters of civil or religious conduct, although they were themselves neither priests nor officials. Their pronouncements carried obvious weight. Such behavior is without parallel in Mesopotamia proper, but has significant analogues in Israel. Both the phraseology of these pronouncements and the independent stature of the speakers[27] — a group set apart from the palace and the temple alike — bring to mind inevitably the position of the Biblical prophets. That the parallelism does not extend to the high moral and social level of Biblical prophecy is beside the point. What matters is the actual presence of such an institution and its evident acceptance by the community, a community which dealt also with Benjaminites, featured such centers as *Naḫur* and *Ḫarrān*,[28] and supervised covenants in which the sacrificed animal was "an ass's foal" (*ḫayāru mār/bin atānim*),[29] the term having an exact correspondent in Biblical poetry. The unique thing, then, about Biblical prophecy is not the institution itself but the sublime heights to which its leading exponents in Israel were able to raise it.

Related examples have been gleaned from documents found in Arrapkha and Nuzi, two Hurrian centers to the north of Babylonia. We have here, as in Mari, an extra-Mesopotamian society under marked Mesopotamian influence. In each case the written language was Akkadian. In each case, too, local practices without direct antecedents in Mesopotamia proper came to be prominently reflected in the Bible. The so-called Nuzi parallels, however, are in many ways more significant and far-reaching than the Mari ones, and for good reason. Nuzian society was an eastern exponent of Hurrian culture which had its main centers in the Harran area. Since the same area also served as the home of the family from which Abraham and his descendants branched off, they would naturally be expected to follow their settled Hurrian neighbors in various practices and customs. It is only a matter of the accidents of discovery that the pertinent evidence should have turned up at Nuzi and not at Harran. The results would be the same either way. Those that we have so far are highly illuminating. They have unlocked for us various Biblical passages whose meaning had been a puzzle to countless generations of commentators and exegetes.

Thanks to these parallels, virtually every detail of the patriarchal narratives is now in its proper and authentic focus. The episode involving Abraham, Sarah, and Hagar; the repeated wife-sister motif; the transfer of the birthright from Esau to Jacob; Jacob's position in Laban's household; the removal of the *teraphim* by Rachel — these and various other details are now clarified by a mass of material dating practically from the age of the Patriarchs themselves. The recovered true meaning of these passages has almost invariably proved to be different from the explanations proposed by Biblical commentators, ancient and modern.[30] All of which shows that scholarly ingenuity and anachronistic moral judgments are doubtful substitutes for first-hand evidence, when the intricate fabric of a complex and remote society is under review. The patriarchal narratives in the Bible are no longer so many disjointed fragments from an ancient work of a writer or writers with an inventive turn of mind. They are all set against a background which contemporary records have fully authenticated. If much of their import was lost early in their transmission, it is because these narratives were committed to writing several centuries after the events in question, and hundreds of miles away from the scene of these happenings. The fact that they were recorded at all, even though their meaning was not always clear at the time, is part of the process that made of the Bible a sacred work for all time. By the same token, however, the outside influences that are reflected in these accounts are important, though by no means decisive. And in one way or another these influences point back to Mesopotamia, or one of its close neighbors and disciples.

We come, finally, to Mesopotamia proper as the source of certain cultural motifs and attainments which the Bible has incorporated. With regard to literary motifs, in particular, it is of little consequence whether any given one reached Israel by the direct route or indirectly. Where the original source is not in doubt, the mode of dissemination has only an incidental importance. An outstanding example of such a motif transmitted at second hand has already been cited in the case of the account of the Flood. That account, however, was but one of a number that came to be combined into a more or less connected section, which is now embodied in Genesis 1–11. This is the so-called *Urgeschichte*, or Primeval History. In it will be found nearly all the literary traditions of Mesopotamia which the Bible had reason to appropriate. It is in order, therefore, at this point to cast a quick glance at these chapters as a unit.

It should cause little, if any, surprise to discover that much of the content of the early chapters of Genesis points unmistakably to Mesopotamia. The historical scheme of the Pentateuch is to start out with Primeval History, continue with the History of the Patriarchs, and end up with the Birth of a Nation. The founding Patriarch came from Mesopotamia; he had been bidden to leave that land for the very purpose that is to become the leading theme of the Bible, namely, the quest of an enduring and universally valid way of life. The story of the ages anterior to the period of Abraham should, therefore, bear the distinctive imprint of his original homeland. That it does so in fact is but further proof that the account as a whole is based on genuine traditions instead of being the invention of some imaginative writer, or school of writers.

The truth of the foregoing statement should have been recognized by the critics long ago. To this day the diverse critical schools have been unable to arrive at anything like a consensus in regard to the authorship of various parts of the *Urgeschichte*. The current criteria for "J" and "E" fail to work in this section. The positing of "J²" has not helped matters; indeed, there are those who argue that the identifications "J" and "E" in these particular chapters should be reversed. Others would see here the hand of an altogether different writer, "L" or "S."[31] All this would seem to be so much misapplied ingenuity. The *Urgeschichte* is not on a par with the later narrative for the simple reason that the material for the former had come from the outside. The original formulation could not be obliterated so thoroughly as to be made of a piece with the rest in every minute detail. The writer who adopts an established literary piece does not have the same freedom as he enjoys in retelling a theme nurtured by oral tradition. The difference in the nature of the material would be bound to be reflected formally. The sundry elements of the *Urgeschichte* were obviously subject to definite restrictions in their handling.

Now the very scheme of the *Urgeschichte* as an introduction to more recent history is a known Mesopotamian convention. We find it in the Sumerian King List, and its popularity is attested by the Hurrian version of successive world rulers. Like its Mesopotamian analogue, the Biblical record goes back to the dim ages before the Flood, except that the various dynasties of antediluvian Mesopotamia are replaced in the Bible by a similar number of individuals with correspondingly abnormal lifetimes. The details have thus been changed, some of them, no doubt, in transit; but the basic concept has come through unaltered.

Enough has been written about the close agreement between the Babylonian and the Biblical accounts of creation to require no more than a bare mention in the present summary. This time, however, the basic concept has been changed, in conformance with the incomparably loftier religious level of the Bible. But the correspondence in incidental detail is obvious to all who have examined the Biblical and the Akkadian material side by side.[32]

The episode of the Fallen Giants (Gen. 6:1–4) may seem troublesome as a thinly disguised remnant of stark paganism. It need not be, if we view it in its due perspective. The tale of divine beings who were guilty of unseemly acts, which they sometimes carried to the point of savage family battles, was taken over from Mesopotamia by the Hurrians, was transmitted from them to the Hittites, and cropped up eventually in Greek and Phoenician sources. It was thus a motif subscribed to by most of the areas known to the Bible. As such it could not be ignored. Neither could it be condoned. Eventually it found its proper place at the beginning of the story of the Flood, where it could serve as the natural motivation for the universal catastrophe and punishment which the Bible made of the Flood.

Another Mesopotamian theme which is utilized critically by the *Urgeschichte* is the celebrated account of the Tower of Babel. Here a whole complex of data accurately reflecting the Babylonian environment has been made the basis for a strong indictment of the underlying religious beliefs and practices.[33] But the original material had to be known well before it could be effectively criticized. And such knowledge presupposes contacts of a more than casual nature.

Lastly, the Nimrod fragment (Gen. 10:8–12) is still another instance of intimate knowledge of Mesopotamian history and culture. And the subsequent popularity of this particular hero is a good example of the extent to which Mesopotamian seeds could be acclimatized in Palestinian soil.[33a]

Taken altogether, the *Urgeschichte* embodies a considerable portion of Israel's literary heritage from Mesopotamia. It was not at all a static legacy, as we have just seen; its contents were transformed, often substantially, and were brought into harmony with Israel's spiritual progress. But the influence of the original source could never be completely obliterated; the various cultural links between Mesopotamia and the home of the Bible continued in force.

It goes without saying that the links and influences which have just been alluded to were not confined to historiography and literature. The most significant ones, in fact, have yet to be cited. They are less tangible perhaps than the foregoing, and more difficult to evaluate at first glance; but they are also more vital by far in the final analysis. I refer to the basic question of law and government.

The discovery of the Code of Hammurabi brought in its wake a long series of studies aimed at comparing the Babylonian laws with the Covenant Code of Exodus 21:2–23:19 and related passages elsewhere in the Pentateuch. The results proved to be suggestive but inconclusive. The differences were no less impressive than the similarities. Subsequent finds, however, and studies of other collections of cuneiform laws — the Assyrian, the Neo-Babylonian, and the Laws of Eshnunna, all these in Akkadian; the Sumerian laws of Lipit-Ishtar and Ur-Nammu; the Hittite Laws — have helped to place the whole question in a truer focus. And the steady flow of documents pertaining to the practice of law, notably from Nuzi, Alalakh, and Ugarit, has further broadened the basis of comparison with the Covenant Code. The laws of Hammurabi were manifestly but one aspect a of larger pattern that represents cuneiform law. When that pattern is viewed as a whole, the discrepancies between it and the Covenant Code are sharply reduced. And the Biblical laws emerge as an integral component of a juridical field that covered the entire Fertile Crescent.

To state the same results in a different way, the various societies of the Fertile Crescent came one by one under the legal influence of Mesopotamia. That influence manifests itself on the surface through the wide use of the cuneiform script and the popularity of the legal document. But the Covenant

Code is sufficient to demonstrate that it was possible also to use other scripts — at least in course of time — and still stay within the same legal orbit.

Yet the script, the document, and the similarity of many of the legal provisions, do not in themselves imply that the content of the law was necessarily homogeneous throughout. There were obvious differences, either original or residual, within the cuneiform field, particularly in Hurrian and Hittite territories. The Biblical laws contribute their quota. The prevailing relationship, in other words, is essentially one of form. The content followed suit in many instances; but in some it did not.

Nevertheless, the acceptance of even the outward forms alone would imply in this context a considerable degree of cultural compatibility. For, what is involved is the recognition of a legal system impersonally conceived. And the natural corollary is a type of government that could be reconciled with such a system; in short, a non-autocratic concept of state. It is in this field, as we have seen, that Mesopotamia achieved its most constructive results at home and wielded its most pervasive influence abroad. And it is in this field, too, as will be shown presently, that Israel had its strongest ties with Mesopotamia.

The objection might be raised at this point that we really do not know whether the formal practices that are incidental to the spread of the Mesopotamian legal system to other countries were actually followed in Israel as well; hence the correspondence between the respective concepts of state, if valid at all, might have to be ascribed to unrelated developments. Any doubts, however, on this particular score can be quickly dispelled. It is true that, for a variety of reasons, the customary script of Palestine was other than cuneiform, and that the clay records, so common elsewhere, are all but absent in this instance. Nevertheless, there is internal evidence to the effect that literacy was not a rarity in ancient Israel. Moreover, legal transactions as mirrored in the Bible were conducted in a manner that was original with Mesopotamia.

Attention has already been drawn to the fact that the Hebrew term *sefer* "document" is itself a loan from Akkadian. In cultural borrowings of this kind the article usually comes with its name. That the drawing up of such documents was a common occurrence as early as the period of the Judges is known from Gideon's experience with Succoth: when he needed a list of the uncooperative inhabitants of that city, Gideon had apparently no trouble in picking up a local youth who wrote down for him the names of the guilty (Jud. 8:14) — to be used in due time for purposes of a rather grim lesson. For legal transactions we may use two pertinent illustrations, which span the long period between the age of the Patriarchs and the last days of Judah. When Tamar, in proper disguise, needed to arm herself with definite proof that her visitor was her own father-in-law Judah, she asked for a pledge consisting of his cylinder seal, the cord on which it was worn, and a staff which, in this context, stands for the Babylonian *bukannu*, a symbol signifiying that the transaction was legally in order (Gen. 38:18). The seal, of course, was a means of attestation peculiar to Sumer, and later the foremost material witness of the expanding civilization of Mesopotamia. All three objects stood Tamar in good stead when the identity of her visitor became a matter of her life or death. The other illustration is contained in Jeremiah 32, a chapter that is memorable for many other things as well. The prophet's remarkable transaction with Hanamel is duly recorded, sealed, and witnessed (v. 10), just as was done normally wherever "cuneiform law" had found a foothold. We need look no farther for evidence that the outward forms associated with the legal system of Mesopotamia were scrupulously observed in Israel.

What, then, is the situation in regard to the concept of state that is attested in the Bible? This question has become in recent years the subject of heated controversy in which the main point at issue is whether or not the idea of divine kingship was central to Biblical thought. The affirmative answer has currently the support of the "Scandinavian School" of Biblical scholarship,[34] which in turn has marked affinities with the "Myth-and-Ritual" approach to the larger issues of society in the ancient Orient. But this interpretation has met with strong and determined resistance. The arguments of the opposition[35] are based on many solid facts which have yet to be refuted. The material that has been summarized in these pages cannot but lend added weight to these arguments.

It is one of the basic assumptions of the divine kingship school of thought that this ideology was common to the ancient Near East as a whole, and that Israel shared these views as a rightful member of the larger community. Yet this assumption is based on a faulty premise. It does not begin to do justice to Mesopotamia, and it cannot be upheld in the case of the other lands of the Fertile Crescent. In Mesopotamia, as was shown earlier, the attempts to invest the king with divine authority were limited as to time and locality, short-lived in effect, and never associated with the stronger rulers. The prevailing culture rejected all such pretensions as alien to its spirit.[36]

The same applies by and large to the areas that were culturally affiliated to Mesopotamia. This was either the result of such affiliation or, at a minimum, a factor that contributed to it in the first place. The only major center that stood out in contrast, by subscribing wholeheartedly to the concept of divine kingship, was Egypt. But Israel was on the same significant count plainly within the Mesopotamian orbit, in common with the rest of the Fertile Crescent. The ideological curtain that thus separated Egypt from its neighbors in the Near East was a more formidable barrier than any conceivable physical obstacle. And the resulting dichotomy was not to disappear altogether even after the respective civilizations had run their full course.

The alleged universality of the concept of divine kingship in the Near East is thus itself a myth. In the case of Israel, the contrary view, which regards kingship as secular and man-made, has the support of many concrete occurrences in written form. These sources have the added advantage of going back to the very inception of kingship in Israel; what is more, most of them are certified as impeccable by the documentary analysis.

It was "the people" who "elevated Saul to kingship" in Gilgal (I Sam. 11:15). Upon Saul's death, "the men of Judah . . . anointed David to be king over Judah" (II Sam. 2:4). "All the elders of Israel" followed suit (*ibid.* 5:3), but not until they had exacted a safeguard against autocracy in the form of a solemn "covenant." Similarly, "all Israel" was disposed to approve Rehoboam as king, following the death of Solomon (I Kings 12:1). But when the people saw that the king had been won over by elements opposing liberal reforms, they summoned Jeroboam before "the assembly" and "made him king over Israel" instead (v. 20).[37] The reference to the assembly in this connection is especially noteworthy.

Other passages, which are regarded as secondary, reflect the same policy and procedure, thus showing that this attitude was not confined to any single school or class. Thus, when the Philistines became a mortal threat to the Israelites, and the older system of loose tribal confederation was no longer equal to the task, "all the elders of Israel" came to Samuel demanding a drastic change: "Establish for us a king to lead us like all the nations" (I Sam. 8:5). Samuel sought to dissuade them, but "the people refused to listen" to his remonstrances. They insisted, "No, we must have a king over us, that we, too, may be like all the nations" (*ibid.* 19–20). Obviously, it is the people who were the ultimate king-makers; and such authority on the part of the people is literally "democracy." The right of the population to extend an offer of kingship, or to withdraw that offer, as witnessed with Rehoboam and Jeroboam, would surely be impossible to reconcile with the concept of a divine ruler. And the people's insistence on having a king "to lead us like the other nations" can point to only one kind of ruler: not one who, as a god, was above law and responsibility, but the kind that had long been known to Mesopotamia and its whole orbit. The term "nations" in this case must refer, then, to the peoples of the Fertile Crescent as opposed to Egypt.

There is one further important fact implicit in the reference to outside nations. The people who demanded such a king, in discarding the previous system of "judges," were consciously importing the new institution from other societies. The ultimate source in this particular case was manifestly Mesopotamia, where the restrictions imposed on the authority of the ruler were the same as those that Rehoboam was so ill-advised to reject. It was the same source that gave to the neighbors, including Israel, the appropriate legal forms and the other instruments of civilization that went with such forms.

Thanks to this affinity with Mesopotamia, which goes back far into the past, Israel was able to go on to its own unique and enduring achievement, in filling the vast spiritual vacuum that had caused Abraham to leave Mesopotamia and proceed to the Promised Land. That the original promise was fulfilled remains to this day one of the great wonders of history. The credit, however, for giving Israel its all-important start, physically and culturally, belongs to ancient Mesopotamia.

D. Colophon

In summary retrospect, there are several things that stand out from the mass of detail comprising the political and cultural history of Mesopotamia. Throughout the span of some two millenniums which written documents have rendered articulate, the pattern that confronts us is one of sustained ethnic and political change. Yet side by side with the rapid succession of peoples and states, there is the steadying influence of cultural cohesion. A superior kind of unity is achieved through change — cultural cooperation through the diversity of the underlying elements. The joint civilization that emerges is able to transcend ethnic, geographic, and political barriers. And it becomes a magnet that attracts an ever widening circle of adherents.

If there was any single feature that was responsible for the great appeal of Mesopotamian civilization, we cannot discover it in Mesopotamian religion, the local solution of the basic problem of alignment between society and the universe. It is true that this particular solution must have been, at first, in harmony with the concurrent societal system — involving the relation of the individual to society; for, progress could not be possible otherwise. Over the centuries, however, Mesopotamian religion did more to impede continuous advance than to promote it. It may well have been an important factor in the eventual collapse of Assyria and Babylonia.

The really constructive factor at home, and a potent magnet to outsiders, was Mesopotamia's secular development — in regard to man on earth as distinct from the gods in heaven. Through the indigenous instruments of law, government, and writing, Mesopotamian civilization reached out to many cultures near and far. In due time it evolved into a society common to the Fertile Crescent as a whole. Neither Israel nor Greece was to prove immune to these far-reaching influences.

When we of today reckon our years by the sun, our weeks by the moon, and identify our days after the planets; when we look at our time-pieces to tell the hours, the minutes, and the seconds, in conformance with a circle of 360 degrees and the sexagesimal system of counting; when we break up the natural sciences into their component disciplines; when we approach the babel of known languages through the medium of internal analysis; when we write our official documents, our scientific calculations and conclusions, our literary creations, and our private letters; when we reaffirm our belief in laws impersonally conceived and in a government that is a safeguard against autocracy — when we do these and countless other things, we are utilizing, consciously or unconsciously, the results of an immemorial experiment in living in which ancient Mesopotamia played a leading part throughout the first half of recorded history.

The Mesopotamian design for living, in so far as the relation of the individual to society was concerned, was popular at home and attractive abroad for the simple reason that it worked; and it worked because it embodied certain basic and enduring truths. This significant attainment outlasted the parent civilization itself, as well as its numerous clients and successors, and it entered eventually, enriched by the independent contributions of Israel and of Greece, into the mainstream of Western Civilization.

B. EGYPT — THE KINGDOM OF THE "TWO LANDS"

by J. A. Wilson

1. FIRST THINGS

A. "The Two Lands"

THE INFLUENCE of the cultures of ancient Egypt and Mesopotamia on world history has been profound and lasting. To be sure, life in classical and modern times has been different from that in the most ancient Orient. To be sure, we have so different an outlook on ourselves and our universe that we cannot completely understand the ways and the psychology of those ancients. The Hebrews and the Greeks are closer to us in modes of thinking. Yet the Sumerians and the Egyptians opened the door to civilized times and gave us forms and institutions which we still take for granted: — family life, government, law, social behavior, writing, education, and the beginnings of science. They gave us chairs and tables, villages and houses, tools and weapons of metal, and a fully structured architecture. They gave us a calendar and a formal art and literature of high complexity. One could go on with the list. In our own day we are experimenting with changes in some of those ancient Oriental forms: — tools of plastic, chairs and tables which do not rest on four legs, houses which are not rectangular boxes, punch-cards and computing machines instead of writing, applied power from machines instead of muscles, metropolitan cities instead of villages, and a science which is more focused upon the future than upon the past. Even in such experimentation the legacy from the ancients will continue to be strong.

The influence of Egypt and Mesopotamia was also negative. The Greeks, building upon the forms which they had inherited from the Babylonians and the Egyptians, rejected the ancient Oriental attitudes towards those forms. The Greeks sloughed off the older myth-controlled mind of the ancient Orientals and gave us rationalism, causality, and the scientific mind — a world open to man's understanding, not the exclusive province of the gods.

Even more importantly, the Children of Israel built a nation and a religion on the rejection of things Egyptian. Not only did they see God as one, but they ascribed to him consistency of concern for man and consistency of justice to man. This revulsion against the unaccountability of the Egyptian gods and against the "flesh-pots" of Egypt profoundly affected Judaism and therefore Christianity. Like the Greeks, the Hebrews took forms from their great neighbors; like the Greeks, they used those forms for very different purposes.

The ancient Egyptians had no consistent name for their nation. They did refer to their country as *Kemet*, "the black (Land)," contrasting the alluvial soil with the surrounding desert, but this was more often a geographical epithet than a political term in earlier history. Only in late times did the Greek form Αἴγυπτος, that is, Egypt, evolve, probably from a name for the district of Memphis, *Hi-ku-Ptah*, "House of the Spirit of (the god) Ptah." They normally referred to their country as "this land" or, more commonly, as "the Two Lands," for they were always conscious of the difference between Upper Egypt, the two banks of the Nile running north from the First Cataract to the area of Memphis, and Lower Egypt, the Delta at the north. The Hebrew *Mizraim* also employs the dual for Egypt, although the Bible uses another term for Upper Egypt, *Pathros*. The modern Arabic name for Egypt is *Misr*.

After a long prehistory, ancient Egyptian history may be taken as running from the beginning of the dynasties about 3000 B.C.E. to the Roman conquest in 30 B.C.E. or to the Christianization of the land in the second century C.E. and the consequent obliteration of the older culture.

Since Greek times, the history of ancient Egypt has been divided into thirty-one dynasties, the First at the beginning of written history about 3000 B.C.E. and the Thirty-first ending with the conquest by Alexander the Great in 332 B.C.E. The dynasty of the Ptolemies ran from 306 to 30 B.C.E. In the older history there were three political plateaus, the Old Kingdom or pyramid age (Third through Sixth Dynasties, 2700–2200 B.C.E.), the Middle Kingdom or feudal age (Twelfth Dynasty, 2000–1800 B.C.E.), and the New Kingdom or imperial age (Eighteenth through Twentieth Dynasties, 1570–1100 B.C.E.). We call the intervening times of troubles the First Intermediate Period (2200–2000 B.C.E.) and the Second Intermediate Period (1800–1570 B.C.E.). Late times include the Ethiopian period, with the Twenty-fifth Dynasty (725–663 B.C.E.), the Saitic revival in the Twenty-sixth Dynasty (663–525 B.C.E.), and the Persian period (525–332 B.C.E., with interludes of Egyptian reassertion).

Egyptian chronology has a wide margin of uncertainty about 3000 B.C.E., is relatively close after 2000 B.C.E., and becomes fairly precise after 663

B.C.E. The First Dynasty may have begun before 3100 or, with less likelihood, after 2900 B.C.E. The Nineteenth Dynasty may have begun as early as 1318 or as late as 1304 B.C.E.

B. The Land along the Nile

Northeast Africa is essentially a rainless country and has been so in historical times. Egypt is a long oasis, the gift of the Nile and particularly of the inundation each summer. The Nile brought not only a spate of floodwater but also fresh alluvial soil, which was a natural fertilizer. With this rich black soil in sharp contrast to the neighboring desert, with abundant natural resources, and with a crowded urbanized life as over against the sparse existence in nearby regions, the Egyptians saw their land as exceptionally favored by the gods. They were "the People"; the Nubians, the Libyans, and the Asiatics had to live like the beasts of the highlands.

Equatorial and tropical rains in Africa produce the White and Blue Niles, which join at Khartum in the Sudan for their final nineteen hundred miles north to the Mediterranean. In hundreds of thousands of years the Nile carved a trough out of the sandstone and limestone desert, and it has deposited alluvial soil within that trough to make life possible. Brief areas of harder stone cut across the bed of the river, making six cataracts, which have formed natural frontiers. South from the Fourth Cataract there is some annual rainfall, and from the eighth century B.C.E. on this area had a provincial culture which the Bible calls Cush or Ethiopia. The region between the Third and First Cataracts is Nubia. Egypt proper lies north of the First Cataract. Upper Egypt ran from the First Cataract to the pyramid area near Memphis — or to the region of Abydos, if one includes Middle Egypt in the listing — and Lower Egypt ran from the apex of the Delta to the Mediterranean. Our experience with maps makes it difficult for us to remember that Upper Egypt lies to the south, Lower Egypt to the north.

The six hundred miles from the First Cataract to Memphis (near modern Cairo) cut through sandstone and limestone cliffs, which are parts of the Libyan desert to the west and the Red Sea hills to the east. The valley runs in width anywhere from one to twenty-four miles. Then from the region of Cairo the Delta fans out, with a maximum width at the north of 125 miles. Anciently there were at least five forks of the Nile in the Delta; today there are but two.

The inundation has a regularity, with waters rising in July and beginning to subside in September. Egypt's prosperity depends upon a good inundation and the planned retention of the flood waters for a maximum period. The ancient system was to run the flood into catch basins and hold it there; the canal system was more common in the Delta and in the Faiyum. Well-sweeps to lift the water appeared in ancient times, although the most common method was probably lifting by pots or buckets. Irrigating waters, an annual increment of new fertile soil, and a warm climate made Egypt one of the richest agricultural countries in the world. With Mesopotamia so distant, the Egyptians could look upon their poor neighbors and feel the assurance that their gods were good.

Another advantage of ancient Egypt was relative security. To the west lay the forbidding Libyan desert, with a relatively thin strip of habitable land along the Mediterranean coast. Nubia to the south was a poor land, with the only major approach on the Nile. At least a hundred miles of Red Sea desert insulated the east. At the northeast the wilderness of Sinai permitted movement to only a limited force. Invaders who tried to come by sea had to penetrate the narrow Nile mouths. It is true that Egypt was successfully invaded by the Hyksos, Assyrians, Babylonians, Persians, and Macedonians, but only when the state was weak or divided. By the same token, Egypt's hold on an Asiatic empire had to be supported by a fleet which controled the eastern Mediterranean, because land communications were so difficult.

The prevailing wind has always been from the north, bringing cool temperature across the Mediterranean and pushing sailboats southward against the current of the Nile. In the spring the south wind from the desert may rise and produce sandstorms, which lay a "thick darkness" over the land; they are a perennial plague of Egypt.

The northern part of the Delta was brackish, and, until Alexander the Great founded Alexandria, no important city lay on the Mediterranean. Pelusium (Sin), which Ezekiel 30:15 calls the "stronghold of Egypt," was probably a frontier fortress. Some of the chief cities were Tanis (Zoan) and Raamses in the east Delta; Mendes, Busiris, Sais, and Bubastis (Pibeseth) in the middle Delta; Heliopolis (On) and Memphis (Noph) at the apex of the Delta and near modern Cairo. Agriculturally rich Middle Egypt always had large cities like Siut or Hermopolis; and Abydos was a place of pilgrimage, as the seat of Osiris, god of the dead. Southern Upper Egypt was poorer; its chief center was Thebes (No), one of the capitals of Egypt, and Assuan (Seveneh) guarded the First Cataract.

Egypt was an agricultural land, but not a land of isolated farm houses. Large commercial cities were rare, but agricultural villages were everywhere. The black soil was so precious that farmers lived in tightly built villages and went out to their fields. To maintain the maximum acreage, the villages were always built in the same places, and today most of the ancient settlements are buried deep under the risen alluvium. Therefore, in contrast to Mesopotamia, our knowledge of domestic life is limited. There was always the desert nearby for burial, so that tombs and mortuary temples have survived in these sands. Tombs and temples were of stone, whereas village houses and even royal palaces were of mud brick. These accidents of survival have made the Egyptian emphasis on life after death seem to us a morbid preoccupation with death, which it was not.

In the concept of the state there was no such thing as private property, since the king was a god and everything belonged to him by divine right. However, in practice Egyptians treated soil, houses, cattle, and chattels as their own. They certainly paid taxes on these properties. In what way and to what degree temples, priests, kings, and queens were taxed remain, obscure. Usage may have varied from age to age. Women were persons at law in ancient Egypt and enjoyed respectable standing in general.

The black soil was too valuable to be cut up by permanent roads, and the Nile or its branches was always near to serve as the artery of traffic. From prehistoric times on, the Egyptians were a river-faring people, and very early they took their boats out onto the open sea. Trade with Phoenicia or Crete may have been in Egyptian or in foreign ships, but on the Red Sea the Nile-built vessel was dominant for the trade southward to the land which they called Punt, for incense, myrrh, gums, and ivory.

To Asia the chief road left Egypt near modern Kantarah, cut across north Sinai, and reached Palestine near modern Gaza. This was a usable road for caravans, but for armies on the march there might not be enough water. It was necessary to police and fortify the water holes along the way, or else one large flock of sheep might make a station stop impossible. Since the water holes were police and communication posts, this may be why Moses led the Children of Israel "by way of the wilderness" rather than "by way of the land of the Philistines" (Ex. 13:17–18), the chief road.

The base for Egypt's wealth and power was agricultural. Barley was the chief crop, with barley bread and beer the staples of life. Wheat and emmer were less important in the economy. Flax made the linen of Egypt prized in the ancient world, and the Egyptians were scornful of those clothed in wool or the skins of animals. Vegetables and melons were abundant. The grape was cultivated in marginal lands: — the fringes of the Delta, the Faiyum, and the oases. Papyrus from the marshes was a valuable product and export, as a standard writing material.

Domestic animals were important in the Egyptian economy. Although there was no such emphasis on sheep and wool as in Asia (Gen. 46:34), large cattle were abundant, and hides went into the export market. The donkey was the earlier animal of traffic. The camel was very rare until Persian times. The horse was introduced about 1700 B.C.E., and the Egyptian horse market was flourishing in Solomon's time (I Kings 10: 28–29). Fish, the goose, and the duck were regular elements in the Egyptian diet.

The cliffs along the Nile were rich in stone for buildings and statues, from hard materials like granite and basalt to softer stones like limestone and alabaster. One contrast between Egypt and Mesopotamia was that the former could build colossal monuments of stone, whereas the latter had to rely upon brick. Until the Iron Age, Egypt was also fortunate in her command of deposits of minerals: — copper in the Red Sea hills but especially in western Sinai, gold in the Red Sea hills and in Nubia. Two of ancient Egypt's great assets were copper for tools and weapons and gold for purchasing power. When the Iron Age came in about 1150 B.C.E., Egypt had to buy this new medium from abroad, and her relative strength in the world fell off.

The Sinai mines for copper and turquoise brought the Egyptians into contact with Semitic Bedouin, and her first imperial pretensions were in that area. A byproduct of this association seems to have been that the Semites were impressed with Egyptian writing, but they rejected the complex hieroglyphic system and took over individual pictures to form the basis of the first alphabet. This must have occurred before 1400 B.C.E. in Sinai.

Ancient Egypt was self-sufficient in most basic commodities. A major lack was good construction wood. From early historical times there was a brisk trade with Phoenicia for cedar, fir, and cypress. Cedar resin also became a desired import for the embalming process. Olive oil was an early import from Asia. Tin, silver, and iron were lacking and had to be brought from abroad. Otherwise, the foreign trade was in luxury items: — lapis lazuli, obsidian, marquetry, and metalwork from Asia; ivory, incenses, gums, and rare skins from Africa.

In physical race the ancient Egyptians belonged to the Mediterranean stock: short, slight, dark of hair and eyes, but not dark of skin color, with a light growth of hair on face or body. They were like the South Semites or the Hamites. Shortly before history a broad-skulled people of unknown antecedents appeared, but these were soon absorbed into the dominant type. The Negro did not appear on the Sudanese horizon until about 2000 B.C.E. Negro characteristics were never prominent in the Egypt with which the

Thebes: New Kingdom. Horses and mules at the harvest field.
Oriental Institute, University of Chicago.

Egyptian gardener drawing water; painting on tomb of Ipui at Thebes (XIX Dynasty).

Methethy — Overseer of the Office of Crown Tenants. Late Vth Dynasty, ca. 2450 B.C.E. From Sakkarah. Wood with gesso and paint.

Nelson Gallery Atkings Museum (Nelson Fund) Kansas City, Missouri, U. S. A.

King Djoser of IIIrd Dynasty, statue from Sakkarah.

Gizeh. Head of diorite statue of King Khaf-re with hawk whose wings are spread around king's head. IVth Dynasty, ca. 26th Cent. B.C.E.

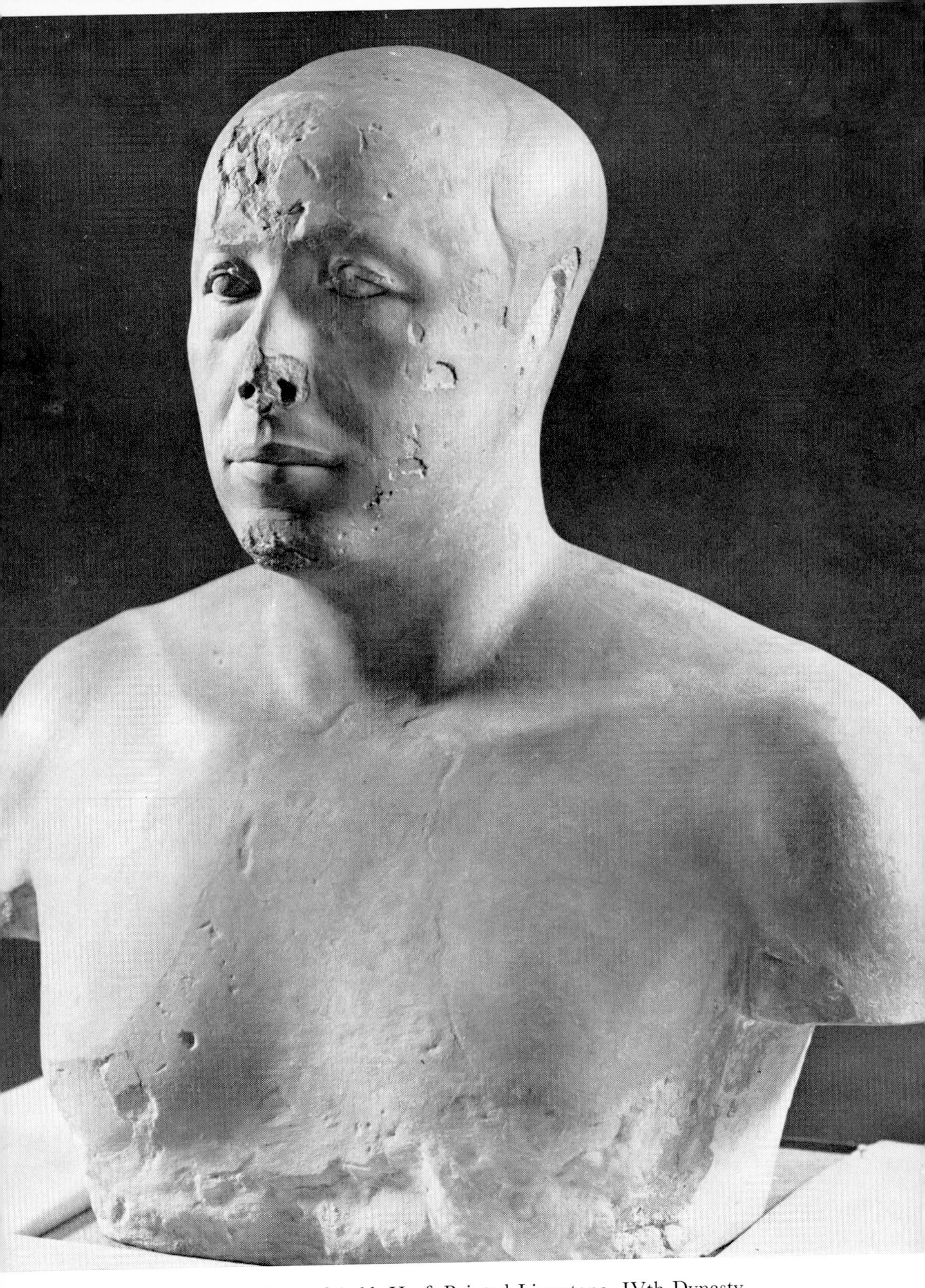

Portrait Bust of Ankh-Haef. Painted Limestone, IVth Dynasty.
Museum of Fine Arts, Boston.

Pepi II on mother's lap.
Brooklyn Museum.

Abusir pyramid field (reconstructed).
Oriental Institute, University of Chicago.

Deir el-Bahri from cliffs above.

Potter at his wheel. Old Kingdom.

Upper part of basalt statue of Thut-mose III.
XVIII Dynasty. 15 Cent. B.C.E.

Philistines as shown in Egypt.

Hebrews had contact, except for such Ethiopian pharaohs as Tirhakah (689 B.C.E.).

The ancient Egyptian language shows relations to Semitic and Hamitic, which may themselves have been one original stock. Since many root words were the same in Egyptian and Semitic, borrowing by one from the other was easy and common. Like Semitic, Egyptian wrote only in a consonantal skeleton, with the unwritten vowels subject to grammatical change in speech. This is one of the reasons why it is difficult to render ancient names consistently. When sources in Greek give Ramesses, Rampses, or Rapsaces and sources in cuneiform Riamashshi for the pharaoh here called Ramses, there is clearly basis for scholarly divergence.

In Egypt, before Christian times, it has been impossible to separate out the dialects which we believe were present. The influence of the priestly control held writing to certain norms. The classical phase of the language was maintained by the priests with little change for nearly three thousand years. This is what was carved in pictures on stone and is therefore called hieroglyphic. A cursive form of hieroglyphic was adapted for rapid writing with a pen on papyrus or other medium, and we call this hieratic. The more colloquial language which appeared increasingly after 1350 B.C.E. had the stages of Late Egyptian and Demotic (Persian times and later), and in Christian times it was written in an expanded Greek alphabet and we call it Coptic.

C. Before the Beginning

History begins with writing, and before history there was a vast prehistoric period. With some gaps, archaeologists have traced human products in the Nile Valley from the crude fist hatchets of the Old Stone Age down to the rippled and polished flint knives at the beginning of history. Back in geologic ages, the northeast African plateau had been well watered. As it gradually dried up, life became possible only in a few oases, the greatest of which was the Nile Valley. Hunting in the uplands became an inadequate supplier of food. Just how man brought domesticated plants and animals into the river valley remains uncertain; but men did leave their roving habits and settle down in villages on the margins of the land watered by the Nile. The basic social unit was shifting from the tribe to the village community.

The last stages of the prehistoric we call the predynastic. It is superfluous here to identify the predynastic cultures step by step. Gradually certain amenities were introduced, such as containers made of pottery, better tools, metal implements, granaries for storage, linen in place of hides, houses with inner sectioning into rooms, with doors and windows, and luxury items, such as jewelry, cosmetics, and amulets. Things made of foreign materials show a modest trade. Worship of gods and a belief in survival after death are shown by figurines, amulets, and the food, drink, and clothing placed in the graves. More and better grain made a richer diet and permitted the population to increase. Weapons and broken bones show that communities were competing with each other for possession of territory.

As the population increased, there were new demands upon the land. It was not enough to herd a few animals down to the swamps which fringed the Nile, nor to depend upon the natural watering of the Nile, while teasing a few marginal plants with a hoe. The marshes had to be cleared and drained for fields. Irrigation works were necessary to carry the water farther from the Nile and hold it longer. About the time that man moved into history, major irrigation works and the animal-drawn plow made possible an agricultural revolution. Thus the community changed from the small agricultural village to the spreading province. Life became complicated. Some men became specialized as potters, weavers, smiths, merchants, or sailors; other men became rich and powerful and emerged as local rulers.

In theory the process would be an enlargement by competition and conquest, from the village to the city state to the province to the nation. Human history has a way of outwitting theory, and we do not know how Egypt became a nation with such apparent abruptness. Nor do we know the economic, political, and spiritual forces which moved the Egyptians from their primitive state of prehistoric times into the civilization of historic times. From the physical materials we can see in their graves, they were ready to move into a life of balanced complexity. But what forces produced this revolutionary change?

One factor can be detected. Just before the beginning of the dynasties there appeared in Egypt certain elements which were borrowed from Mesopotamia. These certainly included the cylinder seal, massive brick architecture decorated with recessed panels, and certain artistic forms, such as a hero standing between two rampant lions. They may have included a more advanced metallurgy and the idea of writing, with its method of setting down objects and concepts in recognizable pictures. The hieroglyphic system was not taken, lock, stock, and barrel, from the Babylonians, but the Mesopotamian use of picture writing seems to antedate the Egyptian, so that the general idea may have been appropriated. Since no comparable borrowing by Mesopotamia from Egypt has been found, the priority of

Sumerian civilization may be conceded, and the Mesopotamian influence may have been the catalyst which precipitated Egypt into civilization. No one argues conquest or colonization of Egypt by the Sumerians; trade connections may provide the answer. By the Third Dynasty, when Egypt was phrasing her own independent cultural forms, these borrowings from Mesopotamia had disappeared or had become vestigial.

D. Through the Door of History

Three factors coincide about 3000 B.C.E., the beginning of writing and therefore of history, the beginning of that complexity and refinement of life which we call civilization, and the beginning of the dynasties. A family from Upper Egypt succeeded in conquering all of the effective parts of the land and founding the first nation in world history. In later tradition the founder of the First Dynasty was called Menes. Although the credit to a single individual is dubious, the family from Abydos in Upper Egypt did unify the land and set up a capital at Memphis, near the point where Upper and Lower Egypt meet. Probably the conquest and unification had been preceded by many years of preliminary action, and certainly it required several generations after Menes to complete the acceptance of the new rule and to organize the new state. The first two dynasties, lasting perhaps three centuries, were occupied in working out the forms of the new nation.

The new atmosphere called civilization had its amenities and its penalties. Men's names might now live beyond their times through written records. Great quantities of workers could be mobilized for public works. Art and architecture could be promoted by patronage, and science likewise. Metallurgy had become so facile that stone implements fell out of use, except for ancient rituals. The purposes of the state led to an exploitation of the Sinai mines, which was imperialistic. People of dignity had to suffer through the use of new domestic machines, sitting up stiffly on chairs at tables or sleeping awkwardly on beds. Only the poor could be comfortable on the floor. A middle class of agents appeared: — clerks, artisans, artists, stewards, accountants, physicians, and tax collectors.

At the top rested the king. He was the god Horus, the "Distant One" who saw all from on high. His was the state and all that was in it. He *was* the state. There is evidence in the first two dynasties of judicious royal marriages with local princesses to weld the new nation. For the most part the royal blood was different because it was divine. Only a god could own and operate this new mechanism, the state, which was composed of so many divergent elements. He was not of Abydos or Memphis, he was not of

Upper or Lower Egypt. He was the god Horus, he was the embodiment of the two goddesses who respectively stood for Upper and Lower Egypt. The divinity of kingship may be an African principle rather than Asian. It certainly provided a dogmatic formula for the acceptance of the new rule.

The dogma of divine kingship also presented problems. A god is dreadfully unapproachable and untouchable. Thus his immediate entourage must consist of his priests and those who share his divine blood. In the earlier, smaller court the chief ministers of the state had to be royal princes and personal servants who were consecrated priests. This was possible as long as the governmental staff was small and uncomplicated.

It took a long time to work out the forms and activities of the state and to secure its acceptance throughout the land, the centuries covered by the first two dynasties. There is evidence in the Second Dynasty either of a rebellion or of a brief change in the official dogma, when the god Seth competed with the god Horus as the embodiment of kingship. Thereafter the dogma went back to its former assertions.

Kings, queens, and nobles were buried in mud-brick *mastabas*, tombs with sloping sides, flat tops, and that paneled decoration which had been borrowed from Mesopotamia. In the First Dynasty there is evidence of a grisly practice. Around the burial of royalty or nobility lie the simpler graves of servants, apparently laid to rest at the same time as their master. The dogma must have asserted that he had servants in this world and that his patrician existence in the next world would demand the same servants. This mass sacrifice soon disappeared, except for one instance in the Sudan under the Twelfth Dynasty. In Egypt the later practice was to equip the tomb with models or pictures of servants, whom the mortuary religion would make effective agents for the deceased in the next world.

2. FROM TRIUMPH TO FAILURE

A. The Age of the Pyramids (2700–2250 B.C.E.)

BY THE BEGINNING of the Third Dynasty, about 2700 B.C.E., Egypt had matured sufficiently to express the forms of her new culture in her own terms. That expression produced one of the great ages of world history, the pyramid age. Djoser (or Zoser) built the Stepped Pyramid near Memphis, the first large monument constructed entirely in hewn stone. To be sure, the hand of tradition still rested upon this huge tomb: — the stone was cut into small bricks following the material used in the past, and some of the stone was carved to imitate the reed or wooden elements of previous architecture. Nevertheless, there was brilliant genius in this complex of structures. This first pyramid consisted of six superposed *mastabas*, each smaller than the one under it, the monument rising 190 feet and dominating the landscape from its cliff at Sakkarah. The halls of the attached temples have a remarkable lightness and airiness, considering the fact that man was working with an entirely new medium in stone. Credit for this architectural revolution goes to Djoser's brilliant minister, Ii-em-hotep (or Imhotep). This man was later revered as one of Egypt's great sages and ultimately became a god of medicine.

This was the formative period for Egyptian expression. Art was moving into that poised and two-dimensional form by which the Egyptians expressed their belief in eternal life. Architecture employed mass for the same purpose. It is likely that medicine was still relatively experimental at the time, laying down the practices and attitudes which later ages followed without question. Although we do not have enough literature from this period for certainty, it appears that the language was leaving its earlier forms and moving into the classical expression which we call Middle Egyptian. For a time Egypt was creative. Later, after she had created forms which were satisfactory, she abandoned experimentation and became firmly retentive.

Under Djoser the bureaucracy was expanded and reorganized, to meet the needs of a more complex state. The government was still a theocracy, vested in the person of the king as a god; the king's sons continued to hold the most responsible offices; and there was no distinction made between priestly and civil offices; but the assigment of authority to individuals to act in the king's name was the first large step toward the building up of a secular bureaucracy, which ultimately might act with some independence of the palace. From the Third into the Fifth Dynasty Egypt was markedly king-centered. The flat-topped *mastaba* tombs of the princes and nobles clustered close to the pyramid of the king. He was the only one who by definition was firmly assured of an eternal and blessed life, because he was a god who never died. If he needed his court for eternal rule in the next world, then they might have eternal life in his service. The general psychology is similar to that of the sacrificed servants of the First Dynasty, even though the association now was a tomb built nearby rather than death at the same time.

The Fourth Dynasty (about 2650–2500) was the peak of Egypt's material and artistic glory. It was the period of the first true pyramids, the excellent structures of Snefru at Dahshur and the three pyramids of Gizeh: the Great Pyramid, built as a tomb for Khufu (or Cheops), the Second Pyramid, for Khaf-Re (or Chephren), and the Third, for Men-kau-Re (or Mycerinus). The Great Pyramid was rightly one of the Seven Wonders of the ancient world. Originally 481 feet high, it covered an area of nearly thirteen acres. Its side in ancient cubits was 440, while the height was 280 cubits; this 11–7 ratio was a characteristic of several other pyramids, giving a 51°51′ slope. Despite the tremendous mass, despite the fact that man had worked in hewn stone for only about a century, it was one of the most precisely finished monuments in world history. The trueness in leveling the stone platform upon which it sits, the exactness in angle of its four corners, and the consistent length of its four sides show superb fidelity and craftsman's conscience. The fitting of its massive casing blocks was so precise that a knife blade cannot be run down between them. The majestic monument was constructed with what we should consider imperfect tools: — no cranes or pulleys, no wheeled vehicles, no tools of firm metal; only sloping ramps, rockers to maneuvre the blocks, copper instruments, and manpower.

While the labor on the Great Pyramid and other such royal tombs was certainly a forced draft of the men who could be deployed in the area, there is no cause for lofty indignation at the brutality of these kings. Forced labor under arbitrary conditions was a normal exaction by the ancient state, and the drafted persons were housed, fed, and clothed during the time of their labor. Indeed, since the major period of work was when the Nile was at its highest, the construction work did provide employment during the agriculturally slack season, even though the king did not intend it as a benevolent gesture.

The building of the greatest monument in the world as a mere tomb for a king was uneconomical, but it was one of the achievements which made Egypt great. Here was the one unescapable exponent of the ability to do mighty things. As the pyramid made a great impression upon foreigners visiting Egypt, anciently and today, so it must have impressed the Egyptians. They could look up at it and say: "We can do mightily!" One historian has expressed the pyramid's successful achievement as a symbol of eternal life in these words:

> It seems probable that the Pyramids, which have borne inanimate witness to the existence of their creators for nearly five thousand years, will survive for hundreds of thousands of years to come. It is not inconceivable that they may outlast man himself and that, in a world where there are no longer human minds to read their message, they will continue to testify: 'Before Abraham was, I am.'[1]

Certainly a new nation needs something upon which to test its powers. With an adequate accomplishment, it will have the self-confidence to go on to other achievements. It is a simplified exaggeration to say that the tremendous power of the pyramids made ancient Egypt. Nevertheless, the pyramids were very visible and very impressive; no other factor gave the new nation such a sense of inner power.

By the Fourth Dynasty writing had become competent to meet the normal needs of government and religion. The enlarged bureaucracy and the demands of a national tax register every other year must have filled the archives. "The Two Lands" retained a curious dualism within unity; the chief storehouses of the state were named in pairs, suggesting that the imposts of Upper and Lower Egypt were separately deposited and separately administered.

Statuary, relief sculpture, and painting had become sophisticated enough to render carefully organized and lively scenes, as well as the depiction of mortals in the serene expectation of immortality. Early in Egyptian history art was more successfully "Egyptian," in its capture of the tranquil assurance of eternity, than it was in the following 2,500 years. These were great accomplishments, effected within a relatively short apprenticeship.

We moderns who find Egyptian art two-dimensional, static, and bland must realize that the static was just what the ancient sought. The burning desire was to live forever. All the art from this early period comes from tombs and temples, the places at which that desire was asserted. Art avoided motion, emotion, anxiety, aging, illness, or violence, and presented the king or noble eternally young. Servants, children, and animals might be shown in strain or excitement; the lord was shown calmly poised for eternity. For its purpose the art was thoroughly successful.

However inspiring the monument might be when finished, it was a burden on the state to build a pyramid for every king. The extreme focus upon the divine person of the king was subject to challenge. The Fifth Dynasty (about 2500–2350 B.C.E.) saw the rise of two other gods. The sun-god Ra (or Re) of Heliopolis gained political power by forcing the acknowledgement that he was the father of the ruling king. Osiris, the god who had died but still lived as ruler in another world, came into prominence as the god of the dead, and kings who died thereby became Osiris. Further, there was a centrifugal force within the state. The royal family and court now had a lesser activity in the government, whereas outlying officials were wielding greater authority, even though claiming loyal service to the king. Nobles who no longer felt a need for clinging to the king's divine immortality began to build their tombs in their own home districts. An age of great achievement had fostered enough self-confidence so that the nobles felt that they might gain the good life, in this world and the next, away from the king. The texts kept on asserting full fidelity to the crown, but a new air of brash self-assertion had crept in.

A warning should be issued about the precise historical value of Egyptian inscriptions. That was a world of the frequent and unexpected activity of the gods. It was a world of divine myths and miracles. Truth lay in conformance to the divine order, with no hint of skeptical questioning, no interest in natural cause and effect. The "portraits" of ancient Egyptians, in art and in texts, sometimes showed elements of personal features or character, but these were overlaid with the bland stereotype most acceptable to the gods. Within the divine order the king was an omniscient and infallible god, and men faithful to this belief might be rewarded with eternal happiness.

Similarly, every orthodox inscription shows the king bringing order and success to the nation by superhuman discretion and power. This was conformance to the truth of faith, rather than to objective observation. Texts which were written out of this psychology of devotion have to be tested against any other knowledge we have. It is disconcerting for the historian to read that the Fifth Dynasty king Sahu-Re recorded a victory over a certain Libyan family, that nearly two centuries later the Sixth Dynasty king Pepi II conquered the same family, and that more than seventeen centuries later the Ethiopian pharaoh Tirhakah again conquered the identical family. The national faith that Egypt was always victorious over the Libyans used the same illustration over and over again, giving this "truth" the support of familiar tradition. The historian will accept his data at face value, unless there is a clear reason for distrust; but he must be ready to modify his acceptance as soon as new materials put the previous interpretation in a new light.

The Fourth Dynasty kings had been buried at Gizeh in their soaring pyramids. The Fifth Dynasty kings were buried a few miles south of Gizeh, with architectural complexes which featured sun-temples, thus showing the newly established power of the god Ra. The Sixth Dynasty kings were buried still further south, at Sakkarah. The decreasing size of the pyramids and the falling off of technical perfection in the structures are evidence of the diminishing authority of the king.

The decentralization of the state which we have noted in the Fifth Dynasty continued in the Sixth (about 2350–2200 B.C.E.). Autobiographies in the tombs of provincial nobles show a self-confidence verging on arrogance. We are told of the successive stages in the careers of officials in terms which suggest that they rose to power by their own energies and abilities, rather than by the grace of the ruler. The wisdom literature, containing the practical advice of a father to his son, also reflects this pragmatic and materialistic self-reliance, as we shall see in section 2 C. below.

This assertiveness appeared in the records of Egypt's foreign relations. To the south there was an energetic penetration into Nubia and the Sudan. From the First Cataract caravans were led southward by nobles, who had the tasks of facilitating the flow of trade, of securing favorable alliances with Nubian princes, and of enlisting Nubian soldiers for the Egyptian army. A basic import from the Sudan was cattle, but there was a greater stated interest in luxury goods: incense, gums, ebony, ivory, and leopard skins.

One charming text tells about the explorer to the south who was bringing back a dancing pygmy for the entertainment of the boy king Pepi II. The young ruler wrote a letter to the explorer, urging the greatest care of the pygmy on the homeward journey. "When he goes into the ship with you, have careful men who will be around him on both sides of the boat, watching so that he does not fall into the water. And have careful men who sleep around him in his cabin at night, and inspect ten times a night. My Majesty wants to see this pygmy more than all the products of Sinai or Punt."[2]

Relations with Asia had been active since predynastic times, when archaeology shows that there were exchanges between Egypt and Palestine in pottery and stone vessels.[3] Egypt wanted olive oil, obsidian, lapis lazuli, and timber. Snefru, the first king of the Fourth Dynasty, recorded as significant the arrival of forty shiploads of cedar in one year of his reign.[4] He further put the mines of Sinai in so active a basis that he later became one of the patron deities of that region.

Byblos (Gebal) in Phoenicia became the particular trading post for cedar, fir, and cypress, and thus the shipping port for other Asiatic products. Obviously this was to the economic advantage of both Byblos and Egypt. A temple excavated at Byblos shows strong Egyptian influence, indicating the presence there of a merchant colony from the Nile. At this stage we are not discussing imperialism, with control by Egyptian soldiers and commissioners. The princes of Byblos were independent, finding their prosperity in active commercial relations with the Nile. The kings of Egypt were anxious to promote good fraternal relations with their junior partners in Phoenicia. In the excavations at Byblos have appeared scores of alabaster vases inscribed in hieroglyphic with the names of Egyptian kings. In some cases they carry record of the royal jubilee in Memphis. These must have been gifts from the king of Egypt to the prince of Byblos, in recognition of satisfactory relations.

Further to the south, in Palestine, the situation was not so advantageous to the Egyptians. Very few Old Kingdom pieces have appeared in the archaeology of Palestine. Probably the official commerce between Phoenicia and the Nile went across the sea by boat and not through Palestine by land caravan. About 2325 B.C.E. there was an active problem for Egypt. Although the Egyptians loftily described their enemies as "sand-dwellers," these were obviously not desert nomads, for they lived in villages, with orchards and vineyards. Apparently the first area of conflict was in southern Palestine. Five successive military campaigns were mounted to check this opposition. In the inscription of a certain official named Uni, we read that the Egyptian army consisted of drafted soldiers, "many ten-thousands" — surely an exaggeration — from Egypt, Nubia, and Libya. Uni claims that His Majesty's "punishment" of the "sand-dwellers" crushed their land and killed them "by many ten-thousands."[5] Yet these raids failed to stamp out the hostility, and a final campaign had to be mounted, further to the north and by sea transport. The term "Antelope Nose" may refer to the Carmel Range.

> When it was said that backsliders because of something were among these foreigners in Antelope Nose, I crossed over in transports with these troops. I made a landing at the rear of the heights of the mountain range on the north of the land of the sand-dwellers. While a full half of this (Egyptian) army was still on the road, I arrived, I caught them all, and every backslider among them was killed.[6]

The implication is that this final campaign ended the war. However, restlessness in Palestine and changes in its population were probably some of the reasons for the fall of the Old Kingdom about a century later. We shall see that in the First Intermediate Period, following the Old Kingdom, the Asiatics took advantage of Egyptian weakness to trickle across the frontier and into the Delta.

The forces which brought an end to this great period of world history are generally clear, even though the detail sometimes evades us. First and foremost was the weakening of the central power and authority of the king through the independence of his officials and nobles. Not only was there a great proliferation of official titles, but some of these titles were weakened when they were conferred on several persons in competition. For example, under the Fifth Dynasty there was only one "Governor of Upper Egypt," and he enjoyed extraordinary powers, because he was the viceroy and taxmaster for the south of the land. By the end of the Sixth Dynasty there were several Governors of Upper Egypt at the same time, and their services to the crown must have been nominal. Apparently the king now had to cultivate provincial nobles by conferring upon them titles which were formerly of high position and power. A similar situation seems to involve that highest of palace officials, the Vizier or Prime Minister. Under the Fourth Dynasty a royal prince held this function. Under the Fifth Dynasty it was held by one noble alone — unless there was one vizier for Upper Egypt and another for the Delta. At the end of the Sixth Dynasty we find many viziers. Although it is assumed that the king was then forced to grant the title right and left, it is also possible that provincial rulers had become strong enough to arrogate it to themselves.

Another index of the independence of outlying powers appears in the charters of immunity issued to a number of temples in the Fifth and Sixth Dynasties. At Dahshur, Abydos, Coptos, and probably other places, the temples secured from the king formal decrees exempting them from the obligation to supply forced labor for the state. Although these did not free them from taxes in goods, the immunity from the labor draft was a distinct privilege, and it shows that the temples had so much power that the king was obliged to defer to them. The following extract on behalf of the temple of Osiris at Abydos is from the Fifth Dynasty.

> I give no man the right to take away any priests who are in the district in which you (the Chief Priest) are, for the corvée or for any other work of the district, except to do service for the god himself in the temple where he is and to conserve the temples in

> which they are. Throughout eternity they are exempt by the decree of the King of Upper and Lower Egypt, Nefer-iri-ka-Re. There is no title to them in any other service. (Similar clauses are provided for temple serfs and equipment.) Any official or courtier or agricultural officer who shall act contrary to these provisions which I have decreed shall [be removed from office] and turned over to the law court, while the house, fields, people, and everything in his possession shall be forfeited, he himself being put on any corvée.[7]

According to tradition Pepi II reigned ninety-four years, and there is evidence in support of the tradition. The reign seems to have been both long and inert. Most of the disintegration of the state occurred when it was clear to ambitious provincial rulers that the god-king was powerless or indifferent. When the state was already breaking into fragments, a Queen, Nitocris, succeeded to the throne for a brief rule. Although she could hardly have wielded much power at the time and although she certainly built no great pyramid, the legend of her rule persisted into Greek times, when tradition said that she was "the noblest and loveliest of the women of her time, who built the third pyramid." We shall see that in ancient Egypt women did sometimes occupy the throne.

B. The Gods of the Land

Any description of this culture must start with the flat dictum that the gods ruled everything. There was no such thing as impersonal natural causation; there was only the action of some god. The Nile flooded because a god willed it, or it fell off badly because a god was displeased for some reason — perhaps a reason unknown to man. The king of Egypt won a victory, not because he had superior forces, tactics, or position, but because he was a god. In such a myth-making mentality there could be no separation of church and state, there could be no secular life which was not drenched by religion. Before we examine the literature as reflecting the culture, we must examine the religion.

Ancient Egyptian religion was a polytheism, which, in the course of three thousand years, showed a high complexity. Within certain firm principles it had a flexibility which permitted it to change with the passage of time. Certain generalities may be laid down, but no simple analysis will do justice to the changes appearing over the millennia. We shall therefore come back to religion in sections 2 E., 3 C., 4 B., and 5 B. below.

For the ancient Egyptian, existence was not contained in sealed compartments: divine vs. human, living vs. dead, animate vs. inanimate, man vs. animal, animal vs. plant. Being was a spectrum within which one category might blend with another. Gods might manifest themselves in animals, plants, mountains, wind, or water. Kings were gods, and lesser men might be recognized after death as having been gods. Men sought magic spells to permit them to take temporary form as animals, plants, or amulets. In a world where the miraculous was always possible, no phenomenon could be penned within a single category.

Even abstractions might be deities, as "Truth" was a goddess and "Command" and "Fate" were gods. The unseen god Amon, whose name meant "Hidden", might be invisible as air or wind, or he might manifest himself in a stone statue, a bull, a ram, or a goose. The statue or animal he used was not in itself a god — only the place for a god to function.

The gods were potentially ever present and ready to intervene in any aspect of life. Science could not work out a rational explanation of climate or weather, plant and animal life, astronomy, or medicine. Since consecutive causation was of no importance, history was concerned with the present generation and had only an annalistic interest in the past. To be sure, the gods had given something of their own at the creation; it was therefore necessary for the present to try to vault over the recent past and try to go back to the good which was at the beginning. The culture looked backward and not forward.

The gods were natural, regional, and functional. Examples of natural or cosmic gods are the sun-god Ra, the sky-goddess Nut, the star god Orion, or the goddess of the north wind Mehit. Regional gods were originally found in a single shrine, as Neith was goddess at Sais, Ptah was god at Memphis, and Khnum was the god of the First Cataract. Functional gods had to do with aspects of life, as Ma'at was goddess of truth or justice, Hat-Hor was goddess of love, and Anubis was a god of the dead. In the fluidity of the Egyptian system there were identifications and mergers, so that single definitions do not hold. Thus Thoth, the regional god of Hermopolis, became cosmic as a god of the moon and functional as the god of wisdom and writing. A god who was both regional and functional was the king of Egypt, for he had the land as his and he had the function of rule.

By the time the myths of the gods were written down they had already become complex. From our modern point of view they might also seem to be self-contradictory. Since everything was possible to the gods, mere man should not question alternative explanations of the same phenomenon. For example, the creation story was told in several different ways about a single god and in varying terms about other creator gods. Every important shrine of Egypt claimed to have participated in the creation. These varying explanations of the same act were not felt to be inconsistent; rather, they strengthened the concept by making it broadly characteristic of divinity: creation is a continuing process of power by any god, and it is a part of the divinity of any important god.

Similarly, Osiris became the dying god and the god of the dead, because (a) he was drowned in the Nile and thus was identified with its annual renewal in the flood period, or (b) because he was cut into pieces and strewn around the land by his wicked brother Seth and thus shared in the annual revivification of every part of Egypt, or (c) because he was smothered in a wooden chest by Seth and this was caught in a tree, so that he thus became identified with plant life and its annual rebirth. If you are not arbitrary, these different myths converge and are the same.

A religious state could never admit any division between the sacred and the secular, particularly when the head of the state was a god. In earlier Egypt there was no distinction between a priest and a lay official. The high official in his service to the state was civil administrator, priest of the temple, priest of the god-king, and even commander of the army. In that campaign which Uni led against the "sand-dwellers" of Palestine, the officers were nobles, courtiers, governors, mayors, caravan leaders, and chief priests. Only after 1500 B.C.E., when the exacting demands of a large and complex state made professionalism necessary, do we find full-time priests and full-time civil servants. Even then the dogma of a theocratic state and the myth-making mentality of the Egyptian refused to admit that there could be any final separation between the religious and the secular.

Egypt consisted of two narrow strips of fertile soil along the Nile, hemmed in by arid deserts. The people lived in villages of mud-brick within the fields. Now the slow accumulation of Nile-carried alluvial soil has buried these villages deep. However, the desert was always near at hand for the stone structures of eternal life, the temples and tombs. Thus we are well informed on the official religion, shown in the great temples, and on the mortuary religion, shown in the tombs. We have little knowledge about the simple faith or private devotions of individuals, as to whether personal religion corresponded closely to official, or about the faithfulness with which the tomb scenes and texts illustrated the daily life of persons. Any analysis of ancient Egyptian religion must suffer from this incompleteness of evidence.

We have already seen that gods tended to merge attributes. Hat-Hor might be goddess of love, goddess of the sky, and goddess at Dendereh. There was another process of syncretism, whereby similarity or competition was resolved by blending. Various falcon gods all came to be Horus, and similarity of status or purposes permitted outright mergers, such as Amon-Ra or Atum Re-Har-akhti, two in one or even three in one.

The cosmic gods were paralleled in Asia, as were the cosmic myths, such as the creation story or the myth about the destruction of mankind by an angry god.[8] The theological system of Heliopolis had a progressive myth for the creation of the universe. The god Atum, whose name means "All," took his place upon a little mound of earth rising out of the waters of chaos and brought into being the elements of the cosmos. Just so, new life seems to rise annually out of the receding flood waters of the Nile. Atum's own two children were Shu, god of air, and Tefnut, goddess of moisture. These two in turn produced Geb, the earth-god, and Nut, the sky-goddess — the firmament below and the firmament above. Geb and Nut produced the mated couple Osiris and Isis, forces of life and regeneration, and the mated couple Seth and Nephthys, with Seth the force that threatened life. The Ennead or "Nine" gods just listed were the corporation of supreme gods, specifically in the theology of Heliopolis, but also generally in Egypt. The successive separations of elements in this myth show broad general similarity to the creation story in Genesis.

Another important myth was the Osiris saga. If we select the main components from the several variations, Osiris had been a ruler in this world, and his wicked brother Seth killed him by trickery, thereby taking over the rule. Isis, the good sister-wife of Osiris, succeeded in reclaiming her husband's body and giving it some new life by her magic. Thus Osiris, the king who had died but who lived on in death, became the god of the dead, and the kings of Egypt became Osiris at death, thus continuing their rule in another realm. Isis also hid from Seth in the Delta marshes and there brought forth her son Horus, who tried to avenge Osiris by challenging his uncle Seth for earthly rule. Ultimately Horus won this contest and thus became the principle of kingship; every living king of Egypt was Horus. Seth became god of storm, of the desert highland, and of foreign lands.

If one seeks to establish the supreme god of the Egyptian pantheon, there is difficulty. Atum had a clear title to priority as the creator. Ra was dominant as is the sun in Egypt. Har-akhti, or Horus triumphant upon the horizon, was a ruling god. By the end of the Eleventh Dynasty a god of the new capital, Thebes, emerged as Amon and was soon united with Ra as Amon-Ra, the imperial god. A similar merger produced a composite of ruling forces in Atum Re-Har-akhti. This syncretism was not monotheistic: gods might blend for combination of powers, but they were also distinct in specific function, as a spectrum is one but the colors are many.

Ptah, an earth-god, was a creator-god in his independent myth and the patron of arts and crafts. His shrine was at Memphis, and, when that city became the capital, Ptah's power rivaled that of Ra at Heliopolis across the river. Other deities include Montu, a god of war at Thebes; Bastet, the cat-headed goddess of joy at Bubastis; and the ibis-headed Thoth, god of Hermopolis, the moon, and wisdom.

From the beginning of history the king of Egypt was called Horus, a god of rule on earth, assured of a happy eternal life. Although lesser persons had burial equipment and offerings, so that they certainly hoped for some sort of existence after death, this may have been as shadowy and restricted as it was in Asia. However, the king would be a king in the next world and there would need his court, his officials, and his servants. Thus they might live forever if they served him. Throughout Egyptian history the mortuary texts asserted that a proper burial was an "offering which the king gives," even though the individual himself might have taken the entire cost and responsibility. We have seen that in the Fifth Dynasty the decentralizing tendency moved the tombs of the nobles away from the immediate vicinity of the king's pyramid out into their home provinces. Despite this physical independence, the dogma continued to insist on their devoted service to the ruler.

Since human psychology offers so many facets, any generalization about people's attitudes will be only partially true. Such a generalization is that the ancient Egyptians had no fear of death. On the contrary, they confidently asserted that life would continue. The texts in the tombs are almost arrogantly confident; the scenes on the tomb walls are lively, gay, and even humorous. As the Nile came close to death each year and then revived triumphantly, and as the sun died each evening and then was reborn each morning, so must the life of man surmount death. From earliest times down to 1200 B.C.E., the prevailing psychology was that the gods had given the Egyptians a very full life and they would continue this richness after death. Only in the late period, after Egypt's superiority had been challenged by other powers and life had become more disciplined and restricted, did the mortuary religion strike a more somber note, as we shall see in section 5 B. below.

The Egyptian faith that an abundant life might be eternal and that the future existence would repeat the rich aspects of this life was in contrast to the dim and uncertain future life of the Babylonians or the Hebrews. One reason for this difference must lie in the geographic security and assurance of annual prosperity in Egypt. Further, a man's future held some hope: there was some encouragement for a man to better his status in the world, to rise to higher position. Of course, we base such a statement on the records left by kings and nobles, because peasants and slaves have left us no records. But even they worked in rich fields, which contrasted sharply with the marginal lands of nearby countries. Even they could hope for continued service in such continued abundance.

Since the king was a god, there was no need for impersonal, written, and codified law, because the word of the god-king was always available and always superseded any other word. In contrast to Mesopotamia and the Hebrews, ancient Egypt has left us no law code, nor is there reference to codified law before 700 B.C.E. To be sure, there must have been unwritten customary law in the various parts of Egypt, perhaps different in the north from the south. Magistrates administered justice throughout the land, making their decisions in the name of the king. But a god who is the embodiment of rule upon earth is also the personal embodiment of law. A code of law would only have competed with him.

We know something about service at the tombs, but we know little about temples and priestly service in the Old and Middle Kingdoms. The temples were modest, relative to the mighty structures which would appear in the New Kingdom. The priesthood was not yet a full-time service but was staffed from the high personnel of the state, in conformance with the principle that a sacred culture made no distinction between the secular and the ecclesiastical. The governor of a province was likely to be a high priest in the local temple. Many of the lay priests served the temples in rotating shifts.

Just as the great resources of the nation were employed to build the king's pyramid tomb, to provide him with rich burial equipment, and to furnish him with a mortuary service in perpetuity, a similar allocation of resources and time was available for the nobles. A man's eternal home was a *mastaba* of stone, built heavy to last forever. In large measure his survival depended upon perpetual service on his behalf. As an "offering which the king gives," fields were set apart as an endowment to provide income for goods and mortuary service. From these fields barley and flax might be made into bread, beer, and linen to be offered at the tomb, or they might be used to purchase other mortuary offerings and to pay the priests to make the offerings and to recite prayers at the tomb in perpetuity. These goods and services were in addition to the cost of building the tomb, furnishing it at burial, and carrying out an elaborate funeral ceremony. This setting aside of large economic resources and their accumulation over the centuries very seriously ate into the prosperity of Egypt. In flourishing times the bill could be paid. In any period of breakdown, this disproportionate economy would be swept aside to the advantage of the living.

Throughout Egyptian history the word of highest moral quality was *ma'at*, which may be translated as "right" or "order" or "conformity," as "truth" or "justice," or sometimes as "righteousness." The Egyptians had no word which we may translate as our moral "good." *Ma'at* was the quality which man had to render to the king and which the king was pleased to render to the gods. Sometimes *ma'at* was simply the orderly seasons of the sun, moon, and inundation; sometimes it was the arbitrary order imposed by the government; sometimes it was truth or veracity in speech. It was a virtue which had been given at creation. Since it was also good administration, one epithet of the vizier was the "High Priest of *Ma'at*." We shall see how the interpretation of *ma'at* altered in later ages.

C. The Tombs and Temples Speak

It is the desire of every historian to serve only on the wings of the stage, while his actors speak their own lines. This is not always possible, because many pages are missing from the actors' script, so that the historian has to serve as prologue, entr'acte, scene shifter, and epilogue. But the words — even the selected and translated words — of the ancients do give a basis for the reader to judge their minds and hearts.

The Old Kingdom tombs had certain standard claims and prayers, which were repeated often, with minor variations. Here is one example: —

> The king favored me. My father made a will for me, for I was . . . [one beloved] of his father, praised of his mother, whom all his brothers loved. I gave bread to the hungry, clothing to the naked, and I ferried across him who had no boat.
>
> O ye living who are upon earth, [who may pass by this tomb in] going downstream or upstream, and who may say: 'A thousand loaves of bread and a thousand jugs of beer for the owner of this tomb!' — I will intercede for their sakes in the cemetery. I am an effective and equipped spirit, a reciter-priest who knows his (magic) speech. But as for any man who may enter [this] tomb [unlawfully, I will seize his neck] like a bird, and he shall be judged for it by the great god.
>
> I was one who said what is good and repeated what was liked. I never said anything evil to a potentate against anybody, for I desired that it might go well with me in the presence of the great god. I [never judged two persons] in such a way that a son was deprived of his father's property.[9]

To illustrate the earlier flattering reliance upon the king and the later independence of nobles, we shall contrast an inscription from the early

Fifth Dynasty with one from the late Sixth Dynasty. For the first, the king is Sahu-Re.

> The Chief Physician Ni-ankh-Sekhmet said in the presence of His Majesty: 'May this thy spirit, beloved of Ra, command that a stone false-door be given to me for this tomb of mine of the cemetery.' His Majesty had two stone false-doors brought for him from (the) Troia (quarries). They were placed in the columned hall of the palace (named) 'The White Crown of Sahu-Re Appears.' The two high priests of Memphis and the artisans of the mortuary workshops were assigned to them, so that the work on them might be done in the presence of the king himself. The stone-cutting went on every day, and every day there was an inspection of what had been done on them in the court. His Majesty had texts(?) put on them and had them painted blue.
>
> His Majesty said to the Chief Physician Ni-ankh-Sekhmet: '(I swear), as these my nostrils are in health, as the gods love me, you will depart in honor to the cemetery at a good old age!' I praised the king greatly and thanked every god for the sake of Sahu-Re, for he knew the wish of the entire court. When anything issues from the mouth of His Majesty, it comes to pass immediately, and the god has given him innate knowledge of things, for he is more august than any (other) god. Do you love Ra? Then you shall thank every god for the sake of Sahu-Re, who did this for me. I was honored by him. I never did anything evil to anybody.[10]

Under Pepi II, the governor of a province in Middle Egypt was named Djau. In his tomb at his home in Deir el-Gebrawi he expresses no need for a close and servile attachment to the king.

> I buried my father, the Count Djau, more splendidly and more beautifully [than] any [peer] of his who was in this southland. . . . Now I have had myself buried in the same tomb with this Djau, in order that I may be in the same place with him — not at all because I lacked the wherewithal to make two tombs — but I did it so that I might see this Djau every day, so that I might be in the same place with him.[11]

Reference was made above on page 282 to the campaign which Uni led against the "sand-dwellers" of Asia. When his army returned to Egypt, they sang this song of triumph:

This army returned in safety,
After it had hacked up the land of the [sand]-dwellers!
This army returned in safety,
After it had crushed the land of the sand-dwellers!
This army returned in safety,
After it had thrown down their enclosures!
This army returned in safety,
After it had cut down their fig-trees and their vines!
This army returned in safety,
After it had thrown fire into all their dwellings!
This army returned in safety,
After it had killed troops among them by many ten-thousands!
This army returned in safety,
[After it had captured] from them many, many prisoners![12]

Military verse is not the highest form of literature.

From the end of the Fifth Dynasty there begins a remarkable series of inscriptions carved inside the royal tombs, the Pyramid Texts. This elaborate and varying body of inscriptions writes down those ritual charms which were first used at the royal burial and then in the continued priestly service of the pyramid. Included are texts for the feeding and equipping of the dead king, for protecting him against all imaginable perils, prayers for his well-being, magical charms to promote his powers in the other world, hymns to the gods, and fragments of myths. These were the grandfather texts for the Book of the Dead a thousand years later. The first extract guarantees that the king will rule in the next world by identifying him with the creator-god Atum and Anubis, a god of the dead.

> O King Unis, thou hast not at all departed dead, thou hast departed living! For thou sittest upon the throne of Osiris, with thy scepter in thy hand, that thou mightest give command to the living, and with the grip of thy wand in thy hand, that thou mightest give command to those hidden of place (the dead). Thy arm is Atum, thy shoulders are Atum, thy belly is Atum, thy back is Atum, thy rear is Atum, thy legs are Atum, and thy face is Anubis. The regions of Horus serve thee, and the regions of Seth serve thee.[13]

In the zeal to bring the king into paradise, men or gods might be threatened or cajoled. Here are two extracts.

> Everyone who may speak evilly against the name of King Unis when thou goest up — (the god) Geb has decreed that he shall be a

> pauper in his own town, so that he will flee and be exhausted.
> Every god who will not build the staircase of this King Meri-Re for him, when he goes up and when he ascends to heaven — he shall have no offering bread, he shall have no sunshade, he shall not wash himself in the basin, he shall not smell the joint of meat, he shall not taste the leg of meat. . . . It is not really this King Pepi who says this against you, O gods; it is magic which says this against you, O gods![14]

The most remarkable of the Pyramid Texts has been called the "Cannibal Hymn," because the dead king takes into himself the powers of other gods by eating them up. Consequently they are in terror when he appears.

> The heavens pour down rain, and the stars are beclouded,
> The Bows (in the sky) are shaken, and the bones of the earth-god tremble, . . .
> When they see King Unis appearing as a soul,
> As a god who lives on his fathers and feeds on his mothers. . . .
> It is King Unis who eats up men and lives on gods. . . .
> It is King Unis who eats their charms and devours their powers.
> The biggest of them are for his morning meal,
> Their middle-sized are for his afternoon meal,
> The littlest of them are for his evening meal,
> And their old men and women are (good only) for his kindling. . . .
> He has carried off the hearts of the gods, . . .
> Their magic is in his belly.
> The dignities of King Unis cannot be taken from him,
> For he has swallowed the knowledge of every god![15]

In substance the most remarkable text is that known as the Memphite Theology. Its purpose was to glorify the god of Memphis, Ptah. To do so, it makes the act of creation by him an act of intellect. The phenomena of the universe were conceived by the mind (Egyptian "heart") and brought into being by the spoken command (Egyptian "tongue"). When Ptah conceived the ideas and commanded them, the creator-god Atum, who was the "All," was brought into being.

> There came into being as the heart and there came into being as the tongue something in the form of Atum. . . . Thus it happened that the heart and tongue gained control over [every] (other) member of the body, by teaching that he (Ptah) is in every body and in every mouth of all gods, all men, [all] cattle, all creeping things,

> and (everything) that lives, by thinking and commanding everything that he wishes. . . .
>
> Thus all the gods were formed and his Ennead was completed. Indeed, all the divine order really came into being through what the heart thought and the tongue commanded. . . . (Thus justice was given to) him who does what is liked (and punishment to) him who does what is disliked. Thus life was given to him who has peace and death was given to him who has sin. Thus were made all work and all crafts, the action of the arms, the movement of the legs, and the activity of every member, in conformance with the command which the heart thought, which came forth from the tongue, and which gives value to everything.
>
> Thus it happened that it was said of Ptah: 'He who made all and brought the gods into being.'[16]

The Memphite Theology is remarkable, not only because creation arises out of the intellectual activity of a god, but also because that creation gave the "value" or "dignified worth" to everything created. Never again did Egyptian thinking reach this high plane.

The oldest example of the long current Egyptian wisdom literature is the instruction of the Vizier Ptah-hotep to his son and successor. The main principle laid down in this Old Kingdom setting of practical advance in the world was the value of effective speech. The king advised the vizier to "teach him first about speaking."

> Do not let your heart be puffed up because of your knowlege; do not be confident because you are a wise man. Take counsel with the ignorant as well as the wise. The (full) limits of skill cannot be reached, and there is no skilled man equipped to his (full) advantage. Good speech is rarer than the emerald, but it may be found with maidservants at the grindstone.

The practical advice included polite and useful etiquette when dining with an important host.

> If you are one of those sitting at the table of a man greater than yourself, take what he may give, when it is set before you. You should keep your gaze on what is before you and not stab him with many stares. . . . Let your face be cast down until he speaks to you, and you should speak only when he addresses you. Laugh after he laughs, and it will be very pleasing to his heart, so that what (ever) you may do will be pleasing to his heart.

The official should be fair when people come to him, but perhaps he would be able to content them merely by listening.

> If you are one to whom petition is made, be calm as you listen to the speech of the petitioner. Do not rebuff him before he has swept out his body or before he has said what he came for. A petitioner may like attention to his words more than the carrying out of what he came for. . . . It is not (necessary) that everything about which he has petitioned should come to pass, but a good hearing is soothing to the heart.

Although generous and faithful dealing with one's wife was good in itself, it may be that the chief reason was that she would produce children.

> If you are a man of standing, you should set up a household and love your wife at home as is fitting. Fill her belly; clothe her back; ointment is the prescription for her body. Make her heart glad as long as you live, for she is a profitable field for her lord.[17]

That was a bustling, extroverted, pragmatic world. It had never known failure, and it could not conceive of failure. Success, high standing, and wealth were proper goals. The challenge was still to come.

D. Material Values Fail (2250–2000)

Tradition of Greek times said that the Seventh Dynasty consisted of seventy kings, who reigned for seventy days. This absurdity is only an exaggeration of the chaotic situation of the First Intermediate Period. The collapse of the proud state seemed sudden and absolute. If we followed the king-lists from Greek times blindly, we should have to fit about 150 kings into a similar number of years. The first observation to make is that the Seventh to Eleventh Dynasties were not successive. Seven and Eight, continuing the old rule at Memphis, may have overlapped with Nine, beginning a new rule at Herakleopolis near the Faiyum; and the Tenth at Herakleopolis certainly overlapped with the Eleventh, beginning a new rule at Thebes. In other words, the state was split by competition. In addition, many provincial nobles continued to act independently and even to arrogate to themselves prerequisites of kingship.

Texts about this period bewailed the governmental chaos, the overturn of social classes, the neglect and robbery of the tombs, the cessation of foreign trade, and the infiltration of Asiatic Bedouin into the Delta. The human desire to find a scapegoat prompted the Egyptians to place the blame for the time of troubles upon these Asiatics. In reality it was the weakness of the state which left the borders unguarded, until a slow but steady influx of Bedouin amounted to a major problem.

Politically the First Intermediate Period witnessed extreme weakness, the rapid dying away of the ruling family at Memphis, the limited power of the new family at Herakleopolis, and finally the emergence of a new family at Thebes far to the south. Generally speaking, one may speak of feudalism in the Period and afterward into the Middle Kingdom, provided that one does not define that term narrowly to what was later known in Europe. For example, the nobles of Siut in Middle Egypt paid allegiance to Herakleopolis and supported her in the war against Thebes; yet here and later such provincial nobles showed a decidedly independent spirit.

The literary texts which deal with this period give us both the clearest and the most agitated idea of the chaos of the time.[18] "The land is helter-skelter, and nobody knows what results will come about, which is hidden from speech, sight, or hearing.... I show you the land topsy-turvy. What had never before happened has happened. Men will take up weapons of warfare, so that the land lives in confusion. . . . I show you the son as a foe, the brother as an enemy, and a man killing his own father."

The neat order which had defined the desert and the sown land, the provinces, and the "people" themselves was destroyed: "Why really, the desert is spread throughout the land! The provinces are destroyed. Barbarians from outside have come to Egypt. . . . There are really no people anywhere."

On the one hand, it is complained that there is no government, and, on the other, that there is nothing left but bureaucracy. "Why really, the government clerks have been removed! The grain sustenance of Egypt is a mere come-and-get-it. Why really, the laws of the enclosure are put out-of-doors! Men actually walk on them in the highways, and the poor tear them up in the streets." Yet "the land is diminished, but its administrators are many; bare, but its taxes are great; short on grain, but the (tax) measure is large, and it is measured to overflowing!"

The king-god who should be ruling the land is no longer honored. "See, he who was buried as a falcon-god now lies on a mere bier. What the pyramid hid has become empty. See now, it has come to the point where the land is plundered of the kingship by a few irresponsible men. See now, it has come to the point where men rebel against the serpent on the brow of the king . . . which should make the Two Lands peaceful."

The distrust which lay upon the land affected these weak kings, and one of them had to advise his son and successor not to kill those nobles with whom he had once recited in school. "Do not kill: it is of no advantage to you. You should punish with beatings and arrests, . . . except for the rebel, when his plans are discovered, for the god knows the treacherous of heart, and the god condemns his sins in blood. . . . Do not kill a man when you know his good qualities, one with whom you once chanted the writings."

The stable society which had been based on position and power was now overturned. "Why really, the land spins around as a potter's wheel does! The robber is now the possessor of riches." "Why really, poor men have become the owners of treasures! He who once could not make himself a pair of sandals is now the possessor of riches." "Why really, all maid-servants make free with their tongues! When their mistresses speak, it is burdensome to the servants." "Doorkeepers say: 'Let us go and plunder.'. . . The laundryman refuses to carry his load. . . . Foreigners have become people everywhere!"

That once prized quality of good speech might now be a danger. "Men will [treat] fellow-citizens as hateful, in order to silence the mouth that speaks. If a statement is answered, out goes an arm with a stick, and men say: 'Kill him!' "

In place of the former trade with other countries there is now only a miserable internal commerce. "No one really sails north to Byblos today. What shall we do for cedar for our mummies? . . . They do not come, and gold is lacking. . . . How important it now seems when the oasis-people come carrying their provisions for feasts: reed-mats, . . . plants, . . . and birds!"

Although these texts again and again lament the penetration of Asiatics into the Delta, one king expressed his lofty scorn for the Bedouin warriors. "Now, the miserable Asiatic — it goes badly with the place where he is, afflicted with water, difficult with many trees, its roads painful because of the mountains. He does not live in a single place, for his legs are made to wander. He has been fighting since the time of Horus, but he does not conquer, nor can he be conquered. . . . Do not trouble yourself about him: he is only an Asiatic. . . . He may rob a single person, but he does not lead against a town of many citizens."

It is important to linger over these expressions of confusion and distress, because they show the political and social turmoil, as well as the bewilderment over a world turned upside-down. In the next section we shall see what answers the Egyptians gave to their first failure.

A political newcomer rescued Egypt from her distress. As it had been in the union for the First Dynasty, as it would be in the deliverance by the Eighteenth Dynasty, the conqueror came from the south. More than four hundred miles south of Memphis lay the hitherto unimportant town of Thebes, worshipping a local war-god Montu. Thebes succeeded in uniting

Upper Egypt by conquest and then challenged Herakleopolis. We do not know how many generations were committed to this war, but with apparent abruptness the ruler of Thebes, Mentu-hotep I of the Eleventh Dynasty, won and succeeded in reuniting the land about 2050 B.C.E. This king's effective power may also be seen in the tomb he built at Thebes. In the majestic desert bay called Deir el-Bahri, his architects constructed a terraced and colonnaded temple surmounted by a small pyramid. It was an artistic innovation, which was later imitated and surpassed by the great queen Hat-shepsut.

About 2000 B.C.E. — we use the specific date of 1991 — a new family came to power in Thebes. The Intefs and Mentu-hoteps of the Eleventh Dynasty gave way to the Twelfth Dynasty Amen-em-hets and Sen-Userts. The name Mentu-hotep had shown devotion to the god Montu; the name Amen-em-het showed devotion to a new god, Amon. The Middle Kingdom is another story, reserved for section 3 A.

E. What Values are Lasting?

From the standpoints of literature and of moral values the First Intermediate Period was a remarkable Age. The Old Kingdom had built confidently in terms of material success. From the start the Old Kingdom had achieved such magnificent results that it entertained no doubts about the good life. A man was active and shrewd; thereby he rose to high position and power; thereby he achieved material wealth. With his wealth he built a massive tomb and endowed it with goods and services, so that he might live forever. The anarchy of the First Intermediate Period swept away these insurances for eternal life; it unseated the families of position and wealth. It thereby upset the confidence that the Old Kingdom way was the only way. In the search for eternity, what values might last, after all?

The literary texts applying to the Period gave various answers. One man looked at the ruins of life and pondered suicide. In a series of measured stanzas he contrasted the loneliness of this world with the privileges of the next world. Death and only a hope of eternity were better than today's despair.

To whom can I speak today?
  One's fellows are evil;
  The friends of today do not love.
To whom can I speak today?
  Hearts are rapacious;
  Every man seizes his neighbor's goods. . . .
To whom can I speak today?

There are not righteous;
The land is left to those who wrong . . . .
To whom can I speak today?
The sin which treads the earth,
It has no end.
Death is in my sight today
Like the recovery of a sick man,
Like going out again after a confinement.
Death is in my sight today
Like the odor of myrrh,
Like sitting under an awning on a breezy day . . . .
Death is in my sight today
Like the longing of a man to see his house again,
After he has spent many years in captivity.
Why surley, he who is over yonder
Will be a living god.
Punishing the sin of him who commits it.
Why surely, he who is over yonder,
Will stand in the boat of the sun,
Sending its choicest offerings to the temples.
Why surely, he who is over yonder
Will be a man of wisdom,
Not hindered from appealing to Ra when he speaks.[19]

Another reaction to the time of troubles was the advice to forget the old values and make the most of today. The old tombs were now neglected, even those of the wisest of men; we can know nothing about paradise; then why not enjoy one's self now?

Generations pass away, and others remain
Since the time of the ancestors.
The gods who lived formerly rest in their pyramids,
The blessed dead also, buried in their pyramids,
And they who built houses — their places are nonexistent.
See what has become of them!
I have heard the words of Ii-em-hotep and Hor-dedef,
With whose counsels men speak so much —
But what are their places now?
Their walls are broken apart,
And their places are as though they had never been!
There is no one who comes back from over yonder,

> That he may tell how they are and what they need,
> That he may still our hearts,
> Until we too travel to the place where they have gone.
> So — let your desire have play . . . as long as you live! . . .
> Make holiday, and do not grow tired of it!
> See, no man is allowed to take his property with him.
> See, no one who departs comes back again![20]

There were more sober-minded answers to the problem. One prophet recited the woes of the time, and then pointed his finger at the king and declared that the ruler who should have been the good shepherd of his people had really fostered the confusion by neglecting his duties. "Authority, discernment, and justice are with you, but it is confusion which you would set throughout the land, together with the noise of contention. See, one man thrusts against another when men conform to what you have commanded. If three men go along a road, they are found to be two men: it is the greater number that kills the lesser — does then the herdsman love death"?[21] This was more than *lèse-majesté;* in the Egyptian setting it was sacrilege. Exceptional times produced an exceptional attitude.

The desire for a good ruler produced messianic prophecy, as when the "wise man of the east," Neferti, stood before a king and foretold the troubles of the First Intermediate Period and then the deliverance by the first king of the Twelfth Dynasty, Ameni (Amen-em-het I). "Then it is that a king will come, belonging to the south, Ameni, the triumphant, his name. . . . Rejoice, ye people of his time! . . . There will be built the Wall of the Ruler, and the Asiatics will not be permitted to come down into Egypt that they may beg for water in the customary manner, in order to let their beasts drink. And justice will come into its place, while wrongdoing is driven out."[22] The fact that we may recognize this story as prophecy after the fact of the Twelfth Dynasty's success does not remove it from the category of messianic literature.

The most striking reaction to the overthrow of material values was the search for moral values. If riches and power were not lasting, perhaps moral character might endure. A king advised his son not to rely upon a mighty tomb with abundant offerings. Men's gratitude was a better monument. "Do not be evil; patience is good. Make your memorial last through the love of you. . . . As a reward, the god will be thanked, (and there will be) praises because of your goodness and prayers for your health." As an offering to the gods, "more acceptable is the character of a man upright of heart than the ox of the evildoer." The gods will judge the dead on the basis of good deeds. "You know that the council which judges the deficient are not lenient on the day of judging the miserable.... Do not trust in length of years, for they regard a lifetime as but an hour. A man remains over after death, and his deeds are placed beside him in heaps. Indeed, existence yonder is for eternity, . . . and he who reaches it without wrongdoing will exist yonder like a god, stepping out freely like the lords of eternity."[23]

In a world where position and power were no longer so important, good character was defined as social conscience. The king should be the sleepless shepherd of his people. Even a peasant had an innate right to justice, and a famous story tells about a farmer from an oasis who was cheated of his property by an official. The peasant stood before the Chief Steward of the palace and demanded restitution of his goods, because justice (*ma'at*) is the impartial gift of the gods. "Does the hand-scales go wrong? Does the stand-balance lean to the side? Is even the god Thoth indulgent? — Then you also may work mischief. ... Now justice lasts to eternity; it goes down into the cemetery with him who does it. When he is buried and interred, his name is not wiped out upon earth, but he is remembered for goodness. That is a principle of the word of god."[24] It is good to report that the peasant finally did receive justice.

This leveling down of kings and nobles, this raising up of the common man even reached its climax in a statement that all men were created equal in opportunity. A text has the creator-god saying: "I have made the four winds that every man might breathe thereof like his neighbor in his time. . . . I have made the great inundation that the poor man might have rights in it like the great man. . . . I have made every man like his fellow."[25]

The leveling out process particularly affected the next world. Under the Old Kingdom, the king alone was a god while living and after death; in life he was Horus, in death he was Osiris. One who was not a king became an "effective spirit" in death, but not a god. Now in the First Intermediate Period the nobles seized upon the royal prerogatives. They also became Osiris in death, so that by definition as divine they might live forever. The Pyramid Texts of the Old Kingdom, restricted to kings and then opened also to queens, were now taken over for the benefit of nobles also. As they were written on the wooden coffins of the period, we call them Coffin Texts. Very definitely they state the same after-death deification of the nobles as had applied to royalty in the earlier period. Even a provincial noble might enjoy the magic of the "Cannibal Hymn." Even though they did not reach down for the benefit of the masses, their extension downward from the god-king to the amorphous group of the nobility was a step in the direction of democratization, one of the first in the world.

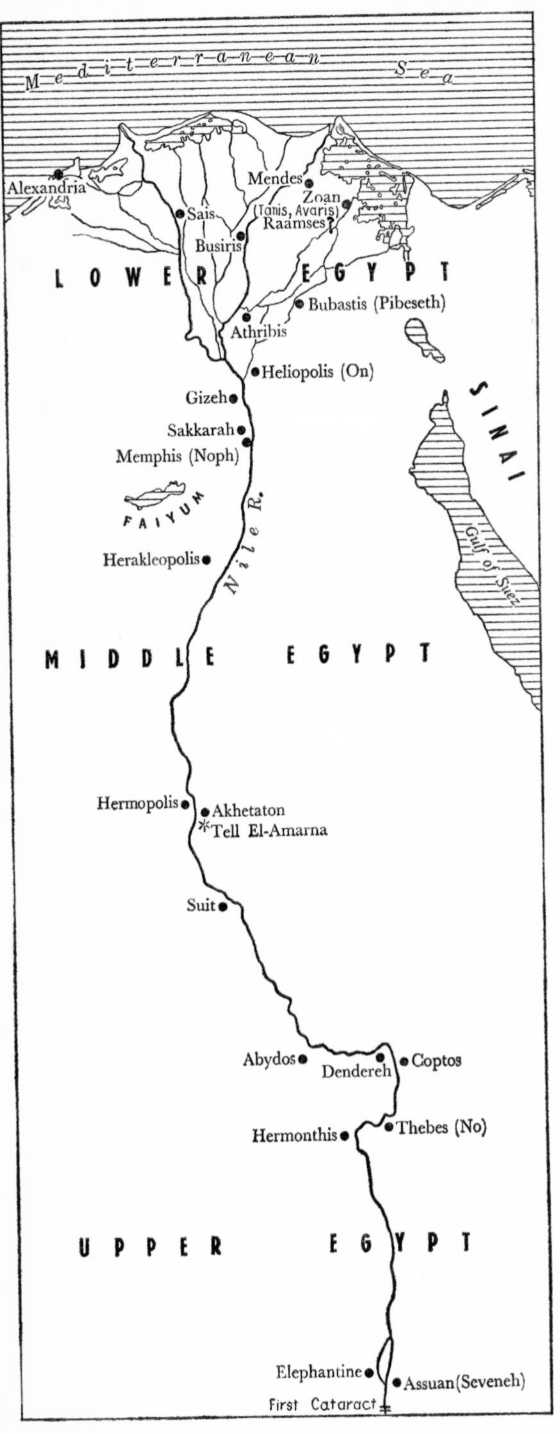

Ancient Egypt

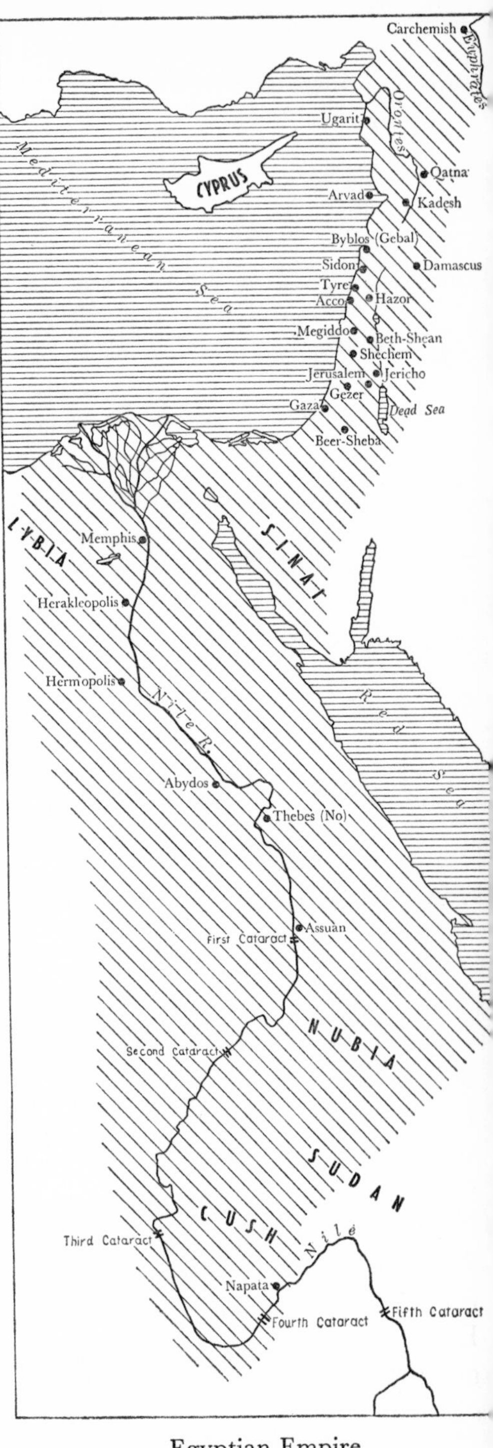

Egyptian Empire

3. THE SEARCH FOR NEW MASTERY

A. Restoration and Crisis Again (2000–1500)

LATER AGES looked back at the Twelfth Dynasty as a classical era of Egyptian history. The literary works of the time were copied for eight hundred years. In Greek days a legendary hero Sesostris borrowed his name and a magnification of his deeds from the kings named Sen-Usert of this Dynasty. Certainly they were remarkable rulers, who, operating within the restrictions of a semi-feudal state, accomplished great things for Egypt. That they were conscious of restoring the land to some of its past glory is indicated by the fact that the first king, Amen-em-het I (1991–1961), took as a ruling name "Renaissance."

The problem which the dynasty had to face was that the people had witnessed the degrading of kingship and had tasted the privileges of independence. The feudal nobles wanted to hang on to their separate powers. Thus about 1928 B.C.E. the governor of the Oryx Nome stated that in the 43rd year of King Sen-Usert I, corresponding to his own local 25th year, he committed 400 of his own troops to accompany the royal army on an expedition into Nubia.[1] Both the independent dating and the independent army are significant.

The Twelfth Dynasty gave to Egypt strong and conscientious government. The statues of these kings show faces lined with care, in contrast to the serenity of the Old Kingdom. It was worth while for the feudal lords to associate with the central government. New agricultural land was won by large-scale irrigation works, particularly in the Faiyum, and by better use of the Nile inundation through observation posts south of the Second Cataract to estimate the expected volume of the flood. The gold lands of Nubia became a major enterprise of the state, to be held by imperial power. A chain of frontier fortresses was maintained in Nubia, and a fortified trading post was established south of the Third Cataract. There the Egyptian high commissioner was buried in a tumulus, surrounded by a great number of attendants and servants, who were interred with him in a sacrifice reminiscent of those mass burials in Egypt under the First Dynasty.

In contrast to Africa, there was no empire in Asia, no resident garrisons or commissioners. An exception lies in the copper and turquoise mines of Sinai, which were reopened with energy and with the cooperation of the local sheikhs. Palestine and Syria were cultivated with trade, royal gifts to local rulers, and cultural leadership from Egypt. That few Egyptians resided in Asia is shown by the fact that the hieroglyphic inscriptions found there commemorate kings rather than commoners. That proportion would change under the New Kingdom, which did have an Asiatic empire. To keep caravan routes open at least one military raid was made by Sen-Usert III, as far as Shechem in Palestine.[2] Otherwise there was no attempt at military control. Byblos and Ugarit on the Phoenician coast were points of active commercial relations, and royal gifts from Egypt to the princes of Phoenicia and Syria maintained neighborly cordiality.

This dynasty, in its alertness to cultivate the loyalty of the Egyptians themselves, even resorted to a literature of propaganda and commissioned writers to compose stories, wisdom texts, and prayers to the glory of the new ruling family. These texts were given such wide distribution that some of them became classics of Egyptian literature for several centuries.[3]

Nevertheless, it was not easy sailing, and there was a conspiracy within the palace during the reign of Amen-em-het I. He has left us a posthumous account of the attack upon him by his own bodyguard at night. Messages to and from the dead were not uncommon in Egypt.

> It was after supper, when evening had come. I had taken an hour of rest, lying upon my bed, for I had become weary. . . . Then the weapons which should have taken care of me were brandished, and I was like one crumbled, crumbled to dust. . . . I awoke at the fighting, being by myself, and I found that it was a hand-to-hand conflict of the guard. If I had made haste with weapons in my hand, I should have made the cowards retreat helter-skelter. But there is no one valiant at night, and there is no fighting alone.[4]

We know about these troubles also from the story of a certain Si-nuhe, who was an official of the royal harem, that part of the palace where doting mothers were always scheming on behalf of their sons. While Si-nuhe was on a military campaign in Libya, secret word of Amen-em-het's assassination came, and the crown prince hurried back to the capital. Si-nuhe accidentally overheard the message. "My heart was distraught, my arms flung out, and trembling fell upon all my limbs. . . . I set out southward, but I did not plan to reach this capital city, for I knew that there would be civil disorder, and I did not expect to live after him." No explicit reason is given for his terror, but obviously he feared implication in the conspiracy. Ultimately the self-exile reached Syria and had a successful career there as a local potentate. When old age came, he realized that no proper Egyptian should die and be buried outside of Egypt, so he sued for pardon, piously exclaiming that there had been no reason for his flight. The king was graciously pleased to welcome him back to Egypt, and there is a humorous scene in which the desert-clad Si-nuhe appears at court. With a straight face the king said to the queen: "Here is Si-nuhe, come as a Bedu, in the garb of the Asiatics." The queen kept up the solemn act. "She gave a very great shriek, and the royal children all clamored together, and they said: 'It isn't really he, O Sovereign, my lord!' " In a happy ending, the political exile was "under the favor of the king's presence until the day of (final) mooring had come."[5]

The Story of Si-nuhe was one of four Middle Kingdom texts which the Egyptians copied over and over again for centuries; it is known to us on five papyri and about twenty ostraca, those scraps of pottery or stone upon which schoolboys practiced. The other three classics were the wisdom text of Amen-em-het I, in which he told about his assassination; a hymn to the Nile inundation; and a wisdom text which glorified the profession of the government clerk and derided other careers.[6] Other writings, which might appeal to us moderns as having more literary quality, were not so popular, so that we assume that these four were highly acceptable to the government and thus went into the curriculum of the schools.

There was a change in the Middle Kingdom attitude toward the Asiatics at the Sinai mines. Whereas the Old Kingdom had sent soldiers to exploit the mines and had carved pictures showing the king slaughtering the Bedouin, the Middle Kingdom cultivated the Asiatic sheikhs and tried to bring them into the outer orbit of Egyptian culture. These chieftains were proud to be pictured on monuments at the mines, with their names and titles written in hieroglyphic. This association probably was a factor in the ultimate Semitic adoption of Egyptian pictures to write a Semitic alphabet.

It was a different matter at the southern frontier, where the gold mines were being exploited. There garrisoned fortresses held back the Nubians — who were not at this time Negroes. Sen-Usert III set up boundary stones at the Second Cataract, in order to "prevent any Nubian from crossing it, traveling north by land or with a ship, or any herds of the Nubians, except for a Nubian who shall come to do trading in Iqen or on a commission." On one of these stelae he tried to encourage his frontier soldiers by a scornful depiction of the Nubian. "The Nubian hears only to fall down at a word: it is answering him that makes him retreat. When one is aggressive against him, he turns his back; but when one shrinks back, he begins to be aggressive. They are not a people of worth; they are poor and broken of spirit. My Majesty has seen them; it is not a lie."[7]

We can only guess at the forces which led to the disintegration of the Middle Kingdom. Although the kings were successful in promoting the prosperity of the land, there must have been a structural weakness in a state which was still highly decentralized. Under ineffective kings, the fealty of the nobles would slacken. There were movements of new peoples in Asia and Africa, which cut down the profitable foreign trade. At the end of the Twelfth Dynasty there were brief and weak reigns, including one queen. At the beginning of the Thirteenth, a new struggle for power began, the Second Intermediate Period.

From the 19th century comes a group of strange documents, the "execration texts," used for the ceremonial cursing and thwarting of the king's enemies. The name or title of such a foe was written in a set formula upon a pottery bowl or upon the clay figurine of a bound captive. This inscribed object was then ceremonially smashed — so perishes every adversary of the king! Several Egyptians were so cursed, and from their names they seem to have been rebellious members of the royal family. Magic of this kind averted evil thoughts, speeches, plots, and dreams. Actual and potential enemies in Nubia and Libya were so cursed. The most interesting set of names comes from Asia, cursing the rulers of Ashkelon, Shechem, Lachish, Beth-shemesh, Acco, Tyre, and so on. As applied to Jerusalem, the formula ran: "The Ruler of Jerusalem, Yaqar-'Ammu, and all the retainers who are with him; the Ruler of Jerusalem, Sez-'anu, and all the retainers who are with him — who may rebel, who may plot, who may fight, who may talk of fighting, or who may talk of rebelling — in this entire land!" Clearly the king of Egypt was nervous: there were enemies in his own family, and he feared hostility from abroad. If he could not win their good will, he could confound them by magic. The towns of Palestine seem to have been ruled by Semitic princes, who felt no loyalty to the throne of Egypt.[8]

The Second Intermediate Period (1778–1570), like the First, started with the breaking of the state into parts, with a weakened rule from Thebes and a competing dynasty in the Delta. A feeble state could not maintain its frontiers, so that Asiatics penetrated the Delta before 1700 B.C.E. This time it was no trickle of Bedouin; the invaders entered with military force. Tradition calls them the Hyksos or, by an incorrect etymology, the "Shepherd Kings." The word "Hyksos" in Egyptian meant simply "rulers of foreign countries," which does not enlighten us on their origin. The center of their power was a great encampment at Avaris in the northeast

Delta, either at the place later called Tanis or Zoan or else a short distance to the south. Similar fortification enclosures of beaten earth have been seen in Palestine and Syria.

The "Stela of the Year Four Hundred," found at Tanis, has been used for the argument that the Hyksos started their rule of Egypt shortly before 1700 B.C.E. This was erected at the very end of the Eighteenth Dynasty, to commemorate four hundred years of rule by the god Seth. For the Egyptians he was the god of foreign countries, and he was here depicted in the costume of a Baal or a Hadad of the Asiatics. The stela ignores the hated Hyksos and claims that 400 years before 1320 B.C.E. an Egyptian god of Asiatic lands began to rule at or near Tanis.[9]

The Hyksos introduced into Egypt, Palestine, and Syria certain new factors — the horse and chariot, the composite bow, a heavier sword, body armor, and their rectangular fortresses of beaten earth. We do not know the ultimate source of these new elements. However, insofar as the Egyptians were concerned, the Hyksos were Asiatics, and they applied to them the same terms (*'Aamu* and *Retenu*) as they had applied to their Asiatic neighbors. Hyksos personal names which can be identified often prove to be Semitic like Jacob-har and Samuqen. Perhaps the factors of power came from distant Asia, but it was the people of Syria-Palestine who introduced them into Egypt and thereby conquered and ruled.

Although Egyptian inscriptions picture the Hyksos as arrogant and impious, this was no barbarian horde. They seem to have been active merchants, introducing a new series of weights into Egypt. A recently discovered stela tells of "hundreds" of Hyksos ships with rich cargo at a port in Egypt. Objects bearing the names of Hyksos kings have been found all over the Near East. They adjusted to Egyptian ways, adopted Egyptian names as kings, and commissioned good Egyptian works of art.

The question whether the Hyksos age includes the time of Joseph and the beginning of the Israelite sojourn in Egypt has been debated since the time of Josephus. The problem is too complicated to be argued here, and certainly the Hyksos as a whole cannot be equated with the Children of Israel. Those who argue for a date about 1225 B.C.E. for the Exodus point to the 430 years of sojourn in Exodus 12:40–41 and reach a date of about 1655 for the entry of the Israelites. A Semitic king might more readily have appointed Joseph as his chief minister. On the other hand, the Egyptian names in the Joseph story are certainly from much later times. On a basis of truth the story may have received a haggadic coloring. Egyptian texts give us nothing on Joseph, the Sojourn, Moses, or the Exodus.

The Hyksos kings at Avaris tolerated the existence of weakened rulers at

Thebes, held the Delta firmly, and exacted tribute from the rest of Egypt. In the course of time the Egyptians acquired the new weapons of warfare. About 1580 a Theban king named Ka-mose found the situation intolerable. His counselors urged him not to provoke a war: he stood in peaceful relation with the Asiatics to the north and the Nubians to the south; the Egyptians were permitted to pasture their cattle in the Delta; war might endanger the advantages they still held. Ka-mose brushed aside the counsel of his nobles and started a war of liberation.[10]

Ka-mose succeeded in pushing the Hyksos back into the northeast Delta, but it was reserved for the following king, Ah-mose I, to drive them out of Egypt, reunite the land, and thus start the Eighteenth Dynasty (1570–1315) and the New Kingdom. After three campaigns, Ah-mose captured Avaris. The war then shifted to Palestine, where the town of Sharuhen was besieged for three years before it fell. Clearly the Hyksos had fallen back upon their homeland in Asia. For a few generations the new dynasty was too busy with the political restoration of Egypt to undertake more than occasional raids into Palestine-Syria.

B. Imperial Triumph (1500–1375)

In art, architecture, language, and literature, the Egypt which emerged from the Hyksos domination was very like that of the Middle Kingdom. Yet the humiliation of having been ruled by foreigners had made a real difference in the national spirit. Ended was the lofty complacency about Egypt's superiority to her neighbors. In the past a deep love of and pride in their home had turned the interests of Egyptians inward. Now the shock of being for once inferior changed them, and they looked outward. As Sinai was held for copper, as Nubia was held for gold, so now must Asia be held for security. Imperialistic patriotism swept the land. In the Egyptian texts it was no longer "the army of his majesty," but "our army," that took the field to seek revenge.

To be sure, the new Asiatic empire was not set up immediately, nor did it happen without some opposition. The conquest was between those who believed that the old ways of commerce and cultural dominance were adequate and the new imperialists. The protagonists in the struggle were Queen Hat-shepsut and young King Thut-mose III. She and her non-military policy had the first success. The youthful Thut-mose, although he had been crowned as king, was thrust into inactivity and obscurity. Hat-shepsut seized power and proclaimed herself, not queen, but king, so that she might rule as a god. For eighteen years (1486–1468) she ruled with vigor. Egyptian energies were devoted to reconstruction, building enterprises, and foreign trade. Her beautiful terraced temple at Deir el-Bahri surpassed, in its fidelity to its setting, the Eleventh Dynasty temple which had been its inspiration. Within the temple she devoted major space to displaying her building activity and a commercial enterprise, the expedition down the Red Sea to the land of Punt for incense, myrrh, ivory, ebony, gold, apes, and leopard skins. For a thousand years Egypt had enjoyed economic dominance on the Red Sea, and the Queen was interested in reasserting that advantage. Punt probably lay both on the Somali coast in Africa and in Arabia Felix in Asia to the south of the Red Sea. If it is not the Biblical Ophir, it is a good counterpart thereof.

The masterful queen suddenly fell from power and disappeared from history. Her statues were smashed to bits, and her name was hacked out of the monuments. Within a few months, her young relative Thut–mose III (1490–1436) set out to establish an empire in Asia. The warlike party had won out. Thut–mose III was a man of military and administrative ability. He devoted seventeen campaigns to subduing Asia, founded an empire running through Palestine, Phoenicia, and central Syria, and affecting north Syria, and he introduced the military and civil controls to hold the area. His fame dominated Syria for a century. In Egypt his throne name, Men-kheper-Re, gave magical authority to scarabs for a thousand years.

Thut–mose described his initial campaign in May, 1468 B.C.E., as the punishment of a "rebellion," which was a self-righteous falsehood.[11] He also described himself as the "smiter of the rulers of foreign countries (*hikau-khasu* or potentially Hyksos) who had attacked him." The memory of the disgrace of the domination by the Hyksos was a powerful motive in the thrusting of Egypt's frontier northward from Sinai to north Syria.

This "rebellion" consisted of a coalition of 330 princes of Palestine and Syria, "each one having his own army." Since little city-states were involved, the entire confederacy was not very large in manpower. The presiding leader was the prince of Kadesh on the Orontes. From the south had come such towns as Gezer, Jaffa, Aijalon, and Beeroth; from the Plain of Sharon came Aphek and Soco; from northwest Palestine came Acco and Achshaph; from the Valley of Jezreel came Megiddo, Dothan, and Beth-shean; from Transjordan came Ashtaroth and Edrei; Merom and Hazor were from Galilee; and Syria sent Damascus, Aleppo, and Carchemish. Major Phoenician cities like Tyre and Byblos did not join the coalition, probably wishing to maintain their trade with Egypt.

The coalition gathered at Megiddo in the Plain of Jezreel, to gain the potential advantage of the shelter of the Carmel Range against the advancing Egyptian army. Thut-mose moved with energy and daring. The loose Asiatic army probably trusted too much to the protection of the mountain range, because the pharaoh threw his forces successfully through the Megiddo Pass. The battle on the following day was a quick Egyptian victory. While the Egyptian soldiers were busy looting the rich camp of the enemy, the demoralized Asiatics fled for safety within the walls of the city. Megiddo was then encircled with a moat and wooden wall and subjected to a seven months' siege. The booty was great: — more than two thousand horses, two thousand cattle, and twenty thousand sheep; abundant gold, silver, metalwork, and inlaid furniture. Since the victory had come just at the time of the Palestine harvest, the Egyptian armed reaped 450,000 bushels of wheat, "in addition to what was cut as forage by His Majesty's army."

In December what was left of the starving enemy inside Megiddo surrendered. Thut-mose was magnanimous. He stripped them of their possessions, he took away their horses and chariots, but he let them return to their homes after taking an oath of fealty to his person. As a mark of vassaldom they went home on donkeyback. Never again did a large Syrian-Palestinian group unite to oppose Egypt.

In the following nineteen years Thut-mose III conducted further campaigns in Asia. Some involved fighting against Kadesh on the Orontes or the state of Mitanni in upper Mesopotamia. Others were mere parades of power, to keep the awe of the pharaoh alive in his new empire. On the eighth campaign Thut-mose enjoyed the diversion of an elephant hunt in the marshes of Syria, and the herd was reported as numbering 120.

The newly won territory was organized with resident garrisons, high commissioners, and a courier service. Phoenician ports were seized and equipped for the conqueror's use. The cedar groves of Lebanon were made an Egyptian preserve. The pharaoh generously maintained local princes upon their thrones, but wisely took their sons and brothers to Egypt as hostages. The princelings were brought up at the Egyptian court, until their fathers died and they might succeed to the throne. This combination of clemency and force welded an empire which was remarkably loyal to Egypt for a century.

Thut-mose's son, Amen-hotep II (1439–1406), undertook two vigorous Asiatic campaigns to show that there would be no lapse of control.[12] On the first of these in the Plain of Sharon he captured a knightly courier "of the Prince of Naharin, carrying a letter of clay at his throat." That international correspondence in cuneiform on clay tablets which is so well-known from the Tell el-Amarna Letters was already a diplomatic factor in the area. On the second campaign Amen-hotep fought in the general vicinity of Sharon again and brought back to Egypt nearly 90,000 prisoners. Among them were 3,600 *'Apiru*, which approximates the Egyptian writing for the term *Habiru* or *Hapiru* in cuneiform. These were listed separately from 15,000 desert Bedouin and from more than 50,000 settled inhabitants of Palestine-Syria, either on the basis of location or way of life. Thus this term enters the Egyptian records, with the controversial problem of its relation to the "Hebrews" — merely as a descriptive term or as a later delimitation for one people.[13]

The new empire made profound differences in Egyptian culture. Many Egyptians now lived abroad in towns of Palestine and Syria, while vast numbers of Asiatics, ranging from hostage princes to captive slave laborers, lived in Egypt. The works of art and luxury products of Asia appealed to the Egyptians, and trade was active. It was no longer possible to believe that the gods cared only for Egypt, when that land so ardently wanted to hold other countries. Shrines for the gods of the Nile Valley were set up in Asia, and the Egyptians living abroad erected inscriptions to such Semitic deities as Baal and Anath. Within Egypt there were priests of Baal and Ashtoreth. Literature was invaded by foreign words, such as *migdol* for fortress and *markabah* for chariot. Parents would soon begin to give their children names from Asia, such as Ben-Anath, "Son of Anath," or Pa-Khura "the Horite."

As wealth flowed into Egypt, ostentation became the mark of cosmopolitan sophistication. Art was profoundly affected: it became livelier, more naturalistic, and softer in line; it sacrificed some of the emphasis on eternal life by becoming interested in the immediate activities of the day. The lively influences of Crete upon art were stronger than the more formal patterns of Asia. Temple architecture showed the new imperial pride and the new wealth by expanding toward the colossal. When Egypt's troubles with the state of Mitanni were settled, the pharaoh was graciously pleased to take a Mitannian princess as wife. Thus the august Egyptian palace was invaded at the top level; at the lower level it had already been peopled with slaves in the kitchen and weaving rooms. To a marked degree the empire egyptianized Asia, and to a marked degree Egypt was asiaticized.

Three generations of such triumph brought the imperial magnificence of Amen-hotep III (1398–1361), who regarded Egypt's efforts as crowned with unassailable success. It looked as though Syria and Palestine gratefully accepted the Egyptian peace; their vassal status had the compensation of orderly prosperity. Phoenicia and Crete enjoyed valuable commerce with the land on the Nile. Mitanni, which was fading as a power, was in peaceful alliance with Egypt. The Hittites, Babylonians, and Assyrians were not yet ready to challenge Egypt in Syria; their kings exchanged letters and royal gifts with the pharaoh. Amen-hotep and the commoner Tiy, whom he had made his chief queen, contented themselves with careless enjoyment of the fruits of conquest.

C. A Disciplined People

On the face of it, it would seem that the Egyptians might have relaxed: they had proved their point; they had conquered the world. Their own land was producing vigorously in crops, copper, and gold; other lands were sending to them products, which they proudly labeled "tribute," whether it was exacted by force, was secured in trade, or came by an exchange of gifts. They now had tens of thousands as captive slaves in Egypt to do the laborious work; they had thousands of foreigners serving in the army, so that the burden of military duty was no longer so heavy. Now, after the pattern of the elegant Amen-hotep and Queen Tiy, was the time for placid enjoyment.

However, it was not proving to be so easy. Imperialism brought obligations as well as privileges. Frontiers hundreds of miles away were uncertain. The peril of the Hyksos had given way to the peril of Mitanni, which was now giving way to the peril of the Hittites, which would be followed by the perils of the Sea Peoples and the Libyans — always some threat to security. Under such shadows the people must always be held in readiness.

Egyptian culture had hardened in two ways. On the one hand, a crack had appeared in the sacred state. The demands for larger and more complex administration were heavy in the civil government and in the temple government. Instead of the same persons serving easily as officials and priests, full-time professionals were now necessary. The army also had become professional, instead of being a seasonal militia. Thus the civil service, the army, and the priesthood all had defined their full-time responsibilities. To be sure, there were occasional individuals who might be both Vizier of Upper Egypt and High Priest of Amon; and there were families in which different members held high civil, priestly, and military titles. But a secularization had appeared, in which the civil service was competing for power with the priesthood, and both were competing with the army.

On the other hand, the power of the church over the state became tighter in one important respect. The responsibility for undertaking a military campaign or a major civil enterprise was great, but it might be shifted: — consult a god. The oracle of an important god in his temple became a controlling factor. The word of the god-king became less weighty. Before the pharaoh undertook a campaign, he sought the sanction and support of the god Amon-Re — perhaps also of other gods. If the god blessed the campaign, and if the campaign was successful, the god deserved rich reward. A lion's share of the booty in gold and silver, in manufactured goods, in cattle, in lands, and in captured slaves went to the temples of the land. From the Eighteenth into the Twentieth Dynasty the great temples of Egypt became fabulously wealthy in goods and persons, thanks to grateful pharaohs. Managing the estates of a temple was big business.

The empire blossomed in one generation and was maintained for about five. The advantages of being within this great enterprise were obvious, and certain families were engaged from the beginning. They became a ruling clan in Egypt, passing important offices from father to son. The pharaoh increasingly became the palace captive of his civil and religious bureaucracy, for the concerns of the state were far too complex for him to control in detail. Let his loyal nobles handle the details.

What about the small landed class, the middle class of agents, artists, and artisans, and the great masses? What was left over of that tentative surge toward democracy of the First Intermediate Period? Practically nothing. It is interesting to note that those documents which were most nearly equalitarian, like the story of the indignant peasant, were rarely copied in the New Kingdom. Such individualism would be difficult in a state which demanded a disciplined unity of its people. Obedient conformance would better suit a nation with vast demands upon its energies. The quality of *ma'at* was now becoming "order" in terms of ungrudging compliance. We shall see later how this changed the religion of the people, in section 5 B.

As the ruling group became wealthier and more engrossed in their administrative interests, a wider cleavage opened between them and the lower classes. In a similar way, the great gods became wealthier and more concerned with universal matters, and a new cleavage opened between them and the common worshipper. There was a greater insistence that a god is unknowable. Amon was the "hidden" of form, name, and shrine. When he was carried out in procession, his image was concealed by a cloth. Ra had a secret name of power, which he withheld from men and from the other gods.[14] Mankind really existed only as the god might manifest himself; without him they were as nothing. "All eyes see through thee, and they have no fulfillment when thy majesty sets," was said to the sun-god. "When thou settest in the western horizon, then they sleep in the manner of death."[15] An old text which had earlier currency was now used frequently and prominently. It tells how the sun-god Ra found that mankind was rebellious and plotted something — we are not told what — against the god. Ra first started to destroy them, then repented and let the remnant live.[16] Thus the state dogma asserted that men were other than gods.

For the mortuary religion, the Pyramid Texts of the Old Kingdom and the Coffin Texts of the Middle Kingdom were succeeded by the Book of the Dead, characteristically written on papyrus for placing in the tomb. The former liveliness and self-assertiveness had disappeared from this body of texts. The deceased no longer won eternal happiness so much on his own merits and momentum from this world. Now he had to be equipped by religion and magic against mysterious perils on his journey to paradise. The Book of the Dead, prepared by the priesthood, detailed these pitfalls and dangers and gave man the means to overcome them. The Book of the Dead was not a canonized book in the sense of our Bible: nearly every manuscript has variants from others. In its fullest form it contained a lengthy denial of guilt, to be recited in the presence of the forty-two gods who would judge the dead, "who live on them who keep up evil and who drink their blood on that day of reckoning up character." It is interesting to see that many of the forty-odd sins listed are ritual in character, in addition to the moral: "I have not killed. . . . I have not stolen. . . . I have not been covetous." Purely ritual seem to be such as: "I have not neglected the (appointed) times and their meat-offerings. I have not driven away the cattle of the god's property. I have not stopped a god on his procession. ... I have not blasphemed against my local god."[17] A constraint of form and obedience had closed down upon the once happy Egyptians. Unity demanded that they be submissive without raising questions.

4. THE CHALLENGES TO POWER

A. The Universal God (1375–1300)

AN EGYPTIAN PEACE imposed by conquest and administrative control had obvious advantages of order and regular commerce. But also obvious to the Asiatic subjects of Egypt were the possible pleasures of independence. This was centuries before Ezekiel (30:6) proclaimed: "They also that uphold Egypt shall fall, and the pride of her power shall come down," but the first seeds of that hostility were being sown by empire. The period of international correspondence visible in the Tell el-Amarna Letters opened with a few signs of dissatisfaction in Asia. Even though each Syrian prince wrote to the pharaoh in terms of slavish devotion, he might take the opportunity to advise his liege lord that some other prince was behaving treacherously. The prince of Gebal (Byblos) humbly fell "seven times and seven times beneath the feet of the king, my lord," and begged the pharaoh to stop the territorial aggrandizement of the prince of Amurru.[1] At the same time the prince of Amurru was writing to protest his doglike loyalty. When the Egyptian capital ignored these accusations as local jealousies, those Asiatics who were experimenting in separatism were emboldened to continue.

Egypt was preoccupied with an internal contest for power. The new professionalism had brought division among the civil service, the army, the priesthood, and the royal court. Because of the needs of the government bureaus, schools were now training boys to be clerks rather than priests. The newly professional army wielded the effective police power for the state. The temples held huge lands, great bodies of workers, and an income guaranteed by the pharaoh. While these three services were competing for power, pharaoh himself saw his divine authority slipping from him.

This contest helped to precipitate the Amarna Revolution, headed by the heretic pharaoh, Amen-hotep IV (1369–1353), who later changed his name to Akh-en-Aton. In the past the culture had been flexible enough to accept change without revolution. The new trends in art, architecture, literature, and religion had already worked their way into the culture without much opposition. The important gods were now universal, no longer restricted to Egypt alone. The demand for services was bringing new families up toward the ruling group. Foreigners were factors within the state, even in the palace. The daughter of commoners had become the honored queen of Amen-hotep III. Change was in the air.

Universalism in religion — a god for all mankind — narrowed devotion down to one god, which was a step toward monotheism. The life-giving disk of the sun, called the Aton, had been worshipped two generations before Akh-en-Aton's reforms. Even though new trends do strain relations between conservatives and radicals, Egypt had previously been able to compromise and adjust. Now the pharaoh found himself increasingly the puppet of the high civil servants and the high priests. To regain his former pre-eminence, he seized upon the new trends as materials for a revolution.

Amen-hotep III had appointed his son coregent, and the formal break with the past came while the older king was still alive, without apparent objection from him. Although Amen-hotep III and Queen Tiy did not join their son in abandoning the old capital at Thebes, they did allow themselves to be depicted in the new modernistic art. In the sixth year of his reign the young king moved away from Thebes, which was dominated by the god Amon. He changed his name from Amen-hotep, "Amon is Satisfied," to Akh-en-Aton, probably meaning "It is Well with the Aton." The young heretic moved his capital more than two hundred miles northward to a virgin site, Akhet-Aton, near modern Tell el-Amarna, and he took a vow never to leave this new garden city. In a vigorous attempt to concentrate worship upon the life-giving sun-disk, the Aton, he sent agents throughout Egypt and the empire to remove from the inscriptions the names of gods, particularly that of the hated Amon. The revolutionary break had been made. In the next section we shall consider whether this may be called monotheism.

Akh-en-Aton was not physically strong. His ancestors, in setting up empire, had exhibited skill, endurance, and muscular power.[2] He was not strong enough to follow their precedent, and he turned to spiritual, artistic, and intellectual leadership. The Amarna art exaggerated the naturalistic trends of the immediate past with sketchy and animated scenes, which were almost caricatures of the older sedate art. Since the pharaoh was long-jawed, narrow-shouldered, and potbellied, so his attendants were also pictured, in imitative flattery. Formerly, Egyptian art had been detached from the here-and-now, in order to achieve timeless and spaceless eternity. In an excess of candor, the cloistered life of the palace was now opened up to public view, with scenes of the royal family in affectionate intimacy.

There were pictures of the immediate present in the capital city, with a story-telling as lively as that of a Greek vase painting.

In a break with the past, Akh-en-Aton appointed as administrators new people, who repaid him for their suddenly advanced status by a servile loyalty. Since the old families who had administered the state were now removed from power, there was no experience in the problems of government. The Asiatic empire went to pieces, there was difficulty in controlling the army, and some taxes went uncollected.

The Tell el-Amarna Letters and the Hittite archives tell the story of the troubles in Syria-Palestine. Not only did Syrian princes try to snatch for themselves little states, but a new power, the Hittite Empire, moved out of Anatolia to seize territory in north Syria. Those princes who remained loyal to the pharaoh lost their thrones when he ignored their appeals for help. For example, the prince of Gebal was forced to flee from his town and seek asylum farther south.

In Palestine the princes saw the empire crumbling, and some of them, such as the ruler at Shechem, intrigued for personal power. Mobile invaders, the *'Apiru* or *Habiru* roamed the land to their own advantage. The loyal prince of Jerusalem pled for only fifty Egyptian soldiers to hold the land for pharaoh, but the capital at Amarna was too preoccupied to send additional troops. The northern part of the empire fell away to the Hittites; the southern part was carved up into small independent states.[3]

At Amarna there was trouble. Probably Akh-en-Aton's ailment was progressive. His beautiful wife, Nefert-iti, fell from favor and was exiled to a northern suburb. Akh-en-Aton had six daughters but no son to aid him in rule. He married his eldest daughter to a young relative, Smenkh-ka-Re, and made the youth his coregent. Smenkh-ka-Re (1355–1352) returned to Thebes and permitted the worship of Amon to be resumed. Although Akh-en-Aton would not leave his capital or desert his god, a compromise which was virtually a surrender was necessary to save the rule of the dynasty.

After Akh-en-Aton's death, Smenkh-ka-Re disappeared from view. Another son-in-law, Tut-ankh-Aton, changed his name to Tut-ankh-Amon (1352–1344), thus protesting his capitulation to the forces of reaction, abandoned the capital at Amarna, and returned to Thebes and the appeasement of Amon.[4] When he also died while quite young, an elderly relative of the family, Eye, reigned briefly. Then the commander of the army, Hor-em-heb (1340–1315), seized the throne to restore order to a confused and resentful state. He put down rebellion and corruption vigorously.[5] Later Egyptian records made him the first legitimate pharaoh after Amen-hotep III, thus wiping the names of the Amarna family from history as heretics.

By an accident of survival, the little tomb of Tut-ankh-Amon in the hills west of Thebes escaped ancient tomb robbery and was discovered in 1922 C.E. Its rich and vivid furnishings have opened our eyes to the excitement of the Amarna period.

B. Heresy

Of the many temples and priesthoods in the land, three had come to be preeminent under the empire: those of Ra at Heliopolis (On), of Ptah at Memphis (Noph), and of Amon-Re at Thebes (No). In particular, the high priest of Amon-Re at the temple of Karnak in Thebes was a powerful official, with strong family ties into the civil bureaucracy and with strong influence over the king through the use of the oracle of the god. These temples had been greatly enriched by the booty and captives brought home by victorious armies. By 1200 B.C.E. the various temples of Egypt would own at least one–eighth of the arable land and possibly as much as one–tenth of the population. Much more than half of this ecclesiastical holding would belong to Amon-Re. In addition to the loot which came to this god in return for his blessing foreign campaigns, the god was a major beneficiary from the gold mines of Nubia, and the pharaoh made generous annual offerings.

When the break of the Amarna Revolution came, the priesthood and the civil service stood together on the conservative side. The new force, the army, saw its advantage with the pharaoh. Even this modernistic revolution had its reactionary aspect: Akh-en-Aton was trying to restore that dogmatic primacy of the king as a god which had been effective in earlier times.

Akh-en-Aton did not invent new forms. They were already present in art, literature, and theology: the new fluidity and excitement in art as the result of foreign contacts, the colloquial story-telling, the universalism of gods, and even the Aton as a god. There was, however, originality in the fresh ardor with which these elements were presented. Another old factor was the revolution's emphasis on the principle of *ma'at*, "truth," which came to have the sense of "candor": naturalism in art, openness in architecture, the use of the speech of the day instead of the already dead classical language, the royal family in public view, and the worship of the sun-disk out in the open air. These were protests against the remoteness of the former temple and palace.

Akh-en-Aton's religion expressed the devotion to a single god, the

Aton or sun-disk, as a creating and sustaining power. The pharaoh referred to the Aton as the "sole god, like whom there is no other." The god was not restricted to Egypt, but was the universal supporter of all mankind and all life everywhere. In his commitment to one god and in the violent break with the older religion, Akh-en-Aton had his agents hack out of the inscriptions the name of the god Amon, frequently the names of other gods, and often the words "the gods" or "all the gods." For the king there was but one god.

Sun-worship in Egypt had existed from the beginnings. Aton as a god was two generations older than Akh-en-Aton. Syncretism, whereby two or more divine forces might merge into one, was centuries old. Hymns addressing a deity as the "sole god," with a flattering emphasis and an exclusive focus of worship, had appeared centuries earlier. Universalism was a product of the century-old empire: when Egyptians regarded foreign countries as worth holding, Egyptian gods became gods of the world. But Amon — Amon was the "hidden one," unseen and unknown in a mighty temple. Under the principle of *ma'at*, "truth," the Aton was to be worshipped out in the open air, where the public might see.

Akh-en-Aton's beautiful hymn to the Aton gives the essence of the new faith: one god for all the world, the creator and maintainer of life.

> Thou appearest beautifully on the horizon of heaven,
> Thou living Aton, the beginning of life!
> When thou art arisen on the eastern horizon,
> Thou hast filled every land with thy beauty. . . .
> When thou settest in the western horizon,
> The land is in darkness, in the manner of death. . . .
> Every lion is come forth from his den;
> All creeping things, they sting.
> Darkness is a shroud, and the earth is in stillness,
> For he who made them rests in his horizon.
> At daybreak, when thou arisest on the horizon,
> When thou shinest at the Aton by day,
> Thou drivest away the darkness and givest thy rays.
> The Two Lands are in festivity every day,
> Awake and standing upon their feet. . . .
> All the world, they do their work. . . .
> How manifold it is, what thou hast made!
> They are hidden from the face (of man).
> O sole god, like whom there is no other!

Thou didst create the world according to thy desire. . . .
The countries of Syria and Nubia, the land of Egypt,
Thou settest every man in his place,
Thou suppliest his necessities:
Everyone has his food, and his time of life is reckoned.
Their tongues are separate in speech, and their natures as well.
Their skins are distinguished,
As thou distinguishest the foreign peoples. . . .
Thou art in my heart, and there is no other that knows thee,
Save for thy son (Akh-en-Aton),
For thou hast made him well-versed in thy plans and thy strength.[6]

The similarity of this hymn to the 104th Psalm in thought and structure is very marked, even though it is impossible to assume a direct connection between the Egyptian and the Hebrew. Atonism was a fervent nature-worship and made no demand upon the worshipper beyond loving gratitude. There was little ethical content in the new faith. Atonism thus stood in contrast to the categorical demands which Hebrew monotheism made upon man for an upright life.

Two gods were worshipped at Amarna. Akh-en-Aton and Nefert-iti gave their sole adoration to the Aton, whereas all of Akh-en-Aton's followers gave their sole adoration to the pharaoh. For them he was the source of good in this life and also in the next, since the old mortuary gods had been eliminated. It is true that there was a father-son relationship between the Aton and the king, so that they might be considered parts of the same godhead. But Akh-en-Aton's claim that there was no other that knew the Aton except himself did make the god exclusively his.

Since Akh-en-Aton's worship of a single god came earlier than the monotheism ascribed to Moses, some writers have argued that Atonism was the inspiration source for the Hebrew faith. The problem is difficult, but a direct lineage seems impossible. The means whereby an exclusive doctrine in Middle Egypt, later suppressed as heretical, might reach a Moses in the Delta perhaps a century later are doubtful. Further, the whole character of Mosaism was anti-Egyptian, based on the faith that the Israelite God had defeated the pharaoh and pharaoh's reliance upon Egyptian gods. Everything points to disconnection, rather than connection.

A majority of writers on the subject have treated Atonism as a genuine monotheism. Because the system had certain flaws in its exclusive focus on one being, we prefer to define it as a sincere but incomplete approach to monotheism, too early in world history to have achieved pure monotheism.

Sakkarah. Tomb of Mereruka. VIth Dynasty. Detail of scene on North wall; boys playing games. Oriental Institute, University of Chicago.

Syrian tribute-bearers, bringing ointment, horn, quiver, vessels, rhyton, and child, on wall painting of tomb 63 at Thebes. Oriental Institute, University of Chicago.

The god Anubis leads the deceased toward the balance, where his heart is weighed against Maat; papyrus of Hu-nefer.

Mortuary scenes from late New Kingdom Tomb.
Oriental Institute, University of Chicago.

Head of Akh-en-Aton.

Portrait bust of Queen Nefert-iti,
from Tell el-Amarna.
Oriental Institute, University of Chicago.

King Akh-en-Aton and Queen Nefert-iti standing with offerings for the sun-god Aton, on balustrade at Amarna.
Photograph, Metropolitan Museum of Art, New York.

Karnak; Temple of Amon. Gross aisle of great Hypostyle Hall, looking southwest.
XVIIIth Dyn., ca. early 14th Cent. B.C.E.
Oriental Institute, University of Chicago.

Statue of Ramses II.
Turin Museum.

Abu Simbel. XIXth Dynasty. Facade of the Great temple from the northeast.
Oriental Institute, University of Chicago.

King Mer-ne-Ptah wearing nemes headdress, from Thebes.
Photograph, Metropolitan Museum of Art, New York.

It was a courageous attempt to simplify and cleanse the murky forces of the day.

Despite the fact that Atonism was proscribed as heretical, it left its mark on Egyptian religion, as the innovations in art and literature also left their marks. There remained the universalism of gods, and there remained the attempt to simplify divinity down to a single god for adoration and humble gratitude, as we shall see in Section V b. Thus, if one insists upon finding some connection between Egyptian religion and Mosaic religion, such ideas may have been current in the Delta or in Egyptian temples in Asia at the time of Moses. It will still be true that the religion of the Children of Israel was an independent religion, based upon independent experience, particularly the deliverance from Egypt.

C. Clashing Empires (1315–1150)

The Nineteenth Dynasty (1315–1205) introduced a new family, with a new political alignment. The names of the Eighteenth Dynasty, Amenhotep and Thut-mose, had shown dedication to Amon of Thebes and to Thoth of Hermopolis. The Nineteenth Dynasty names, Ramses, Seti, and Mer-ne-Ptah, expressed devotion to northern gods, Ra of Heliopolis, Ptah of Memphis, and Seth of the northeast Delta and of foreign countries. Within a generation the capital city would become Raamses (or Rameses) in the northeast Delta; Thebes would become a traditional and seasonal capital and the seat of a provincial government. Egypt's concerns had moved north.

Military interests and a desire to restore empire are shown by the succession of military pharaohs. General Hor-em-heb was succeeded by two who had had army careers, Ramses I and his son Seti I (1314–1304). The determination of Seti I to recapture the older glories appears in the term which he applied to the beginning of his reign — the "Renaissance."

Reconquest of the empire was a first concern of the new dynasty. In his first regnal year Seti I campaigned from the Suez frontier to the hills of Galilee, put down an attempt by Palestinian princes to unite, and seized the town of Beth-shean on the Jordan. Subsequently he defeated the *'Apiru* or *Habiru* of Mount Jarmuth near Beth-shean. He realized the importance of good communications and maintained the caravan stations across north Sinai. When the land of Canaan was again under control, Seti was able to face the major enemy and to campaign against the Hittites in Syria. There may have been no conclusive battle between the two powers, but the pharaoh was successful in taking Kadesh on the Orontes and setting up a triumphal stela in that town.[7]

At home Seti I's energies were devoted to the continuing problem of checking administrative abuses. At Thebes and Abydos he carried out major building operations. In particular, his temple at Abydos shows a restraint and delicacy far surpassing the other work of the dynasty.

Some modern works call Ramses II (1304–1238) "the Great," but it is doubtful that he earned the epithet. He did reign sixty-seven years, and in that time he built tremendously, but he also showed an overweaning arrogance in appropriating the monuments of the ancestors for himself. His military successes were doubtful, but his propaganda of triumphant conquest was blatant.

In his fifth regnal year (1300 B.C.E.), Ramses II fought against the Hittite king Muwatallis at Kadesh on the Orontes. As allies the Hittites brought such city-states of north Syria as Carchemish, Aleppo, and Ugarit, some of the older regions of Asia Minor like Arzawa and Kizzuwadna, and some of the new "Sea Peoples" of the eastern Mediterranean, such as the Dardanians and the Mysians. On his side Ramses had as mercenaries some of those Sea Peoples, the *Sherden*, who were later to give their name to the island of Sardinia. The ethnic composition of the armies offers a chapter in the protohistory of the classical world. In the battle the Egyptians failed to gain their objectives, although Ramses boasted mightily of victory.[8] In his later campaigns he fought chiefly in Palestine, and it may be that he avoided the main Hittite army.

The world was changing. The Sea Peoples were pressing insistently upon the Hittite flanks and causing uneasiness to the west of Egypt; Assyria was gaining in strength. Hatti and Egypt had to resolve their difficulties against these new threats. About 1284 the two countries entered into a treaty of alliance and mutual assistance,[9] and about 1270 the new peace was confirmed by the marriage of the middle-aged pharaoh to the daughter of the Hittite king.

> So the daughter of the Great Prince of Hatti marched to Egypt, while the infantry, chariotry, and officials of His Majesty accompanied her, mingling with the infantry and chariotry of Hatti. . . . They ate and drank together, being of one heart like brothers, without shunning one another, for peace and brotherhood were between them, after the manner of the god himself, Ramses. . . . So she was beautiful in the heart of His Majesty, and he loved her more than anything. . . . And so it was that, if a man or a woman proceeded

> on their mission to Syria, they could reach the land of Hatti without fear around about their hearts, because of the greatness of the victories of His Majesty.[10]

The final thirty-three years of Ramses II's long reign were unmarked by major incident, although the restless Sea Peoples were using the time of peace to harass the borders of Hatti and Egypt.

The name of Ramses II looms large upon the monuments of Egypt, since he built extensively and also appropriated older monuments for himself. He encouraged the soldiers in his military encampments to worship his statues as divine. The Great Hypostyle Hall of Karnak at Thebes was completed by him, and he built the majestic rock-cliff temple of Abu Simbel in Nubia. In the Delta the royal residence city of Raamses was named after him, so that serious consideration must be given to the possibility that he was the Pharaoh of the Oppression, who forced the Children of Israel to work on the cities of Pithom and Raamses (Ex. 1:11). However, Egyptian texts offer no supporting evidence, either on the enforced toil of the Israelites or on an exodus in the reign of his successor.

In his long reign Ramses II produced a swarm of royal princes, many of whom died before their father. His fourteenth son, Mer-ne-Ptah (1238–1226), must have been an old man when he succeeded to the throne. He had pressing problems to the north and west. The aggression of the Sea Peoples was threatening the existence of his Hittite ally, so that the pharaoh sent shipments of grain to keep Hatti alive. In his fifth year the Sea Peoples, including the Achaeans and Lycians, united with the Libyans, to attempt an invasion of the western Delta. A poem commemorating a victorious Egyptian campaign against this alliance ends with the only mention of Israel in Egyptian literature, and the monument has therefore been named the "Israel Stela."

> The princes are prostrate, saying: 'Mercy!' . . .
> Desolation is for Libya; Hatti is pacified;
> The Canaan is plundered with every evil;
> Ashkelon is carried off; seized upon is Gezer;
> Yanoam is made as if non-existent;
> Israel is laid waste, he has no offspring;
> The Horite land has become a widow for Egypt!
> All lands together, they are pacified.[11]

This is a poetical outburst, not corresponding to specific facts. However, it does know of the Israelites as a people in or near Canaan about 1234

B.C.E. In the hieroglyphic writing, the word "Israel" is determined with signs for people rather than for settled place, suggesting that they were nomadic or semi-nomadic at the time. This date must then be considered in relation to an exodus and a wandering in the wilderness. There may have been one exodus from Egypt in the thirteenth century B.C.E., but forty years of wandering before approaching the land of Canaan make it difficult to regard Mer-ne-Ptah as the Pharaoh of the Exodus.

The Nineteenth Dynasty ran out its course with feeble kings succeeding one another rapidly, with one queen ruling. Then for a brief time, perhaps 1205–1197, there was an interregnum, in which Arsu, a Syrian (in the text "Horite"), seized the throne of Egypt. Probably he had not invaded the land; he may have been an Asiatic chamberlain serving at the palace, who was able to take over the rule. Such foreigners had high position; for example, we know that at the court of Mer-ne-Ptah a chief herald was a Semite named Ben-ozen. There is some doubt about the reading of "Arsu" as a name, and nothing more is known about this episode. A generation later the account ran as follows: —

> Afterwards other times came in empty years, and Arsu, a Syrian with them, made himself prince. He set the entire land as tributary before him. One man joined another that their property might be plundered. They treated the gods like humans, and no offerings were presented in the temples.[12]

A new dynasty, the Twentieth (1197–1090), appeared to "cleanse the great throne of Egypt." Its only important figure was Ramses III (1195–1164). His chief responsibilities lay in the warding off of invasions of the Delta, twice from the west by Libyans, and once (1185) from the north by Sea Peoples. The latter advanced on sea in war galleys and on land in great ox-carts, with their women, children, and household goods. Among them were the Philistines, and, although Ramses III did thwart their attempt to invade the Egyptian Delta, they soon settled down in Palestine and gave their name to that country.[13] At the end of his reign the pharaoh still held territory in Canaan, for his mortuary testament guaranteed for Amon the Palestinian towns which he had given that god. Within a generation after his death the Asiatic empire finally collapsed, the Sinai mines were abandoned, and Egypt withdrew into her shell.

Ramses III lost his life in a conspiracy which originated in his own harem. The court which tried the plotters was composed of palace officials, among them the Semitic butler Mahar-Baal. When the accused of higher ranks were found guilty, they were permitted to take their own lives; the lesser criminals were executed.[14]

In his posthumous will — probably promulgated by his son — Ramses III confirmed the Egyptian temples in their holdings. The detailed figures are difficult to relate to the area and population of Egypt, but it seems possible that the great temples held no less than ten per cent of the people and twelve per cent of the agricultural land, while the temple of Amon-Re at Karnak owned one person out of every fifteen and one acre out of every ten. The vested power of the temples was certainly extraordinarily high.[15]

The reigns of the later kings of the dynasty were weak and usually brief; all were named Ramses. There came a series of misfortunes: inflation, famine, strikes by government workers, plundering by idle soldiers, and official corruption. About 1125 B.C.E. the large-scale robbing of the Egyptian tombs began and was unchecked for a full generation, with the result that the royal and noble tombs at Thebes were thoroughly looted. There is no evidence that the government took — or even wanted to take — energetic measures to stop this pillage. The dynasty ended with the last of the kings named Ramses a feeble palace puppet, controlled by the viziers of Upper and Lower Egypt, the High Priest of Amon, and the commander of the army.

D. Literature from Schoolboys

The need of the government for trained writers, to be clerks in the bureaus, paymasters, and letter writers, produced in the Nineteenth and Twentieth Dynasties secretarial schools from which we have several collections of papyri and ostraca upon which the schoolboys wrote their exercises. They give us a remarkable picture of the literature used for teaching. Some old classics were standard, such as the story of Si-nuhe, the wisdom text of Amen-em-het I, a hymn to the inundation, and a text glorifying the trade of the scribe over other callings. One dreary "teaching" consisted simply of a catalogue of phenomena in the universe, listed in series: "sun, moon, star, Orion, . . .; king, queen, crown prince, . . .; castle, settlement, house, room, . . .; breast, upper spine, back, rib, . . .," and so on for hundreds of items.[16] The poor schoolboy, laboriously penning such lists, had to get the right spelling, penmanship, and association of elements. His master held him to his task with discipline: "the ear of the boy is on his back, and he listens when he is beaten."[17]

Other items in the curriculum had greater interest. There were model letters, of the type that a government clerk might be expected to write as reports. For example, from a fortress on the northeast frontier there might be a record that the officials there "have finished letting the Bedouin tribes of Edom pass the Fortress of Mer-ne-Ptah . . . which is in Tjeku, to the pools of Pithom of Mer-ne-Ptah . . . which are in Tjeku, to keep them alive and to keep their cattle alive." Another model letter tells of the pursuit of two slaves who have run away into the desert, presumably Sinai. "When my letter reaches you, write to me about all that has happened to them. Who found their tracks? Which watch found their tracks? What people are after them?"[18]

Such letters might illustrate some of the official propaganda, such as the joy of heaven and earth at the accession of Mer-ne-Ptah to the throne. "The water stands and is not dried up; the inundation lifts high. Days are long, nights have hours, and the moon comes normally. The gods are satisfied and content of heart. One lives in laughter and wonder."[19]

One popular composition was a long letter in which one scribe belittles the abilities of another with heavy-handed sarcasm.

> You are sent on a mission to Syria at the head of the victorious army, to crush those rebels called 'young men.'[20] . . . The number of men is too great for you, whereas the provisions are too small for them. . . . The Bedouin look on furtively, saying: 'O wise scribe!'[21] Midday is come, the camp is hot. . . . O What's-Your-Name, what does it mean, this beating of us? (The writer jeers at his correspondent's ignorance of Palestine.) Come, set me on the way southward to the region of Acco. Where does the Achshaph road come in? At what town? . . . Where does the mountain of Shechem come? . . . Where does the courier make the journey to Hazor? What is its stream like? . . . Let me know the way to pass Megiddo. . . . The narrow valley is dangerous with Bedouin, hidden under the bushes. Some of them are four or five cubits high . . . and fierce of face. Their hearts are not mild, and they do not listen to wheedling. . . . You think that the enemy is behind you. Trembling seizes you. If only you had a hedge of shrubs, so that you might put it on the other side![22]

In these schoolboys' miscellanies there were stories, such as the tale of the capture of Jaffa, when an officer under Thut-mose III introduced his soldiers into the town hidden in baskets.[23] Or there was the glorification of the residence city Raamses.

> The Residence is pleasant in life; its fields are full of everything good; it is full of supplies and food every day, its ponds with fish, and its lakes with birds. Its meadows are green with grass; its banks bear dates; its melons are abundant on the sands. . . . Its granaries are so full of barley and emmer wheat that they come near to the sky. . . . Come, let us celebrate for it its feasts. . . . The young men of (the city) are dressed up every day, with sweet oil on their heads and newly dressed hair. They stand beside their doors, their hands bowed down with flowers.[24]

Also there were myths for the schoolboys to copy, such as the story telling how the god Ra had a mysterious name of power which he concealed from the other gods. The goddess Isis by her magic tricked the august Ra into revealing this name for her benefit and the benefit of her son Horus.[25] Even less complimentary to divine beings was the myth of the contest between Horus and Seth for the rule, a story treating the mighty gods as childish, inconstant, and jealous. Even though the story comes out right, in that Horus does win the rule and Seth is confined to being a thunder-god, one is left puzzled at such attitudes of bawdy irreverence.[26]

It may be surprising to find love songs in the miscellany used for schoolboys, but youth mature early in the Orient. In any case, the songs are romantic and nostalgic, rather than erotic. The first example is the shy maiden, meeting the young man on the road.

> My heart intended to see Nefrus,
> So that I might sit in her house.
> But I found Mehy driving on the road,
> Together with his gallants.
> I did not know how to get out of his sight,
> So that I might pass him freely by. . . .
> See, if I pass by before him,
> I shall tell him of my flutterings;
> 'See, I am yours,' I shall say to him.
> And he will boast of my name
> And assign me to the foremost harem
> Of those who are in his retinue.

The other example is the love-sick lad, who longs for "the sister," as these texts call the beloved.

> Seven days to yesterday I have not seen the sister,
> And a sickness has invaded me. . . .

> If the chief of physicians come to me,
> My heart is not content with their remedies. . . .
> The sister does better for me than any remedies;
> She is more to me than the collected writings. . . .
> If she opens her eye, my body is young again;
> If she speaks, then I am strong again;
> When I embrace her, she drives evil from me —
> But she has gone away from me for seven days![27]

A culture lays before its schoolboys what it considers its wisest guidance. These texts give a good sampling of Egyptian taste.

5. A LOWLY KINGDOM

A. Division and Confusion (1100–663)

SHORTLY BEFORE 1100 B.C.E. the High Priest of Amon at Thebes sent an emissary to Byblos (Gebal) in Phoenicia, to secure cedar for the sacred boat of the god. The story does not mention the reigning pharaoh, because he was then of no importance. It was the independent ruler of Tanis (Zoan) who found a Syrian ship for the messenger Wen-Amon. In the Palestinian harbor of Dor, then ruled by some of the Sea Peoples, Wen-Amon was robbed of his gold and silver. When he reached Byblos, the Phoenician prince brusquely refused to deal with him on credit alone; Egypt had to pay in advance. Formerly Egypt had sent as many as six ships loaded with goods to pay for cedar — "What are these silly trips they have had you make?" Finally, after a year of misadventures and insults, new payment came from Egypt, and Wen-Amon received the cedar.[1] The story is a vivid illustration of the low esteem into which Egypt had fallen — in that very Phoenician town which had once been so pro-Egyptian. Verily, Egypt had already become that "lowly kingdom" which Ezekiel (29:14) was to prophesy.

"The Two Lands" had split in two, with Tanis and Thebes working cooperatively but independently. Thereafter Egypt was rarely united and never firmly united. Solomon's Egyptian queen may have been the daughter of one of the small Delta dynasts, with whom Solomon was trading in horses and chariots.

From this time forward the history of ancient Egypt is subordinate to that of other cultures. Here and in section 5 C. we summarize briefly, to round out the picture.

Rule by foreigners became a normal. A descendant of Libyan mercenaries, Shishak or Shoshenk, founded the Twenty-second Dynasty (940–745) and made a raid into Palestine (I Kings 14:25) as the only important move in two centuries. Egypt gradually broke into small fragments, from which she was rescued only by outside rule. At the Fourth Cataract on the Nile a Cushite or Ethiopian dynasty had come into being. About 725 B.C.E. the Cushite pharaoh Pi-ankhi raided Egypt and brought the land into unified subjection.[2] His son Tirhakah (689–664) tried unsuccessfully to hold off the Assyrians under Esarhaddon. When the Assyrians conquered the land, they recognized certain local princes as their vassals in city-states.

B. The Quiet Gods

The earlier Egyptian religion had been characterized by assurance and self-confidence. Egypt was the best of all possible worlds, and the Egyptians would be successful in this world and the next. Scenes and texts in the tombs had asserted this flourishing faith. As early as the Nineteenth Dynasty, a change had appeared in the tombs of the nobles. In place of a gay and lusty emphasis upon the abundant things of this world, which would be richly extended into the next life, the scenes began to show the mortuary services and to chart the perils of the journey into the other world. The statement no longer was: this is a good life and it will last forever; now the emphasis had become: life itself is restricted and the passage to the hereafter is restricted; only rigorous conformance to the practices of the mortuary religion can win eternal life for a man. When the joy of living disappeared, the future also had some uncertainty.

This new sobriety appeared also in personal religion. Formerly a father had encouraged his son to a life of pushing activity: be alert and well-trained, and you will get ahead; the smart man or the impartial administrator can acquire for himself the rewards of this life. Now the emphasis had become resignation to one's lot in life: entrust yourself to the arms of the god; he alone can cure your woes and reward you for submissiveness. Little room was left for individual initiative. The deities Fate and Fortune had become powerfully controlling of human destiny. The good man was no longer the "knowing one;" he was now the "silent one."

This humble piety appeared particularly in two types of documents: dedicatory tablets set up by relatively modest people, often to relatively modest gods, and the instructions which a father gave to his son. For the first time the Egyptian was aware of a sense of sin — not the ritualistic denial of wrongdoings, but a contrite admission of error in general.

Little stelae carried the confession that an individual had committed wrong and that a god had punished him. The god was right and just in this punishment, and now the worshipper prayed for the god's mercy and healing.

> Do not punish me for my numerous sins, for I am one who does not know his own self, I am a man without sense. I spend the day following after my own mouth, like a cow after grass.
> I knew neither good nor evil. When I did the deed of transgression

> against the Peak (a goddess), she punished me, and I was in her hand by night as well as day. . . . She smites with the smiting of a savage lion. She pursues him who transgresses against her. . . . But when I called to my mistress, I found her coming to me with sweet breezes. She showed mercy to me, after she had let me see her hand. She turned about to me in mercy; she made me forget the sickness which had been upon me. See, the Peak of the West is merciful, when one calls to her!

The son of an artisan in Thebes was stricken with serious illness after he had somehow offended the god Amon. Later his father set up a grateful stela.

> Thou art Amon, the lord of the silent man, who comes at the voice of the poor man. If I call to thee when I am distressed, thou comest and rescuest me. Thou givest breath to him who is weak; thou rescuest him who is imprisoned.... Supplications were made to (Amon) before his face and in the presence of the entire land, on behalf of the Outline Draftsman Nakht-Amon, when he was lying ill and in a state of death, when he was under the power of Amon because of his cow.

We are not told what sin the son had committed against the sacred cow. The god answered the prayer, and the young man recovered from his illness. The father continued with a statement that the normal nature of man is sin, but the normal nature of god is forgiveness — after punishment.

> Though it may be that the servant is normal in doing wrong, still the lord is normal in being merciful. The Lord of Thebes does not spend an entire day angry. As for his anger — in the completion of a moment there is no remnant, and the wind is turned about in mercy for us.[3]

Because we can make contrasts with earlier literature, the wisdom texts most strikingly show the new piety and quietude.[4] Under the Old Kingdom, the Vizier Ptah-hotep had urged his son to cultivate effective speech. Now the clerk Ani advised his son: "Do not talk a lot; be silent and you will be happy. Do not be talkative. Clamor is the abomination of the dwelling of god. Pray with a loving heart, with all the words hidden, and he will do what you need, he will hear what you say, and he will accept your offering." Whereas Ptah-hotep had counseled his son to treat his wife well, because "she is a profitable field for her lord," Ani suggested that one's love for his mother should be the basis for his love for his wife. "When you are a young man and take a wife and are settled in your home, set your attention on how your mother gave birth to you and all her bringing you up as well. Do not let (your wife) blame you, nor may she raise her hands to the god, nor may he hear her cries.[5]

The most remarkable exponent of the new piety is the advice which the agricultural official Amen-em-Opet gave to his son, perhaps in the seventh century B.C.E.[6] Sections of this text are extraordinarily like passages in the Book of Proverbs. Indeed there is little doubt that the instruction of Amen-em-Opet was an original for Proverbs 22:17–24:22. In particular, the sectioning of the Egyptian text into thirty chapters and its terminal words: "You see these thirty chapters: they entertain and they instruct" have permitted us to point the Hebrew vowels in Proverbs 22:20 to read: "I have written to you thirty (sayings) of counsels and knowledge."

Give your ears, hear what is said,
Give your heart to understand them.
To put them in your heart is worth while,
But it is damaging to him who neglects them.
Let them rest in the casket of your belly,
So that they may be a key in your heart.
At a time when there is a whirlwind of words,
They will be a mooring-stake for your tongue. . . .

As for the passionate man of a temple,
He is like a tree growing out in the open.
In an instant's time it loses foliage,
And its end is reached in the shipyards. . . .
Whereas the truly silent man holds himself apart;
He is like a tree growing in a garden.
It flourishes and doubles its yield;
It stands before its lord.
Its fruit is sweet; its shade is pleasant;
And its end is reached in the garden. . . .

If you find a large debt against a poor man,
Make it into three parts, forgive two, and let one stand.
You will find it like the ways of life;
You will lie down and sleep soundly; in the morning
You will find it like good news.
Better is praise as one who loves men
Than riches in a storehouse;
Better is bread, when the heart is happy,
Than riches with sorrow. . . .

Do not spend the night afraid of tomorrow —
At daybreak what is tomorrow like?
Man does not know what tomorrow is like.
God is always in his success,
Whereas man is in his failure.
The words which men say are one thing,
But what the god does is another. . . .

Do not laugh at a blind man nor tease a dwarf
Nor injure the affairs of the lame.
Do not tease a man who is in the hand of the god,
Nor be fierce of face against him if he errs.
For man is clay and straw, and the god is his builder.
He tears down and builds up every day.
He makes a thousand poor men as he wishes,
Or he makes a thousand men as overseers,
When he is in his hour of life.
But how joyful is he who reaches the West,
When he is safe in the hand of the god!

In this world, where man was failure and only god was success, where man was but the clay for the god to build, the West, that is, the next world, was no longer a triumph and a merit; it had become a compensation for patient suffering in this life. The "silent man" would finally be "safe in the hand of the god." These texts, under those unifying influences which had played upon Egypt centuries earlier, regularly use the singular, "the god." If this is not monotheism, it is a clear focus on man's worship on his own personal god.

As the Egyptians were bidden to be patient and uncomplaining, to avoid passion or protest, the forms of their religion became more rigid. There was a greater emphasis on scrupulous carrying out of ceremonial acts at the temple. The temple paraphernalia became more important. For example, the sacred animal, which had been only one possible means for the unseen god to make an appearance, now became sacred in itself and began to receive worship. Formerly the sacred bull or the sacred cat had been just one of the temple's treasured elements. Now it was treated as holy, so that all other bulls or cats shared somewhat in this sanctity.

In late times there was more recourse to magical texts and magical apparatus; there was more recourse to the oracle of the god for any purpose, however trifling. Alexander the Great was doing a very Egyptian thing when he made the dangerous trip to Siwah in the western desert, to consult the oracle of Ammon.

As the exuberant spirit was squeezed out of Egyptian religion, formal acts became much more important.

C. To the End (663–30)

Those Egyptians whom the Assyrians had left in local rule attempted a brief age of independent glory, the Saite Period or the Twenty-sixth Dynasty (663–525). The strength of the pharaoh in large part was dependent upon foreign mercenaries from Greece and Asia Minor. There were attempts to stir up trouble by fomenting rebellion against Babylonia in Palestine. Psammetichus I besieged Ashdod, and Pharaoh Necho led an ill-fated expedition through Megiddo to Carchemish on the Euphrates in 606–05. A generation later Pharaoh Hophra intrigued unwisely, without committing his forces. Egypt was proving to Judah to be the "broken reed" that Isaiah denounced.

Parallel to the ritualism in religion, the Saite Period showed a marked archaism, attempting to recapture ancient glories. Very old monuments were excavated, restored, and imitated. Entire scenes were copied from older tombs to ornament new burials. Earlier statues were copied with striking success. The classical literature was studied anew, in an attempt to reproduce its form and spirit. Officials received ancient and now meaningless titles. Essentially this was merely imitative; it lacked inner spirit.

In 525 B.C.E. Egypt fell like an overripe fruit into the hands of the Persians under Cambyses. Persian rule was formal and correct, but the Egyptians staged several abortive rebellions. In this period we learn from manuscripts about the Jewish military colony at Elephantine near the First Cataract.[7] Then in 332 B.C.E. Alexander the Great conquered the land with no difficulty.

Alexander's Macedonian successors set up the Ptolemaic Dynasty (305–30), based on the new city of Alexandria. That capital enjoyed a career as a vigorous commercial city and a center of intellectual life, with its famous Library and Academy. Yet there was no cohesion in the nation. Cleopatra's wiles could not hold off the ultimate fate, and in 30 B.C.E. Egypt became a vassal of Rome. Roman taxation was so oppressive that the Egyptians finally stopped trying. When Christian missionaries in the second centry C.E. proclaimed that the next world would redress the damages of this world, the land went over to the new religion in great numbers. The ancient Egyptian game was played out.

6. THE FINDING OF ANCIENT EGYPT

A BRIEF STATEMENT on the history of Egyptology will be useful to clarify the abilities and limitations of this study. The beginnings of Egyptology lay in Biblical and classical studies. Thus the start was from texts written outside of Egypt. Ancient history, field archaeology, decipherment and translation of texts, and Biblical studies have come to be parts of a larger whole. Until the written and unwritten materials from ancient Egypt became large enough to force concentration upon them for their own sakes, a central curiosity about Egypt rested on the Biblical account. About 1890 controlled techniques of field archaeology, which had been worked out in Egypt, particularly through the analysis of pottery, were transferred to Palestine. There has always been a close relation between Egyptian and Palestinian research.

The study of ancient Egypt combines history, with the analysis of texts, and archaeology, with the analysis of physical materials. Although the last stage of the ancient language, Coptic, persisted in the liturgy of the Egyptian Christian Church, the earlier phases of the language and the ability to read hieroglyphic, hieratic, and demotic had been lost after the introduction of Christianity into the land. Two centuries ago hieroglyphic was assumed to be an involved and occult writing. Before Schliemann's dramatic results at Troy ninety years ago, there was little interest in field excavation. The Bible and the classical writers gave us most of what we knew about Egypt.

When Napoleon Bonaparte led a military expedition to the Nile in 1798, he brought with him a staff of historians and scientists. Their observations and recordings touched off a vigorous interest in ancient Egypt. Wealthy amateurs began to collect statues and papyri with enthusiasm. Among the discoveries by Napoleon's army was the Rosetta Stone, containing the same text in Greek and in two forms of Egyptian: hieroglyphic and demotic. This was to prove the critical element in Champollion's decipherment of hieroglyphic in 1822. Meanwhile, the opening up of Egypt to Western enterprise enriched the public and private museums with materials for study. In the first half of the nineteenth century industrious copying expeditions brought back to Europe a wealth of scenes and texts for scholars to work on. Digestion of the new materials was slow. As yet philology was in its undisciplined infancy, there was only looting rather than excavation, and history was still written in Biblical and classical terms.

In 1850 a Frenchman, Auguste Mariette, began in Egypt a series of recorded clearances of major monuments and became the dominant figure in the land for thirty years, thus starting a French control of the Egyptian antiquities service which lasted until about ten years ago. In Mariette's service to the Khedive of Egypt and in the psychology of the time, the work was a search for show pieces, rather than a scientific interest in all materials in their archaeological setting. Yet he did point the way admirably.

In the 1880's three figures appeared who changed the study of ancient Egypt to a discipline of higher standards. The young Frenchman, Gaston Maspero, came to direct the antiquities service for a full generation. He was a philologist and historian of genius, and he was able to use the ancient source materials to full advantage. A young German, Adolf Erman, brought order and accepted rules to the study of Egyptian grammar, permitting more reliable translation. A young Englishman, Flinders Petrie, revolutionized field archaeology everywhere by his insistence that every bit of excavated material must be respected, recorded, and published. Petrie made a neglected material, ordinary pottery, the critically decisive factor for excavations which lacked inscriptions. He brought the same kind of control to archaeology that Erman brought to language. Petrie's long and successful career included work in Egypt, Sinai, and Palestine. No other single figure contributed so much to our knowledge of the physical materials and the sequence of culture.

An inevitable result of the abundance of new materials and new insights was a shift of focus from Egypt's connections with the Hebrews, Greeks, and Romans to the process of Egyptian culture in itself. Because we know so little about the Delta, where the contact with Asia was strongest, work in Egypt has produced regrettably little evidence to answer specific questions about Biblical relations. Ironically, recent excavations in Palestine and Phoenicia have produced testimony on the Egyptian influence abroad.

About the beginning of the twentieth century Americans entered the scene and contributed two notable figures. George A. Reisner of Harvard University advanced Petrie's techniques to new standards of precision and excavated with great success in the pyramid area and in the Sudan. James H. Breasted of the University of Chicago became America's most widely recognized ancient historian and produced books on Egyptian texts, history, and religion which still carry great weight.

We can only know ancient Egypt partially. Our materials appear under the chances of survival and discovery, and they must represent a very tiny sampling of three thousand years of a culture. The surviving documents almost always give us only the official side of the case and rarely suggest that there might be any other side. The masses were illiterate and have left us almost nothing. We have temples and tombs, but rarely towns, houses, or even palaces. We have much from Upper Egypt, very little from the teeming Delta. In view of the gaps, the consistency of the picture is all the more remarkable.

The ancient Egyptian language is certainly not as well known as Hebrew or Greek. Nor does excavation permit the same detailed analysis within a larger setting which is possible in Greek or Roman archaeology. However, Egyptology has reached a mature understanding of careful methodology, has blocked in with success most of the stages of Egyptian history, has attained a certain understanding of the way the Egyptians thought, and is now able to present a consistent and significant story.

7. EGYPT AND THE BIBLE

EGYPT AND PALESTINE are close neighbors. Despite the barrier of the Sinai Wilderness, caravans can go from Gaza to the Delta in five days, with waterholes along the way. Both the Bible and the Egyptian records attest the practice of Semitic herds entering the Nile Valley for pasturage, when their own lands were dry. From prehistoric times there was a continuous trade in such materials as olive oil and wood. The mines in Sinai used Semitic tribes in their seasonal operations. Particularly after the Egyptian empire was established in Asia, there was a constant interflow of relatively skilled and educated people between the two areas.

Egypt looms large in the Bible. The Lord's deliverance of the Children of Israel from Pharaoh's bondage was a tremendous experience, creating a unity which solidified Hebrew faith and made the Hebrew nation. Before that time there had been the sojourn of Abraham and the service of Joseph in Egypt. After that time there came Solomon's alliance with Pharaoh and the raids and intrigues of the later rulers of Egypt. Jeremiah, after his denunciations of Egypt, had to seek refuge at Tahpanhes (Daphnae) in the Delta. Hebrew and Egyptian scribes had the same respect for traditional wisdom, so that one would expect a constant interchange of ideas and modes of expression.

It is therefore disappointing that the Egyptologist can offer so little specific confirmation of the details in the Bible account. Abraham, Jacob, Joseph, Moses, Aaron, and Jeremiah are absent from the Egyptian records. There is no confirmation that a people called Israel were sojourners or workers in Egypt. Despite ingenious attempts to explain miracles,[1] there is no record of the plagues of Egypt or of a calamity to the Egyptian army in a Sea of Reeds. These elements bulk so large in the Bible that we have a feeling that they must inevitably appear in Egyptian inscriptions. Does it affect our confidence in the Biblical account that events of such sweeping and dramatic importance should be lacking from the Egyptian records?

Below we shall list some general factors which do accord with the account in the Bible. Here we check off some reasons why we should not expect specific corroboration. First, the vast majority of our so-called historical inscriptions from Egypt appears in religious texts carved in stone in temples and tombs; we have very few official reports. Second, what has survived to our day is a very small proportion of what once existed. Third, the Israelite contacts were in the Delta, from which almost nothing of an official character has survived. Fourth, the Egyptians did not normally distinguish specific tribes or peoples among their foreign captives, lumping them all under one or two generalized terms. Fifth and most important, Egyptian records were always positive, emphasizing the successes of the pharaoh or the god, whereas failures and defeats were never mentioned, except in some context of the distant past. All of these are valid reasons why events of importance may have failed to appear in the material which has survived to our day.

The Egyptologist can make many comments on the coloration of the Biblical story. Not all of these comments are helpful. It is possible that Joseph served a Hyksos pharaoh in the seventeenth century, yet the perfectly good Egyptian names in the Joseph story — Potiphar, Potipherah, Asenath, and Zaphenathpaneah — are characteristic of the eleventh century or later. Some of them do not occur before that time. The fact that these names *are* Egyptian — as are the names Moses, Hophni, Phinehas, and the first part of Puti-El — is significant. Similarly, much of the background color of the Joseph story can be matched from Egyptian sources: — seven years of famine,[2] the importance of storehouses, the interpretation of dreams, the death of Joseph at the ideal age of one hundred and ten years, and much more. We are dealing with an authentic memory about an Asiatic prominent in the court of an Egyptian king, but that memory was later filled out with a pious elaboration of detail drawn from later times. The intention of that later coloration was not to deceive but to authenticate.

When we come to the story of the sojourn and the exodus, we see a similar textual construction — elements which are genuinely Egyptian in character, but other factors of embarrassment in details. For example, while seventy of Jacob's people went down into Egypt (Gen. 46:27), something like two million persons seem to have departed in the exodus (Ex. 12:37). So large a number could not have lived in the eastern Delta: when Napoleon went to Egypt in 1798, the population of the entire land of Egypt was estimated at something a little over two million. Even today such a number cannot be accommodated in the eastern Delta. These numbers have received a later pious magnification to accommodate into the tradition all of those who came to be known as Hebrews. It is as if all the present Americans came over in the Mayflower — as, spiritually, they did.

Further, we must recognize that exact numbers are less at home in an emotional setting than large and exciting figures, which may persuade us that we all belong to God's providence. The religious truth of the Bible does not rest on numbers.

It is possible to list an impressive series of contacts and parallels between the Egyptians and the Hebrews. To consider only texts, an Egyptian wisdom book is directly related to a section of the Book of Proverbs;[3] the hymn to the sun disk by Akh-en-Aton is remarkably like the 104th Psalm;[4] the phraseology and images in Egyptian love songs can be paralleled in Canticles;[5] there was an elaborate code for the interpretation of dreams;[6] and so on. These demonstrate that the Hebrews borrowed from or shared with Egypt common interests and common expressions in proverbs, songs, and omens, just as the Hebrews shared with Mesopotamia common elements in myths and laws. It may further be argued that the Hebrews enriched what they borrowed by making it consistently expressive of God's purposes for man. The Egyptian sages wrote separate documents, within a more easy-going psychology and with little ethical force. The Hebrew sages gathered their writings together into a single canon, with a consistent moral and ethical purpose.

After these genuine relations have been recognized, it must be said that the major influence of Egypt upon the Hebrews was negative. Within the relatively poor land of Canaan the Israelites struggled to hold their people together, to achieve unity and common religious purpose. Next door to them lay the famous land of Egypt, rich, powerful, showy, and sophisticated. To a rural and solemnly dedicated people, the urbane and wordly-wise culture of Egypt was both a fascinating lure and a corrupt abomination. The complicated maze of Egyptian gods, richly enthroned inside towering temples, would be abhorrent to a people of more rigid standards, particularly those who had been bondsmen in the land of those gods. This is not to say that the Children of Israel were rural simpletons; they had a logic and finality to their thinking, which the supple-minded Egyptian never achieved. Yet there was something of the attraction and repulsion which a rural man finds in the pitfalls of a great city. There is a great truth to the story of Moses' flight from his Egyptian education and of his revelation in the burning bush. He cast off the borrowed Egyptian coating in favor of something uniquely for his people. Thus Hebrew religion took form as a rejection of the eclectic complexity and empty power which the Israelites felt in the Egyptian religion.

The history of the people who settled in Canaan added to this rejection of Egypt and Egyptianism. Some Semites had been in Egypt among the

Hyksos, had been driven out, and had been followed into Palestine by the army of Pharaoh. Then in the fifteenth century, the Asiatic empire had been conquered by force. For most of three centuries the peoples of Palestine and Syria had been subjected to Egyptian rule. In the Amarna period they tried to break out of this control, which was reasserted by the Nineteenth Dynasty, and it was not until the mid-twelfth century that Palestine was finally freed from Egyptian domination. We today are seeing a hatred of European colonialism, and we can understand how these Asiatics must have felt about the Egyptians.

There were also real Egyptian bondages. Tens of thousands of Asiatics were carried into the land of the Nile, there to be in some kind of slavery. A few of them were relatively privileged, as household servants in the kitchen, the butler's pantry, or the weaving rooms.[7] Most of them were subjected to heavy labor, in quarries or on major building projects. They had a reason to hate Egypt.

Whether they lived in the land of Canaan or had sojourned in Egypt, practically all of those who formed the Hebrew people had experienced some resentment against the land of the pharaohs. Thus the message that the God of the Children of Israel had defeated the powerful Egyptian gods, had outwitted Pharaoh, had released Asiatic slaves and brought them safely through the wilderness to Canaan served as a rallying call for the people in and around Palestine. A god who had smitten the Egyptians, but who had passed over the Children of Israel was a god deserving the devotion of all men who resented Egypt and wanted a protector god of their own. In this negative way, Egypt was the major binding force for those who formed the Hebrew people.

After they had won their independence and achieved national status, they could deal with the Egyptians in wary diplomatic terms, as one sovereign people with another. Solomon might wed the daughter of a Delta pharaoh. The kings of Judah might intrigue with the later pharaohs against the threats from Mesopotamia. Cultural exchange might then be recognized. Hymns which saluted the power or the mercy of divine beings might be used for Amon or for Yahweh, just as the same architectural elements might be used in each country. These were only forms of expression. A Palestinian temple was essentially different from an Egyptian temple, even though each might use columns with the same floral capitals. The essential being of Yahweh was different from the essential being of Amon, even though each might use the same expressions in hymns. Such common factors may be listed with appreciation. Yet the glory of the God of Israel remained in the fact that He had delivered His people out of the land of Egypt.

EPILOGUE

by E. A. Speiser

THE VOLUME just concluded has dealt with the ancient Near East as a background for the Biblical experience. Several of the books to follow will concentrate on the principal facts and aspects of Biblical history itself. The prelude should foreshadow some of the sequel: To what extent was this background normative? What threats and what promises did it hold for the future? Were the threats overcome and the promises fulfilled?

It is plain enough in retrospect that the Bible as a whole originated and was sustained as history, though not history in the ordinary sense of the term. The aim of its writers and compilers was not primarily to give a chronicle of events in the lives of outstanding individuals, a history of a state or group of states, or even a biography of a particular nation. The reader who might be interested in such things is told time and again where he can find them: in the Book of the Wars of the Lord, the Book of Jashar, the Chronicles of the Kings of Israel, or the Chronicles of the Kings of Judah. The central theme of the Bible is something very different. It is the history of a society embarked on a special quest, the quest for an enduring way of life, a way of life possessing universal validity. Everything else is subordinated to and co-ordinated with that single dominant theme. The Bible is thus essentially the record of a unique experience of mankind.

That experience, however, neither occurred nor continued in a vacuum. The people of the Bible, throughout the long span that this work covers, were an integral part of a pioneering, dynamic, and enormously sophisticated region which we now call the ancient Near East. It is only by starting with that common background that we can discover, evaluate, and understand the difference between the message embodied in the Scriptures and the joint testimony of other contemporary records, the basic difference between the enduring and so much that was to prove ephemeral.

Both Mesopotamia and Egypt, the two senior partners of Israel in the regional enterprise of the ancient Near East, had their own distinctive ways of life. Each of these was achieved by a great and self-sufficient civilization. Each served its followers well, since the pertinent civilizations flourished simultaneously over a period that covers one half of the total recorded history of mankind. Historic Israel could not but be aware of the impact of Egypt and Mesopotamia, culturally no less than politically. But what of proto-historic Israel, the inchoate and amorphous group on its way to evolving into a nation?

On this last point, the Bible itself provides us with a substantial body of evidence. It is stated explicitly and repeatedly that the original home of the Patriarchs was in Mesopotamia, and this attribution is now abundantly corroborated by local Mesopotamian sources. There is scarcely a cultural detail in the patriarchal narratives in Genesis that has not been confirmed and elucidated by numberless documents from Babylonia, Mari, Nuzi, Alalakh, and elsewhere. Nor is this all. The history of the Patriarchs is introduced in the Bible by a section on Primeval History (Gen. 1-11). Virtually every episode in that long-familiar section about the childhood of mankind can be correlated today with rich cuneiform source material. At an earlier stage of Assyriological studies this relationship could be viewed as an indication of wholesale and unacknowledged dependence of the Bible on Mesopotamia. Indeed, the "Babel-and-Bible" school of interpretation went so far as to brand this tie as a case of outright infringement, in that Mesopotamian copyright had been flagrantly violated. Further study has placed that verdict in its proper perspective: it was hasty and vitiated by half-truths. To be sure, the connections between Mesopotamian material and the early chapters of Genesis are more intimate and numerous than even the pan-Babylonian interpreters supposed, and the basic content is indeed Mesopotamian. Yet this is precisely what the Biblical record itself would lead one to expect. If Abraham migrated from across the Euphrates, and his group had not started out with a total cultural blank, the pre-Israelite traditions of the Bible should abound in Mesopotamian detail. It is the very presence of such detail that bears out its authenticity. Any other result would be cause for suspicion.

More significant still is the fact that, although Mesopotamian material is prominent in the pre-patriarchal and patriarchal narratives of the Bible, that material was not incorporated mechanically. Most of it shows traces of unconscious or deliberate criticism. The account of Creation in the Bible is a majestic reflection of a monotheistic regime of the universe. The rivers of Eden can all be located in Mesopotamia, where they belong, but Paradise itself is no longer the domain of countless competing gods. The Flood has a distinct moral motivation, unlike its Sumerian and Babylonian prototypes. And the story of the Tower of Babel, while expressly Babylonian in its stated locale, is a severe indictment of Mesopotamian beliefs and practices. It is this critical attitude towards concepts which are admittedly and demonstrably Mesopotamian that is the real key to the very origin of the Biblical process. That process was in its inception a protest against a way of life which the Patriarchs had every reason to know well. The rest of it was taken up with a search for positive values.

In the light of these facts, the beginning of the patriarchal narrative, which also marks the actual start of the Biblical process, assumes extraordinary significance. It takes up, with seeming abruptness, Abraham's departure from Mesopotamia for a destination and on a mission that will be disclosed in due time (Gen. 12). The purpose soon proves to be spiritual and is always remembered as such (Josh. 24); and the mission is duly solemnized by God's covenant with Abraham. The destination, accordingly, becomes the Promised Land. The terms in which the call is announced leave no room for doubt that to the narrator, and his tradition, this was a turning point in the life of the Patriarch, a genuine experience and not just a pious invention or a fanciful literary elaboration. As such, it was honored by a long line of later Biblical writers, all of whom saw in God's covenant with Abraham the real foundation of the spiritual history of Israel. The covenant with Abraham becomes thus one of two dominant notes that the Bible is to feature as recurrent refrains. It is the key event that set the Biblical process in motion.

How does Abraham's migration from Mesopotamia, which the Bible immediately shows to be the heart of the matter, accord with the independent facts of the cultural history of Mesopotamia? It was pointed out earlier in this book that the country which Abraham was thus bidden to leave had achieved prodigious social gains alongside an ever-growing spiritual deficit. The societal solution which Mesopotamia had evolved was to influence many other lands, Israel included. In matters of law and government in particular, Israel was an apt and faithful, if not always conscious, disciple of Mesopotamian civilization. But the concurrent religious beliefs and practices of the Land between the Rivers lacked similar appeal. Israel, for one, rejected them outright. Now this rejection was natural enough in the prophetic age. For by then Israel's course had long been set, and the spiritual content of Mesopotamia could be appraised on the evidence of uncounted centuries. But there could be little hindsight in Abraham's drastic move. In his day most of Mesopotamia's history still lay ahead. Abraham's appraisal had to be made in terms of contemporary facts, and of long-range prospects. Yet the stated reasons for the Patriarch's journey to the Promised Land agree so closely with religious conditions in Mesopotamia during the patriarchal period — conditions that we have begun to understand only recently — as to rule out mere coincidence. For tradition, it should be recalled, ascribed the move to a need for a healthier religious climate. Had Abraham or tradition tried to invent an excuse for the fateful journey to the Promised Land, neither could have improvised a motive that fitted the actual facts half as well. The migration was a resolute protest. For all her notable social strides, Mesopotamia was to the Patriarchs a good place to leave behind. The protest could have been aimed only at the spiritual content of the native civilization. And without such a protest the Biblical process could not have commenced.

Arrival in Canaan brought the Patriarchs into contact with the world view of the Egyptians. Now if the Mesopotamian way, with its congenial features of government and society, was to Israel's forefathers an urgent reason for departure, then the Egyptian way, with its deified king and unrelieved totalitarianism, could scarcely be viewed as anything short of abomination. For the seed that had been planted by Abraham had not been left untended. There was time for it to strike root in the course of the intervening centuries. The original motivating ideal now had a cherished tradition behind it. It also had a worthy spokesman to reaffirm it. Just as the protest against Mesopotamia had been spearheaded by a native of that country, someone who could speak from direct experience, so too the implacable opposition to Egypt came from a native of the pharaonic land. In fact, who could have better reason to rebel against the divine pretensions of the royal house of Egypt than a man who had been brought up as a member of the royal household? In this respect, tradition gains much in credibility in its account of Moses' youth. In any case, the aspect of Moses that history permits us to reconstruct with maximum safety is not so much that of legislator or religious leader as that of liberator, but a liberator from much more than mere physical oppression. For the exodus from Egypt was above all an act of liberation from intolerable spiritual bondage imposed by the Egyptian way of life. Small wonder, therefore, that the remembrance of the Egyptian horror was to become the other dominant note in all Biblical history. Only an indelible spiritual experience could have left so deep an imprint on the whole national consciousness.

Migration under Abraham emerges thus as the answer of Israel's founders to the religious solution of Mesopotamia, and liberation under Moses marks Israel's rejection of the Egyptian world view. These are two acts of resolute defiance of the ruling civilizations of that age, far-sighted moves to be commemorated ever after by unceasing reference to the Covenant and the Exodus. Together they constitute Israel's declaration of spiritual independence and the true foundation of the Biblical experience.

Time was to vindicate eventually the judgment and the faith of the leaders who saw beyond the great positive contributions of Egypt and Mesopotamia. For in turning against its two major neighbors, Biblical society focused unerringly on their main underlying weaknesses. The ultimate collapse of Egypt was surely conditioned by that country's monolithic way of life. And the crushing weight of the religious structure of Mesopotamia was to become one of the decisive factors in the downfall of its distinctive civilization. It should be stressed, however, that the end came in each instance after millenniums of pioneering historic achievement, preceded by immemorial centuries of proto-historic effort. Thanks to our vastly increased knowledge of the ancient Near East, which this volume has attempted to summarize, we know now how much Israel had learned from both Egypt and Mesopotamia. If it had not been for their prior labors, Israel might not have fared so well in going on from where they left off, or in starting afresh where they had failed. The very strides that had been made in material, societal, and intellectual fields helped to emphasize the existing spiritual vacuum. The mission that Israel took on was to counteract that vacuum. Once accepted, this mission was pursued with unparalleled dedication and single-mindedness of purpose. The all but universal acceptance of the results is a true measure of the success attained. How these results were accomplished is the central theme of the volumes that follow.

NOTES AND BIBLIOGRAPHY

PART ONE: THE ENVIRONMENTAL FACTOR

THE LAND OF ISRAEL

MORPHOLOGY

1 Num. 34:3–13; Josh. 12:1–6.
2 Isa. 65:10.
3 I Chron. 27:29; Menahot 87, a.
4 Ex. 13:17.
5 Jeraq in Arabic. Meron is the modern name; the ancient Hebrew name is unknown.
6 Hazur in Arabic.
7 Known for its recently discovered ruins and burial caves.
8 II Sam. 1:21.
9 II Kings 9:27.
10 Mishnah: Rosh ha-Shanah II, 4.
11 The city Adam. Josh. 3:16.
12 II Kings 17:5.
13 II Sam. 13:23.
14 Josh. 17:15.
15 Jud. 4:5.
16 I Sam 1:1.
17 "The mountains are round about Jerusalem." Ps. 125:2.
18 II Chron. 20:26.
19 Gen. 37:14.
20 Josh. 11:16.
21 This type of cave is called "Harabbah" in Arabic.
22 Ps. 42:7.
23 Gen. 13:10.
24 Jer. 49:19; 50:44.
25 In the map of Medeba a ship sailing the Dead Sea is shown.
26 Ps. 68:16, 23.
27 Deut. 3:10.
28 This sandstone, known as the Nubian sandstone, is an aquifer.
29 II Sam. 18:8.
30 Isa. 15 and 16; Heshbon, Medeba, Elealeh and Nebo which had been within Israel are here included in Moab.
31 Ps. 83:8.
32 Jer. 49:16; Ob. 3–4.

GEOLOGY

Bibliography

Avnimelech, M.: "Etudes geologiques dans la region de la Shephelah en Palestine," 1936, *Travaux Lab. Geot. Univ. Grenoble*; "Decline's of Palestine's countryside," *Palestine and Middle-East*, vol. XVII, 1945; *Tzefunoth sal'e artzenu* (The Secrets of our Rocks), Israel, 1948; "Contribution to the Knowledge of the Quaternary Oscillations of the Shoreline in Palestine," *Atti I-o Congr. Intern. Preistoria e Protostoria Mediterrana*, 1950, (1952); "Late Quaternary Sediments of the Coastal Plain of Israel," *Bull. Res. Counc. Israel*, II (1952), No. 1; "The Influence of the Geology of Jerusalem on its Development" (in Hebrew with English summary), Judah and Jerusalem, The Twelfth Archaeological Convention, Jerusalem, 1957, 129–136.

Ball, M. W. & D., "Oil Prospects of Israel," *Bull. Amer. Ass. Petrol. Geol.*, 37 (1953), No. 1.

Bentor, Y. & Vroman, A., *Ha-mapa ha-geologit shel ha-Negev*, 1951.

Blake, G. S., *The Stratigraphy of Palestine and its Building Stones*, Jerusalem, 1935.

Blanckenhorn, M.: "Syrien in seiner geologischen Vergangenheit," *Bericht d. Ver. Naturkunde zu Cassel*, 1891; "Syrien, Arabien und Mesopotamien," *Hdb. Regionalen Geol.*, 5 (1914), No. 4.

Hull, E., "Memoir on the Geology and Geography of Arabia Petraea, Palestine and Adjoining Countries, *Survey of Western Palestine Palest. Expl. F.*, 1889.
Lartet, L., "Essai sur la géologie de la Palestine et des contrees avoisinantes," *Ann. sc. geol.*, 1869–1871.
Picard, L.: "Structure and Evolution of Palestine with comparative notes on neighbouring countries," *Bull. Geol. Dept., Hebr. Univ.*, 4 (1943), No. 2–4; "The Structural Pattern of Palestine" (Israel and Jordan), *Intern. Geol. Congr., Alger.*, 1952, fasc. 14, sect. 13; "History of Mineral Research in Israel," *Israel Economic Forum*, 6 (1955), No. 3.

FAUNA

1 O. Abel, *Lebensbilder der Tierwelt der Vorzeit*, Jena, 1922, 75–160, F. S. Bodenheimer, *Ha-Ḥai be-Arẓoth ha-Miqra* (abbreviated below as *H.A.M.*), I, Jerusalem, 1951, 26–35.

2 D.M.A. Bate, *The Stone Age of Mount Carmel*, I, Oxford, 1937, 139–233.

3 C.R. Conder, *Palestine*, 2nd ed., London, 1891, 216.

4 N. Glueck, *The River Jordan*, Philadelphia, 1946, 5–11.

5 F. S. Bodenheimer, *H.A.M.*, II, Jerusalem, 1956, 328–392.

6 R. A. S. Macalister, *The Excavations of Gezer*, I, London, 1911.

6a. D. M. A. Bate, in P. L. O. Guy, *Megiddo Tombs*, Univ. Chicago Press, 1938, 209–210.

7 St. Willibald, *The Hodoeponion of Saint Willibald*, Pilgrims Text Soc., III, London, 1891.

8 Seligmann.

9 Steier, "Pferd," in: *Pauly Realencyclopaedie der klassischen Altertumswissenschaften*, 38. Halband, Stuttgart, 1938, 1430 f.

10 H. Rothert, *Transjordanien: Vorgeschichtliche Forschungen*, 1938.

11 W. F. Albright, *From the Stone Age to Christianity*, Baltimore, 1940, 196. Cf. also, J. P. Free, "Abraham's Camels," *JNES*, 3 (1944), 187–193. F. S. Bodenheimer, *H. A. M.*, Jerusalem, I, 1951, 58–60, II, 1956 339–347.

12 F. S. Bodenheimer, *H. A. M.*, I, Jerusalem, 1951, 334 f.

13 A. Reifenberg, *Ancient Hebrew Seals*, London, 1950, 28 and 36.

14 F. S. Bodenheimer, "Barburim Avussim," *Leshonenu*, 1947, 45–46.

15 F. S. Bodenheimer, in *Ergebnisse der Sinai-Expedition* (1927) *der Hebr. Univ.*, Leipzig, 1929, 45–88.

16 Mukaddasi, *Description of Syria, incl. Palestine*, Pilgrim's Text Soc., III, London, 1886.

17 E. Speiser, "One Hundred New Selected Nuzi Texts," *AASOR*, XVI (1935), Note to no. 77.

R. Pfister and L. Bellinger, "The Textiles," in *The Excavations of Dura-Europos*, Final Report IV, 2. New Haven, 1945.

F. S. Bodenheimer, *H.A.M.*, II, Jerusalem, 1956, 305–310.

18 E. A. Speiser, *Language*, 12 (1936), 121–26.

19 F. S. Bodenheimer, *H.A.M.*, II, Jerusalem, 1956, 310–313.

20 F. S. Bodenheimer, *H.A.M.*, II, Jerusalem, 1956, 313–316.

21 F. S. Bodenheimer, *Animal Life in Palestine*, Jerusalem, 1935, 16–28.

F. S. Bodenheimer, *Ha-Ḥai be-Ereẓ Yisrael*, Tel Aviv, 1953, 73–93.

PREHISTORY

1 B.P. — "before the present."

2 See Cesare Emiliani, *Scientific American*, Feb., 1958, 54–63, with full correlations.

3 In 1961 two University of California physicists, G. H. Curtis and J. A. Evernden, announced that they had succeeded in dating the Australopithecine Zinjanthropus discovered by L. S. B. Leakey in East Africa two years before, about 1,750,000 B.P. (see the joint paper in *Nature*, 191, p. 478, and for a popular account see *National Geographic*, October, 1961, pp. 564–589 and 590–592). Since paleontologists agree in dating the fauna of the Zinjanthropus deposit in or about Upper Villafranchian, before the first Pleistocene glaciation, this potassium-argon dating conflicts directly with the Emiliani correlation. Some geologists are very skeptical about such a precise date, since potassium-argon is being used to date rock deposits a billion years old. Since its half-life is about 1,300,000,000 years, the statistical uncertainty of dating becomes very high when only the past few million years are involved. As a matter of fact, the potassium-argon ratio was later applied to the basalt bed *under* the remains of Zinjanthropus and a much shorter lapse of time, about 1,300,000 B.P., was found (G. H. R. von Königswald, W. Gentner, H. J. Lippolt, *Nature*, 192, p. 720; cf. W. L. Straus and C.B. Hunt, *Science*, 136 [1962], pp. 293 ff.). Under the circumstances it will be necessary to await further light. Nothing, however, can alter the established fact that the lapse of time since the end of the last glaciation was estimated by most Pleistocene geologists at twice the true figure before radiocarbon settled the question once for all. We must remember that American geologists estimated the end of the Wisconsin (Würm) glaciation at about 25,000 years ago, as recently as 1950, whereas it is now fixed about 11,000 B.P. Dating by enriched carbon has reduced the *floruit* of Neanderthal man in Palestine from 150,000-120,000 B.P. to 50,000–40,000 B.P. Furthermore, the Emiliani correlation on the basis of de Vries' date after 70,000 B.P. for the end of the Riss-Würm interglacial, yields a duration of about 50,000 years (in no case more than about 60,000) for the Würm glaciation, which agrees extraordinarily well with G. S. Blake's generally overlooked estimate of 50,000 years for the time required to deposit the three stages of the Lisan Terrace just south of Jericho. This result is based on the fact that the alternating varves (laminations) of the 400 feet of deposit in three stages can easily be counted (Blake, *Geology and Water Resources of Palestine*, Jerusalem, 1928, pp. 24 f.), though the figure may have to be raised somewhat. In the face of such observations, the proposal of the Lamont Laboratory of Columbia University to stretch the glacial part of the Pleistocene back over 800,000 years with the aid of ocean bottom cores (*Science*, 22 Feb., 1963, 727 ff.; *Scientific American*, January, 1963), does appear premature. *Dies diem docet!*

4 In the light of what is said in note 3, it may be that the Australopithecines of East Africa are to be dated well under a million years ago. In the present welter of chronological opinion, this view remains quite possible. If the Urey-Emiliani system is proved to be wrong in principle, the date may be earlier. Sooner or later we may expect evidence of vital significance from the northern valley of the Jordan, as shown by the work begun near Ubeidiya, south of Lake Kinnereth. Here, in a clear Villafranchian context, were discovered (1959) fragments of human fossils, including an incisor tooth and two small but remarkably thick bits of human cranial bone. On the whole picture see M. Stekelis, L. Picard, N. Schulman and G. Haas, "Villafrancian Deposits near Ubeidiya in the Central Jordan Valley (Preliminary Report)" in *The Bulletin of the Research Council of Israel*, Vol. 9G, No. 4 (1960), and Emmanuel Anati, *Palestine before the Hebrews*, 1963, 59 ff. I wish to thank Drs. G. Haas and L. Picard for several very informative

letters on the subject (particularly G. Haas on 23 October, 1962, and L. Picard on 12 December, 1962 and 31 January, 1963).

5 It may well be that the "pebble" culture claimed by Leakey in East Africa and by Stekelis in the Jordan Valley is to be retained, but when one recalls the story of Rutot's eoliths in Belgium and of Reid Moir's rostrocarinates in England, one hesitates to accept it until there is more and better evidence. At best the Australopithecines seem only to have struck flints of suitable shape and size together to obtain cutting edges. Raymond Dart's "osteodontokeratic" culture, making "tools" out of horns and bones, is much better established for the Australopithecines of South Africa (Dart, *Adventures with the Missing Link*, New York, 1959).

6 For the most recent survey of the fossil man situation see W.E. Le Gros Clark on "The Crucial Evidence for Human Evolution" in *Proceedings of the American Philosophical Society*, 103 (1959), 159–172. It should be remembered that Clark has not yet been influenced appreciably either by the genetic point of view of such men as Theodosius Dobzhansky or by the drastic lowering of dates which is following use of carbon and oxygen isotopes in dating the Pleistocene.

7 See Howell in *Proceedings of the American Philosophical Society*, 103 (1959), p. 20. But the lapse of time involved is probably too small to warrant any evolutionary inferences.

8 See their joint paper on "Pathology and the Posture of Neanderthal Man," in *Quarterly Review of Biology*, 32 (1957), 348–363. Dr. Cave announced some further observations along the same lines at the International Congress of Zoology which met in London, July, 1958.

9 See especially Leo Picard, *Structure and Evolution of Palestine*, 1943, 104 ff.

10 *Op. cit.* (note 4), p. 15.

11 *Op. cit.*, 15 ff.

12 *Op. cit.*, 18–24.

13 See the convenient discussion by E. Anati, *Palestine before the Hebrews*, 1963, 89–99.

14 Stewart and Solecki, *Year Book of the American Philosophical Society, 1958* (Philadelphia, 1959), 274–278 and 403–407, with references to previous publications.

15 For the contemporary development of Upper Palaeolithic in Eastern Mesopotamia and Iran see the 1963 article by Ralph Solecki referred to above. He dates the beginning of the earliest culture of this age (the Baradostian) about 36,000 B.P. (34,000 B.C.E.).

16 See F. C. Howell, *op. cit.*, 24 ff.

17 For the latest information about these phases of the Epipalaeolithic see especially Anati, *Palestine before the Hebrews*, 1963, 119 ff., and Solecki (1963).

18 See *Antiquity and Survival*, II (1957), 91–110.

19 See *Antiquity*, XXXIII (1959), 7 f.

20 For subsequent work at 'Enan see J. Perrot, *IEJ*, 10 (1960), 14-22, and E. Anati, *Palestine before the Hebrews*, *passim* (see his index). No detailed report on the results of M. Stekelis' excavations at Naḥal Oren, which has also yielded a Mesolithic village, have yet been published; see Anati, *op. cit.*, *passim* (as indexed) for his chief results.

21 See K. Kenyon, *Archaeology in the Holy Land*, 1960, 42 f.

22 The sensational discoveries of James Mellaart at Hacilar and Çatal Hüyük in southwestern Anatolia (since 1959) have demonstrated the existence of a flourished pre-ceramic culture closely resembling that of Jericho in essential respects, but richer. Chronologically the two cultures seem to be quite parallel; the Anatolian culture antedates the middle of the sixth millennium, as shown by radiocarbon counts.

23 Kathleen Kenyon, *Digging Up Jericho*, 1957, p. 84, prefers to date these statuettes in the period of Jericho IX, but the resemblances in technique between them and the plastered heads cannot be dismissed lightly. Jericho IX possessed an entirely different culture.

24 The same kind of treatment of skull of the deceased has been found by J. Mellaart to be true of Hacilar; it has also been found in the interior of New Guinea

Even in the eastern Pacific, the excavations of Robert C. Suggs in the Marquesas have yielded comparable preservation of skulls in family shrines, dating between ca. 500 and 1000 C.E. (Suggs, *The Hidden Worlds of Polynesia*, 1962, p. 93).

25 See W. F. Albright, *The Archaeology of Palestine*, 1949, p. 66 and cf. J. Kaplan, *IEJ*, 8 (1958), 160, note 24, where further references will be found.

26 *IEJ*, 1 (1950–51), 1–19 and folding chart.

27 See *BASOR*, 48 (1932), 10–13, where the writer's sketch of Chalcolithic chronology is substantially correct throughout, requiring only expansion to bring it up to date.

28 See J. Kaplan, *BASOR*, 159 (1960), 32–36, and No. 162, p. 21. For a general survey of the Chalcolithic cultures of Palestine see E. Anati, *Palestine before the Hebrews*, 1963, 285 ff.

29 See especially Jean Perrot, *IEJ*, 5 (1955), pp. 17 ff., 73 ff., 167 ff., and M. Dothan, *ibid.*, 6 (1956), 112 ff.

30 *The Pottery of Palestine from the Earliest Times to the End of the Early Bronze Age*, 1937, 32 ff.

31 These dates follow the minimal Egyptian chronology, originally proposed by the writer and now accepted by most German scholars, which places Menes and the beginning of the First Dynasty about 2850–2800 B.C.E. If the date must be raised, all comparable Palestinian dates must also be raised.

32 See Kathleen Kenyon, *op. cit.*, (note 14), 95 ff. and pl. 34 on p. 136.

33 On the still unpublished Ma'adeh material see provisionally the writer's *Archaeology of Palestine*, p. 70.

THE LANDS TO THE NORTH

SYRIA

1 According to Xenophon, the boundaries of Syria extended east of the Euphrates until its tributary, the Habor River, which signifies that *Aram* must have been included in Syria. The Talmudic definition of Syria is the land outside of Israel which was conquered by David, a "private conquest" which enjoyed none of the sanctity of the soil of the Holy Land. Rabbinical authorities imposed some of the religious obligations applicable to the Holy Land also upon residents of Syria, but these obligations were considered controversial and, practically speaking, from early Medieval times onward no differentiation whatsoever was made between Syria and the other Gentile lands. An extreme opinion is expressed in the Mishnah (*Ḥallah IV*,11): "He that owns [land] in Syria is as one that owns [land] in the outskirts of Jerusalem."

2 The name Syria is a Greek misnomer for Assyria which is the *Asshur* of the Bible. Herodotus relates that Συροι (the Syrians) is the name which the Barbarians call 'Ασσυροι. The Septuagint and also Josephus locate Aram in Syria; Strabo and Poseidonius identify *Aram* with Syria.

3 The "promise" of the land is mentioned for the first time in Gen. 15:18, where it refers to the territory from the River of Egypt, i. e., the Pelusiac branch of the Nile (to the east of the present Suez Canal) which had already dried up even in ancient days, up to the south-eastern bend of the Euphrates near Tapascus (the Biblical Tiphsah). According to Talmudic tradition, the Promised Land extended to Taurus Amanus in the north-west. The actual expression "The Promised Land" is found neither in the Old Testament nor in the Talmudic Literature. It appears for the first time in Greek, in the writings of Paul (Hebrews 11:9).

4 Hos. 14:7; Cant. 5:15; Isa. 60:13; Ps. 29:5.

MESOPOTAMIA

1 Gen. 8:4; II Kings 19:37.

2 Deut. 11: 24.

3 II Kings 17:6; 18:11.

4 II Kings 19:12; Isa. 37:12.

5 Gen. 29:2.

6 Ezek. 1:1; Ezra 8:21.

7 Isa. 14:23.

8 G.M. Lees and N. L. Falcon, "The Geological History of the Mesopotamian Plains," *Geographical Journal*, 118 (March, 1952), 24—39.

9 Dan. 8:2.

10 Gen. 14:1—5.

THE REGIONAL ENVIRONMENT

1 This theme will be developed in Part III A, "Mesopotamia."

PART TWO: THE ETHNO-LINGUISTIC FACTOR

LINGUISTIC DATA

SEMITICS

1 Cf. Pinchos Wechter, "Ibn Barun's [ca. 1100] Contribution to Hebrew Philology," *JAOS*, 61 (1941), 172-87.

2 Cf. Theodor Benfey, *Geschichte der Sprachwissenschaft und orientalischen Philologie in Deutschland*, Munich, 1869.

3 Edmund Castellus' admirable *Lexicon heptaglotton* (London, 1669–1686) was a companion volume to the London Polyglot. The Syriac part of it was reprinted by Joh. David Michaelis (Goettingen, 1788) and was still used within living memory. The Hebrew part, likewise reprinted by Michaelis (1790; Steinschneider, *Bibliogr. Handbuch*, no. 368/3) was highly esteemed at the time, but was, of course, superseded by Gesenius. On Michaelis (1717–91) cf. R. Smend, *Johann David Michaelis* (Festrede... zur akadem. Preisvertheilung, Goettingen, 1898).

4 *The Book of Jonah in four Oriental Versions, namely Chaldee, Syriac, Aethiopic* [*sic*] *and Arabic*, London, 1857. Wright's Arabic text is not from the Polyglot.

5 In point of fact it is much to be regretted that the comparative study of Semitic Bible versions has entirely gone out of fashion. It is eminently useful, as a linguistic rather than as a theological pursuit, less for the reasons given by Wright than as a means of acquiring familiarity with the differences among the Semitic languages, esp. as regards syntax and idiom.

6 Hebrew had no part in the development of Oriental studies in France during the 19th century: Mayer Lambert, in *Le Livre du Centenaire de la Société asiatique* (1822–1922), Paris, 1922, 105–6.

7 G. Hoffmann, *Syrisch-arabische Glossen*, I, Kiel, 1874, VII.

8 Cf. I. Y. Kratchkovsky, "A Martyr for Arabic Literature," *Among Arabic Manuscripts*, tr. T. Minorsky (Leiden, 1953), 163-9; in the Russian original, 3rd ed., (1948), 166–71. Michaelis was one of Reiske's persecutors: Smend (quoted in note 3), 12–3.

9 For a Turkologist's view on the detrimental effect of this set-up upon Turkish studies see J. Benzing, *Einführung in das Studium der altaischen Philologie und der Turkologie*, Wiesbaden, 1953, 6,7,64, etc.

10 A. Baumstark, *Oriens Christianus*, 4 (1904), 208–9.

11 A. Goetze, *Language*, 17 (1941), 136–8.

12 "Ya'udic" is described as an "independent language" by Joh. Friedrich in an appendix to his *Phoenizisch-punische Grammatik* (*AnOr* 32, Rome, 1952), 153–62; cf. F. Rosenthal, *JAOS*, 72 (1952), 172. It follows from our general preference for the "multilingual" approach that we are, on principle, willing rather to put up with "Ya'udic" than with "Old Aramaic with a strong admixture of Phoenician." On the vocalization of Y-'-d-y see B. Landsberger, *Sam'al*, 22, n. 42. Cf. now S. Moscati, *Studi Orientalistici in onore di G. Levi della Vida*, II, Rome, 1956, 206–8.

13 Uniate Jacobites are called "Syrians," and Uniate Nestorians "Chaldaeans."

14 The teaching of Nestorius was condemned at the Council of Ephesus in 431. The Jacob or James after whom the Monophysite Jacobites are called died in 578.

15 The "Assyrian" community of Jerusalem belongs to this group.

16 Practically all Aramaic-speaking ("Kurdish") Jews are now in Israel, where their dialects can be studied at leisure. Although Christian communities still exist in several towns and villages, there seems to be a widespread urge to emigrate. On the Chaldaeans of Tellkef cf. Desmond Stewart, "The New Babylon": I, *The Twentieth Century*, October, 1955, 324–35; "their promised land is Detroit, a section of which is now called New Tal Kayf."

17 F. Rosenthal, *Die aramäistische Forschung*, Leiden, 1939, 104–5, calls this type of Aramaic "Jungaramäisch," not "Westaramäisch," so as to convey that the opposite is rather Old than East Aramaic.

18 Cf. Johann Fück, *Arabiya, Untersuchungen zur arabischen Sprach-und Stilgeschichte* (Abhandl. Sächs. Akad., Philol. -hist.Kl., 45/1), Berlin, 1950. An important review by A. Spitaler, *BiOr*, 10 (1953), 144–50; also J. Cantineau, *BSL*, 48 (1952), *110–3.

19 The only historical and comparative, as well as descriptive, grammar of any modern Arabic dialect is still Wilh. Spitta's (1853–83) *Grammatik des arabischen Vulgärdialektes von Aegypten*, Leipzig, 1880 (an interesting, if not always strictly relevant, review by Ign. Goldziher, *ZDMG*, 35 [1881], 514–29). Nowadays Arabic dialects are mostly used for experiments in descriptive techniques.

20 C. Rabin, *Ancient West-Arabian*, London, 1951. Cf. J. Cantineau, *BSL*, 48 (1952), *119–24; E. Littmann, *Orientalia*, 21 (1952), 386–92; F. Rosenthal, *JAOS*, 72 (1952), 173–4.

21 For the older bibliography cf. F. Hommel, *Süd-arabische Chrestomathie*, Munich, 1893. Maria Höfner, *Altsüdarabische Grammatik*, Leipzig, 1943, is authoritative, but relies too one-sidedly upon Classical Arabic, and the glottogonic and "psycholinguistic" digressions will irritate many readers.

22 Cf. Wolf Leslau, *Modern South Arabic Languages*. A bibliography, *Bulletin of the New York Public Library*, August, 1946, 3-29. Two important recent works are W. Leslau, *Lexique soqotri* (Collection linguistique p.p. la Société de Linguistique de Paris, vol. 41), Paris, 1938; Ewald Wagner, *Syntax der Mehri-Sprache* (Deutsche Akademie der Wissenschaften zu Berlin, Institut für Orientforschung, Veröff. Nr. 13), Berlin, 1953.

23 This is an instance of the remarkable vitality of grammars by pupils of Heinrich Ewald (1803–75). On this great scholar cf. Julius Wellhausen's article in the *Festschrift zur Feier des hundertfünfzigjährigen Bestehens der Kgl. Gesellschaft der Wissenschaften zu Göttingen* (Berlin, 1901), 63–81; cf. also Rubens Duval, *Journal asiatique*, 1905, I, 366–8.

24 Nöldeke is the outstanding instance of that curious phenomenon, "the unmistakeable gift of the Low Saxon race for Oriental studies," cf. Jacob Wackernagel, *Kleine Schriften*, 514.

25 W. Porzig, *Die Gliederung des indogermanischen Sprachgebiets*, Heidelberg, 1954; Cf. A. Martinet, *Word*, 11 (1955), 126–32.

26 Or South-"East"? W. Leslau's article in *JAOS*, 63 (1943), 1–14, is called "South-East Semitic (Ethiopic and South-Arabic)," but the running title is "South-West Semitic" (thus also p. 7, n. 17).

27 The last attempt known to the writer is J. Kurylowicz, "Le système verbal du sémitique," *BSL*, 45 (1949), 47–56.

28 Berber (Kabyle) *ifərrən* "he chooses" as against *yəfrən* "he chose" was compared with Akkadian *isakkan* as against *iskun* as early as 1882 by Francis William (brother of John Henry, Cardinal) Newman, *Libyan Vocabulary* (London, 1882), 33; he also expressly rejected Hanoteau's term "idée (forme) d'habitude" for "the present Tense." For the doubling in *isakkan* he was indebted to A.H. Sayce, on whom cf. J.H. Greenberg, *JAOS*, 72 (1952), 2 with n.5.

29 *BiOr*, 10 (1953), 89–90. A sceptical attitude is also taken by A. Klingenheben, "Die Praefix- und die Suffixkonjugationen des Hamitosemitischen," *Mitteilungen des Instituts für Orientforschung*, 4 (1956), 211–77, and by F. Rundgren, *Ueber Bildungen mit š- und n̠-t̠-Demonstrativer im Semitischen*, Uppsala, 1955, 320 ff.

AKKADIAN

[1] The standard work on Akkadian linguistics is W. von Soden, *Grundriss der Akkadischen Grammatik*, 1952.

[2] This is the traditional historical form of the name. But the early orthography was not distinctive as to voice, so that written *g* could also represent spoken *k*.

[3] See below, Part III, A, 250–255.

[4] Probably *Warūm*, cf. T. Jacobsen, *Oriental Institute Communications*, 13 (1932), 43 f.

[5] Cf. below, Part III, A, 250–255.

[6] The language itself was, of course, spoken — and written — before that date; it was, moreover, the source of a number of loanwords in Sumerian.

[7] The same is true of the corresponding pl. forms.

[8] See G. Bergsträsser, *Einführung in die semitischen Sprachen*, 1928, 8.

[9] Speiser, "Studies in Semitic Formatives," *JAOS*, 56 (1936), 22 ff. Ugaritic represents a special case, cf. *id.*, *JCS*, 6 (1952), 81, n. 4. For the situation in Aramaic see below.

[10] Thus Akk. *yā-ši(m)* "to me," Agau *yi-š*; Akk. *yā-ti* "me," Agau *ye/i-t*; see J. Barth, *Die Pronominalbildung in den semitischen Sprachen*, 1913, 26.

[11] For a comprehensive statement on Semitic, note H. J. Polotsky, above, Part II, B, 99–111.

[12] For this particular *t*-form, which has nothing to do with the reflexive *-t-*, see A. Goetze, *JAOS*, 56 (1936), 324 ff.

[13] For the Akkadian dialects in general, see v. Soden, *op. cit.*, 2 ff.

[14] For a host of far more subtle distinctions which do not, however, fall within the scope of the present account, see the pioneering study by B. Landsberger, *Islamica*, 2 (1926), 355 ff.

[15] In these two examples the hyphen stands for a vowel which could be *a*, *i*, or *u*.

[16] For secondary passives with *-t-* cf. v. Soden, *op. cit.*, 121 ff.

[17] Cf. Speiser, *Language*, 14 (1938), 196 ff.

[18] *Ibid.*

[19] A.H. Gardiner, *Egyptian Grammar*, 1927, 234 ff., and H. J. Polotsky, below, Part II, A, 127–130.

[20] The standard statement on this subject is that by S. R. Driver, *A Treatise on the Use of the Tenses in Hebrew*, (2nd ed.) 1881, 83 ff.

[21] See Bauer-Leander, *Grammatik des Biblisch-Aramäischen*, 1927, 116, 142, 169 f.

[22] Speiser, *JCS*, 6 (1952), 89, n. 52.

[23] I have dealt with this subject at length in "The 'Elative' in West-Semitic and Akkadian," *JCS*, 6 (1952), 81 ff.

[24] Speiser, "The Durative Hithpa'el: A *tan*-Form," *JAOS*, 75 (1955), 118 ff.

EGYPTIAN

[1] Cf. Benno Landsberger, *Sam'al. I* (Veröff. der Türk. Histor. Gesellschaft, VII. Serie, Nr. 16), Ankara, 1948, 86–93.

[2] Such a unified account has been attempted by Fritz Hommel, *Ethnologie und Geographie des Alten Orients* (W. Otto's *Handbuch der Altertumswissenschaft*, III. i. 1), Munich, 1926 (1108 pages). The vast learning and fertile imagination of this scholar (1854–1936), to whom Ancient Near Eastern studies are indebted for much that now belongs to the common stock of knowledge, or at least of belief, in many fields (including, e.g., Comparative Egypto-Semitics) will be enjoyed by critical readers.

3 *Kingship and the Gods*, Chicago, 1948; *The Birth of Civilization in the Near East*, London, 1951.

4 It is true that Leo Reinisch (1832—1919) — author of the first Nubian grammar (Vienna, 1879) and pioneer explorer of the Cushitic languages — believed all these languages to be more or less remotely akin to "Hamitic," Nubian occupying an intermediate position between Cushitic and the Nilotic languages; cf. his *Die sprachliche Stellung des Nuba*, Vienna, 1911. Massai was included in Carl Meinhof's *Sprachen der Hamiten*, Hamburg, 1912. It may be recorded here, just to show the part irresponsible arguments sometimes play in such clasifications, that Felix von Luschan, Meinhof's anthropological collaborator, adduced in support of his belief that the Masai were Hamites the circumstance that a certain Masai female reminded him "in her general *habitus*" of Berlin Jewesses; note the chain of associations: Jews — Semites — Hamites.

5 For a trenchant criticism of "much of what has hitherto been standard physical anthropology and reconstructed culture history in Africa" see Joseph H. Greenberg, *Southwestern Journal of Anthropology*, 6 (1950), 8–10, and *Studies in African Linguistic Classification*, New Haven, 1955, 51–5.

6 M. A. Bryan, *The Distribution of the Semitic and Cushitic Languages of Africa* (International African Institute, 1947) gives bibliographies (unfortunately often at second hand and without verification), statistical information, and an excellent map.

7 Cf. J. Tubiana, *BSL*, 50 (1954), vi-vii.

8 A recent study by Wm. E. Welmers, *Word*, 8 (1952), 145–62, 236–51.

9 The main works to be consulted are Aaron Ember, *Egypto-Semitic Studies* [Posthumously], ed. by Frida Behnk (Veröffentlichungen der Alexander Kohut Memorial Foundation. Philolog. Reihe, Bd. 2), Leipzig, 1930; Franz [v.] Calice, *Grundlagen der ägyptisch-semitischen Wortvergleichung. Eine kritische Diskussion des bisherigen Vergleichsmaterials* (Beihefte zur *WZKM*, 1. Heft), Vienna, 1936; Marcel Cohen, *Essai comparatif sur le vocabulaire et la phonétique du chamito-sémitique* (Bibliothèque de l'École des Hautes Études, fasc. 291), Paris, 1947; an important review of the last-named work by Fritz Hintze, *Zeits. f. Phonetik u. allg. Sprachw.*, 5 (1951), 65–87; also J. Cantineau, *BSL*, 44 (1948), *173–80; C. Brockelmann, *BiOr*, 7 (1950), 58–61. Only a very small fraction of the etymologies suggested in these works are more than just suggestions. On comparative grammar we have Ernst Zyhlarz, "Ursprung und Sprachcharakter des Altägyptischen," in *Zeits. f. Eingeborenenspr.*, 23 (1932–3), 25–45, 81–110, 161–94, 241–54 (and separately, Berlin, 1933); rev. by M. Cohen, *BSL*, 34 (1933), *179–82; Werner Vycichl, "Hausa und Aegyptisch. Ein Beitrag zur historischen Hamitistik," *MSOS*, Afr. Stud., 37 (1934), 36–116. Both these works are marred by extravagance.

10 The present writer offers his apologies for still believing in the superiority of grammatical over lexical criteria for the determination of linguistic relationship, after all that has been argued to the contrary by H. Schuchardt, A. L. Kroeber, and other authorities. The argument (Schuchardt, *Rev. internat. des études basques*, 7 [1913], 293 n. 1; *Schuchardt-Brevier*[2] 198, 230; J. H. Greenberg, in *Anthropology Today*, Chicago, 1953, 274) that morphological elements are usually short and therefore have too little phonic substance to permit conclusive comparisons is counterbalanced by the fact that such elements often come in sets (paradigms) and thus allow the comparison to be verified.

11 To operate with such notions as "affinity," "convergence," "Sprachenbund," etc. is inadvisable in our present state of inadequate knowledge.

12 Zyhlarz (quoted in n. 9).

13 The first Egyptologist to express this view was Pierre Lacau, *Notes de grammaire à propos de la grammaire de M. Erman*, repr. from *RT*, 35 (Paris, 1913), 1–2. This was also the stand taken by Marcel Cohen in his various publications, especially *Essai comparatif sur le vocabulaire et la phonétique du chamito-sémitique*, Paris, 1947. The same conclusion was reached, apparently in-

dependently, by Joh. Friedrich in an account of O. Rössler's Akkado-Berber researches, *BiOr*, 9 (1952), 154–7, which called forth a strongly worded priority claim and some critical contributions by Cohen, *BiOr*, 10 (1953), 88–90.

14 Cf. Joseph H. Greenberg, *Southwestern Journal of Anthropology*, 6 (1950), 3–7, and *Studies in African Linguistic Classification*, New Haven, 1955, 46–51.

15 The hope that the language of the Meroitic inscriptions would turn out to be Cushitic has recently been shattered by Fritz Hintze, "Die sprachliche Stellung des Meroitischen," *Afrikanistische Studien D. Westermann . . . gewidmet* (Deutsche Akad. d. Wiss. zu Berlin. Institut f. Orientf., Veröff. Nr. 26, Berlin, 1955), 355–72.

16 Franz Praetorius, *Zur Grammatik der Gallasprache*, Berlin, 1893, is a comparative study of Galla, undertaken with insufficient materials; still valuable, but antiquated. Cf. the same author's "Ueber die hamitischen Sprachen Ostafrika's," *BAss*, 2 (1894), 312–41, and F. Hommel's review thereof, *ZDMG*, 55 (1901), 532–7.

17 Lest it be suspected that this reluctance is due to prejudice against unwritten languages and inability to deal with them, it may be pointed out that the study of (Nile) Nubian, speakers of which often come into contact with travellers and excavators in Egypt, has always been a recognized hobby for Egyptologists. It is mainly due to the work done by Egyptologists that Nubian ranks among the better known African languages.

18 Ad. Erman, "Die Entzifferung der Hieroglyphen," *Sitzungsber. Preuss. Akad.*, 1922, 1–17; F. Ll. Griffith, "The Decipherment of the Hieroglyphs," *JEA*, 37 (1951), 38–46 (repr. from *The Times Literary Supplement*, 1922); H. Sottas, in Sottas and Ét. Drioton, *Introduction à l'étude des hiéroglyphes*, Paris, 1922, 97–115.

19 Cf. P. Marestaing, *RT*, 30 (1908), 22–36.

20 Akerblad, in his *Lettre sur l'inscription égyptienne de Rosette, adressée au Citoyen Silvestre de Sacy* (Paris, an X = 1802; pp. 64–70 contain a generous *Réponse* by the addressee), had made the first step towards the decipherment of Demotic, correctly identifying most of the alphabetic signs.

21 For short biographies, references to full ones, obituaries, etc., cf. Warren R. Dawson, *Who was Who in Egyptology*, London, 1951.

22 Even Coptic syntax was very imperfectly known prior to 1880; Ludwig Stern's (1846–1911) admirable *Koptische Grammatik* appeared in the same year as the *Neuaegyptische Grammatik*.

23 Steindorff later lost interest in linguistics. Strangely enough, this deplorable development coincided with his tenure of the chair of Egyptology at Leipzig, the center of the Neogrammarians, where he was the colleague of K. Brugmann and A. Leskien.

24 *Das aegyptische Verbum im Altaegyptischen, Neuaegyptischen und Koptischen.* A third volume, containing *Indices*, appeared in 1902.

25 Cf. Sethe, *ZDMG*, 77 (1923), 150, note 1.

26 On two points Sethe's attitude was more intransigent than will seem justified today: (1) He refused to consider any possibility of *matres lectionis*; see now T. W. Thacker (qu. in note 27), 7–31. (2) He refused to admit that the "weak" consonants which constitute the accessory element of the so-called Syllabic Orthography are intended as a rudimentary vowel-notation. The present writer is convinced that the opposite view, set forth by W. F. Albright, *The Vocalization of the Egyptian Syllabic Orthography* (*AOS* 5, New Haven, 1934), is sound in principle, — *pace* W. F. Edgerton, *JAOS*, 60 (1940), 473–506. Cf. E. Edel, "Neues Material zur Beurteilung der syllabischen Orthographie des Aegyptischen," *JNES*, 8 (1949), 44–7.

27 The French Egyptologists did not deny that there exists some kind of relationship between Egyptian and the Semitic languages; they merely objected, quite rightly, to the view that Egyptian was a Semitic language (this view found its extreme expression in A. Ember's favorite formula "Egyptian and the other Semitic languages"). They countered the Semitic bias of the Germans by stressing the connections of Egyptian with Berber. To Maspero goes

back the comparison of the Old Egyptian dependent pronoun 2nd fem. sg. *ṯm* (later *ṯn* > *tn* with Berber (Tuareg) *kem*: *RT*, 21 (1899), 197–9.

28 Wolfhart Westendorf, *Der Gebrauch des Passivs in der klassischen Literatur der Aegypter* (Deutsche Akad. d. Wiss. zu Berlin. Inst. f. Orientf. Veröff., Nr. 18), Berlin, 1953; T.W. Thacker, *The Relationship of the Semitic and Egyptian Verbal Systems*, Oxford, 1954; Elmar Edel, *Altägyptische Grammatik. I* (*AnOr* 34), Rome, 1955; C. E. Sander-Hansen, *Studien zur Grammatik der Pyramidentexte* (Analecta Aegyptiaca VI), Copenhagen, 1956.

29 Cf. René Basset, *Manuel de langue kabyle*, Paris, 1887, 35; André Basset — André Picard, *Éléments de grammaire berbère* (Kabylie-Irjen), Algiers, 1948, 262.

30 The 2nd persons owe their *-ā-* to the analogy of the 1st ones.

31 The decline of the inflection of the Pseudo-Participle can be explained without reference to the notion of languishing; see below.

32 The following quotation in justification of "Pseudo-Participle" may be permitted: "Le vocable a un mérite appréciable. S'il est plein de son, il est à peu près vide de sens et, à tout prendre, un non-sens prête moins aux confusions qu'un contresens," Henri Sottas, *RT*, 40 (1923), 78.

33 Since Modern Syriac is a recognized source of analogies for the suffix-conjugation, especially for *sḏm.n.f* (see below), it may be pointed out that the compound tenses of that language offer a striking parallel to the Egyptian tenses compounded with *ḥr* plus Infinitive and the Pseudo-Participle. The phrase *bi-šqa:la* (Infinitive preceded by the preposition "in"), expressing the progressive aspect, is the partner of the Perfect Participle *šqi:la*, fem. *šqilta*, expressing the resultative aspect.

34 When, as frequently happens, the ending of the 3rd m. sg. is left unwritten, the spelling represents the bare stem, and is indistinguishable from a variety of other forms, including the participle. In such cases the decision must be sought from examples exhibiting the identical syntactic pattern in a different person. In normal Middle Eg. orthography the 3rd fem. sg. is usually spelled in full.

35 In the 20th Dyn. the *ḥr* had ceased to be pronounced. It is written irregularly, and sometimes in places where it is inappropriate.

36 There are interesting exceptions from the general rule, e.g. with verbs of motion.

37 W. F. Albright, *RT*, 40 (1923), 70.

38 O. Rössler, *ZDMG*, 100 (1950–1), 491.

39 T. W. Thacker (qu. in note 27), 226–8.

40 The "imperfective" *sḏm.f* can be recognized with certainty only in the last radical *y/w* verbs, which reduplicate the 2nd radical (*mrr.f*).

41 Jos. H. Greenberg, *JAOS*, 72 (1952), 7, likewise claims the *mrr.f* form as the Egyptian representative of *The Afro-Asiatic Present.*

42 Nominal actor and pronominal actor come both after the verbal base and are mutually exclusive. The nominal actor can be separated from the verbal base by intervening words. The pronominal actor, on the contrary, is inseparably attached to the verbal base.

43 *Grundriss der Sprachwissenschaft*, I.i, 124, note*.

44 *Schuchardt-Brevier* [1]220 = [2]273–4.

45 *Some Aspects of the Egyptian Language* from the *Proceedings of the British Academy*, 23 (1937).

46 Relative forms can only be used when the actor is distinct from the antecedent. They correspond therefore only to those relative clauses in which the relative pronoun is the complement (direct or indirect, that is governed by a preposition) or the possessor.

47 The phenomenon of an original present perfect encroaching upon and finally ousting the narrative past is common enough. It has also occurred in Egyptian. In Late Egyptian we have the narrative past *'iw.f ḥr sḏm* by the side of the present perfect *sḏm.f* (doubtless = *sḏm.n.f*); in Demotic only *sḏm.f* survives, serving as narrative past as well. This Egyptian example presents a certain general interest because it is the inflected (synthetic) form which has ousted the phrasal (analytic) form. This suggests the possibility that in

the much more frequent case of the surviving tense being the phrasal one, it was the meaning rather than the phrasal structure as such (thus A. Meillet, "Sur la disparition des formes simples du prétérit," *Linguistique historique et linguistique générale*, I, 149–58) which caused the present perfect to survive. Cf., e.g., A. J. F. Zieglschmid, "Der Untergang des einfachen Präteritums in verschiedenen indogermanischen Sprachen," *Curme Volume of Linguistic Studies*, (Language Monograph No. 7, 1930), 169–78; F. Hartmann, *Gnomon*, 6 (1930), 190–1.

48 Cf. H. J. Polotsky, *Études de syntaxe copte*, Cairo, 1944, 87–91.

49 So far as available information goes.

50 "Egyptian Language and Writing," *Encyclopaedia Britannica*, 11th edition. Griffith's (1862–1934) judgment is valuable on account of his vast practical acquaintance with texts of all periods (except Coptic), in addition to his outstanding mastery of Demotic, and his profound insight into the Egyptian language, embodied in the concise and at first sight sometimes cryptic notes to his Demotic publications.

ETHNO-LINGUISTIC ELEMENTS

SEMITES

1 The following titles may be regarded as a cross-section of the literature on the subject: Th. Nöldeke, "Semitic Languages," *Encyclopaedia Britannica*, 11th. ed., Vol. XXIV, 1911, 617–630; G. Bergsträsser, *Einführung in die semitischen Sprachen*, 1928, "Ursemitisch," 1-19; G. A. Barton, *Semitic and Hamitic Origins*, 1934; S. Moscati, *Geschichte und Kultur der semitischen Völker*, 1953.

2 Cf. H.H. Bender, *The Home of the Indo-Europeans*, 1922.

3 Cf. H. Möller, *Vergleichendes indogermanisch-semitisches Wörterbuch*, 1911.

4 See especially M. Cohen, *Essai comparatij sur le vocabulaire et la phonétique du Chamito-sémitique*, 1947.

5 Contrast, however, W. Vycichl, *Orientalia*, 23 (1954), 219.

6 J.H. Greenberg, "The Afro-Asiatic (Hamito-Semitic) Present," *JAOS*, 72 (1952), 1ff.

7 Cf. above, Part II, A, 1, 109 ff.

8 See *JBL*, 79 (1960), 157 ff.

HURRIANS AND HITTITES

1 Cf. O. R. Gurney, *The Hittites*, 1952; A. Goetze, *Kleinasien*, (2nd ed.), 1957; H. G. Güterbock, "*Ḥeth, Ḥittīm*," *Enc. Miqr.* III, 320–358.

2 Equally old, but minimal in volume, are the traces of Indo-Aryan names and terms as recorded in cuneiform texts.

3 E. A. Speiser, *Introduction to Hurrian*, 1941; "The Hurrian Participation in the Civilization of Mesopotamia, Syria, and Palestine," *Journal of World History*, I (1953), 311–327; "*Ḥōrīm*," *Enc. Miqr.* III, 58–62.

4 J. Nougayrol, *RA*, 44 (1948), 1 ff.

5 W. F. Albright, *BASOR*, 94 (1944), 12–27.

6 See below, Part III, A, 250–255.

7 I. J. Gelb, *Hurrians and Subarians*, 1944; cf. the discussion in *JAOS*, 68 (1948), 1 ff.

8 Notably in the Mitanni letter of Tushratta, written in Hurrian. The name was

evidently a native Hurrian term, and certainly not related to Akkadian *ḫurru* "hole."

9 This used to be read *Ḫaru*, but Akkadian transliterations help to establish the correct form. Curiously enough, the cuneiform writing of the name was once similarly interpreted as *Ḫar-ru* and equated with "Aryans"; but this was before the appearance of explicit syllabic spellings and the independent demonstration that the Hurrian language had nothing to do with Indo-European and its (Indo-) Aryan branch.

10 For details cf. E. A. Speiser, *Introduction to Hurrian.*

11 Cf. J. Nougayrol and E. Laroche, *Le palais royal d'Ugarit*, 1955, pl. 106 and p. 324.

12 Cf. B. Landsberger, "Assyrische Königsliste und 'dunkles Zeitalter'," *Jour. Cuneiform Studies*, 8 (1954), 31 ff.

13 Cf. H. H. Güterbock, "The Hittite Version of the Hurrian Kumarbi Myths: Forerunners of Hesiod," *Amer. Jour. of Archaeology*, 52 (1948), 123 ff.

14 *Die Israeliten und deren Nachbarstämme*, 1906, 328–344.

15 E. A. Speiser, "Ethnic Movements in the Near East in the Second Millennium B.C.," *AASOR*, 13 (1933), 13–34.

16 The first component of this name is written with the logogram ARAD "slave"; it is thus uncertain whether this should be read as Canaanite (*Abdi*) or Hurrian (unknown).

17 Traces of an earlier Hebrew tradition, however, are found in Isa. 17:9, where Greek has "Hivites and Amorites" for the incomprehensible *hḥrš wh'myr* of Hebrew. The first word, though, accords with "Horite" better than "Hivite."

18 See below, Part III, A, 255–265.

AMORITES AND CANAANITES

1 See especially, F. Böhl, *Kanaanäer und Hebräer*, 1911.

2 S. Smith, *The Statue of Idrimi*, 1949, 14 and pl. 3A.

3 D. J. Wiseman, *The Alalakh Tablets*, 1953.

4 Cf. Böhl, *op. cit.*

5 E. A. Speiser, "The Name '*Phoinikes*'," *Language*, 12 (1936), 121–126.

6 Cf. B. Maisler, "Canaan and the Canaanites," *BASOR*, 102 (1946), 7–12.

7 The isolated *Kinaḫ(ḫ)ayau* (Amarna 9.19) is based on the Hurrian form *Kinaḫḫi*.

8 Maisler, *loc. cit.*, p. 11.

9 W. F. Albright, "The Rôle of the Canaanites in the History of Civilization," in *Studies in the History of Culture* (W. G. Leland Volume, 1942), 11–50.

10 For the latest comprehensive discussion cf. J. R. Kupper, *Les nomades en Mésopotamie au temps des rois de Mari*, 1957, 147–244; see also B. Mazar, "'Emorî," *Enc. Miqr.* III, 440–446.

11 Th. Bauer, *Die Ostkanaanäer*, 1926.

12 Thus, e.g., in the old texts from Alalakh: LÚ.IŠ.MAR.TU (AT 247.21, 25; 281.9) and LÚ *ki-zu A-mu-ru-uḫ-ḫi* (AT 277 rev. 4) "Amorite horse groom"; cf. B. Landsberger, *Jour. Cuneif. Stud.*, 8 (1954), 54, n. 103. Note the Hurrian suffix -*ḫi* as an example of the early participation of Hurrians in this Syrian center.

13 See below, Part III, A, 202–212.

14 On a smaller scale, however, such symbiosis is apparent already in the Old Babylonian period; cf. above, note 12. And Hurrian texts of a religious nature have turned up among the documents from Mari.

15 Landsberger, *loc. cit.* (see above, note 12).

16 Cf. Z. S. Harris, *Development of the Canaanite Dialects*, 1939.

17 Cf. the old Alalakh personal names *Sapsi-adu* and *Sapsi-Eda*, alongside *Šapši*

and *Šapši-abi*; see provisionally Wiseman, *The Alalakh Tablets*, p. 145.

18 Note especially *špš amry*, C. H. Gordon, *Ugaritic Handbook*, 93.15.

19 E. A. Speiser, *JAOS*, 75 (1955), 156 f.

20 Böhl, *Kanaanäer und Hebräer*, 53 ff.

21 There is even a fair chance that the Bible has recorded a trace of phonetic differences between Canaanite and Amorite, namely, in the shibboleth incident (Judg. 12:6). To expose hostile Ephraimites, who had sought to pose as Gileadites, Jephthah made them pronounce a test word. As suggested in *BASOR*, 85 (1942), 10–13, the word in question, appears to have been **ṯubbult-* "stream," particularly appropriate at a time when the crossing of the Jordan was involved. The Hebrew-speaking Ephraimites had long lost the ability to pronounce the spirant *ṯ*-sound, which had shifted in their speech to *š*. But the Gileadites of Amorite Transjordan still retained that sound under Amorite influence. The best that the Ephraimites could manage was *subbult*; just so, the present-day Turks and Iranians substitute *s* for the *ṯā*-sound of Arabic. Unhappily, that best was not good enough.

22 G. Dossin, as reported in *Orientalia*, 19 (1950), 509. See also Kupper, *Les nomades*. . . ,179, n. 1.

23 It was indicated above that the pertinent linguistic material cannot always be apportioned with confidence between Canaanite and Amorite. This is especially true of the West Semitic glosses — as distinct from personal names — in the Mari texts. E.g., Mari *šipṭu* has the sense of "reprimand, chastisement" that is basic to Hebrew *šefāṭīm*. Similarly, the conclusion of a treaty between Amorite parties in Mari is signified by the killing of a pure-bred ass, and the phrase for that is *qatālum hayaram DUMU atānim*, for which cf. *'avir ben-'atōnōt* in Zech. 9:9 and the corresponding phrase in Gen. 49:11. Are these idioms, then, Canaanite, Amorite, or proto-Canaanite-Amorite? In other words, was there much Canaanite material in use among the Western Semites of Mari, or Amorite material in the Bible, or a large store of expressions common to both? Any one of these assumptions could be defended on the basis of present evidence, which is another way of saying that the linguistic issue before us remains to be clarified.

PART THREE: THE CULTURAL FACTOR

MESOPOTAMIA

Prelude to History

1 Cf. in general my essay on "Ancient Mesopotamia" in *The Idea of History in the Ancient Near East*, ed. R. C. Dentan, *AOS*, 38 (1955), pp. 37–76, 361–62.

1a (See now, however, J. J. Finkelstein, "Mesopotamia," *JNES*, 21 [1962], 13 ff.= the area within the great bend of the Euphrates, the Middle Euphrates district).

2 J. M. Lees and N. L. Falcon, "The Geographical History of the Mesopotamian Plains," *Geogr. Jour.*, 118 (1952), 24–39. (Hebrew summary in *BIES*, 19 [1955], 198–207.)

3 E. A. Speiser, "Ancient Near East: Cradle of History," in *Mid-East: World-Center*, ed. R. N. Anshen, New York, 1956, pp. 29 ff.

4 Note especially V. Gordon Childe, *Man Makes Himself*, 1936.

5 Cf. R. J. Braidwood, *The Near East and the Foundations of Civilization*, 1952.

6 See R. J. and Linda Braidwood, "The Earliest Village Communities of Southwestern Asia," *Journal of World History*, 1 (1953), 278–310.

7 *Jour. World Hist.*, 1 (1953), 303.

8 Ann Louise Perkins, *The Comparative Archaeology of Early Mesopotamia*, Chicago, 1949; R. J. and N. Braidwood, *loc. cit.*

9 Various other sites, notably Uruk and Ur, have contributed their share, but they are more significant for other periods.

10 Gawra is regarded by some as the type site for a northern sequel to the Obeid phase.

11 Cf. above, n. 6.

12 See Seton Lloyd and Fuad Safar, "Tell Hassuna," *JNES*, 4 (1945), 259 ff., and R. J. Braidwood, *ibid.*, 255–59.

13 Cf. H. Frankfort, *The Art and Architecture of the Ancient Orient*, 1954, 1 f.; for a full treatment of the Samarra style see Braidwood *et al.*, *JNES*, 3 (1944), 47 ff.

14 Cf. M. E. L. Mallowan and J. C. Rose, *Prehistoric Assyria*, 1935; A. J. Tobler, *Excavations at Tepe Gawra*, II, 1950, plates 110–13.

15 It is no longer certain that the Samarra style was part of an independent "culture"; cf. *JNES*, 4 (1945) 258.

16 Cf. Perkins, *op. cit.*, 31.

17 Cf. Mallowan and Rose, *op. cit.*, 25 ff.; Tobler, *op. cit.*, 42 ff.

18 Cf. Speiser, *BASOR*, 65 (1957), 5, and Tobler, *op. cit.*, 177 and pl. 166, no. 123.

19 Speiser, *Excavations at Tepe Gawra*, I, 1935; Tobler, *op. cit.*

20 R. J. Braidwood, *The Near East and the Foundations of Civilization*, Fig. 24, nos. 1–2.

21 Note the bone playing pipes from Gawra, Levels XVII-XII, Tobler, *op. cit.*, pl. 99, b, d.

22 As opposed to "civilization," which is a term reserved for more advanced stages.

23 Miss Perkins, *op. cit.*, 46, is inclined to place the home of the Halaf culture in the Mosul area.

23a C. S. Coon, *Sumer*, 5 (1949), 103–06.

24 For the figurines see Perkins, *op. cit.*, 83 f.; for the seals cf., e.g., Tobler, *Gawra*, II, nos. 92, 95; for the relatively rare painted representations cf. the designs on the pottery from Susa I.

25 Speiser, *Mesopotamian Origins*, 1930, 38 ff.

26 B. Landsberger, *Ankara ... Fakültesi Dergisi* II/3 (1944), esp. pp. 435–37; S. N. Kramer, above, Part II, B, 142–152.

27 Even more instructive in some respects is the example of the word for "plowman" which appears in Sumerian as *engar*, in Semitic as *'ikkār(u)*. Landsberger, *loc. cit.*, 436, regards it as "distinctly proto-Euphratian," i.e., pre-Sumerian. The region which first reflects the advent of the agricultural revolution would naturally be expected to have supplied the term for the basic agricultural implement.

28 See L. Perkins, *Comparative Archaeology*

of Early Mesopotamia, 97.

29 *Ibid.*, 1 ff.; H. Frankfort, *The Birth of Civilization in the Near East*, 1951, 32 ff.; cf. also notes 5 and 6, above.

30 A. J. Tobler, *Excavations at Tepe Gawra, II*, 1950, 30 ff.

31 E. A. Speiser, "Some Sources of Intellectual and Social Progress in the Ancient Near East," in *Studies in the History of Culture* (W. G. Leland Volume, 1942), 51 ff.

32 Cf. Perkins, *op. cit.*, 94, 96; Braidwood, *The Near East*, 34, Fig. 24 1–2.

33 Cf. W. Andrae, *Das Gotteshaus und die Urformen des Bauens im alten Orient*, 1930, 24 ff.

34 The platform for the "temple oval" of the Early Dynastic Period also belongs here in all probability.

35 This conventional form has been retained for the sake of convenience, in preference to the linguistically favored *siqqurratum.*

36 See p. 237.

37 This feature alone was deemed sufficient to suggest the term "Protoliterate" for this period as a whole. For objections to this label on other grounds see above, p. 184.

38 Cf. E. A. Speiser, "The Idea of History in Ancient Mesopotamia," in *The Idea of History in the Ancient Near East* (*AOS* 38), ed. R. C. Dentan (1955), 46 f.

39 See above, note 31.

40 Cf. P. Koschaker, *Abh. sächs. Ak. Wiss., phil. -hist. Kl.*, 42 (1931), 115 f.; listed for use in black magic are "nail-parings, shavings from the armpit, shoes with holes in them, a tattered belt," etc., see E. Reiner, *JNES*, 15 (1956), 143. 44' ff. The hem of the garment is familiar from Mesopotamian business records and from the encounter between Saul and David (I Sam. 15:27).

41 For the basic study on this question see A. Falkenstein, *Archäische Texte aus Uruk*, Berlin, 1936.

42 Cf. H. Frankfort, *Birth of Civilization ...*, 106 f.

43 Cf. note 41.

44 See D. Diringer, *The Alphabet*, 1948, 54.

45 Cf. note 42.

46 *Ibid.*, 100 ff.

47 See note 31.

48 Cf. above, note 23a.

49 For this whole topic cf. Speiser, "The Sumerian Problem Reviewed," in *HUCA*, 23/1 (1950–51), 359 ff.

50 See note 24.

51 An overland migration would presuppose a starting point not too far away, in which case the total absence of tangible linguistic affinities of Sumerian would be all the more surprising. Cf. especially B. Landsberger, as cited in note 26, p. 434.

The Historical Framework

1 Cf. my remarks in "The Idea of History in Ancient Mesopotamia," contributed to *The Idea of History in the Ancient Near East* (ed. R. C. Dentan) 45 (*AOS* 38).

2 The whole issue of Mesopotamian chronology prior to the first millennium B.C.E. is now more than ever a matter of heated debate. Since relative sequence alone is of real moment in this context, no attempt will be made to select absolute dates prior to Neo-Assyrian times. If the low chronology appears to be favored in this survey, it is mainly because its figures are rock bottom. Future revisions, if any, would have to be upward.

3 Th. Jacobsen, *The Sumerian King List*, 1939.

4 Speiser, *AOS*, 38, 50 f.

5 Jacobsen, *op. cit.*, 80, 16–19.

6 See below, p. 238.

7 Jacobsen, *op. cit.*, 86 ff., 4–20.

8 See *ANET*, 72 ff.

9 *Ibid.*, 44 ff.

10 If Gilgamesh should some day prove to point in a different direction, his name was, at most, Sumerianized.
11 See S. N. Kramer, *IEJ*, 3 (1953), 221 ff.
12 See H. Frankfort, *The Birth of Civilization* . . ., 60 ff.
13 His one-man dynasty lasted 25 years.
14 Again employing the figures of the low chronology without prejudice.
15 Cf. Isa. 20:1. Sargon I of Assyria, who antedated Hammurabi by nearly a century and a half, appears to have modeled his regnal name on that of the illustrious Akkadian conqueror. The latter, incidentally, is the first personage in recorded history to be the subject of an exposition legend in which the hero is rescued as an infant from a floating basket; cf. *ANET*, 119.
16 Cf. Speiser, "Some Factors in the Collapse of Akkad," *JAOS*, 72 (1952), 97 ff.
17 *Ibid.*, 100 f., and for repeated suggestion that this term may be reflected in the *Gōyim* of Gen. 14:1, see *ibid.*, 101 note 41.
18 *Loc. cit.*, 100.
19 See Th. Jacobsen, *The Sumerian King List*, 138.
20 Cf. *ibid.*, note 10a.
21 *Ibid.*, 141, 202.
22 I. J. Gelb, *Hurrians and Subarians*, 1944, 100 ff.; cf. Speiser, *JAOS*, 68 (1948), 1–13.
23 See A. Goetze, *The Laws of Eshnunna*, *AASOR*, 26 (1956).
24 *ANET*, 159 ff.
25 See above, Part II, B, 162–169. On the over-all problem of Amorites: bearers of West Semitic personal names, cf. J. R. Kupper, *Les nomades en Mésopotamie au temps des rois de Mari*, 1957, 147–247.
26 Published as *Archives royales de Mari* (Abbr. ARM) both in transliteration and translation, and in autographed copies (Louvre XXII ff.).
27 ARM, I 60.6; II 13.29.
28 ARM, II 37; cf. M. Noth, "Das alttestamentliche Bundschliessen im Lichte eines Mari-Textes," in *Gesammelte Studien zum alten Testament*, 1957, 142 ff.
29 See especially G. Dossin, "Benjaminites dans les textes de Mari," *Mélanges Dussaud*, 981 ff.
30 See *Orientalia*, 25 (1956), 317 ff. (For this age as a whole see now D. O. Edzard, *Die "zweite Zwischenzeit" Babyloniens*, 1957.)
31 This long-familiar form has been retained here for the sake of convenience; the correct form is in all probability *Ḫammurapi*.
32 See Gelb, *JNES*, 13 (1954), 210 f. (Khorsabad List 10 and SDAS List 9).
33 Landsberger and Balkan, *Belleten* 14, 220.
34 G. Bergsträsser, *Einführung in die semitischen Sprachen*, 1928, 46.
35 It was probably the intrusive Amorites, with their fresher grasp of the phonemic pattern of Semitic, who were responsible for the important reform in Babylonian orthography whereby voiced and voiceless consonants could be indicated in writing. The inherited Sumerian orthography lacked the means to do this.
36 See W. v. Soden, *Die Welt des Orients*, 1948, 193, and *Herrscher im alten Orient*, 1954, 29 f.
37 ARM, IV 20.
38 Cf. *Ugaritica*, I, 16, note 2 for the expressed desire of the king of Aleppo to see Zimrilim's palace. In those days it was not a short trip.
39 Perhaps ARM, II, 33.
40 G. Dossin, *Syria*, 1938, 117.
41 Dr. H. Lewy (*Mélanges Isidore Lévy*, 1955, 243, note 5) maintains, however, that Hammurabi was actually Zimrilim's friend and protector, and that the destruction of Mari took place in or after the fifth year of Hammurabi's son Samsuiluna.
42 For some of the literature which relates to the material from Nuzi, cf. Speiser, *Journal of World History*, 1 (1953), 312, note 2, and add. C. H. Gordon, *The Biblical Archaeologist*, 3 (1940), 1 ff.; on the question of the form of this name, see Speiser, "Nuzi or Nuzu?" *JAOS*, 75 (1955), 52 ff.
43 Cf. Gen. 2:13; 10:8, as distinct from the more numerous Biblical passages in which *Kūš* refers to Ethiopia. (See now *Festschrift Johannes Friedrich* [1959], 475 f.) The Nuzi form receives independent support from the familiar Hellenistic *Kossaîoi*.
44 See especially B. Landsberger, *JCS*, 8 (1954), 64 f.

45 B. Landsberger, "Assyrische Königsliste und 'Dunkles Zeitalter,'" in *JCS*, 8 (1954), 31 ff. (cf. above note) and subsequent issues.
46 A. Alt, *Die Herkunft der Hyksos in neuer Sicht*, 1954; and cf. J. A. Wilson, below, pp. 306 ff.
47 Notably the building inscription of *Tišari/Tižadal*, J. Nougayrol, *RA*, 42 (1948), 1 ff.
48 For the linguistic remains of the Kassites see now K. Balkan, *Die Sprache der Kassiten*, *AOS*, 37 (1954).
49 R. T. O'Callaghan, *Aram Naharaim*, 1948, 56 ff. Not all the names, however, which are given there can be accepted as Indo-Aryan.
50 There is a good possibility that Heb. *sūs*, Akk. *sisū* "horse" is ultimately related to Latin *equus*, Indo-Iranian *áçva*. But certain irregularities in the behavior of the respective forms, both within Semitic (written with a special *s*-sign in Ugaritic) and Indo-European may indicate a common source elsewhere.
51 Notably so in the Mitanni letter of king Tushratta; see my *Introduction to Hurrian*, 1941, 2. Idrimi of Alalakh refers to the king of Hurri as "the great king"; S. Smith, *The Statue of Idrimi*, 1949, pl. 10, 43–4 (and p. 16).
52 See D. J. Wiseman, *The Alalakh Tablets*, 1953, Nos. 128 and 15; cf. my review, *JAOS*, 74 (1954), 21.
53 The pre-Hurrian name of the site was *Gasur* and the bulk of its population was 'Subarian" as distinct from Hurrian.
54 For the Habiru question see the comprehensive works by J. Bottéro, *Le problème des Ḫabiru*, 1954, and M. Greenberg, *The Ḫab/piru*, 1954.
55 Cf. in particular J. A. Knudtzon, *Die El-Amarna Tafeln*, (1915), No. 4.
56 E. Weidner, *AfO*, 13 (1939-40), 109 f.
57 E. Ebeling, *Mitt. d. altor. Ges.*, 12/3 (1938); W. G. Lambert, *AfO*, 18 (1957-58), 38 ff.; W. v. Soden, *Herrscher im alten Orient*, 70 ff.
58 Note Nimrod's association with "the land of Shinar," Gen. 10:10.
59 Cf. above, note 43.
60 For a more detailed treatment of this whole question, cf. my article "In Search of Nimrod," *Eretz-Israel*, 5 (1958), 32* ff.
61 *Ibid.* If the separate equations of Ninos with both Nimrod and Tukulti-Ninurta I are valid, Nimrod can be none other than Tukulti-Ninurta.
62 Cf. J. R. Kupper, "Le recensement dans les textes de Mari," *Studia Mariana* (1950), 99 ff.; (Speiser, *BASOR*, 149 [1958], 17—25.)
63 ARM, I 42. 20.
64 Cf., e.g., *RA*, 36 (1939), 172 ff.
65 See J. J. Finkelstein, *JCS*, 7 (1953), 133f.
66 For a detailed discussion see H. Frankfort, *The Art and Archaeology of the Ancient Orient*, 1954, 84 ff.
67 *ANET*, 279.
68 Cf. *ANEP*, fig. 355. The phrase "son of Omri" was used in a political rather than genealogical sense.
69 He was one of the sons of Tiglath-pileser III; cf. *AfO*, 9 (1933-34), 79.
70 II Kings 19:36f.; Isa. 37:37 f.; II Chron. 32:21; cf. also the Babylonian Chronicle (CT 34. 46 ff.) iii 34 ff. For the complex question of the murder of Sennacherib cf. B. Landsberger and T. Bauer, *ZA*, 37 (1926-27), 68 ff., and B. Meissner, *Sitz. Pr. Ak. Wiss., phil. hist. Kl.*, 1932, 250 ff. Note also, R. C. Campbell Thompson, *The Prisms of Esarhaddon and Ashurbanipal*, 1931, 8, and A. L. Oppenheim, *ANET*, 288.
71 Cf. the literature cited in the above note, and add A. T. Olmstead, *History of Assyria*, 1923, 337 ff.; H. Lewy, "Nitokris-Naqi'a," *JNES*, 11 (1952), 264 ff. For a probably Canaanite origin of the name see Meissner, *loc. cit.*, 258, note 1.
72 Landsberger-Bauer, *loc. cit.*
73 Thompson, *loc. cit.*
74 Cf. H. Frankfort, *Kingship and the Gods*, 1948, 264.
75 Cf. v. Soden, *Herrscher*, 119.
76 See Olmstead, *op. cit.*, 401.
77 Speiser, *AOS*, 38, 47 f.
78 For the better form Nebuchadrezzar cf. Jer. 21:2; in fact, the consonantal text reflects correctly the original *Nabū- kudurri-uṣur.*

The Cultural Component

1 Cf. E. A. Speiser, "The Ancient Near East and Modern Philosophies of History," *Proc. Am. Philos. Soc.*, 95 (1951), 583 ff.

2 *Vorderasiatische Bibliothek*, VII, 254. 15.

3 Speiser, *AOS*, 38, 47 f.

4 Speiser, *JAOS*, Supplement 17 (1954), 15.

5 This is a point, of course, that has been made many times, often under the heading of "God, man, and the state." I have had occasion to refer to it in several different connections. It is of particular importance in the present context.

6 See above, pp. 182 f.

7 Cf. H. and H. Frankfort, *The Intellectual Adventure of Ancient Man*, 1946, 24.

8 *ANET*, 93.

9 Rosh ha-Shanah I, 2.

10 Zichronoth, Verse 12 (See also *BASOR*, 149 [1958], 24.)

11 Speiser, *AOS*, 38, 43.

12 Gilg. XI 197.

13 *ANET*, 65 f. (Creation Epic III 130–38).

14 *ZA*, 43 (1936), 98. 31. For the same phrase in the Bible cf. *JAOS*, 75 (1955), 120.

15 Cf. Speiser, *Orientalia*, 25, 317 ff.

16 Gilg. XI 35; cf. *ANET*, 93, note 188.

17 *ANET*, 81 col. v.

18 S. N. Kramer, *ANET*, 44 ff.; T. Jacobsen, *JNES*, 2 (1943), 165 f.

19 Speiser, *AOS*, 38, 51; *ANET*, 114.

20 *AOS*, 38, 53, note 44; *Yale Or. Ser.*, X 31, x, 43 f.

20a For a survey of Mesopotamian rulers whose names were written with the divinity-sign, see W. W. Hallo, *Early Mesopotamian Royal Titles* (*AOS* 43, 1957), 56 ff.

21 To the extensive older literature on the subject add now J. A. Wilson, "The Royal Myth in Ancient Egypt," *Proc. Am. Philos. Soc.*, 100 (1956), 439 ff.

22 Speiser, *AOS*, 38, 62.

23 *Ibid.*, 44, note 22.

24 Cf. F. Thureau-Dangin, *Rituels accadiens*, 1921, 144.

25 Speiser, *JAOS*, Supplement 17 (1954), 14; cf. also *id.* "Ancient Law and Civilization," *The Canadian Bar Review*, (1953), 863 ff.

26 C(ode of) H(ammurabi) rev 25, 96–98.

27 Cf. *AOS*, 38, 69; add W. von Soden, *BiOr*, 10, 8–12; W. G. Lambert and O. R. Gurney, *Anatolian Studies*, 4 (1954), 65 ff.

28 Lit. "remote is god's plan" (*nesi milik ilim*), B. Landsberger, *ZA*, 43 (1936), 50.

29 J. Nougayrol, *RB*, 59 (1952), 250.

30 For the text see *Keilschrifttexte aus Assur religiösen Inhalts*, 10–11 "obv." 14–19.

31 Gilg. VII iv 45–51 (*ANET*, 87).

32 Gilg. X (Assyrian Version) vi 26–35.

33 Gilg. Meissner Fragment iii. Cf. *ANET*, 90, where I rendered, however, the last line as "task [of mankind]," in common with various earlier editors. In view of the common phrase *šipir sinništim*, lit. "woman's work," I am now inclined to regard the present restoration of the missing word as probably superior. The impact of the passage as a whole, one of the greatest in all early literature (the fragment is Old Babylonian), is not affected either way. Cf. Eccl. 7:9; 9:7–9.

34 There is a curiously widespread misconception that the plant carried with it the gift of immortality. Yet Utnapishtim had just finished telling Gilgamesh that immortality was beyond his reach. Besides, the name of the magic plant is "Man Can Be Made Young in His Old Age" (Gilg. XII 282), and that clearly spells out "rejuvenation."

The Expanding Orbit of Mesopotamian Civilization

1 See above, 188 f.

2 Speiser, "Some Sources of Intellectual and Social Progress in the Ancient Near East," *Leland Volume* (Menasha, Wisconsin, 1942), 51–62.

3 See especially A. Falkenstein, *Archaische Texte aus Uruk*, Berlin, 1936, 43 ff.

4 B. Landsberger, *Die Fauna des alten Mesopotamien*, Leipzig, 1934.

5 R. Campbell Thompson, *A Dictionary of Assyrian Botany*, London, 1949.

6 R. Campbell Thompson, *A Dictionary of Assyrian Chemistry and Geology*, London, 1936.

7 Cf., e.g., L. F. Hartman and A. L. Oppenheim, "On Beer and Brewing Techniques in Ancient Mesopotamia," *JAOS*, Supplement 10 (1950).

8 See O. Neugebauer, *The Exact Sciences in Antiquity*, Copenhagen, 1951.

9 Note particularly T. Jacobsen, in *Materialien zum sumerischen Lexikon* (abbr. MSL) IV (Rome, 1956), 1*–50*; and for general orientation cf. S. N. Kramer, above, A2.

10 R. Hallock and B. Landsberger, MSL, IV, 129 ff.

11 Cf., e.g., P. Kahle, in Bauer-Leander, *Historische Grammatik der hebräischen Sprache*, Halle, 1922, 93.

11a MSL IV, 13,* 21* n. 1.

12 This whole subject was treated in a special monograph by H. Zimmern, entitled *Akkadische Fremdwörter als Beweis für babylonischen Kultureinfluss* (Leipzig, 1915). But this work is now badly out of date. Added material is presented in B. Meissner's *Babylonien und Assyrien*, II, Heidelberg, 1925, 283 ff. and in the works listed in notes 4–6, 8, above. In metrology cf. the Hebrew and Greek forms for "minah"; and in jurisprudence a good example is Gr. *arrabōn*, Heb-Aram. *'rb*, Akk. *erubātu*, all relating to "pledge." The sociolegal term which Akkadian knew as *muškênum* traveled not only to various other Semitic languages but to French and Italian as well; see *Orientalia*, 27 (1958), 19–28.

13 Inscription of *Tiẓadal*, king of Urkish, cf. J. Nougayrol, *RA*, 44 (1950), 3 ff.

14 Inscription of Arisen, king of Urkish and Nawar, *RA*, 9 (1912), 1–4.

15 Speiser, *Introduction to Hurrian*, 1941, 61 f.

16 See especially P. Koschaker, "Keilschriftrecht," *ZDMG*, 89 (1935), 27; cf. Speiser, "Early Law and Civilization," *The Canadian Bar Review*, 31 (1953), 874 f.

17 The ancient capital of the region.

18 For a good example of Nuzian correspondence with the Code of Hammurabi cf. *JBL*, 74 (1955), 254 n. 11.

19 H. G. Güterbock, *JAOS*, Supplement 17 (1954), 19.

20 G. G. Cameron, *AOS*, 38 (1955), 83.

21 Speiser, "An Intrusive Hurro-Hittite Myth," *JAOS*, 62 (1942), 98 ff.; H. G. Güterbock, *Kumarbi*, 1946, 105 ff.

22 Güterbock, *op. cit.*, 115.

23 *Ibid.* The Phoenicians often acted as intermediaries between the Hurrians and the Greeks.

24 Speiser, *Jour. World Hist.*, 1 (1953), 325 f.

25 KUB XXVII 38 iv, 8 ff.

26 Cf. E. Ebeling, *Die babylonische Fabel* (Mitt. altor. Ges. II/3 [1927]), 47 f.

27 Cf. A. Malamat, "'Prophecy' in the Mari Documents," *Israel Exploration Society*, 4 (1955), 2–12; W. von Soden, *Die Welt des Orients*, 1, 1947 f., 397 ff.

28 Personal names such as Bibl. Nahor often reflect older place names; cun. *Naḫur* lay near *Ḫarrān*/Haran.

29 ARM, II 37. 6, 11; cf. Gen. 49:11, Zech. 9:9; cf. above, notes 28–29 [p. 368].

30 Cf. Speiser, *Jour. World Hist.*, 1, 1953, 323 f.

31 Cf., e.g., R. H. Pfeiffer, *Introduction to the Old Testament*, 1941, 142 ff., and 159 ff.

32 And it is testified to by such informed writers of the conservative school as A. Heidel, *The Babylonian Genesis*, 1942, 1951.

33 Cf. Speiser, *Orientalia*, 25 (1936), 317–323.

33a Cf. *Eretz-Israel*, 5, 32* ff.

34 See especially Ivan Engnell, *Studies in*

Divine Kingship, 1943; G. Widengren, *Sakrales Königtum im Alten Testament und im Judentum*, 1955.

35 For a recent detailed statement cf. M. Noth "Gott, König, und Volk im Alten Testament," *Gesammelte Studien*, 1957, 188-229.

36 See above, 239 f.

37 For the examples just cited see Noth, *op. cit.*, 211 f.

EGYPT

First Things

Bibliography

SECTION B. THE LAND ALONG THE NILE. Hermann Kees, *Ancient Egypt. A Geographical History of the Nile*, University of Chicago Press, 1961; Karl Baedeker, *Egypt and the Sûdân*, Leipzig, 8th ed., 1929; A. Lucas, *Ancient Egyptian Materials and Industries*, London, 3rd ed., 1948; for the language, Sir Alan Gardiner, *Egyptian Grammar*, Oxford University Press, 3rd ed., 1957.

SECTION C. BEFORE THE BEGINNING. S. A. Huzayyin, *The Place of Egypt in Prehistory*, Cairo, 1941; V. Gordon Childe, *New Light on the Most Ancient East*, New York, 4th ed., 1952, and *What Happened in History*, Penguin Books, 1943; Robert J. Braidwood, *The Near East and the Foundations of Civilization*, Eugene, Oregon, 1952; Elise Baumgartel, *The Cultures of Prehistoric Egypt*, 2 vols., London, 1947–60; A. Scharff, *Die Frühkulturen Aegyptens und Mesopotamiens*, Leipzig, 1941; J. Vandier, *Manuel d'archéologie égyptienne*, Vol. I, Paris, 1952.

Also for this section and the following: H. Frankfort, *The Birth of Civilization in the Near East*, Indiana University Press, 1951; Rushton Coulborn, *The Origin of Civilized Societies*, Princeton, 1959; *City Invincible. A Symposium on Urbanization and Cultural Development*, ed. by C. H. Kraeling and R. M. Adams, University of Chicago Press, 1960.

SECTION D. THROUGH THE DOOR OF HISTORY. See list at end of preceding section: also Henri Frankfort, *Kingship and the Gods*, University of Chicago Press, 1948.

From Triumph to Failure

1 Arnold Toynbee, *A Study of History* (Abridgment, Oxford University Press, 1947), 30.

2 Breasted, *Ancient Records*, I, §§ 351–54.

3 Helene J. Kantor, *JNES*, I (1942), 174 ff.; II (1952), 239 ff.

4 Breasted, *Ancient Records*, I, § 146.

5 Quoted on page 292.

6 *ANET*, 227–28.

7 *Ibid.*, 212.

8 *Ibid.*, 3–7, 10–11.

9 Breasted, *Ancient Records*, I, §§ 328–31.

10 *Ibid.*, §§ 238–40.

11 *Ibid.*, §§ 382–83.

12 *ANET*, 228.

13 *Ibid.*, 32. The regions of Horus and of Seth were Lower and Upper Egypt.

14 Both *ibid.*, 327. Meri-Re is another name of Pepi I.

15 Erman, *Literature of the Ancient Egyptians*, 5–7.

16 *ANET*, 4–6.

17 *Ibid.*, 412–13.
18 *Ibid.*, 414–18, 441–46.
19 *Ibid.*, 405–07.
20 *Ibid.*, 467.
21 *Ibid.*, 443.
22 *Ibid.*, 445–46.
23 *Ibid.*, 414–18.
24 *Ibid.*, 407–10.
25 *Ibid.*, 7–8.

Bibliography

SECTION A. THE AGE OF THE PYRAMIDS. Ahmed Fakhry, *The Pyramids*, University of Chicago Press, 1961; I. E. S. Edwards, *The Pyramids of Egypt*, London, rev. ed., 1961; Somers Clarke and R. Engelbach, *Ancient Egyptian Masonry. The Building Craft*, Oxford University Press, 1930; W. S. Smith, *The Art and Architecture of Ancient Egypt*, Penguin Books, 1958, and *A History of Egyptian Sculpture in the Old Kingdom*, London, 2nd ed., 1949.

SECTION B. THE GODS OF THE LAND. Jaroslav Černý, *Ancient Egyptian Religion*, London, 1952; Henri Frankfort, *Ancient Egyptian Religion*, Columbia University Press, 1948, and *Kingship and the Gods*, University of Chicago Press, 1948; H. Frankfort and others, *The Intellectual Adventure of Ancient Man*, University of Chicago Press, 1946 (abridged as *Before Philosophy*, Penguin Books, 1949); Alan H. Gardiner, *The Attitude of the Ancient Egyptians to Death and the Dead*, Cambridge University Press, 1935; James H. Breasted, *Development of Religion and Thought in Ancient Egypt*, Scribner's, 1912 (now Harper's paperback, 1959); Adolf Erman, *Die Religion der Aegypter*, Berlin and Leipzig, 1934; Hermann Kees, *Der Götterglaube im alten Aegypten*, Leipzig, 1941; Jacques Vandier, *La Religion égyptienne*, "Mana," Paris, 1944.

SECTION C. THE TOMBS AND TEMPLES SPEAK. From previous listings, particularly *Ancient Near Eastern Texts;* Breasted, *Ancient Records*, and *Development of Religion and Thought.* Adolf Erman, *The Literature of the Ancient Egyptians*, London, 1927.

SECTION D. MATERIAL VALUES FAIL. Herbert E. Winlock, *The Rise and Fall of the Middle Kingdom in Thebes*, New York, 1947, and *Excavations at Deir el Bahri, 1911–1931*, New York, 1942; Hanss Stock, *Die erste Zwischenzeit Aegyptens*, Rome, 1949.

SECTION E. WHAT VALUES ARE LASTING? Breasted, *Development of Religion and Thought;* Wilson, *The Culture of Ancient Egypt.*

The Search for New Mastery

1 Breasted, *Ancient Records*, I, §§ 518–23.
2 *ANET*, 230.
3 G. Posener, *Littérature et politique dans l'Égypte de la XIIe dynastie*, Paris, 1956.
4 *ANET*, 418–19.
5 *Ibid.*, 18–22.
6 *Ibid.*, 418–19; 372–73; 432–34.
7 Breasted, *Ancient Records*, I, §§ 651–60.
8 *ANET*, 328–29; W. F. Albright, *BASOR*, 81 (1941), 16–21; 83 (1941), 30–36.
9 *ANET*, 252–53.
10 *Ibid.*, 230–34. Preliminary report by Labib Habachi on a new stela in *Annales du Service des Antiquités de l'Égypte*, LIII (1955), 195–202.
11 *ANET*, 234–38.
12 *Ibid.*, 245–48.
13 Moshe Greenberg, *The Hab/piru*, New Haven, 1955; Mary F. Gray, *HUCA*, 29 (1958), 135–202.
14 *ANET*, 12–14.
15 *Ibid.*, 368.
16 *Ibid.*, 10–11.
17 *Ibid.*, 34–36.

Bibliography

SECTION A. RESTORATION AND CRISIS AGAIN.
H. E. Winlock, *The Rise and Fall of the Middle Kingdom in Thebes*, New York, 1947; Hans Stock, *Studien zur Geschichte und Archäologie der 13. bis 17. Dynastie Aegyptens*, Glückstadt and Hamburg, 1942; Pahor Labib, *Die Herrschaft der Hyksos im Aegypten und ihr Sturz*, Glückstadt, 1937.

SECTION B. IMPERIAL TRIUMPH.
Particularly, Gardiner, *Egypt of the Pharaohs*; Steindorff and Seele, *When Egypt Ruled the East.*

SECTION C. A DISCIPLINED PEOPLE.
The chapters on Egypt in Frankfort and others, *Before Philosophy.*

The Challenges to Power

1 *ANET*, 483–84.
2 *Ibid.*, 243–45.
3 *Ibid.*, 483–90.
4 *Ibid.*, 251–52.
5 Kurt Pflüger, *JNES*, 5 (1946), 260–76.
6 *ANET*, 369–71.
7 *ANET*, 253–55; *Journal of Egyptian Archaeology*, VI (1920), 99–116; B. Grdseloff, *Études égyptiennes*, II, Cairo, 1949.
8 *ANET*, 255–56; Sir Alan Gardiner, *The Kadesh Inscriptions of Ramesses II*, Oxford University Press, 1960.
9 *ANET*, 199–203.
10 *Ibid.*, 256–58.
11 *Ibid.*, 376–78.
12 *Ibid.*, 260.
13 *Ibid.*, 262–63.
14 *Ibid.*, 214–16.
15 *Ibid.*, 260–62. H. D. Schaedel, *Die Listen des grossen Papyrus Harris*, Glückstadt, 1936.
16 Alan H. Gardiner, *Ancient Egyptian Onomastica*, 3 vols., Oxford University Press, 1947.
17 Erman, *Literature of the Ancient Egyptians*, 189.
18 *ANET*, 259.
19 *Ibid.*, 378.
20 The word *nearin* is used, as in I Kings 20:14, etc.
21 Hebrew, *sofer yodeʿa,* as a sarcasm.
22 *ANET*, 475–79.
23 *Ibid.*, 22–23.
24 *Ibid.*, 471.
25 *Ibid.*, 12–14.
26 *Ibid.*, 14–17.
27 *Ibid.*, 467–69.

Bibliography

SECTION A. THE UNIVERSAL GOD.
Steindorff and Seele, *When Egypt Ruled the East;* Gardiner, *Egypt of the Pharaohs;* J. D. S. Pendlebury, *Tell el-Amarna*, London, 1935; H. Frankfort, ed., *The Mural Painting of El ʿAmarneh*, London, 1929; Penelope Fox, *Tutankhamun's Treasure*, London, 1951; O. R. Gurney, *The Hittites*, Penguin Books, 1952.

SECTION B. HERESY.
Particularly the histories by Breasted, Gardiner, and Steindorff and Seele.

SECTION C. CLASHING EMPIRES.
See the General Bibliography.

SECTION D. LITERATURE FROM SCHOOLBOYS.
Adolf Erman, *The Literature of the Ancient Egyptians*, London, 1927; Alan H. Gardiner, *The Library of A. Chester Beatty. Description of a Hieratic Papyrus . . .*, Oxford University Press, 1931, and *Hieratic Papyri in the British Museum. Third Series. Chester Beatty Gift*, London, 1935; Ricardo A. Caminos, *Late-Egyptian Miscellanies*, London, 1954; G. Lefebvre, *Romans et contes égyptiens de l'époque pharaonique*, Paris, 1949.

A Lowly Kingdom

1 *ANET*, 25–29.
2 Breasted, *Ancient Records*, IV, §§ 796–883.
3 All three texts, *ANET*, 379–81.
4 Rudolf Anthes, *Lebensregeln und Lebensweisheit der alten Aegypter* (*Der alte Orient*, XXXII,2), Leipzig, 1933.
5 *ANET*, 420–21.
6 *Ibid.*, 421–24.
7 Latest treatment, Emil G. Kraeling, *The Brooklyn Museum Aramaic Papyri*, New Haven, 1953.

Bibliography

SECTION A. DIVISION AND CONFUSION.
The histories of Gardiner and Breasted; H. von Zeissl, *Aethiopen und Assyrer in Aegypten*, Glückstadt, 1955.
SECTION B. THE QUIET GODS.
Jaroslav Cerný, *Ancient Egyptian Religion*, London, 1952; chapters on Egypt in H. Frankfort and others, *Before Philosophy;* Adolf Erman, *Die Religion der Aegypter*, Berlin and Leipzig, 1934. For the Wisdom of Amen-em-Opet, see *Journal of Egyptian Archaeology*, XII (1926), 191–239.
SECTION C. TO THE END.
P. G. Elgood, *The Later Dynasties of Egypt*, Oxford, 1951; F. K. Kienitz, *Die politische Geschichte Aegyptens vom 7. bis 4. Jahrhundert vor der Zeitwende*, Berlin, 1953; G. Posener, *La première domination perse en Égypte*, Cairo, 1936; E. Bevan, *A History of Egypt under the Ptolemaic Dynasty*, London, 1927.

The Finding of Ancient Egypt

Bibliography

Chapter I in Gardiner, *Egypt of the Pharaohs;*
Warren R. Dawson, *Who was Who in Egyptology*, London, 1951.

Egypt and the Bible

1 For example, C. S. Jarvis, *Yesterday and Today in Sinai*, Houghton Mifflin, 1932. Such attempts to find natural explanations for miracles ignore the fact that a miracle is effective because those who believe in it are convinced that it was accomplished contrary to natural causes. Historically the belief in a miracle is itself an energetic force.
2 *ANET*, 31–32.
3 *Ibid.*, 421–25.
4 *Ibid.*, 369–71.
5 *Ibid.*, 467–69.
6 *Ibid.*, 495. The Index of Biblical References, *ibid.*, 504–07, gives many more parallels.
7 Cf. W. C. Hayes, *A Papyrus of the Late Middle Kingdom in the Brooklyn Museum*, Brooklyn, 1955, esp. p. 99.

General Bibliography for Ancient Egypt

James H. Breasted, *A History of Egypt*, Scribner's, New York, 1909; chapters in *Cambridge Ancient History*, Cambridge University Press, Vols. I-III, 1923–25; Sir Alan Gardiner, *Egypt of the Pharaohs*, Oxford University Press, 1961; William C. Hayes, *The Scepter of Egypt*, 2 vols., New York, 1953, Cambridge, Mass., 1957; W. S. Smith, *Ancient Egypt as represented in the Museum of Fine Arts*, Boston, 4th ed., 1960; George Steindorff and Keith C. Seele, *When Egypt Ruled the East*, University of Chicago Press, 2nd ed., 1957; John A. Wilson, *The Culture of Ancient Egypt*, University of Chicago Press, 1956 (published in 1951 as *The Burden of Egypt*); É. Drioton and J. Vandier, *Les Peuples de l'orient méditerranéen. L'Égypte*, Paris, 3rd ed., 1950; A. Scharff and A. Moortgat, *Aegypten und Vorderasien im Altertum*, Munich, 1950.

The Legacy of Egypt, ed. by S. R. K. Glanville, Oxford University Press, 1942; A. Erman and H. Ranke, *Aegypten und ägyptisches Leben*, Tübingen, 1923; R. Engelbach, *Introduction to Egyptian Archaeology*, Cairo, 1946; W. Helck and E. Otto, *Kleines Wörterbuch der Aegyptologie*, Wiesbaden, 1956; Jack Finegan, *Light from the Ancient Past. The Archaeological Background of Judaism and Christianity*, Princeton, 2nd ed., 1959; *The Bible and the Ancient Near East. Essays in Honor of . . . Albright*, ed. by G. Ernest Wright, Doubleday, New York, 1961.

Ancient Near Eastern Texts relating to the Old Testament, ed. by James B. Pritchard, 2nd ed., Princeton, 1955; James H. Breasted, *Ancient Records of Egypt*, 5 vols., University of Chicago Press, 1906–07; James B. Pritchard, *The Ancient Near East in Pictures relating to the Old Testament*, Princeton, 1954.

INDEX OF PROPER NAMES

DISCARDED
Adirondack Community College Library